HOMER BETWEEN HISTORY AND FICTION IN IMPERIAL GREEK LITERATU⎯

CW00820083

Did Homer tell the 'truth' about the Trojan War? If so, how much, and if not, why not? The issue was hardly academic to the Greeks living under the Roman Empire, given the centrality of both Homer, the father of Greek culture, and the Trojan War, the event that inaugurated Greek history, to conceptions of Imperial Hellenism. This book examines four Greek texts of the Imperial period that address the topic – Strabo's *Geography*, Dio of Prusa's *Trojan Oration*, Lucian's novella *True Stories*, and Philostratus' fictional dialogue *Heroicus* – and shows how their imaginative explorations of Homer and his relationship to history raise important questions about the nature of poetry and fiction, the identity and intentions of Homer himself, and the significance of the heroic past and Homeric authority in Imperial Greek culture.

LAWRENCE KIM is Assistant Professor of Classical Studies at Trinity University, San Antonio. His research focuses on Greek literature and culture under the Roman Empire.

Editors
SUSAN E. ALCOCK, Brown University
JAŚ ELSNER, Corpus Christi College, Oxford
SIMON GOLDHILL, University of Cambridge

The Greek culture of the Roman Empire offers a rich field of study. Extraordinary insights can be gained into processes of multicultural contact and exchange, political and ideological conflict, and the creativity of a changing, polyglot empire. During this period, many fundamental elements of Western society were being set in place: from the rise of Christianity, to an influential system of education, to long-lived artistic canons. This series is the first to focus on the response of Greek culture to its Roman imperial setting as a significant phenomenon in its own right. To this end, it will publish original and innovative research in the art, archaeology, epigraphy, history, philosophy, religion, and literature of the empire, with an emphasis on Greek material.

Titles in series:

Athletics and Literature in the Roman Empire
Jason König

Describing Greece: Landscape and Literature in the Periegesis *of Pausanias*
William Hutton

Religious Identity in Late Antiquity: Greeks, Jews and Christians in Antioch
Isabella Sandwell

Hellenism in Byzantium: The Transformations of Greek Identity and the Reception of the Classical Tradition
Anthony Kaldellis

The Making of Roman India
Grant Parker

Philostratus
edited by Ewen Bowie and Jaś Elsner

The Politics of Munificence in the Roman Empire: Citizens, Elites and Benefactors in Asia Minor
Arjan Zuiderhoek

Saints and Church Spaces in the Late Antique Mediterranean: Architecture, Cult, and Community
Ann Marie Yasin

Galen and the World of Knowledge
edited by Christopher Gill, Tim Whitmarsh, and John Wilkins

Local Knowledge and Microidentities in the Imperial Greek World
edited by Tim Whitmarsh

Homer Between History and Fiction in Imperial Greek Literature
Lawrence Kim

Epiphany and Representation in Graeco-Roman Culture: Art, Literature, Religion
Verity Platt

HOMER BETWEEN HISTORY AND FICTION IN IMPERIAL GREEK LITERATURE

BY

LAWRENCE KIM

CAMBRIDGE
UNIVERSITY PRESS

University Printing House, Cambridge CB2 8BS, United Kingdom

Cambridge University Press is part of the University of Cambridge.

It furthers the University's mission by disseminating knowledge in the pursuit of
education, learning and research at the highest international levels of excellence.

www.cambridge.org
Information on this title: www.cambridge.org/9781107485297

First published 2010
First paperback edition 2015

A catalogue record for this publication is available from the British Library

Library of Congress Cataloguing in Publication data
Kim, Lawrence Young, 1970–
Homer between history and fiction in imperial Greek literature / by Lawrence Kim.
p.   cm. – (Greek culture in the Roman world)
ISBN 978-0-521-19449-5 (hardback)
1. Greek literature – History and criticism.   2. Homer – In literature.   3. Trojan War – Literature
and the war.   4. Literature and history – Greece – History – To 1500.   I. Title.   II. Series.
PA3086.K56   2010
880.9′351 – dc22   2010029759

ISBN 978-0-521-19449-5 Hardback
ISBN 978-1-107-48529-7 Paperback

For my parents

Contents

Acknowledgments

This book began, many incarnations ago, as my Princeton doctoral dissertation, and I am indebted to those who encouraged and patiently endured my initial attempts to come to grips with the Imperial reception of Homer: my director Froma Zeitlin, my committee members Bob Kaster and Ruth Webb, as well as Andrew Ford and John Ma. During the process of revision, I have benefited from conversations with a number of colleagues, particularly Stephen Hinds, Melissa Mueller, Egbert Bakker, Erwin Cook, Andrew Faulkner, Tim Power, Joel Walker, and Adam Rabinowitz. At later stages of this project, Tim Whitmarsh, Craig Gibson, and Ewen Bowie offered criticism, advice, and support, and Richard Hunter and Karen Ní Mheallaigh generously shared work in advance of publication (on Dio's *Trojan Oration* and Lucian's *True Stories*, respectively) from which I have learned a great deal. I am fortunate to have worked with Michael Sharp, Liz Hanlon, Sarah Roberts, and Anna Zaranko at Cambridge University Press as well as the Series editors and the readers, whose prompt and incisive comments have improved the work immeasurably.

Portions of this book were written in Seattle, Philadelphia (generously funded by a Loeb Classical Library Foundation Fellowship in 2005–6), Wiesbaden, New York, Ann Arbor (where I participated in a 2008 NEH Summer Seminar on *Homer's Readers: Ancient and Modern*), and of course Austin. I am grateful to my friends and family in all of those places for their emotional and intellectual support during the long gestation period of this project. Of these, I especially want to thank my sister, Eleana, with whom I could always commiserate over the difficulties of the writing process, the trio of New-York-based classicists – Mark Buchan, Joy Connolly, and Brooke Holmes – who always made time to see me on my visits back home, and finally my mother and father, Jae Jin and Yung Duk Kim, who have been patient, supportive, and encouraging through this long journey, and to whom this book is dedicated.

Finally, deserving special thanks are two people without whom this book could not have been written, or at least without whom the end result would have been far poorer. Jim Porter read and meticulously critiqued several drafts of the book, forcing me to rethink and reconceive central aspects of my thesis as well as numerous lesser points of detail, even if in the end I know that I have not addressed all of his concerns. Sira Schulz tirelessly read and edited more versions of this book than either of us care to remember, clarified my arguments, continuously engaged in conversations about the intricacies of my texts, and spent several years living with the specter of an unfinished book haunting our household. I could not imagine a better companion with whom to navigate the ups and downs of life inside and outside academia.

Note on texts, translations, and abbreviations

Abbreviations of ancient authors and texts are those found in the *Oxford Classical Dictionary*³ or, if not provided there, those in Liddell, Scott, and Jones, *A Greek-English Lexicon* (an exception are the works of Lucian, which follow *LSJ* rather than the *OCD*). Periodicals are referred to by the abbreviations in *L'Année philologique*. Translations are my own unless otherwise attributed. I have tried to translate the titles of all ancient works into English (e.g., *Trojan Oration*) rather than using a Latin (*Troicus*) or transliterated Greek (*Troikos*) version; the one major exception is Philostratus' *Heroicus*, where I retain the Latin title. As for transliteration of Greek names into English, I have preferred to Latinize them whenever possible.

Greek and Latin texts are cited, quoted, and translated from the standard Oxford Classical Text (e.g., Aristotle, Herodotus, Homer, Lucian, Plato, Thucydides), or, where none exists, the most recent Teubner edition (Maximus of Tyre, Philostratus, Plutarch, [Plutarch] *On the Life and Poetry of Homer*, etc.). The following authors and texts are exceptions, either because no OCT or Teubner exists, or because the edition listed is considered superior. In the case of the *Lives of Homer*, I refer to West's recent Loeb rather than the more commonly used OCT (T. W. Allen, ed. (1912) *Homeri Opera*. Vol. V. Oxford: 184–268) because of West's more user-friendly system of numbering the *Lives*. Finally, fragments of ancient authors are referred to by number and editor's name (e.g., Crates F 91 Broggiato); full references to these editions are listed in the Works cited under the editor's name. The exceptions are fragments of the Presocratic philosophers and of ancient Greek historians, which use abbreviations (DK, *FGrH*) for the standard collections; the full references are listed below.

Dio Chrysostom: Arnim, H. von (1893) *Dionis Prusaensis quem vocant Chrysostomus quae exstant omnia*. 2 vols. Berlin.
DK = Diels, H. and Kranz, W., eds. (1952) *Die Fragmente der Vorsokratiker*. 6th edn. Berlin.

Eustathius, *Commentary on Homer's Iliad*: Valk, M. van der, ed. (1971–87) *Eustathii archiepiscopi Thessalonicensis. Commentarii ad Homeri Iliadem pertinentes ad fidem codicis Laurentiani.* 4 vols. Leiden.

FGrH = Jacoby, F., ed. (1923–) *Die Fragmente der griechischen Historiker.* Leiden.

Heliodorus, *An Ethiopian Tale*: Rattenbury, R. M. and Lumb, T. W., eds. (1960) *Héliodore. Les Éthiopiques.* 2nd edn. 3 vols. Paris.

Heraclitus, *Homeric Problems:* Buffière, F., ed. (1962) *Héraclite. Allégories d'Homère.* Paris.

Lives of Homer: West, M. L., ed. (2003) *Homeric Hymns. Homeric Apocrypha. Lives of Homer.* Cambridge, MA.

Porphyry, *Homeric Questions (Iliad)*: Schrader, H., ed. (1880–2) *Porphyrii Quaestionum Homericarum ad Iliadem pertinentium reliquias.* Leipzig.

Ptolemy the Quail: Henry, R., ed. (1962) *Photius. Bibliothèque.* Vol. III. Paris: 51–72. For fragments not in Photius, see Chatzis (1914).

Scholia to Homer, *Iliad*: Erbse, H., ed. (1969–88) *Scholia Graeca in Homeri Iliadem (scholia vetera).* 7 vols. Berlin.

Scholia to Homer, *Odyssey*: Dindorf, W., ed. (1855) *Scholia Graeca in Homeri Odysseam ex codicibus aucta et emendata.* Oxford.

Strabo, *Geography*: Radt, S., ed., tr., comm. (2002–9) *Strabons Geographika.* 8 vols. Göttingen.

Theon, *Progymnasmata:* Patillon, M. and Bolognesi, G., eds. (1997) *Aelius Théon. Progymnasmata.* Paris.

CHAPTER I

Introduction

Imperial Homer, history, and fiction

Near the beginning of his treatise *Against Celsus*, the third-century Christian scholar Origen conveys the difficulty of his project, a defense of the Gospels' account of Jesus, by an analogy to Greek example:

> Before we begin the defence [of Jesus], we must say that an attempt to con-firm almost any story as having happened, even if it is true (πᾶσαν ἱστορίαν, κἂν ἀληθὴς ᾖ . . . ὡς γεγενημένην), and to produce complete certainty about it, is one of the most difficult tasks and in some cases is impossible. Suppose, for example, that someone says the Trojan War never happened (μὴ γεγονέναι), in particular because it is bound up with the impossible story (διὰ τὸ ἀδύ-νατον προσπεπλέχθαι λόγον) about a certain Achilles having had Thetis, a sea-goddess, as his mother . . . How could we defend [the historicity of the Tro-jan War] (κατασκευάσαιμεν), especially as we are embarrassed by the invention (ὑπὸ τοῦ . . . πλάσματος) which for some unknown reason is woven alongside the opinion, which everybody believes, that there really was (περὶ τοῦ ἀληθῶς γεγονέναι) a war in Troy between the Greeks and the Trojans?[1]

It is probably no accident that Origen selects the Trojan War to illustrate the difficulty of substantiating "true" stories as fact. The war is poised at the chronological end of the 'mythological' era and the beginning of Greek history, and while the legends surrounding it are more human-centered and less fantastic than those concerning previous heroic generations, they still feature the divine apparatus and enough "invention" or "fiction" (πλάσμα) to render problematic any simple correspondence to historical reality.[2] The anxiety engendered by these problems is well expressed by Origen; like nearly all ancient authors he was caught in an uneasy negotiation between his firm belief in the reality of the Trojan War and a suspicion that the stories told about it were not completely accurate. How then does he propose to verify its truth? Origen can only suggest the following technique: to

---

[1] Orig. *Contr. Cels.* 1.42.
[2] Origen's other examples – Oedipus, the Seven against Thebes, the return of the Heraclidae – similarly fall into the 'late' period of Greek legendary tradition.

I

accept a significant portion of the story as true, dismiss other parts as gratification of certain people (διὰ τὴν πρός τινας χάριν), and interpret the rest allegorically (τροπολογήσει).

Origen does not mention Homer by name, but establishing the historical details of the Trojan War naturally hinged on assessing the accuracy of its most important narrative source. Homeric poetry commanded an immense cultural authority throughout antiquity, but was generally recognized, at least implicitly, as *historical fiction* about the people and events of the heroic age.[3] I mean by this simply that Homeric epic was believed to be a basically accurate account of an historical event to which a certain amount of invention and elaboration had been added. The problem, for those who chose to tackle it, was differentiating the historical truth from the poetic fiction – in other words, negotiating a balance between the contrasting images of Homer as poet and historian.

In this book, I look at four Imperial Greek texts that address, in very different ways this question of Homer's historical reliability, that is, of whether or not he told the 'truth' about the Trojan War and Odysseus' wandering (and if so, how much; and if not, why not): Strabo's *Geography*, Dio Chrysostom's *Trojan Oration*, Lucian's satirical novel *True Stories*, and Philostratus' fictional dialogue *Heroicus* (chs. 3–6 respectively). Chronologically, the works, spaced out at intervals of approximately sixty to seventy years, span the first two centuries of the Roman Empire, with the first roughly dating to the later part of the reign of Augustus and the consolidation of the principate, and the last to the waning days of the Severan dynasty and the advent of the third-century crisis. The critical tradition to which these authors belong, however, extends back to earlier eras, and I devote a chapter (2) to two important previous attempts to address the question – by the Classical historians Herodotus and Thucydides, who are the first extant writers to examine Homer critically on historical grounds. There remains, however, at the heart of their efforts a tension between Homer's historiographical and his poetic objectives which is never satisfactorily resolved. As I show in Chapter 3, Strabo, in his long, intense, and convoluted defense of Homer's historical and geographical accuracy, tries desperately to reconcile these two conflicting images of Homer – as diligent historian and 'mythmaking' poet. Chapters 2 and 3 are thus primarily focused on elucidating the presumptions about Homeric poetics that underlie these discussions of his historical reliability – for example, how he composed his poems, how he shaped historical matter into fictional form, the nature of his

---

[3] Veyne (1988), 21. See further Ch. 2 below.

motivations and intentions (aesthetic, historiographical, etc.) – as well as exploring the image of Homer himself implied or explicitly stated by these critics.

Strabo's (inevitable) failure to create a coherent image of Homer could be seen as marking the point at which critics started moving in a different direction, away from the earnest but ultimately futile strategy of attacking the issue head-on, and toward the more self-conscious, oblique, and parodic approach characteristic of the Second Sophistic, and which we find on display in the works of Dio, Lucian, and Philostratus. These three authors expand upon and transform the issues raised in the earlier works concerning Homer, his poetry, and the 'reality' represented and fictionalized in that poetry, and I devote considerable space to mapping out precisely how they reformulate and re-imagine important elements of the Homeric historiographical tradition.[4] The Second Sophistic authors' attitudes toward Homer are profoundly influenced by the vital and authoritative role that the literature and history of the distant past played in defining the Imperial Greek elite sense of self-worth and social identity. As a result, their investigations of Homer's relation to the heroes and the War often raise (to different degrees) more general questions concerning the validity and authority of ancient literary and historical tradition in Imperial culture: what is at stake in believing Homer's account of the Trojan War? What is the place of the past in the culture of the present? What role, if any, should Homer and the heroic age play in the definition of 'Greekness'? In fact, I argue that one of the reasons that Dio, Lucian, and Philostratus choose to write on the topic is precisely because it provides so many possibilities for exploring such broader issues.

As we shall see, exploiting the tension between Homer's capacities as poet and historian becomes an ideal way of wryly commenting on the Imperial Greek obsession with the past and satirically undermining commonplace claims to the poet's authority and sagacity. The historiographical conception of Homer had always courted the risk of deflating Homer's exalted reputation, because it involved thinking about Homer as an actual human being as opposed to a divinely inspired sage. Dio, Lucian, and Philostratus push this further, vividly portraying Homer in a variety of amusing ways: an itinerant, improvisatory liar; a sighted Babylonian consorting with his characters in the afterlife; a traveling poet raising the ghost of Odysseus on Ithaca. Moreover, their re-inventions of Homer are

---

[4] I should emphasize that I am not interested in answering or exploring the actual historical accuracy of Homeric poetry – e.g., whether the Homeric world reflects Mycenaean times, the Dark Age, etc. – but only ancient responses to the question.

situated in self-consciously literary works (epideictic speech, short novel, and fictional dialogue, respectively) that introduce new, fictional 'histories' in competition with those of the poet. The texts thus play with their audiences' notions of belief by destabilizing their investment in the 'truth' of the two cornerstones of the Greek literary and historical past – Homer and the Trojan War – but they also inscribe their authors as the descendants of Homer, as fellow composers of 'fictions' about the ancient heroes.[5]

In the remainder of this introduction, I want to sketch out briefly some of the background against which the texts examined in this book should be viewed: the extent and power of Homer's influence in Greek culture, his status as a symbol of Hellenism, and the variety of interpretative techniques applied to his poetry. The interest my four Imperial texts evince in questions of Homer, history, and fiction sets them within a critical tradition that stands somewhat apart from the dominant trends of ancient Homeric reception, which tend to be preoccupied with moral, theological, philological, or rhetorical matters.[6] I show how this 'historical' approach to Homer (which boasts a distinguished pedigree in antiquity) is closely tied to the post-classical construction of Greek identity and investment in the heroic past. I then narrow the focus onto the three Second Sophistic authors' creative attempts to critique this conception of Homer and the past, and demonstrate how the particular combination of interests found in their texts – in Homer's historiographical qualities, in the figure of Homer, and in explicit commentary on his poetry – marks them as a distinct group within the larger body of Homeric continuations, rewritings, and revisions so popular in the Imperial period.

IMPERIAL HOMER

Throughout antiquity, the influence of Homer upon Greek literature and the authority he exercised over Greek culture were tremendous, so much so that his sheer ubiquity has discouraged any large-scale attempt to chart

---

[5] After all, Homeric poetry, particularly the *Odyssey*, was often at the center of ancient debates about the nature of truth, lies, and fiction. See, e.g., Pratt (1993), 55–94; Grossardt (1998).

[6] There is no good synthetic account of Homer's place in Imperial Greece; admittedly the topic is an enormous one, and studies tend to focus (as this one does) on more restricted aspects of Homeric reception or criticism. For instance, Kindstrand (1973) examines Dio, Aristides, and Maximus of Tyre; Zeitlin (2001) conveys an idea of the vast quantity of material, despite her focus on Homer and visuality; Buffière (1956) treats primarily the allegorical tradition and is arranged thematically. Hunter (2004), 250–3, is brief but insightful.

his ancient reception.[7] Under the Empire, the reverence for Homer is as enthusiastic as ever; Homer was, to paraphrase Dio Chrysostom, "the beginning, middle, and end" of culture.[8] Similarly, for Heraclitus, the (first century CE?) author of a work defending Homer through allegorical interpretation, the poet accompanies the educated person through every stage of life:

From the very first age of life, the foolishness of infants just beginning to learn is nurtured on the teaching given in [Homer's] school. One might almost say that his poems are our baby clothes, and we nourish our minds by draughts of his milk. He stands at our side as we each grow up and shares our youth as we gradually come to manhood; when we are mature, his presence within us is at its prime; and even in old age, we never weary of him. When we stop, we thirst to begin him again. In a word, the only end of Homer for human beings is the end of life. (Heraclit. *All.* 1: tr. Russell)

The continuous, even oppressive, presence of Homer suggested by this passage can be compared to Dio's (joking?) claims for the poet's wide-ranging influence as an ambassador of Hellenism to the farthest corners of the globe: so well known is Homer that his poetry has been translated in India and the Indians, who do not even see the same stars as the Greeks, yet listen with rapt attention to the stories of heroes such as Achilles, Priam, and Hector of whom they have no other knowledge.[9] And it was commonplace to assert, as the second-century Platonizing philosopher-rhetor Maximus of Tyre does, that *all* of life and the universe could be found in his poetry:

It was with his soul that Homer toured every quarter of the world and saw everything that there was to be seen, all the movements of the heavenly bodies, all that happens on earth, the councils of the gods, the different natures of men, the shining of the sun, the dances of the stars . . . household management, war, peace, marriage, farming, horsemanship, all kinds of arts and crafts, different languages and customs, men lamenting, rejoicing, grieving, laughing, fighting . . . (Max. Tyr. *Or.* 26.1)

These passages speak to the pervasive way in which Homer dominated Imperial Greek cultural life, and their claims are supported by a glance at the literature of the period, in which Homer is quoted with the frequency

---

[7] The comments of Lamberton (1992), vii n. 1, are still valid almost twenty years later: "For the ancient reception of Homer, even general discussion of the influence of the epics is lacking, though admittedly the task would be so enormous that it would require writing a history of Greek and Latin literature from the perspective of Homeric influence." For brief attempts see Richardson (1993) and Lamberton (1997).

[8] Dio Chrys. *Or.* 18.8: Ὅμηρος δὲ καὶ πρῶτος καὶ μέσος καὶ ὕστατος.

[9] Dio Chrys. *Or.* 53.6–8.

and familiarity consonant with his monumental authority: to appeal to an august witness, to prove a point, to spice up one's discourse with a literary allusion, to provide an appropriate moral example.[10] The vision of Homer as source of an eternal wisdom, whether moral, philosophical or theological, particularly inspires the allegorical strand of Homeric interpretation that flourishes in the period, from Heraclitus' *Homeric Problems* and Maximus' *Discourses*, to Ps.-Plutarch's *On Homer* and the writings of the Middle Platonist philosopher Numenius of Apamea.[11]

Homer thus looms large in the Imperial landscape, but it is important to emphasize the significant if subtle differences in the nature of Homer's exalted status from that of previous eras. The distinction lies not so much in the kinds of assertions made about him, which are already found in the Classical period. Homer is called 'divine' in Aristophanes and Plato and frequently referred to elsewhere as the wisest of men;[12] his status as an 'instructor' in technical matters is familiar from the boasts of characters like Plato's Ion and Xenophon's Niceratus, who claim to have learned the arts of generalship, household management, rhetoric, and chariot-racing from the poet;[13] and Plato's famous discussion in *Republic* 2–3 testifies to a widespread ethical interest in the Homeric heroes as *exempla*, one that was also reflected in what we know of lost works such as Antisthenes' Homeric discourses, Hippias' *Trojan Discourse*, or Alcidamas' *Mouseion* (all from the late fifth to the early fourth century BCE).[14] Examples of quoting Homer to reinforce or illustrate one's arguments abound in Plato, Xenophon, Aristotle, and Aeschines,[15] and offer a glimpse of the cultural capital that accrued to those among the elite who were able to cleverly sprinkle their discourse with Homeric testimony.[16] Similarly, all of the major modes of

[10] A sample of scholarship studying the Homeric citations of various Imperial authors: Bouquiaux-Simon (1968) on Lucian; Kindstrand (1973) on Dio, Maximus, and Aelius Aristides; Moraux (1987) on Galen; D'Ippolito (2004) on Plutarch.

[11] The literature on Homeric allegory is vast; Buffière (1956) is a general survey, while Bernard (1990) is more specifically attuned to the Imperial period. For an introduction to Heraclitus, see Russell and Konstan (2005); more in-depth are Chiron (2005) and Pontani (2005). On Ps.-Plutarch, see Hillgruber (1994) and on Numenius, Lamberton (1986), 54–77.

[12] Classical references to Homer as "wisest" (σοφώτατος): Pl. *Alc.* 2 147b, *Tht.* 194e, *Leg.* 776e; Xen. *Mem.* 1.4.2, *Symp.* 4.6; Isoc. *C. soph.* 13.2; Aeschin. *In Tim.* 1.141. As "divine" (θεῖος): Ar. *Ran.* 1034; Pl. *Phd.* 95a2; *Certamen* 214, 309, 338 Allen. In general on these issues, see Graziosi (2002), 150–9.

[13] Pl. *Ion* 541b; Xen. *Symp.* 3.6, 4.6–7.

[14] Antisthenes' extant works: *Ajax* and *Odysseus* (14, 15 Caizzi); titles: 1 Caizzi = Diog. Laert. 6.15–18; for discussion, see Giannantoni (1990), 331–7. Hippias: *FGrH* 6 T 3 = Pl. *Hp. mai.* 285d. On the moral content of Alcidamas' *Mouseion*, Richardson (1981).

[15] Halliwell (2000) is an excellent treatment of Plato's use of poetic quotation as testimony; see 95 n. 5 for previous bibliography. On Aristotle, see Hillgruber (1994), 20–1. On the use of Homer and other poetry in Athenian lawcourts, see Ford (1999b).

[16] Ford (2002), 194–7.

reading and interpreting Homer – allegoresis, critiquing verisimilitude or narrative logic, paradigmatic moralizing, ethical and theological critiques, philological inquiry, etc. – can be traced back to the fifth and fourth centuries BCE or earlier.[17]

But while the manner in which Homer was praised, as well as the basic principles of interpreting, using, and criticizing his poetry, remain fairly constant throughout antiquity, the nature of Homer's authority, the symbolic value of his poetry, changes radically in the wake of Alexander the Great's conquest of the Persian Empire and the subsequent expansion of Greek rule throughout the Eastern Mediterranean. Much of this transformation was the result of Homer's position at the heart of the remarkably standardized educational system established throughout the Hellenistic world. In practical terms, the teaching of Greek language and culture was necessary for the continued administration of Greek rule over largely non-Greek populations from Egypt to Bactria. By virtue of its universality and conventionality, however, Greek education also becomes a key marker of Hellenic identity, an acquired trait common to inhabitants of the geographically and ethnically diverse Hellenistic kingdoms.[18] In this context, familiarity with Homer, whose poetry was ensconced at the very beginning of the curriculum, became closely associated with learning Greek, and by extension with *being* Greek.[19] This marks a significant difference from the Classical period, when knowledge of Homer may have been valued (and was probably expected) in an educated elite citizen (at least in Athens), but was not seen as an integral part of citizenship or self-worth among the citizen body at large, much less a defining symbol of an abstract 'Greek' identity.[20]

---

[17] For overviews of Classical critical approaches to Homer, see Richardson (1992) (=[1993], 25–35), supplemented by Apfel (1938) on the fourth century BCE. Ford (1999a) treats the early development of allegorical criticism; see the discussion of Classical allegoresis below in Ch. 2, 35–7. The genre of Homeric problems and solutions that originated in the fourth century gives a good idea of the variety of classical criticism: no work survives intact, but we possess the 25th chapter of Aristotle's *Poetics*, which summarizes his *Homeric Problems* (F 366–404 Gigon; Hintenlang [1961]), as well as the fragments of Zoïlus of Amphipolis, the so-called *Homeromastix*, or, "scourge of Homer" (*FGrH* 71; Gärtner [1978]), and those of a number of lesser-known authors.

[18] Morgan (1998), 21–5. Marrou (1956), 162–70 is still good on this. For a broader view of the new sense of Greek identity in the Hellenistic period, see Burstein (2008).

[19] Hunter (2004), 246: "Through Homer one learned Greek and Greekness."

[20] The ideological linking of Greek identity and education was, however, articulated in the fourth century BCE by Isocrates (see Too [1995]), whose views had considerable influence in later antiquity. We know very little about Classical education and the curriculum, but from the reticence of the Athenian orators (aside from the special case of Aeschines) to quote or refer to Homer, one can infer that such appeals might not have resonated in the same way with democratic juries and audiences as they would have in elite, aristocratic circles.

The canonization of Homer's poems as the greatest and most important works of Greek culture is another index of this transformation of the poet's symbolic value in the Hellenistic world.[21] The founding father of the new political landscape, Alexander himself, was said to have been an ardent admirer of Homer and Achilles;[22] and while Classical authors call Homer 'divine,' it is only in the Hellenistic period that we hear of *Homereia*, or temples built in honor of Homer and featuring a statue of the poet, in cities such as Alexandria and Smyrna.[23] The well-known allegorical relief by Archelaus of Priene known as the 'Apotheosis of Homer,' where he is shown being crowned by a personified *Chronos* (Time) and *Oikoumene* (the inhabited world) as *Muthos* and *Historia* prepare a sacrifice in his honor, is a surviving testament to Homer's new status.[24] Homer's poems are the twin foundational texts of Greek culture and thus an object of study and prestige; to obtain the 'best' manuscripts or produce the authoritative edition of his poetry is to establish proprietary ownership over the greatest symbol of Greek culture.[25] The critical work on Homer's text by scholars such as Zenodotus of Ephesus, Aristarchus of Samothrace, and Crates of Mallus thus forms an essential part of the cultural projects of Hellenistic monarchies at Pergamum and Alexandria (and to a lesser degree in Macedonia), aimed at establishing continuity with both the Classical and Archaic Greek past as well as advertising the legitimate 'Greekness' of the new regimes.[26]

Whereas the early philosophers and Plato had famously attacked Homer's claims to moral, theological, and philosophical authority, Stoicism, which would become the most influential philosophical movement to arise in this period, valorized Homer as an illustrious predecessor, a stance that would contribute greatly to the increasing faith in the poet's universal wisdom so characteristic of the Hellenistic and Imperial periods.[27] Even the Epicurean philosopher and critic Philodemus of Gadara (first century BCE), despite his sect's well-known disdain for poetic wisdom, wrote a

---

[21] Succinct overview in Zeitlin (2001), 195–203.   [22] E.g., Plut. *Alex.* 8 (Homer), 15 (Achilles).

[23] Ael. *VH* 13.22 on the temple and statue of Homer set up by Ptolemy Philopator (221–205 BCE); Str. 14.37 and Cic. *Arch.* 9 on the Homereion at Smyrna. For discussion, see Brink (1972).

[24] Newby (2007), 169: the lower register of the relief is an allegorical narrative of "Homer's dominance over all forms of human literature and learning." On the Archelaus relief, whose date is uncertain, see Brink (1972); Zeitlin (2001), 197–200; and Newby (2007), who provides a full bibliography of earlier scholarship.

[25] Erskine (1995) on Homeric philology in Alexandria and the importance of establishing monarchical control over Greek learning.

[26] Too (1998), 115–50, esp. 134–9.   [27] On the Stoics and Homer, see Long (1992).

treatise, *On the Good King According to Homer*, which uses the poet's work as a compendium of precepts and exempla for monarchs.[28]

The prestige enjoyed by Homer in the Hellenistic world continues unabated in the Roman Empire (as demonstrated by the examples from Heraclitus, Dio, and Maximus I quoted above). On the one hand the passage of time and the conservatism of the educational system consolidated the poet's canonical position for each successive generation, but the increased importance of Greek *paideia* ("education" or "culture") in the self-definition of the Imperial aristocratic elite contributes as well.[29] To be labeled *pepaideumenos*, "educated" or "cultured," becomes a social marker of the highest distinction and was dependent on one's mastery of the canonical literature of the Greek past, particularly of the Classical period[30] – a process that had begun in the Augustan era (best on display in the writings of the critic Dionysius of Halicarnassus) and reached its zenith in the so-called Second Sophistic, the renaissance of Greek oratory and letters extending (roughly) from the mid first to the mid third century CE.[31] In fact, so strong is the faith in Homer's role as avatar of Greek culture that he maintains his centrality under the Empire, despite the fact that his non-Attic language and archaic worldview did not always suit the classicizing tendencies of a society more attuned to the style and content of the Attic prose authors of the fourth century BCE.[32] Homer is now firmly established at the heart of Greek *paideia*, a truly colossal figure, the very personification of Greek culture, and even of Greekness itself.[33] In a culture

---

[28] Asmis (1991).

[29] Cribiore (2001), 140–2; 194–7; 205–10, for the technical details. It is perhaps no accident that the most ardent defenses and panegyrics of the poet occur in texts with a strong pedagogical bent, like Dio's *Or.* 18, Heraclitus' *Homeric Problems*, Ps.-Plutarch's *On Homer*, and Maximus of Tyre's popular didactic philosophical discourses. For the characterization of these texts as 'pedagogical' see Russell (2003) on Heraclitus; Lamberton (2002) on Ps.-Plutarch; Trapp (1997), xx–xxii, on Maximus.

[30] Schmitz (1997) is the most thorough statement of the case; see also Connolly (2001) and Webb (2006) on rhetorical education and declamation; Whitmarsh (2001), 90–130, explores the tensions inherent in the notion of *paideia*.

[31] The continued engagement by Imperial writers with the glorified figures, events, and texts of the distant past was one of the primary means by which they negotiated their sense of what it meant to be Greek under the Roman Empire, whether this nostalgia is seen as resistance to or an escape from the realities of Roman rule. Generally Bowie (1970); Swain (1996), 65–100; Whitmarsh (2001).

[32] Swain (1996), 55–6. Aristarchus had claimed already in the second century BCE that Homer was Athenian (Sch. A ad *Il.* 13.197).

[33] The reverence for Homer *in itself* was not necessarily an anti-Roman position – after all, Homer had been a central part of Roman culture for centuries (cf. Farrell [2004]) and could be seen as the cultural and literary foundational text for both Greeks *and* Romans. Nevertheless, because of the way that Greekness came to be increasingly associated with cultural achievements, 'Homer' signified something slightly different for Greek and Roman Imperial elite, as much as their interests and outlooks matched in other ways.

where elite identity was tied up with the literary authority of the classics, to quote Homer, to appeal to his poetry, was part of the continuous process of asserting one's membership in the 'cultured' and therefore 'Greek' elite.[34]

Homer and heroic history

It bears emphasizing that all of the Imperial authors I treat in this book acknowledge Homer's centrality and authority. Strabo is perhaps the most laudatory; he takes the poet's authority for granted on the basis of his antiquity and cultural pre-eminence and vigorously defends Homer's knowledge of history and geography. But even the others, who are capable of more ambivalent attitudes toward the poet, often effusively praise Homer, display a profound knowledge of his poems, and lay claim to his cultural authority throughout their writing. Dio, for instance, whose *Trojan Oration* is the most anti-Homeric of the three sophistic texts, generally extols Homer's virtues elsewhere in his corpus, as attested by his panegyrical comments on Homer that I quoted above, his encomium *On Homer* (*Or.* 53), and other passages sprinkled throughout his discourses.[35]

What sets the four texts I examine apart from the apologetic and encomiastic readings of Homer that are so prevalent in the period is their focus on the relationship between Homeric poetry and the 'history' that it purports to represent. The absence of interest in the historical underpinnings of Homeric epic is perhaps not a terrible surprise in the case of allegorical interpreters, who proceed on the principle that Homer's narrative is not 'real' but only a symbolic representation of the 'truths' that lie hidden in the text.[36] When Maximus calls Thersites "a perfect allegory of an insubordinate citizenry" or sees the quarreling Agamemnon and Achilles as "allegories of the emotions, of youth and authority" (*Or.* 26.5), it is apparent that he was not particularly concerned about the heroes' historicity. But

---

[34] On this general idea, Whitmarsh (2001), 26–38.

[35] E.g., *Orr.* 2, 12, 55, 61. The contrast between Dio's historicizing approach in the *Trojan Oration* and his interpretative attitude toward Homer in the rest of his corpus is significant; see further Ch. 5 below.

[36] The matter is a bit more complicated, given the variety of allegorical techniques and practices. For example, in Heraclitus' defenses of Homer, he sometimes finds it more convenient to 'rationalize'; thus the plague scene in *Iliad* 1 is interpreted as the description of a real plague told in symbolic terms (Apollo = Sun, his arrows = the sun's rays, etc.) rather than Homer revealing a general truth about the connection between the sun and disease (*Homeric Problems* 6–16). A similar, but more interesting example is Porphyry's *On the Cave of the Nymphs* where Porphyry insists that there was a real cave on Ithaca, but that Homer composed a complex allegorical description of it that Porphyry proceeds to decode (on this text see Lamberton [1986], 119–33). Nevertheless these are exceptions to the general aversion to history prevalent in allegorical interpretation in antiquity.

this lack of attention to history is also evident in Ps.-Plutarch's *On Homer*, which tries to prove that Homer knew of, and often 'founded' every field of knowledge, from rhetoric to physics to arithmetic, music, medicine, and law. One would think that Homer's knowledge of the Trojan War and his qualities as a historian would at least warrant a chapter in Ps.-Plutarch's catalog, but the section on Homer's mastery of "historical discourse" and "narratives of past events" (74–90) only praises Homer's ability to vividly describe a wide variety of objects, people, deeds, creatures, etc.[37]

Similarly, examples of moralizing criticism, like Plutarch's *How the Young Man Should Listen to Poetry*, are only concerned with evaluating the *ethical* truth of Homer's poetry (and that of other poets as well) and operate under the (Platonic) presumption that poetry's purpose was to 'teach' proper morals, either by direct precept or through *exempla*. A good example of how Homer was thought to have intentionally fashioned his heroes as paradigms for behavior appears in a speech that opens the section of Athenaeus' *Deipnosophists* (c. 200 CE) entitled *On the Life of the Heroes in Homer*.[38]

Homer, observing that moderation is the first and most appropriate virtue for the young . . . wishing (βουλόμενος) to implant it anew from the beginning onwards, *in order that* [the young] might spend their leisure and their zeal on noble deeds and be doers of good and share with each other, has set up (κατεσκεύασε) a frugal and self-sufficient way of life for everyone, reasoning (λογιζόμενος) . . . that those who abide resolutely in frugality become well-disciplined and self-controlled concerning the rest of life. (Athen. 1.15 [8e–f])

The idea here is that Homer's depiction of the heroes is solely directed at morally didactic ends; there is no question of whether Homer might

---

[37] This is an example of another influential strand of Homeric criticism – the rhetorical – which imagines the poet as the model of oratorical composition and technique, and analyzes the means by which he achieves such a powerful effect upon audiences (often in order to reproduce them in one's own work). Criticism of this sort focuses on Homer's style, arrangement, descriptive skills, diction, and emotional power and is naturally quite common in the Imperial period, dominated as it is by rhetorical training and display: the best example is the encomium of Homer's eloquence in Quintilian, *Inst.* 10.1.46–51, the most well-known, Ps.-Longinus' *On the Sublime*, and the most copious source of such readings is the so-called 'exegetical,' or bT scholia to the *Iliad*, which consistently approach Homer from this perspective (Richardson [1980]; Meijering [1987]; Schmidt [2002]). The most sustained rhetorical analyses are found in the little-known but fascinating treatise *On Figured Speeches B* preserved in the corpus of Dionysius of Halicarnassus (see Schouler [1986] and Heath [2003b]). Technically, the question of Homer's representation of historical reality could have figured in such criticism, since the shaping of the 'facts' into one's narrative was a recognized step in rhetorical composition, but there is almost no inkling of such concern in our sources – if anything, the concern is with Homer's refashioning of previous stories and traditions, rather than 'reality.'

[38] Ath. 1.15–18 (8e–11b). This part of Athenaeus' work is unfortunately only preserved in an epitomized version; the title derives from a parallel reference in the *Suda* s.v. Ὅμηρος.

have been restricted in some way by the necessity to depict the heroes' *real* lifestyle (nor is there in the rest of the speech).[39] This avoidance of history is characteristic of these strands of ancient Homeric criticism prior to the Imperial period as well, and suggests that there is something in the idea of Homer as a historian that is somewhat incongruous with the broader vision of the poet's universal authority. The divergent visions of Homer that underlie these two critical stances provide some further support for this hypothesis. A striking feature of historicizing critiques of Homer is their tendency to historicize Homer as well, that is, imagine the poet as a real, living, breathing person, involved in mundane activities such as collecting information, asking questions, traveling throughout the Mediterranean. In contrast, 'strong' moralizing critics such as the one in Athenaeus, and allegorists and apologists like Ps.-Plutarch, see Homer only in the haziest of terms, as a disembodied force of nature, a mystical and arcane sym- bolist, or a semi-divine creator of complex didactic allegorical narratives; one never gets a sense from their texts of the poet as an actual human being.[40]

In centering their work on the question of Homeric poetry's status as history (and conversely, as myth or fiction), Strabo, Dio, Lucian, and Philostratus thus largely abandon the concerns of the more traditional branches of Homeric reception – the gods, ethics and morality, technical and philosophical wisdom – and instead choose to follow a separate but parallel tradition that treated Homer as if he were a historian. This mode of interpretation or 'use' of Homer (which I discuss in more detail in the next chapter) presumes that Homeric poetry reflected and could be employed as evidence for historical or cultural data about the heroic age. While such historical inquiry into the heroic past could be conducted for purely antiquarian reasons, it was often responding to the important role that the heroic age played in the construction of Greek identity. Efforts to locate and establish concrete connections to heroes are evident already in the Archaic and Classical periods,[41] but the practice takes on a new valence

---

[39] Although it is hard to be sure since the epitome lacks indications of changes of speaker, Athenaeus seems to have structured the discussion of the heroes' life and customs as a debate between the forceful moralizer depicted here (customarily identified as Myrtilus), a 'historicizing' speaker who is concerned with heroic reality, and others whose positions lie somewhere in between; on this, see Heath (2000).

[40] Ps.-Plutarch exemplifies the difficulty involved in integrating a description of Homer's life with an account of his encyclopedic knowledge by sectioning off Homer's biography (2–3) as parenthetical to the main body of his work.

[41] On the early genealogists and mythographers: Thomas (1989), 173–95; Graf (1993), 125–31; Jacob (1994); Fowler (2000).

as Hellenistic cities and kings, predominantly outside of mainland Greece, seek to legitimize themselves by claiming descent or other links to the mythic and heroic past of 'Greece.'[42] As a privileged witness to that age, and particularly of its watershed event, the Trojan War, Homer's influence on conceptions of Greek identity based on genealogy, rather than *paideia*, expanded accordingly.[43] Seen from this perspective, Homer is positioned at the forefront of a culture that cherished its origins, both as its first and greatest poet and as the most respected *historian* of its illustrious past, even if the two roles are not, as we shall see, perfectly compatible.[44]

Criticizing or defending Homer's historiographical accuracy or objectives thus often became embroiled in larger debates about the heroic past and its relevance in the present. For example, the Hellenistic and early Imperial discussions of Homer's geographical accuracy alluded to in Strabo's *Geography* are spurred on by the competing claims of various local historians, cities, and regions to identify themselves with particular heroic events, figures, and sites (most famously, Troy).[45] As we shall see in my discussion of Strabo in Chapter 3, his defense of Homer's historiographical diligence against the skepticism of previous scholars is motivated by a similar desire to retain some sort of authoritative connection to the Greek legendary past. The later Imperial texts also vividly evoke this discourse by their choice of setting: Dio's *Trojan Oration* purports to be delivered at Troy (Roman Ilium) itself, to Trojans who revere their Homeric past, while the conversation depicted in Philostratus' *Heroicus* takes place on the Thracian Chersonese, just across the Hellespont from the Troad and its heroic tombs.[46] But Dio and Philostratus (and to a lesser extent Lucian) exploit this link between Homeric historical criticism and the reverence for the heroic past for very different purposes; questioning Homer's bona fides as a historian permits them to cast doubt on the legitimacy of the poetic and historical tradition so valued by Imperial Greeks. For them, criticizing and satirizing the desire to imagine Homer as a historian becomes a means to question the investment in the heroic past as well.

---

[42] A vast bibliography, but see Jones (1999); Scheer (2003).

[43] Thus while Homer's association with education and *paideia* connected him to a theoretically inclusive conception of Greek identity defined as a body of knowledge that could be acquired, his role as historical witness operates by contrast within a discourse that sees present-day identity as determined primarily by more restrictive notions of 'ancient' ethnicity based on genealogy. Both had their adherents in the Imperial period.

[44] Hunter (2004), 250; Porter (2004), 325.

[45] Cf. Sage (2000) on visits to Troy in the Imperial period and the symbolic value of the city.

[46] On depictions of the Troad in the Second Sophistic, see Trachsel (2007), 387–461; 418–44 on Dio's *Trojan* and Philostratus' *Heroicus*.

FICTIONALIZING HOMER

It should be clear by now that Strabo stands somewhat apart, temporally and temperamentally, from the other three authors I treat in this book. He is something of a transitional figure, still immersed in the intellectual world of the Hellenistic period, yet belonging to the nascent classicizing movement that would define Greek culture under the Empire. As a historian and geographer, Strabo sees Homer as an illustrious predecessor, and his treatment of Homer in the *Geography* (his only surviving work) is thus a relatively straightforward attempt at solving the problem of how to distinguish the 'history' in Homeric poetry from the 'myths.' Dio, Lucian, and Philostratus on the other hand are neither historians nor professional scholars, but rather multifaceted literary writers firmly embedded in Second Sophistic culture.[47] And while their works touch upon historiographical and literary critical issues, they are generically diverse – epideictic oratory, the novel, fictional dialogue; in fact, their choice to tackle Homer and history in specifically non-historiographical texts suggests an interest in fictional literary experimentation. And in contrast to the fairly direct and sober inquiries of Strabo and his predecessors, the Second Sophistic texts display a self-consciously playful and creative attitude toward Homer, the heroes, and the heroic age: Dio's *Trojan Oration* accuses Homer of being a liar and paradoxically asserts that Troy actually won the Trojan War; Lucian's *True Stories* takes the *Odyssey* as its explicit model and tells of the narrator's encounter with Homer, Odysseus, and the other heroes on the Island of the Blessed, and Philostratus' *Heroicus* features a vine dresser offering new information about the Trojan War that he claims to have obtained from the ghost of Protesilaus, the first Greek soldier killed at Troy. While the texts all address the relation between Homer and historical 'reality,' they do so in a provocative, mischievous manner that suggests that their Second Sophistic authors were less concerned with solving the problem of Homer's reliability than with mocking (at different levels of intensity) the presumptions and prejudices sustaining the desire to find a 'solution.' That they simultaneously summon up a picture of Homer himself, while fabricating their own 'fictions' that compete with Homer's, suggest that

---

[47] Dio's eighty surviving works include short dialogues, moral essays, epistles, long public orations on numerous topics, etc. Lucian's specialty is the comic dialogue, but his corpus boasts declamations, *prolaliai* (short prefatory speeches), biographies, a treatise on historiography, and diatribes. Philostratus' surviving body of work is smaller, but similarly varied: dialogues (*Nero, On Gymnastics*, and *Heroicus*), biographies (the massive *Life of Apollonius of Tyana* and the *Lives of the Sophists*), and the *Imagines*, a lengthy series of rhetorical descriptions of paintings.

their texts are also reflections on the authors' own literary relation to their monumental predecessor.

Homeric palimpsests

In their play with Homer, history, and fiction, the Second Sophistic authors are following in the footsteps of a figure who could be called the patron saint of the historical revisionist tradition: the sixth-century BCE lyric poet Stesichorus of Himera. Stesichorus had apparently related, in a poem called the *Palinode*, how he had been blinded by Helen for saying that she had gone to Troy (i.e., Homer's version), and had only regained his sight when he told the 'true' story – that she had never gone there. Although Homer is not mentioned in fragments of the poem that survive,[48] the implication is that his version of the Trojan War was not true, and this is certainly how Plato, the first author who refers to this story, takes it.[49] But by introducing a fantastic and amusing autobiographical tale of divine epiphany and vengeance in order to refute Homer's version of events, Stesichorus deliberately provokes the skepticism of his audience, placing his new 'truth' under the same scrutiny as the recently discredited version of Homer. Stesichorus complicates, rather than simplifies, the issue of Homer's historical accuracy, and thus provides *in nuce* a model for Dio, Lucian, and Philostratus' similarly ambivalent and self-conscious responses to Homer.

Dio's *Trojan*, Lucian's *True Stories*, and Philostratus' *Heroicus* are only three examples among a host of Homeric works written in the Roman Empire that are the heirs, broadly speaking, of the Stesichorean tradition – that is, palimpsestic texts parasitical on and in a close intertextual relationship with the originary Homeric poems. A number of other surviving texts attest to the popularity of this sort of fictional response to Homer in the Second Sophistic, and are as much a testament to the poet's monumental status as the paeans to his wisdom we have already encountered.[50] There are full-scale replacement narratives (Dictys of Crete's *Journal of the Trojan War* and Dares of Phrygia's *On the Destruction of Troy*, which purport to

---

[48] Unless one understands the claim that Stesichorus "blamed" (μέμφεται) Homer (F 193 Davies), made by a second-century CE commentator on the work of Chamaeleon, a Hellenistic literary critic, to mean that Stesichorus did so explicitly.

[49] Pl. *Phdr.* 243a–b. Pratt (1993), 132–6; Austin (1994), ch. 2; Wright (2005), 86–109, whose thorough treatment comes to the intriguing (yet ultimately unpersuasive) conclusion that Plato invented the lines he quotes from the *Palinode* and that the original poem had nothing to do with 'correcting' Homer or the traditional account of Helen.

[50] Bowersock (1994), ch. 1; Hunter (2004), 251.

be eyewitness accounts of the Trojan War written by participants), poetic continuations (Quintus Smyrnaeus' *Posthomerica*; Triphiodorus' *Sack of Troy*),[51] and rhetorical dramatizations of individual scenes (Aelius Aristides' *Or.* 16 [52 Dindorf] *Embassy Speech to Achilles*). Homeric centos, in which verses from his poems are rearranged to create a different meaning, are found in Dio's *Alexandrian Oration* (*Or.* 32.82–5) and Lucian's *Charon*. One could add the numerous biographies of Homer from the period, including *The Contest of Homer and Hesiod*, as well as fictional dialogues such as Dio's *Or.* 58, depicting an acrimonious exchange between Chiron and the young Achilles, Plutarch's *Gryllus* (in which Odysseus and one of Circe's man-pigs debate the rationality of animals), or the Homeric episodes in Lucian's *Dialogues of the Dead*.[52]

On occasion, like our three texts, the palimpsestic work brings Homer into the picture: in Lucian's *Charon*, loosely structured as a reverse *Nekuia* in which Charon comes to the upper world to witness the follies of the living, we hear of Homer getting seasick on board Charon's ferry and vomiting up his verses, now imagined as material objects (which Charon greedily gathers up and commits to memory).[53] And in probably the most successful Imperial literary transformation of the *Odyssey*, Heliodorus' *An Ethiopian Tale*, Homer is revealed to be the hairy-thighed, bastard offspring of an illicit love affair between Hermes and the wife of an Egyptian priest.[54] These examples illustrate how the tone of these rewritings, especially those involving Homer himself, tends to be tinged with humor and a healthy, self-conscious dose of the absurd in a manner typical of many Second Sophistic texts. Homer, in these texts, is still canonical, but that centrality is acknowledged through parody, reinvention, and rewriting. In this respect Dio, Lucian, and Philostratus' efforts to revise, rewrite and undermine the Homeric tradition fit smoothly into the Second Sophistic literary landscape.

---

[51] On Quintus, see James and Lee (2000) and Baumbach and Bär (2007); on Triphiodorus, Paschalis (2005).

[52] These are all examples of "literary transduction" (Dolezel's [1998] term) or "hypertextuality" (Genette's [1997]) – Genette labels Quintus' *Posthomerica* at 178 as a "continuation" and Dictys and Dares' works at 220–1 as "prosifications" of Homer (cf. 177–92 on Homeric continuations from the *Odyssey* to Aymé's *Uranus*). On *Gryllus*, Fernández Delgado (2000) and Casanova (2005); on Aristides' *Embassy Speech to Achilles*, Kindstrand (1973), 215–20. D'Ippolito (2007) examines *Gryllus*, the *Embassy Speech to Achilles*, Dio's *Alexandrian*, and Lucian's *Charon*.

[53] An echo of the painting by Galaton described by Aelian (*VH* 13.22) in which Homer is depicted vomiting his verses, which other poets greedily slurp up.

[54] Heliod. *Aeth.* 3.14.2–4; for Heliodorus and the *Odyssey*: Whitmarsh (1998), (1999), and Hunter (2004), 250–3.

While such texts take pleasure in travestying the most respected representative of Greek culture, they also depend upon an erudite familiarity with the Homeric poems that firmly establishes their authors' credentials as *pepaideumenoi*. The ability to discourse knowledgeably and wittily on Homeric minutiae was prized in Imperial intellectual life, particularly in the sort of occasions for social performance of *paideia* depicted in Plutarch's *Table-Talk*, Aulus Gellius' *Attic Nights*, or Athenaeus' *Deipnosophists*.[55] The participants at these gatherings show off their learning and cleverness by fashioning recondite opinions on questions such as which hand of Aphrodite Diomedes wounded, or why Achilles asks Patroclus to "mix the wine stronger" for the members of the embassy in *Iliad* 9. Did the heroes eat boiled meat, or was it always roasted? What were the names of the men eaten by Scylla?[56] Such discussions drew upon the vast tradition of 'problems and solutions' that had begun in the Classical period, and that has survived predominantly in the Homeric scholia. The controversies could revolve around the kind of historical, moral, or theological concerns that we have mentioned already, but often dealt with problems of narrative verisimilitude and consistency, character, motivation, or plot. The 'correctness' of the answer was often less important than the persuasiveness and originality with which it was proposed.[57] As members of this intellectual milieu, Dio, Lucian, and Philostratus exhibit a thorough grasp of Homeric criticism, and the facility with which they manipulate and transform well-known 'problems' for their own purposes will be evident throughout this book.

What marks their work as a coherent group within the larger fields of erudite Homeric rewritings and learned Homeric commentary is the distinctive combination of three interests: in the historical 'truth' of Homer's account, in the explicit and detailed discussion of Homeric poetry, and in the figure of Homer himself. Of the other Imperial works that engage with Homer, the few that address one or two of these issues fail to take the other(s) into account.[58] For instance, most of the palimpsestic works

---

[55] Johnson (2009) on these "elite reading communities." On such displays of learning as consolidating elite identity, see Schmitz (1997). There is evidence that many educated individuals did not know the entire *Iliad* and *Odyssey*, but I do not believe this applies to any of our authors. Naturally, some books will be quoted or cited more often than others – this hardly proves that a section of the poems that is not mentioned was unfamiliar to a given author.

[56] Plut. *Quaest. conv.* 677e; Ath. 1.25c–e; Aul. Gell. *NA* 14.6.3.

[57] Cf. Jacob (2004).

[58] Another set of texts that I refer to in passing, but do not examine in detail are the various *Lives of Homer* dating from the Imperial period but probably incorporating material from much earlier. The biographies are surprisingly uninterested in Homer's relationship to the historical content of

of the Empire are primarily concerned with re-imagining Homeric characters, narrative, or style. Aristides' reworking of *Iliad* 9 in his *Embassy
Speech to Achilles* is a case in point; an intimate knowledge of the Homeric
hypotext is essential to fully appreciate his project, but it is a purely literary
exercise in trans-stylization, with no explicit concern either for Homer
or for the 'real' events. This is also one of the reasons why I only take
a brief look at the so-called *Troy Romances* of Dictys and Dares,[59] which
are often grouped together with Dio's *Trojan Oration* and Philostratus'
Heroicus (and a chapter [17] of Lucian's dialogue *The Rooster*) as part of the
Homeric 'revisionist' vogue under the Empire – texts that 'correct' Homer's
account and present a new 'truer' version of what happened.[60] A significant difference between Dio and Philostratus' texts and the *Troy Romances*,
however, is that while the latter may *replace* Homer, they never mention or
discuss him (understandably a difficult task, given their claims to be pre-
Homeric).[61] In contrast to the bare-bones narratives of Dictys and Dares,
Dio and Philostratus (and Lucian in *The Rooster*) introduce their 'historical' corrections in counterpoint to a learned and playful interrogation of
Homeric poetry (and Homer himself).[62]

Ptolemy the Quail and literary authority

I would like to conclude with a glance at an erstwhile member of the
Homeric revisionist club whose interests more closely resemble those of
my authors: Ptolemy the Quail, a somewhat mysterious figure active in the
late first or early second century CE, possibly from Alexandria, and probably

his poems, focusing instead on his life as a poet. The *Lives* can be found most conveniently in West
(2003), 295–457, and in Allen (1912), 184–268; Graziosi (2002) examines the biographical tradition
in the Classical era.
[59] Another reason is that the versions of the two texts we possess are later Latin translations of lost
Greek originals (definitely in the case of Dictys, probably in that of Dares) and are thus difficult to
examine as Imperial Greek texts.
[60] On Dictys' and Dares' relation to Homer, see Venini (1981), Merkle (1994), and Usener (1994); for
more on Homeric revisionism, see Ch. 6. Alternatively, the group (sometimes *sans Heroicus*) is seen
as a late manifestation of the tradition, dating back to Xenophanes and Plato, that accused Homer
of being a liar (cf. Wolff [1932]).
[61] The Troy Romances, of course, *implicitly* interact with the Homeric account, as they diverge from,
rationalize, and supplement his narrative, but this is precisely what ties them closer to works like
that of Aristides rather than, let's say, Dio's *Trojan Oration*. In fact, this distinction between explicit
and implicit rewritings is central to Genette's definition of a palimpsestic text ([1997]: 5): "By
hypertextuality I mean any relationship uniting a text B (which I shall call the *hypertext*) to an
earlier text A (I shall, of course, call the *hypotext*), upon which it is grafted in a manner that is *not*
that of commentary" (my emphasis).
[62] For more on Dictys, Dares, and Lucian's *The Rooster*, see Ch. 6.

a scholar or grammarian.[63] His specifically Homeric work, the *Anthomeros* (apparently a twenty-four book verse refutation of the poet), is known to us only by its title,[64] but his *Paradoxical History* shows an interest in Homer and his heroes as well, and, moreover, betrays an irreverent attitude toward these topics reminiscent of that of our authors. The work, which survives only in fragments and a summary by the ninth-century scholar Photius, is a collection of outlandish anecdotes about legendary figures that Ptolemy nevertheless insists were true, or at least vouched for by his sources.[65] While the *Paradoxical History*, as it stands now, is a random, unstructured collection of 'facts' meant to shock and amuse and lacks the thematic cohesion one finds in the work of Dio, Lucian, and Philostratus, it nevertheless provides us with some glimpses of the sort of interests in Homer, fiction, and 'sources' shared by those authors.[66]

Ptolemy enjoys telling unparalleled stories about Homeric heroes that test even the most naïve reader's credulity: for instance, Achilles was so called because one of his lips was burnt off (ἀ-χεῖλος) when Thetis was making him immortal, Odysseus "used to be called Outis because he had big ears" (ὦτα), and Helen and Achilles had a winged child named Euphorion on the Island of the Blessed.[67] Many of these stories are not explicitly tethered to Homer, but there are a few exceptions involving absurd solutions to classic Homeric 'problems.' For instance, Ptolemy breezily deciphers Tiresias' enigmatic prediction that Odysseus' death will come "from the sea," or *ex halos* (ἐξ ἁλός: *Od.* 11.134) by explaining that a witch (a former servant of Circe no less) used her drugs to turn Odysseus into a horse, whom she took care of until he grew old and died. Her name? Halos.[68] And most significantly for my purposes, he tells several unusual stories about Homer

---

[63] On Ptolemy see Tomberg (1968); Bowersock (1994), 23–7; and especially Cameron (2006), 134–59. On his Trojan stories, Grossardt (2006), 62–5; on his connection to Dictys, Dowden (2009).

[64] *Suda*, s.v. Πτολεμαῖος Ἀλεξανδρεύς: Ἀνθόμηρον (ἔστι δὲ ποίησις ῥαψῳδιῶν εἰκοσιτεσσάρων).

[65] Our primary knowledge of the text derives from the summary of its contents in Phot. *Bibl.* 190, 146a–153b, who gives the title as *New* [or '*Strange*'] *History for the Sake of Erudition* (Περὶ τῆς εἰς πολυμαθίαν καινῆς ἱστορίας). The *Suda* (s.v. Πτολεμαῖος Ἀλεξανδρεύς) gives the title as *On Paradoxical History* (Περὶ παραδόξου ἱστορίας); Eustathius also cites this text, often in more detail than Photius, in his commentaries on the *Iliad* and *Odyssey* (on Eustathius' use of Ptolemy, Valk (1971–87) vol. I, cix–cx). Chatzis (1914) includes Photius' summary along with all of the fragments.

[66] The randomness is typical of mythographical collections, as well as second-century CE miscellanies such as Aelian's *Miscellaneous History* or Aulus Gellius' *Attic Nights* that explicitly stress their intentional lack of unity and order.

[67] As these examples illustrate, Ptolemy is particularly fond of using puns, banal etymologies, and other language-related jokes as the basis for his 'new' myths. Helen, Achilles, and Odysseus figure in a significant majority of Ptolemy's heroic anecdotes; e.g., there are at least fifteen 'facts' about Helen listed.

[68] Phot. *Bibl.* 190, 150a12–19.

himself. At one point, Ptolemy reveals that a certain Helen, daughter of Musaeus (and incidentally proud owner of a talking lamb), "wrote a prose account of the Trojan War before Homer from which Homer is said to have taken his *hupothesis* ['plot,' or 'content']."[69] Later he informs us of yet another female 'source,' the appropriately named Phantasia ("Imagination"), an Egyptian from Memphis:

They say that she wrote (συνέταξε) a Trojan War and a narrative (διήγησιν) about the *Odyssey* before Homer and deposited the books (τὰς βίβλους) in Memphis. Homer, arrived there, received copies (τὰ ἀντίγραφα) from the priest Phanites, and composed [his poems] in accordance with her works (συντάξαι ἐκείνοις ἀκολούθως).[70]

These two anecdotes (that glaringly contradict each other) sound very much like the kind of tales about Homer told by Dio, Lucian, and Philostratus: Homer is historicized, deflated, and his authority called into question. Moreover, Ptolemy's portrayal of Homer as a plagiarist, who passes off the work of others as his own, points to Ptolemy's own play with the 'truth'; as I mentioned, Ptolemy meticulously documents the 'sources' of his anecdotes, often specifying the author and work where he has allegedly discovered his information (e.g., the Phantasia story is attributed to a certain Naucrates). While some of these are genuine, the vast majority are otherwise unattested and, as Alan Cameron has convincingly argued, almost certainly invented by Ptolemy himself.[71] Ptolemy, as a forger, is thus engaged in precisely the opposite (if no less fraudulent) activity that he assigns to Homer. This self-conscious play with questions of truth and falsehood, with 'sources' and authentication, situates him very near Dio, Lucian, and Philostratus whose similar testing of their audiences' willingness to believe their new, revisionist accounts constitutes, as we shall see, an essential part of their critiques of Homer.

The Second Sophistic authors, then, are responding to the same anxieties about differentiating history from poetry and truth from fiction that so consumed Origen, who, after all, was a contemporary of Philostratus

---

[69] Phot. *Bibl.* 190, 149b22–6.

[70] Phot. *Bibl.* 190, 151a37–b5; cf. Eust. *Od.* 1379, 62–1380, 1. Homer is mentioned in one other 'fact' – his servant, named Scindapsus, failed to burn the poet's corpse after death, as he had commanded, and was fined a thousand drachmas (Phot. *Bibl.* 190, 152b20–5).

[71] Cameron (2006), restating with new arguments the extreme skepticism of Hercher (1855–6) against Chatzis (1914) and Tomberg (1968), who maintain the authenticity of many of Ptolemy's sources (cf. Dowden [2009] for a cautious defense of Ptolemy). While I share Cameron's skepticism concerning the authenticity of Ptolemy's sources, I wonder whether he seriously intended to deceive his readers (as Cameron thinks) or rather expected them to see his outlandish variants for the fictional creations they are.

and, his Christianity aside, part of the same basic intellectual milieu. But while Origen, much as Strabo before him, is 'embarrassed' by the fictions that have become interwined with historical fact, and frustrated by the intransigence of the problem, Dio, Lucian, and Philostratus embrace and exploit its uncertainties and contradictions to write their own ambivalent and slippery Homeric 'fictions.' Each author problematizes the relationship between Homer and historical reality in their own particular way, but all three cast a bemused and at times satirical eye upon the canonical status of Homer, the reverence for the heroic past of which he was the primary witness, and thus the essential role that both played in the construction of Imperial Greekness.

CHAPTER 2

Homer, poet and historian

Herodotus and Thucydides

For the ancients, Homeric poetry depicted real *historical* people and events. As Carlo Brillante puts it, the Greeks of the Classical period "imagined their heroes as men who had actually lived, inhabiting the same cities and regions in which they themselves, several centuries later, continued to reside."[1] By the Imperial era, physical evidence of the heroic past was everywhere: a papyrus letter in Lycia written by Sarpedon, the tusks of the Calydonian boar in Beneventum, the anchor of the Argo at the mouth of the Phasis.[2] The precise locations of heroic activity, such as the bronze floor of Agamemnon's tent at Aulis (Paus. 9.19.5), were carefully preserved, marked out, and displayed to tourists and travelers; the heroes themselves, in their tombs, or else as the dedicatees of cults, were visited and venerated.[3] The establishment of coherent heroic 'family trees' and genealogies situating the heroes in time and linking them to particular cities and geographical areas contributed to the perception of their reality.[4] On a more quotidian level, the heroic world intruded into ancient social life – from public art to religious practices and ritual, as a source of *paradeigmata* in philosophical discourses, rhetorical displays, and moral diatribes,[5] and as the subject-matter of the epic and tragic poetry which formed the backbone of the Greek and Roman educational system. The historicity of the heroic age was thus taken for granted: it had left visible, tangible traces; it had a

---

[1] Brillante (1990), 94. Cf. Graf (1993), 121–3. Other good expositions: Walbank (1960); Piérart (1983); Veyne (1988); Feeney (1991), 252–62; Dowden (1992), 39–56.

[2] Plin. *HN* 4.53; Procop. *Goth.* 1.15; Arr. *Peripl. M. Eux.* 11. On this topic see Friedländer (1907–13), 367–80, and Casson (1974), 229–61.

[3] For some specific case studies of the relation of hero cults and the legendary Homeric past in the Hellenistic period, see Alcock (1997); and see Ch. 6 on Philostratus' *Heroicus*.

[4] The importance of establishing links to the past can be witnessed by the practice of citing heroic precedent in political disputes throughout antiquity. See Swain (1996), ch. 3, on the Imperial period; Jones (1999) on the Hellenistic; and Erskine (2001) on Hellenistic Troy. For some uses of Homer in this regard, see Richardson (1993), 27.

[5] Buxton (1994), 171–3.

relative chronology and had taken place in identifiable locales; unbroken lines of descent linked it to contemporary Greek society, and it formed the subject matter of an authoritative poetic and religious tradition. The belief in the heroic age held sway throughout antiquity, but seems especially pronounced in the Hellenistic and Imperial periods, when, as I pointed out in the Introduction, new geographical and political realities provided an impetus for Greek-speaking people across the Mediterranean to find links to an illustrious past that was drifting further away with each passing generation.[6]

But if there were very good reasons to believe in the existence and his-toricity of the heroic age, several obstacles stood in the way of accepting that heroic tales were true in every detail. The first-century BCE historian Diodorus Siculus laments the myriad difficulties that bedevil "compilers of ancient mythology" (τοῖς τὰς παλαιὰς μυθολογίας συντατγομένοις: 4.1): the bewildering and contradictory accounts of earlier writers, the impos-sibility of accurate dating, and the impediments to investigation posed by the antiquity (ἀρχαιότης) of the events.[7] Despite these caveats, Diodorus is impelled by the importance of this period to provide an account of these times, although even he acknowledges that he has not been able to adhere to a strict chronology for events prior to the Trojan War (5.1). The heroic age was thus considered fully historical, but distinguished from later history on an *epistemological* basis, as a period for which knowledge was provisional and less susceptible to verification.[8] This distinction already manifests itself in the Classical period, in Herodotus' frequent specifi-cation of certain figures as the "first of those whom we *know*" to have done certain things (as opposed to earlier 'mythic' performers of the same deeds).[9] This is not to say that the heroic period was ignored, but only that such work was recognized as occupying a separate category of ancient historiographical inquiry.[10] In some instances, this field is given a specific name – ἀρχαιολογία, which Plato has the sophist Hippias of Elis define

---

[6] Scheer (2003) is a good overview.

[7] Cf. the similar, if more derisive, remarks of the first-century CE Jewish historian Josephus in *Against Apion* 1.

[8] Leyden (1949–50); Bickerman (1952); Nickau (1990).

[9] E.g., Hdt. 3.122.2: "For Polycrates was the first of the Greeks of whom we know (πρῶτος τῶν ἡμεῖς ἴδμεν) to aim to rule the sea" (see Shimron 1973). Cf. the fourth-century historian Ephorus' decision to begin his universal history with the return of the Heraclidae, eighty years after the Trojan War (*FGrH* 70 T 8).

[10] Herodotus discusses heroic events several times, e.g., his Helen story which I treat below. Ephorus (*FGrH* 70) likewise treats the Trojan War, for example, in F 11–14; cf. F 31 and see in general Bruno Sunseri (1997).

as "the genealogies of heroes and men, and . . . how cities were founded in ancient times."[11]

While many mythographers and genealogists were content to ignore problems of verifiability, verisimilitude, and multiplicity in their collections,[12] others, like Hecataeus of Miletus or Palaephatus (fourth century BCE), critiqued the ancient stories and produced versions they felt were more reasonable. But the only criterion they could use was their own subjective appraisal of the relative plausibility of an individual account; in this sense the 'true' story was what was left over after the 'mythic' or improbable was eliminated. This so-called 'rationalization' technique remained the primary means of sorting out *archaiologia* throughout antiquity, but historians recognized the provisional nature of their task; in the face of such a chaotic and tangled tradition that transmitted so little reliable information about a heroic period ever more distant in time, they could do little more than beg their readers' indulgence. Consider Plutarch's plea at the beginning of his *Theseus* (1.3):

I hope, then, that I would be able, purifying the mythic (ἐκκαθαιρόμενον . . . τὸ μυθῶδες), to make it submit to reason (λόγῳ) and take on the appearance of history (ἱστορίας ὄψιν). But wherever it obstinately defies plausibility (τοῦ πιθανοῦ) and refuses to admit any element of the probable (τὸ εἰκός), I will ask for readers who are generous and can listen patiently to ancient history (ἀρχαιολογίαν).

HISTORICAL CRITICISM OF HOMER

There was one source for the heroic age, however, that commanded more respect and credibility than the others: Homeric poetry. Curiously, most surveys of ancient historical criticism of heroic myth ignore this fact, treating Homeric stories as just another set of myths that were 'rationalized,' and failing to delineate the very different approach applied to Homeric history.[13] After all, in contrast to the other conflicting, anonymous, secondhand tales, the *Iliad* and the *Odyssey* were extensive, detailed, and authoritative narrative accounts of the Trojan War and the Returns, attributed to an individual author, that seemed historiographical in form and content.[14] The narrator sets his account in the past, emphasizes his concern for accuracy, begins his story by identifying the causes of his primary subject, the anger of Achilles, and adheres to a verisimilar narrative, largely eschewing the supernatural.

---

[11] Pl. *Hp. mai.* 285d = *FGrH* 6 T 3. Cf. Diod. Sic. 4.4; Dionysius' Ῥωμαϊκὴ Ἀρχαιολογία; and Josephus' Ἰουδαϊκὴ Ἀρχαιολογία. For *archaiologia* as a branch of ancient historiography, see Bickerman (1952) and Momigliano (1990), ch. 3.

[12] Henrichs (1987).   [13] E.g., Dowden (1992), 39–53; Graf (1993), 121–41.   [14] Strasburger (1972).

The world in which the story is set correlates for the most part with 'real' geography and topography, and is filled with specific detail about the customs, families, histories of the heroes.[15] And even aspects of the works that strike us as non-historical – the frequent speeches and vivid, poetic, descriptions of battles and other scenes – were staples of ancient historiography, which no doubt was heavily influenced by the Homeric model.

Most important, however, was the status of the poet himself. Homer, as I have noted, occupied a central place in Greek education, literature, and culture, and hence enjoyed a certain amount of *a priori* authority.[16] But for historians, his reliability also stemmed from the fact that he was the *oldest* source for the heroic period; Dionysius of Halicarnassus, for instance, calls Homer "the most credible and the *most ancient* of all witnesses" (Ὅμηρος... μαρτύρων ἀξιοπιστότατός τε καὶ ἀρχαιότατος ὤν: *Ant. Rom.* 7.72.3).[17] In other words, studying heroic history presumed belief in the historicity of Homer himself, now thought of as an authentic source situated in historical time. Only a minority of ancient scholars, however, considered Homer contemporary with the Trojan War, with most dating his birth between 50–150 years afterwards.[18] Ascertaining the precise era in which Homer flourished was less important than establishing his proximity to the heroic age, which bestowed on his poetry an evidentiary value surpassing any other known narrative account. The antiquity of Homer, when combined with his canonical authority, explains the abiding faith in his historical reliability; the tragedians, for example, despite their prestige and their detailed dramatic accounts, are rarely cited for 'historical' facts about the heroic age.[19] But one of the peculiar features of historical Homeric

[15] On the different aspects of Homer's 'realism' see the succinct summary of de Jong (2005). Of course Homer's world includes divinities, and the accuracy of the gods' depiction is certainly a major problem for some ancient Homeric critics, especially allegorically minded ones (see Feeney [1991], ch. 1). But many others, including the bulk of those included in this book, either ignore them completely or treat them as inhabiting a world separate from the heroes, with its own internal rules of coherence and consistency. Since Homer chooses to portray them anthropomorphically, they are criticized on that basis if their behavior fails to conform to the norms of their fictional world. Interesting remarks on this in Pavel (1986) and Doležel (1998), 128–31.

[16] On Homer's authority in antiquity, see Lamberton (1997).

[17] On Dionysius' attitude toward 'myth,' see Fromentin (1988).

[18] For the various datings of Homer in antiquity, see Mosshammer (1979), 193–8; Graziosi (2002), 90–124. Homer's temporal distance from the War is evident from his own comments: as one of the *Lives* (*Vit. Hom. Scoral.* II, West 9.2; Allen 5) points out, Homer himself "shows that he is much later in time" (καὶ γὰρ αὐτὸς ὁ Ὅμηρος ὑστεροῦντα πολλοῖς χρόνοις ἑαυτὸν ἀποδείκνυσι) when he says in *Il.* 2.486, "but we only hear the report, we have no personal knowledge." Only Crates (F 73 Broggiato) dates Homer contemporary with the War, and even this is uncertain, since he elsewhere seems to adopt the more traditional dating as contemporary with the Return of the Heraclidae, or eighty years after the War.

[19] But see Falappone (2006).

criticism, as we shall see later in this and subsequent chapters, was the failure
to adequately reconcile the faith in Homer's knowledge of the Trojan War
with the fact that he lived considerably later in time.[20] The belief in the
historicity of the heroic age and that of Homer thus stand together in
a somewhat uneasy relationship; as the most ancient historical source,
Homer must be 'real' and situated on the historical timeline alongside the
equally 'real' Trojan War, but little attempt is made to bridge the gap of a
century or so that lies between them.[21] As will become clear in this chapter,
the seemingly trivial issue lies at the heart of the problems encountered by
historical critics of Homer.

The wealth of historical information that Homeric poetry was imagined
to contain extended far beyond the identities of important players or
the broad narrative outlines of events. A well-known anecdote relates the
role that Homeric poetry supposedly played in a political quarrel between
Megara and Athens in the early sixth century BCE.[22] The different versions
vary in their details and emphases, but the basic story is that the Athenians
cited two lines from the Catalogue of Ships (*Il.* 2.557–8) to prove that the
island of Salamis had belonged to Athens at the time of the Trojan War,
and by implication, still did: "Out of Salamis Ajax brought twelve ships /
and placed them next to where the Athenian battalions were drawn up."
The Megarians countered by claiming that the Athenians had forged line
558 and inserted it into the Catalogue in order to back up their spurious
assertion of ownership. The story is a justly famous one, particularly for
the light it sheds (if genuine) on early notions of a 'fixed' Homeric text.
But what is relevant here is that both cities accept Homer's authority as an
arbiter of inter-polis conflict, and that they presume, already in the sixth
century, that his poetry accurately represented political conditions during
the Trojan War period.[23]

---

[20] The Muses, whom Homer cites as his 'sources,' were of course not an acceptable explanation to the
rationalizing historians of heroic history.

[21] For instance, Aristotle also dated Homer well after the War (placing his birth at the beginning of
the Ionian migration, 140 years after the Trojan War: *On Poets* F 20.1 Gigon (76 Rose) = [Plut.]
Vit. Hom. A.3–4), but he never addresses this temporal distance in his interpretations of Homer's
depiction of heroic culture; cf. Weil (1977), 211. An exception is the second-century Alexandrian
Homeric critic Aristarchus of Samothrace, who also is said to have dated Homer around the Ionian
migration ([Plut.] *Vit. Hom.* B.3), but who differentiates between cultural practices, such as the use
of trumpets, that exist in Homer's time, but not in the heroic age (Sch. D ad *Il.* 18.219; cf. 21.388);
on this see Schmidt (1976), 250–1.

[22] For discussion see Higbie (1997); Graziosi (2002), 228–32. Aristotle, the earliest source, says only
that the Athenians "used Homer as a witness about Salamis" (Ὁμήρῳ μάρτυρι ἐχρήσαντο: *Rh.*
1375b 29–30).

[23] Cf. Hdt. 5.94.2 and 7.153–63 on the Greek allies' appeal to Homer in their embassy to Gelon of
Syracuse with Grethlein (2006).

Such a vision of Homeric poetry as an accurate mimetic reflection of historical reality – Homer as a painter of heroic life – was common throughout antiquity. Aside from the details of historical events, Homer acted as a source for various features of heroic society, government, and lifestyle.[24] Aristotle, for example, claims that Homer "represented" or "imitated" (ἐμιμεῖτο) ancient constitutions (ἀρχαίων πολιτειῶν) in his work and quotes *Il.* 2.391–3, where Agamemnon threatens to kill anyone who hangs back from battle, to prove that kings on military expeditions had the authority to put subjects to death "in ancient times" (ἐπὶ τῶν ἀρχαίων).[25] A more extended example, and one that specifies the *heroic* age and not just a vague 'ancient' era, is the long excursus in Dionysius' *History of Ancient Rome* (7.72–3), where he repeatedly cites Homer as evidence for ancient Greek customs preserved in Roman culture but no longer practiced by the Greeks of his own day, in support of his thesis that the Romans were originally Greek.[26] The use of three-horse chariots, Dionysius asserts, was "an ancient and *heroic* practice (ἀρχαῖον . . . ἐπιτήδευμα καὶ ἡρωικόν) which Homer represents the Greeks as using in battle." In fact, an entire 'primitive' heroic culture was extrapolated from the Homeric poems, as scholars observed the heroes' unfamiliarity with certain basic elements of later Greek life such as writing, coinage, riding horses, and wreathes,[27] and their *autourgia*, that is, their tendency to do most things, like driving chariots, by themselves, even though they had servants (τὸ τ᾽ αὐτουργεῖν ἐλευθέριον μάλιστα εἶναι ἐδόκει τοῖς παλαιοῖς: Sch. H ad *Od.* 1.332).[28] A familiarity with the details of theories of 'heroic simplicity' is on display in a wide variety of ancient texts – moralizing treatises, literary criticism, ethnography, comedy, literary symposia, etc. – and testifies to the pervasive acceptance of Homer's value as a historical source.[29]

---

[24] In the *Poetics* (25.1460a10), Aristotle names "the sort of things that *were* in existence (οἷα ἦν)," but, it is implied, are no longer, as one possible object of poetic imitation.

[25] *Eth. Nic.*1113a8; *Pol.* 3.14, 1285a8–14. The interest in ancient monarchy is reflected also in F 382 Gigon (158 Rose). On Aristotle's antiquarianism, Huxley (1973) and (1979).

[26] Cf. other uses of Homer as evidence at 1.53.4 (on Aeneas and Italy); 2.12.4; 5.74.2 (both on ancient kings).

[27] Vischer (1965), 92–4; Schmidt (1976), 159–64.

[28] Hofmann (1905), 28–31. In addition, the heroes' children often perform tasks later associated with slaves, e.g., herding animals, cleaning tables, bathing guests, and serving wine: Sch. H ad *Od.* 1.332.

[29] Some examples: Plato (*Resp.* 404b–8b) argues (ironically?) that the Homeric heroes' physical constitution was superior to men of his day due to their simple lifestyle; Aristotle (e.g., F 389 Gigon) and Aristarchus (e.g., Sch. HMQ ad *Od.* 3.464) used their belief in heroic simplicity to explain actions and practices in Homer that other critics had found unseemly; the method came to be called solving "from custom" (ἐκ τοῦ ἔθους). Athenaeus devotes a large section of the first book of his *Deipnosophists* (1.8e–19a; 24b–25e) to a debate over the alleged simplicity of heroic culture.

EARLY HISTORICAL CRITIQUES OF HOMER

From a very early stage, however, the assumption that Homer could be depended upon as an accurate depiction of heroic society or the Trojan War was contested. The first surviving critics of Homer's historical reliability are poets: I have already mentioned Stesichorus' foundational criticism of Homer's version of Helen's travels in his *Palinode*. The other early poetic reference to the reliability of Homer's historical account is by Pindar, who suggests that Homer had exaggerated and embellished his story of Odysseus: "And I expect that the story of Odysseus came to exceed his experiences, through the sweet songs of Homer" (*Nem.* 7.20–1).[30] These texts are a good reminder that discussions of the value of Homer's historical information stood alongside the more familiar criticisms (and defenses) of the poet's portrayal of the gods by Xenophanes, Heraclitus, and Theagenes of Rhegium.[31]

The first systematic engagement with Homer and heroic history, however, is that of the genealogists and mythographers active in the late sixth and early fifth centuries, such as Hecataeus of Miletus, Acusilaus of Argos, and Pherecydes of Athens, who were reading Homer as part of their broader investigations of mythic tradition.[32] As the Athens–Megara debate illustrates, Homeric verses mentioning geographical and political details (especially in the *Catalogue*) served as the most popular point of inquiry, as one can see in the remains of Hecataeus' *Periegesis*.[33] But the mythographers also focused on Homer's *story*; Pherecydes' *Troica* naturally did, and two fragments of Acusilaus contain narrative elaborations suggested by Homeric verses.[34] As we move further into the fifth century, more prose studies linked to Homeric content appear: e.g., Hellanicus of Lesbos' *Troica* and the genealogies of the Trojan War combatants by Damastes of Sigeum and Polus of Acragas.[35]

---

[30] Cf. Richardson (1985) and Howie (1998), who links Pindar's statement to Thucydides' similar characterization of Homeric poetry as an exaggeration of the truth in his *Archaeology* (see below); one can also point to the similar sentiment about Homer's enhancement of Odysseus in Philostratus' *Heroicus* (see Ch. 6).

[31] Xenoph. DK 21 B 11 (cf. B 12); Heraclit. DK 22 B 42; Theagen. DK 8 2.

[32] For the use of poetry or myth by early historians in general, see Walbank (1960); Strasburger (1972), 16–20.

[33] E.g., Hecat. *FGrH* 1 F 199, 217, 239, 328. See Nicolai (2003), 86–98, and further Ch. 3 below.

[34] Pherecydes *FGrH* 3 F 136–44. Of Acusilaus' fragments dealing with the Trojan Cycle (*FGrH* 2 F 39–43), F 39 conjectures a story of Aphrodite's motives throughout the Trojan War from *Il.* 3.307 on Aeneas' descendants' future rule of Troy, and F 43 derives a tale of Ithaca's founding by Ithacus and Neritus from *Od.* 20.207. On Acusilaus, see Tozzi (1967).

[35] Hellanicus *FGrH* 4 F 23–31; 138–56; Damastes *FGrH* 5: Περὶ γονέων καὶ προγόνων τῶν εἰς Ἴλιον στρατευσαμένων; Polus *FGrH* 6: Γενεαλογία τῶν ἐπὶ Ἴλιον στρατευσάντων Ἑλλήνων

Unfortunately, very little of this intellectual production survives, and what evidence we possess rarely sheds any light on how these writers used Homer for their historical inquiries. From what we can make out, the earlier generation of writers were mainly concerned with filling in details or elaborating myths left unexplained by Homer. Acusilaus' Homeric forays fall into this category, as does Pherecydes' naming of the six compatriots of Odysseus killed by Scylla (*FGrH* 3 F 140). That is, while it seems that they take the basic historicity of Homer's account as a given, it is difficult to get any sense of their criteria for determining how much to believe. It is also impossible to determine whether they are interested in exploring the legendary tradition or historical reality, or even whether they differentiated between them. What we can say is that among the extant fragments of the first generation of mythographers, there is no explicit *critique* of Homer's historical content; even Hecataeus' famous rationalizations of myths, for example, do not concern Homeric episodes (although this may be due to the vagaries of survival). Only later, in the late fifth century, with Hellanicus do we see an attempt to 'correct' fantastic stories in Homer, such as Achilles' fight with the river Scamander (F 28).[36] But again the fragmentary nature of Hellanicus' interventions renders assessments of his position vis-à-vis Homer's reliability difficult; we know almost nothing about the grounds that Hellanicus had for believing Homer wrong, or how he authenticated or argued for the correctness of his own information.

Fortunately, the two most famous fifth-century historians, Herodotus and Thucydides, provide fairly detailed critical analyses of Homer's accuracy in historical matters, even though their ostensible subject-matter occurred centuries later: Herodotus' excursus on Helen in Book 2 of his *Histories*, and Thucydides' demonstration of the inferiority of the Trojan War in his *Archaeology*. In fact, they are the earliest prose examples of Homeric criticism to have survived in any significant length. These are familiar passages, and the subjects of a number of scholarly studies, but in examining them again, I want to highlight several tendencies of thought and interpretation that inform their attempts to address the question of Homer's reliability. In short, while both authors seek to demonstrate, in different ways, that Homer's objective was not historical accuracy and that

καὶ βαρβάρων. Note that Hellanicus and Damastes also wrote on literary historical topics, see Lanata (1963), 234–9. On early Greek genealogical scholarship, see Thomas (1989), 173ff.; Jacob (1994); Fowler (2000); and for later periods, Bickerman (1952).

[36] This appears to be the only example of a 'correction'; Hellanicus also seems to have tried his hand in solving other Homeric problems: e.g., F 26a. But for the most part the fragments reveal an interest in filling in Homer's narrative by supplying background information and other stories about heroes, places, etc., mentioned only briefly in Homer.

his account was not accurate, they nevertheless seem loath to wholly abandon the poet as a witness to historical truth. The Homer who emerges in the course of their readings is similarly conflicted, a man trying to fulfill poetic and historical objectives, and neither historian manages to produce a unified vision of Homer that satisfactorily integrates these two incongruous motives. Their attempts to resolve this dilemma, however, and particularly the logic that underlies their approaches, remain influential and inform nearly all of the Imperial authors who touch upon the problem of Homer's relation to history.

HERODOTUS ON HOMER AND HELEN

The first sustained engagement with the question of Homer's historical reliability is also one of the most important and influential: Herodotus' famous story of the Egyptian Helen in Book 2 of his *Histories* (2.116–20).[37] The lengthy critique of Homer included in this excursus is unusual; despite his significant literary debts to Homeric epic, Herodotus seldom explicitly engages with the poet.[38] The only general statements he makes are at 2.53, where he dates Homer and Hesiod 400 years before his own time, marks them as the first poets, and asserts that they named and described the gods to the Greeks.[39] He twice appeals to Homeric authority for quite minor matters: at 4.29 a line of the *Odyssey* "testifies" (μαρτυρέει) to Herodotus' opinion concerning the lack of horns on Scythian cattle,[40] and two paragraphs later, he notes that Homer has mentioned the Hyperboreans in the *Epigoni*, "if indeed Homer really is the author of this poem" (4.31). And finally, Herodotus calls Homer's accuracy into question when he dismisses the existence of a river 'Ocean' as a fabrication of "Homer or some other poet" (2.23).[41] This general paucity of reference makes the long, involved discussion in Book 2 all the more significant. In addition, the issue

---

[37] Important treatments of this famous excursus are Neville (1977); Hunter (1982), 50–61; Lloyd (1988), 43–52; Farinelli (1995); Graziosi (2002), 113–18. Cf. the interesting discussion of Ligota (1982), 9–11.

[38] On Herodotus' use of Homer, see, Verdin (1977), 58–62; Marcozzi, Sinatra, and Vannicelli (1994), 164–8; Graziosi (2002), 226–8 (111–13 on Herodotus' dating of Homer); and Nicolai (2003), 98–101, who notes the paucity of Homeric reference in Herodotus in comparison to the fragments of Hecataeus.

[39] Lanata (1963), 228–30; Graziosi (2002), 111–12. At 2.154.4, Herodotus dates the Trojan War 800 years before his time, suggesting that he believed that Homer lived 400 years after the War and the events about which he wrote.

[40] The *Odyssey* line quoted is 4.85, which speaks of "Libya, where sheep grow horns soon after birth" – the argument is that animals in hot climates grow horns quickly, but those in cold slowly, or not at all. On Herodotus' reasoning process here, see Darbo-Peschanski (1987), 129.

[41] One could also argue that the famous account of female kidnapping episodes that opens the *Histories* (1.1–5) constitutes an implicit criticism of the traditional story of the Trojan War as told by Homer.

at hand is a much more serious one; by questioning Helen's presence at Troy, Herodotus takes aim at the very heart of the *Iliad*'s account of the war.

In the course of a chronological account of Egyptian kings, Herodotus informs his readers that after Pheros, son of Sesostris, the kingship fell to a native of Memphis who was called Proteus in Greek. Even in Herodotus' time, we learn, a sanctuary at Memphis sacred to Proteus existed, within which stood a temple dedicated to Aphrodite the Foreigner (ξείνης). Herodotus, familiar with stories placing Helen in Egypt at the time of Proteus,[42] reasons that Aphrodite the Foreigner might actually be another name for Helen. To test his hypothesis, he asks the Egyptian priests at the temple what they know about Helen. According to them, Paris, on his way back to Troy with Helen, had been forced to stop at the Canopic mouth of the Nile due to bad weather, and some of his slaves, learning of a nearby temple of Heracles where runaway slaves could receive sanctuary, took the opportunity to flee and take refuge there. Eventually King Proteus became involved. Appalled to learn of Paris' betrayal of Menelaus' hospitality, he decided to keep Helen and the rest of the stolen property until such time as Menelaus returned to collect them. Paris was forced to leave the country immediately.

This version of events brings up a question that Herodotus puts to the priests: if Helen was not at Troy, what exactly was the Trojan War about? Menelaus himself, say the priests, had told them "the truth of what happened" (τὴν ἀληθείην τῶν πρηγμάτων: 2.119.1). The Greeks had gone to Troy, looking for and demanding Helen. The Trojans, naturally, told them that she was in Egypt with Proteus. Believing that they were being ridiculed, the Greeks besieged the city, and finally took Troy after ten hard-fought years. At this point, they realized that the Trojans had been telling the truth after all, and Menelaus was dispatched to Egypt to retrieve Helen and the rest of his stolen property, where he found them safe and sound. Menelaus, however, was unable to sail home because of contrary winds, and in an egregious display of ingratitude, sacrificed two Egyptian children as offerings to the gods. The Egyptians became angry and pursued him as he sailed off to Libya, but he and Helen eventually managed to escape. On this view, the whole Trojan War was the result of an unreasonable refusal on the part of the Greeks to believe the truth.

---

[42] Lloyd (1988), 47 suggests that this version of the Helen in Egypt story, conspicuously lacking the *eidôlon* so prominent in Stesichorus' *Palinode* and Euripides' *Helen*, "may well have derived from" Hecataeus. See Austin (1994) for a survey of Helen's portrayals in this tradition, which is echoed again by Dio in the *Trojan Oration* (see Ch. 4).

Herodotus pauses to assess this new tale, whose central premise – Helen's presence in Egypt during the Trojan War – conflicts with the better-known and more canonical narratives of the *Iliad* and the *Odyssey*. Nevertheless, Herodotus finds the Egyptian *logos* more convincing than Homer's version. On the one hand, the authority of the Egyptian priests, and the antiquity and value of their information, deriving as it does from an eyewitness source (Menelaus), is considerable here, especially when one considers Herodotus' dating (not mentioned, however, in this passage) of Homer 400 years after the Trojan War. But Herodotus is also swayed by a fundamental implausibility in the traditional story, which he criticizes in an extended display of counterfactual reasoning. I break down the passage (2.120.2–4) to make it easier to understand the logic:

1. If Helen had been in Ilion, then she would have been given back to the Greeks, whether Alexander (Paris) was willing or not.

   a. Surely neither Priam, nor those nearest to him, were so crazy, as to be willing to risk themselves, their children, and the city just so that Alexander could be with Helen.

      i. Even if they were so inclined in the beginning, when not only many of the Trojans were slain in fighting against the Greeks, but also two or three or even more of the sons of Priam himself died in every battle (if the poets are to be believed), in this turn of events, even if Helen had been Priam's own wife, I expect that he would have given her back to the Greeks, in an attempt to escape from the misfortunes at hand.

      ii. Nor was Alexander even heir to the throne, in which case matters might have been in his hands since Priam was old, but Hector, who was an older and a better man than Alexander, was going to receive the royal power at Priam's death, and would not have acquiesced in his brother's wrongdoing, especially when that brother was the cause of great calamity to Hector himself and all the rest of the Trojans.

Although Herodotus doesn't mention the term, he is using the argument from probability (τὸ εἰκός) that was the primary tool for historians evaluating the poetic and mythic tradition.[43] Hecataeus of Miletus is considered to have inaugurated this 'rationalizing' method that pared away the incredible parts of myths to reveal 'probable' versions, but Herodotus is a

---

[43] Hussey (1995), 534, offers the following definition: reasoning by εἰκός involved applying "a probabilistic estimate (not quantified) to questions at some remove from experience...and appeals, necessarily, to antecedently established notions of what is likely or unlikely to happen in some familiar realm."

worthy successor, often judging stories on the basis of his own subjective ideas about physical and psychological likelihood. He rejects stories of a diver who swam two miles underwater, of bottomless springs, of a human Heracles killing hundreds of Egyptians, and doubts the story of the Samian exiles defeating Polycrates, because they sought Spartan assistance after the battle – an act that would not have made much sense if they had won the fight.[44] As in this last example, Herodotus' incredulity toward Homer's tale is directed at its psychological improbability (the curious unwillingness of the Trojans to surrender Helen in the face of a powerful force). In this respect, Herodotus has managed a by-the-book rationalizing critique of Homer's "foolish tale" (μάταιον λόγον: 2.118.1), a phrase reminiscent of Hecataeus' famous labeling of the *logoi* of the Greeks as "ridiculous" (γελοῖοι: F 1).[45]

Homeric hints

So far, Herodotus is performing a classic maneuver against an illustrious predecessor, contesting Homer's authority by ridiculing his version of events as silly and unconvincing, and presenting a more 'probable' option backed up by better sources (deriving from eyewitness testimony no less). But Herodotus also makes some effort to *defend* Homer as well, despite his inaccuracy. He even goes so far as to assert that Homer had learned of the 'true' Egyptian *logos* (δοκέει δέ μοι καὶ Ὅμηρος τὸν λόγον τοῦτον πυθέσθαι), but believed that it was "not as well-suited to epic poetry" (οὐ γὰρ ὁμοίως ἐς τὴν ἐποποιίην εὐπρεπής: 2.116.1) as the version he ended up using. This last formulation has garnered the lion's share of attention among commentators.[46] Herodotus implies that epic poetry has different standards of truth than historical narrative (although he doesn't explain what these are). By thus freeing Homer from the necessity of telling the 'truth,' Herodotus seems to be articulating a nascent conception of fiction that grants Homer some level of control over the content of his poetry.[47]

[44] Hdt. 8.8; 2.28; 2.45; 3.45. On Herodotus and εἰκός, see Lloyd (1975), 160–5; Corcella (1984); and Darbo-Peschanski (1987).
[45] The extended set of subsidiary arguments Herodotus provides probably owes something to sophistic rhetorical technique, to which the concept of εἰκός was also central: Kennedy (1963); Schmitz (2000); Gagarin (1990). Corax and Tisias are supposed to have established the argument from εἰκός in their rhetorical handbooks in the early fifth century (Pl. *Phdr.* 267a–b; Arist. *Rh.* 2.24.11).
[46] E.g., Verdin (1977), 60; Ligota (1982), and the works cited by Farinelli (1995), 25.
[47] As Verdin (1977), 61 n. 25, notes, Herodotus accentuates poetic agency when he says that Homer or some other poet "invented" (εὑρόντα) the name Ocean and introduced it into his poetry (2.23).

I want to call attention, however, to an equally unusual element of Herodotus' argument – his attempt to prove that Homer knew the true version despite not using it. With his "not as well suited for epic" argument, Herodotus had already provided a suitable explanation for the deviation of Homer's narrative from the truth. Nevertheless, he insists that Homer not only knew the 'true,' Egyptian version, but by intentionally leaving hints in the *Iliad* and the *Odyssey* "has *made it clear* that he knew it" (δηλώσας ὡς καὶ τοῦτον ἐπίσταιτο τὸν λόγον: 2.116.1).

As evidence, Herodotus quotes three Homeric passages in which the poet "makes it clear that he knows" (δηλοῖ ὅτι ἠπίστατο: 2.116.6) of Alexander's journey to Egypt:

(1) *Il.* 6. 289–92: Homer mentions that Paris had stopped at Sidon on his way back to Troy with Helen (2.116.3).[48]

(2) *Od.* 4. 227–30: Helen is said to have received drugs from Polydamna, wife of Thôn in Egypt (2.116.4).

(3) *Od.* 4. 351–2: Menelaus explains that he was delayed in Egypt because of poor winds (2.116.5).

To many scholars, Herodotus' decision to cite these passages reflects poorly on his reasoning ability. His explanation of the *Iliad* citation's relevance – Syria borders on Egypt, the Phoenicians rule Sidon, and the Phoenicians live in Syria – is hardly satisfactory, given that it fails to prove that Paris went to *Egypt*. Moreover, the *Odyssey* passages are mentioned in the context of Menelaus and Helen's trip *back* from Troy, and in any case do not discuss Paris.[49]

But modern commentators, in dismissing the relevance of these citations, have forgotten that Herodotus is not claiming to have found unambiguous passages where Homer explicitly mentions elements of the Egyptian version; any such passage would clearly contradict Homer's main narrative. What Herodotus is looking for is much more subtle – certain elements in the text that are slightly out of place, that do not quite fit, but suggest a

---

[48] Incidentally, Herodotus mentions that the *Iliad* passage proves (ἐν τούτοισι τοῖσι ἔπεσι δηλοῖ) that the *Cypria* was not composed by Homer, since in that poem Paris and Helen reach Troy in three days with no layover in Sidon. This passage is often referred to by modern scholars as an indication of Herodotus' critical acumen, since scholars now do not believe the *Cypria* was by Homer. Cf. Neville (1977); Lloyd (1988), s.v. 2.117 = 50–1.

[49] Lloyd (1988), 50: "As the text stands, H. loses as much credit as he gains." Herodotus' failure to explain the relevance of the second two passages, as well as their apparent lack of significance to his point have led many editors to consider them interpolations (e.g., Hude [1927]) despite the univocality of the manuscript tradition. Others have thought that they belong elsewhere in the text (e.g., at 2.119) or else were marginal notations that Herodotus was thinking about inserting later (Legrand (1936), 142 n. 2). I follow Rosén (1987) in retaining the contested passages. See Farinelli (1995), 7–10 for a history of the controversy.

correspondence, however tenuous, to the Egyptian version. For Herodotus, Homer did not go so far as to say that Paris went to Egypt, but by noting Paris' stay in nearby Sidon, he is 'hinting' at the truth. And as Caterina Farinelli has pointed out, Homer's reference to Polydamna and Thôn in the second passage is an aside in his own voice, and not part of Menelaus' narrative of his trip with Helen to Egypt. Neither name appears again, and there is nothing connecting this encounter with anything mentioned in Menelaus' account of their stay in Egypt after the war.[50] Is this an improperly integrated remainder of the 'true' visit to Egypt that Helen made on her way to Troy with Paris?[51] Finally, Menelaus' story of being stranded in Egypt, referred to in the third passage, is also a bit anomalous; there is no explanation offered in Homer as to why he went there at all. The whole episode could well be construed as another 'remnant' of the 'true' version in which he discovers Helen in Egypt *after* the war.[52]

These may be strained connections, but that is precisely the point; they are not meant to stand independently as convincing proof, only to raise suspicions that there is more going on than meets the eye. Each of the passages pinpoints a slight inconsistency or ambiguity in Homer's account of Helen's travels to and from Troy, testifying to Herodotus' intimate knowledge of the Homeric text. These 'problems' are then solved, not by re-integrating them into the narrative, but by reading them as intentionally anomalous; their lack of 'fit' is not the result of carelessness, but premeditation. Homer has placed them in the text in order that skilled readers like Herodotus, so accustomed to scanning visible objects and *logoi* for traces of the distant past, would notice them and realize that the poet did in fact know the truth about Helen, Egypt, and the Trojan War.

'Hidden' knowledge and sophistic interpretation

Herodotus' method of reading Homer bears a close resemblance to that practiced by sophistic interpreters of Homer, who also claim to reveal a

---

[50] Hellanicus (*FGrH* 4 F 153), however, tells a story of how Thôn welcomed Menelaus and Helen, but then tried to rape Helen, and was killed by Menelaus. This clearly occurs on the trip *back* from Troy and does not technically contradict Homer's account.

[51] Farinelli (1995), 12–19.

[52] Herodotus is suggesting that Homer had Menelaus stop off at Egypt on the way back because he was hinting at the 'real' story; he couldn't mention that he was there to get Helen, of course, but why else include the trip at all? There is also an implicit connection between King Proteus and the shape-shifting divinity Proteus whom Menelaus has to wrestle during his stay in Egypt (*Od.* 4.347–570).

'truth' in Homer not accessible to the inexperienced reader.[53] For example, in Plato's *Theaetetus* Socrates mentions interpreters who claim that "when [Homer] *said* (εἰπών) the line 'Ocean, begetter of gods, and Tethys their mother' (*Il.* 14.201, 302) he *meant* (εἴρηκεν) that all things are the offspring of flux and motion."[54] From passages in Xenophon and Plato it seems that a popular term for such a truth was ὑπόνοια – "under-meaning" – in contrast to the more straightforward διάνοια – "thought" or "meaning" – found elsewhere.[55] As the *Theaetetus* example suggests, the logic informs what we call allegorical interpretation, in which the literal, surface meaning, or διάνοια, symbolizes a deeper cosmological, theological, or moral truth (the ὑπόνοια).[56] But in the fifth century ὑπόνοια could also "include any interpretation which disregarded the obvious literal sense of a passage in favor of a more subtle way of taking the words."[57] In a discussion of the cup which Homer says that only Nestor could lift (*Il.* 11.636–7), Antisthenes asserts that Homer is not *talking* (λέγει) about the cup's weight, but is *signaling* (σημαίνει) that Nestor was sober (F 55 Caizzi).[58] Individual critics might differ about the precise content that was "hidden", but they shared the idea that there was more to Homer than met the eye.

Just as in Herodotus, these *huponoiai* were imagined to have been intentionally concealed, or at least obfuscated, by the poets themselves. In the *Theaetetus* example, the allegorists believe that the "ancients have hidden [the theory of flux] by means of poetry" (τῶν ἀρχαίων μετὰ ποιήσεως ἐπικρυπτομένων: 180c–d). Another operative word was αἰνίττεσθαι – to "hint at," or "riddle" – marking a conception of Homeric composition that also conveniently served the needs of those professing to teach

---

[53] Graziosi (2002), 117–18 speaks of the "sophistic color" of Herodotus' argument, as well as his understanding of Homer as a "proto-historian."

[54] Here the same verb is given two different meanings; the second must mean "intend to say" or "meant to say": LSJ s.v. λέγω III.9. On these distinctions, see Pépin (1993), 10; on this passage, see Struck (2004), 44–5.

[55] Xen. *Symp.* 3.6: τὰς ὑπονοίας οὐκ ἐπίστανται; Pl. *Resp.* 378d: οὔτ' ἐν ὑπονοίαις πεποιημένας οὔτε ἄνευ ὑπονοιῶν. Contrast, e.g., *Ion* 530d: πολλὰς καὶ καλὰς διανοίας; *Prt.* 347a: Simonides διανοούμενος.

[56] Cf. Plut. *Quomodo adul.* 19e: "By forcibly distorting these stories through what used to be called ὑπονοίαι but are nowadays called ἀλληγορίαι."

[57] Richardson (1975), 67. But see the comments of Tate (1953), 16–17 and Giannantoni (1990), 339–41. On the much-discussed question of the relationship between the terms ἀλληγορία and ὑπόνοια see Buffière (1956), 45–8; Pépin (1976), 85–92; Montanari (1987); Ford (2002), 72–3, and the works listed in the next note.

[58] Richardson (1975), 79: it "runs counter to the obvious sense of the words, and surely ranks as a ὑπόνοια". So Pépin (1993), 10: "this very specific exegesis which rejects the apparent physical sense and substitutes a hidden moral meaning." Cf. Scodel (1999), 179. On the question of Antisthenes' allegoresis: full list of *pro* and *contra* in Giannantoni (1990), 338–9 n. 41; see in particular the exchange between Höistad (1951) and Tate (1953); Richardson (1975); Pépin (1993).

about Homer.[59] Socrates' assertion in the Ps.-Platonic *Second Alcibiades* that "poetry as a whole (ποιητικὴ ἡ συμπᾶσα) is by nature inclined to riddling (αἰνιγματώδης)" (147c), or Protagoras' celebrated claim that Homer and Hesiod were sophists who disguised their craft in poetic form (Pl. *Prt.* 316d–e) both authorize the non-literal nature of their interpretations by imagining the inclusion of *huponoiai* as an essential part of the poetic process.[60] The rhetoric of 'hidden meanings' is as much about the competitive claims to authority sought by the critic as it is about interpreting Homeric poetry. As opposed to the "many, noble *dianoiai*" provided by rhapsodes like Plato's Ion, a student of a sophist or fifth-century 'Homeric professor' like Metrodorus, Stesimbrotus of Thasos, or Glaucon could learn the more arcane, esoteric *huponoiai* that Homer had reserved for the initiated few.[61] In this way the critic displays his interpretative ingenuity while maintaining that he is only reconstructing what Homer had intended all along.

It is this literary-critical idea of an enigmatic Homer that Herodotus incorporates into his historiographical examination of Homer's reliability. On the one hand, Herodotus is demonstrating his skill in close reading by uncovering bits of the truth within Homer's false, 'poetic' story. But by asserting that the poet is complicit in leaving these traces, he can also co-opt Homer's authority for the version that he did *not* tell. Herodotus has it both ways – Homer is wrong, but still serves as a witness for Herodotus' competing narrative. He uses the tools of historiography – locating a more reliable source, analysis based on probability – to knock Homer from his pedestal, and the tools of poetic interpretation to help him back up on his feet. But the Homer that emerges from Herodotus' exegetical maneuvers is still a somewhat mysterious figure, faithful to his poetic imperatives yet eager to demonstrate, surreptitiously, his knowledge of the historical truth. Herodotus' insistence, at the very earliest stages of the critical tradition, on simultaneously refuting and supporting Homer's historical reliability exemplifies a deeply conflicted way of thinking about Homer's relation to history that will be echoed (and comically exploited) throughout antiquity.

---

[59] Ford (1999a). The 'enigma' is the running theme throughout Struck (2004); see 21–50 on the Classical period.

[60] But see Cole (1991), 55–70, and Ford (2002), 85–6 on the slippage between rhetorical interpretation, which devoted itself to discovering what the poet 'intended' – the "thought" (*dianoia*) contained in his "expression" (*lexis*) – and allegorical interpretation. Once the poet is allowed to "riddle," or "hint" the connection between expression and intention is broken; to connect them again requires a critical intervention that comes rather close to allegoresis.

[61] Pl. *Ion* 530c–d. Ford (2002), 84; cf. (1999a), 44–5. On Stesimbrotus, see Lanata (1963), 240–3; on Metrodorus and Glaucon: Richardson (1975).

Like Herodotus, Thucydides positions his work as a successor and com-
petitor to that of Homer. In the very first sentence, he claims that the wars
of ancient times were not particularly great, and that his own subject, the
Peloponnesian War, is thus "more worth writing about than any of those
which had happened previously" (1.1.1). The so-called *Archaeology*, which
immediately follows, makes it clear that the Trojan War and its chronicler,
Homer, are two of his primary targets: the campaign against Troy is proven
to have been "inferior to its renown and to the opinion now held about
it because of the poets" (1.1.11). And at the conclusion of the *Archaeology*,
Thucydides emphasizes the superiority of the rationalized, realist version of
the distant past that he has just presented over that which "the poets sing,
exaggerating" (ποιηταὶ ὑμνήκασι περὶ αὐτῶν ἐπὶ τὸ μεῖζον κοσμοῦντες:
1.21.1). His own work is thus set in opposition to both the subject-matter
and style of his great poetic predecessor.

Within the *Archaeology*, however, Homer plays a considerable role in
Thucydides' reconstruction of the past.[62] Homer "provides evidence"
(τεκμηριοῖ δὲ μάλιστα Ὅμηρος) that Greece was not united even in his
day, because he neither refers to the Greeks collectively by a single name,
nor uses the negative collective term, *barbaros* (1.3.3).[63] Similarly, Thucydides argues that "in the old days" (τὸ πάλαι: 1.5.1) piracy brought no
shame upon its practitioners, no doubt thinking of Homeric verses such as
Od. 3.71–4 and 9.252–5.[64]

Some of the islanders still even now indicate this (δηλοῦσι... ἔτι καὶ νῦν), as
do the ancient poets (οἱ παλαιοὶ τῶν ποιητῶν), when they ask everywhere the
questions of those sailing whether they are pirates, as if those whom they ask would
not deny the fact, not reproach those who desired to know it. (1.5.2)

And in Book 3, in an excursus on the prehistory of Delos, Thucydides
quotes and analyzes two long passages from the *Homeric Hymn to Apollo*
(which he attributes without question to Homer), concluding that "Homer
thus provides evidence (ἐτεκμηρίωσεν) that there was in ancient times (τὸ
πάλαι) a great assembly and festival on Delos" (3.104.6). We see here some
ideal instances of the use of Homer as reliable witness for historical data.

---

[62] Of the many treatments of Thucydides' criticism of Homer and poetry in general, the best are
probably Verdin (1977), 65–75; Hunter (1982), ch. 1; and Funke (1986), 80–4. Cf. Graziosi (2002),
118–23.

[63] See Gomme (1945) and Hornblower (1991) on 1.3.3, and Verdin (1977), 70–2 for detailed discussion;
cf. the scholia to *Il.* 2.530 and 867.

[64] The lines are identical, but spoken by Nestor and Polyphemus respectively.

The language Thucydides employs in connection with his use of Homer is also significant; for the historian, Homer "provides evidence" (τεκμηριοῖ; ἐτεκμηρίωσεν) of historical data. Τεκμήριον, along with its virtual synonyms σημεῖον and μαρτύριον,[65] was a central term in the language of proof, demonstration, and evidence developed in the fifth century, most conspicuously in the medical, rhetorical, and historical fields.[66] In an historiographical context, the words literally mean 'evidence,' not in the sense of 'proofs,' but 'evident' phenomena, signs that allowed the historian to gain a foothold into the past by enabling a process of inference.[67] The historian scanned available data for such signs, or clues, that would allow an entry into the past – some way, as Herodotus says, "to conjecture (τεκμαιρόμενος) from visible things to those unknown (τοῖσι ἐμφανέσι τὰ μὴ γινωσκόμενα)" (2.33.2).

Such an inferential method is generally aimed at the recovery of non-contemporary history, and Thucydides' use of τεκμ vocabulary in his own voice (that is, outside of the speeches) is largely restricted to discussions of the distant past, such as the *Archaeology*, where he repeats programmatically both at the beginning and at the end that his reconstruction is based on "evidence" (τεκμηρίων: 1.1.3; 1.21.1).[68] Often this evidence is physical or material: Thucydides infers that before Theseus' time Athens comprised only a part of the present city from the τεκμήριον of temple locations, and he calls the Carian graves unearthed during the purification of Delos as μαρτύρια, literally 'witnesses,' of the fact that Delos had been colonized by Carians.[69] But as Thucydides' use of Homer shows, poetry could also be considered a 'relic' of the past; like physical remains or cultural practices 'fossilized' in primitive peoples, archaic poetry preserves vestiges of ancient times down to the present that provides clues for the reconstruction of the past.

Despite Thucydides' disdain for poetry and its vision of the past then, he still feels he can use it to formulate a historical narrative. One possible explanation for this discrepancy is that in the examples we have mentioned

[65] Hornblower (1987), 100–7.
[66] See Lloyd (1966), 424–30; Hankinson (1997); and the relevant parts of Manetti (1993) for overviews.
[67] Connor (1984), 28: "*Tekmêria* are not 'proofs' of incontrovertible evidence, but 'indications' – facts or observations that point in a certain direction." For Herodotus' and Thucydides' use of conjecture: Hunter (1982), 93–107, and Butti de Lima (1996), 138ff. On Herodotus alone, see Corcella (1984), ch. 2; Darbo-Peschanski (1987), ch. 2; Thomas (2000).
[68] On the connection of this kind of reasoning to antiquarianism, or archaeology, see Ginzburg (1999), 38–53.
[69] Thuc. 2.15.4, 1.8.1, 1.3.3. His famous comment at 1.10.1–3 on the ruins of Mycenae, though emphasizing rather their unreliability as evidence and not specifically using the language of proof, takes such inferential procedures for reconstructing the past for granted.

so far, Thucydides reads Homer as evidence of how things were in *the poet's own day*, which the historian dates to a time "much later than the Trojan War" ("Ομηρος· πολλῷ γὰρ ὕστερον ἔτι καὶ τῶν Τρωικῶν γενόμενος: 1.3.3). In other words, no claim is being made about the heroic period about which Homer wrote, but only about the linguistic usage or historical events contemporary with the poet. Homer has no active historiographical role; he is only unconsciously providing evidence of his own time.[70] Thucydides is not lending any credence to Homer's 'embellished' narrative, but only mining his verses for information to which the poet was an unwitting witness.

Thucydides reading Homer

This explanation, however, is not completely satisfactory because Thucydides, as we will see, also uses Homeric poetry as evidence for the history of the Trojan War era, far *before* Homer lived. As part of the *Archaeology*'s overarching argument that the distant past (τὰ ἔτι παλαίτερα) was "not great either in wars or in other respects" (1.1.3), Thucydides tries to prove that the Trojan War also, despite its fame, was not particularly severe or large in comparison with modern conflicts. Much of this demonstration is implicitly based on Homer,[71] and Thucydides even goes so far as to defend Homer's picture of a powerful Mycenae against the archaeological evidence of its fifth-century remains.[72] On two occasions, however, he turns explicitly to Homeric verses in order to extract historical information.

In the first case (1.9), Thucydides asserts that Agamemnon's ability to organize the Trojan expedition was due to the fear aroused by his naval power. In order to prove that Agamemnon had a formidable naval force (not normally associated with Mycenae), Thucydides turns to Homer, noting that "Agamemnon obviously brought with him the greatest number of ships and in addition supplied the Arcadians, as Homer has indicated (ὡς Ὅμηρος τοῦτο δεδήλωκεν)," although he qualifies this last phrase by adding "if he is good enough evidence" (εἴ τῳ ἱκανὸς τεκμηριῶσαι: 1.9.4). Thucydides is a careful reader; he counts the hundred ships attributed to Agamemnon in *Il.* 2.576, but has not forgotten that in lines 2.610–14

[70] Emphasized by Verdin (1977), 69; Funke (1986), 83; and Graziosi (2002), 119–20, among others.
[71] General accounts of the *Archaeology* that discuss Thucydides' use of Homer: Täubler (1927), 103–7; de Romilly (1967), 242–3; Howie (1998); Tsakmakis (1995), ch. 2; Nicolai (2001).
[72] Biraschi (1989), 116. This is not to say, of course, that Thucydides approached Homer acritically; he is careful to acknowledge the possibility of poetic exaggeration, and one suspects that certain passages, like the Catalogue of Ships, were considered more reliable than others. On what Thucydides might have seen at Mycenae, see Cook (1955).

Homer adds that Agamemnon had given sixty more to the Arcadians, who were not a seafaring people. As further proof, Thucydides cites an obscure line from the description of Agamemnon's scepter, "and to be lord of many islands and over all Argos" (*Il.* 2.108). How, Thucydides asks, could he have ruled "many islands" without a navy, given that his power base was landlocked?

Thucydides' inferences appear reasonable and bear witness to his careful attention to Homeric detail, but we should remember that his conclusions are technically valid only for the narrative world of the *Iliad*, and not for historical reality. The leap that Thucydides makes is to assume that the information produced by these conjectures can function as historical data. One might contend that the proviso "if he is good enough evidence" is Thucydides' acknowledgment of the conditional nature of his conjectures, but it only disguises the fact that Homer is Thucydides' *only* evidence for his claim, and it hardly prevents him from assuming the validity of his inferences in the subsequent stages of his argument. In fact, the inclusion of the disclaimer, by raising and then ignoring the issue of Homer's reliability, calls attention to the unanswered question of how Homer would have had access to such historically accurate information in the first place.[73] Thucydides is too conscientious to believe uncritically that Homeric poetry reflects a real, historical world in every detail, but too dependent on Homer as a source to let those suspicions affect his reading practices.

A similar blurring of the boundaries between fiction and history occurs a few paragraphs later at 1.10.3–5 when Thucydides attempts to demonstrate that the Greek force sent against Troy was far smaller than overseas expeditions of the fifth century. Once again, his detailed reading of Homer is prefaced with a disclaimer: "if we can here also trust Homer's poetry, which it is likely that he, being a poet, has exaggerated" (τῇ Ὁμήρου αὖ ποιήσει εἴ τι χρὴ κἀνταῦθα πιστεύειν, ἣν εἰκὸς ἐπὶ τὸ μεῖζον μὲν ποιητὴν ὄντα κοσμῆσαι: 1.10.3).[74] That does not stop him, however, from engaging in a highly detailed analysis of the size and make-up of the Greek expeditionary force, based on the Catalogue of Ships:[75]

---

73 Scholars differ widely on how seriously to take Thucydides' disclaimer here and at 10.3 (discussed below). Verdin (1977), 73–4, uses them to claim that Thucydides did not really trust in Homeric evidence, while Gomme (1945), s.v. 9.4, notes that whatever his excuses, "Thucydides is in fact relying on Homer's authority."

74 The level of detailed argument with which Thucydides analyzes Homer suggests that such caveats were probably *pro forma*. Gomme (1945, s.v. 10.3) suggests that such disclaimers may be an ironic nod to overly skeptical predecessors such as Herodotus; cf. Graziosi (2002), 123.

75 On Thucydides' use and interpretation of the Catalogue, see Marcozzi, Sinatra, and Vannicelli (1994), 169–74. Thucydides is the first extant author to refer to the Catalogue by that name.

Of the twelve hundred ships, [Homer] has represented (πεποίηκε) those of the Boeotians as holding a hundred and twenty men and those of Philoctetes fifty, indicating (δηλῶν), as it seems to me, the largest and the fewest amounts; at any rate there is no mention made in the catalogue of ships concerning the size of any others. That they were all rowers as well as warriors he has indicated (δεδήλωκεν) in the ships of Philoctetes; for he has represented (πεποίηκε) all the oarsmen as archers. It is not likely (οὐκ εἰκός) that many extra passengers sailed apart from the kings and high officers, especially since they intended to cross the open sea with military equipment, and having ships, moreover, with no decks, but equipped in the archaic manner, like pirate ships. To the one examining the average of the largest and smallest ships, not many men appear to have gone, inasmuch as they were sent collectively from the whole of Greece. (1.10.3–5)

This is a remarkable passage. On the one hand, Thucydides has again performed careful calculations, this time of all the ships listed by Homer in the Catalogue (actually 1,186, but 1,200 is a reasonable approximation). But he has also come up with a total – that of the Greek soldiers – from numbers that Homer does not explicitly provide. To obtain this figure, Thucydides takes the two instances where Homer supplies the amount of men on board ships – 120 on those of the Boeotians, and 50 on those of Philoctetes[76] – and then asserts that in these cases Homer was "indicating" (δηλῶν) the largest and smallest contingents; as a result, the average of these two figures would represent the number of men per ship for the whole force. Furthermore, in order to count all of these men as soldiers, rather than slaves, cooks, etc., he posits that Homer has also "indicated" (δεδήλωκεν) that all of those sailing were warriors, when he mentions that on Philoctetes' ships *every* rower was also an archer (*Il.* 2.720). Here we can see the work that δηλοῦν has to do; the verb has a clearly polemical, assertive charge, since what Homer 'indicates' are in fact merely Thucydides' conjectures.

History and fiction

We can also see how the object of Thucydides' analysis once again vacillates between Homeric representation and historical reality. At first, his reference to poets' exaggerative tendencies and his use of the verb πεποίηκε ("he has represented") to describe Homer's activity suggest that the ships which are under discussion are those of the Iliadic world, and not of history.[77] The

---

[76] Boeotian ships at *Il.* 2.510; Philoctetes at 2.719.

[77] Verdin (1977), 73–4 sees Thucydides' use of πεποίηκε as another attempt to distance himself from Homer, and furthermore as a justification for Thucydides' avoidance of making his calculations explicit. The perfect forms of ποιέω, however, are commonly used to refer to poets' conscious shaping of their characters or narratives.

farther Thucydides gets into his argument, however, the more difficulty he
has maintaining this distinction. After claiming that Homer has indicated
that men on board ship were rowers and soldiers, Thucydides supports
his assertion first by pointing to something that Homer has "represented"
(πεποίηκε) in his poetry – that all the oarsmen in Philoctetes' boat were
archers – but then adds a second argument dependent on Thucydides'
own concept of what was "likely" in *reality*: "it is not likely (οὐκ εἰκός)
that many extra passengers (περίνεως... πολλούς) sailed apart from the
kings and high officers, especially since they intended to cross the open
sea with military equipment, and having ships, moreover, with no decks"
(1.10.4).[78] Thucydides' decision not to provide a total number of troops
based on his inferences only adds to the uncertainty as to what Thucydides'
conclusion that "not many men appear to have gone" refers: in Homer, or in
reality?[79]

Thucydides' equivocation with regard to the truth-value of Homer's
descriptions is reflected in the image of Homer implicit in his argument.
First of all, like Herodotus' Homer, the poet's knowledge of the truth
goes without saying; Thucydides' assumption that Homer probably mag-
nified the numbers implies that he knew them to begin with.[80] After all,
why should Homer's numbers have any relation to the truth whatsoever?
Secondly, the Homer posited here, even though indulging in poetic exaggeration, seems very concerned to ensure that his readers are given the
information necessary to calculate the size of the Greek forces as depicted
in his poetry. The two mentions of sailor numbers are intended to convey
the maximum and minimum contingents, while he includes the description of the rower-archers on Philoctetes' boat to allow the extrapolation
of that fact to all the ships.[81] The concept of τεκμήριον, or evidence, has

[78] On Thucydides' use of *eikos*-reasoning, see Butti de Lima (1996), 160ff. For his more general
'rationalizing' approach to Greek poetic tradition in the *Archaeology*, see Hunter (1982), 30–43, and
Biraschi (1989); and Pearson (1942), 29–32, on the similarity of Thucydides' approach to his Ionian
predecessors and later Atthidographers.
[79] 1.10.5. An additional problem: if one does the calculation as directed by Thucydides, the sum appears
to disprove rather than support Thucydides' claim that "not many men appear to have sailed." As
Gomme (1945), 114 puts it, the total would be "102,000, or allowing for some poetic exaggeration,
say 70,000–80,000 – a very large number for an overseas expedition, and much larger that any that
sailed in the Peloponnesian War." Others have argued that Thucydides is emphasizing how small a
number it is for the *entire* force of Greece (de Romilly (1967), 248 n. 2).
[80] As Howie (1998), 95, points out, Thucydides' "argumentation depends on two arbitrary assumptions:
that the Catalog is basically true; and that the Trojan War did last as long as tradition said."
[81] Graziosi (2002), 122: "Homer, like Thucydides, is concerned with giving an accurate account; he is
simply less successful." Thucydides conceives of Homer as, "so to speak, a bad historian." Hunter
(1982), 37, speaks soberly of Thucydides' poor source-criticism.

been turned on its head; instead of the historian scanning Homeric poetry for unconscious traces of the past, such as the unity of Greece or Delian festivals, he now identifies and employs 'signs' that Homer has consciously and enigmatically pre-inserted into his poetry. The act of historical inquiry is imagined as a reconstruction of a predecessor's purposeful and partial presentation of the facts. Thucydides' interpretation of Homer here recalls the search for *huponoiai* we discussed above *apropos* of Herodotus, where the poet is imagined to have intentionally "hidden" information which only the skill of the interpreter can bring to light. The constant reiteration of the verb δηλοῦν (δεδήλωκεν, δηλῶν) with Homer as grammatical subject reminds us that the poet himself is framed as the conscious "revealer" of this information.

Like Herodotus, Thucydides imagines a 'hinting' Homer, aligning himself with those critics who believed that poets expressed themselves in a less than straightforward manner. Thucydides, however, is not recovering 'hidden meanings' that conflict with the literal sense of Homer's text, but inferring facts about the Homeric world that Homer has not directly mentioned, such as Agamemnon's power base or the size of the Greek forces. He does so by imagining what the ships must have been like, the make-up of the crews; later on he will even look into the logistics of the siege of Troy.[82] But caught up in his interpretative prowess, Thucydides fails to distinguish between his reconstruction of the *fictional* world of Homeric poetry and that of the *historical* world which is the object of his larger inquiry.[83] This confusion is symptomatic of a more fundamental split in Thucydides' idea of Homer. On the one hand Thucydides believes that Homer lived well after the Trojan War and as a poet, tended to embellish and exaggerate the truth, but in order to obtain the historical evidence from his poetry that he needs, he has to assume not only that individual verses are accurate down to the last detail, but also that historical accuracy was Homer's objective.

---

[82] The interpretations of this later section, such as his attempt to 'solve' the notorious problem of the Achaean Wall at 1.11, do not make specific reference to Homer or his poetry, and are thus outside the scope of this treatment.

[83] Thucydides is certainly reading the past in light of his understanding of the present; his emphases on sea-power, rule by fear, and the importance of money for warfare certainly fit far better into a fifth-century context than a Homeric one, and will preoccupy him throughout the rest of his work. But there is little reason to doubt that he believed in an unchanging continuity of human motivations and behavior uniting the past and the present, or that he felt that he could demonstrate this very fact from Homeric evidence as well.

Conclusion

Thucydides is thus caught in the same bind as Herodotus, engaged as they both are in a struggle for historiographical authority with an illustrious predecessor. To combat that authority they call Homer's historical reliability into question and demonstrate their mastery over Homer by interpreting his own lines to back up their own, revisionist accounts. But in doing so, they have to concede that Homer did know the truth and that he was interested in conveying some of that truth in his poetry. In other words, they question Homer's devotion to historical accuracy on the grounds that he was a poet, yet still insist upon a certain historiographical impulse on the poet's part. This picture of Homer at odds with himself is the result of an ambivalence toward Homer's identity and intentions that neither Herodotus nor Thucydides ever properly comes to terms with: how to reconcile the aims and objectives of Homer the poet with those of Homer the historian? Thucydides never really sorts out what he thought Homer was doing, conflating Homeric poetry's status as fiction and history, while Herodotus is even more peculiar in this respect, since he clearly distinguishes the two versions of the Helen story on the basis of genre, yet subsequently undermines his own position by positing that Homer managed to indicate his historical knowledge despite his deference to poetic 'appropriateness.'

Part of the problem is that Herodotus and Thucydides are quick to explain why Homer was *un*reliable (because he was a poet), but avoid answering the more difficult question of why one should assume his historical reliability at all. In addition, one might ask, even if Homer had known the truth, why would he, as a poet, have desired historical accuracy? It is perhaps telling that, while Herodotus and Thucydides both date Homer long after the Trojan War elsewhere in their work (400 years later in Herodotus' case, "much later" in Thucydides'), neither brings up that fact in their discussions of his poetry and its truth content. That might have raised questions concerning Homer's access to historical truth that both prefer to leave unexamined.

A more general point that we can draw from these passages is that properly addressing the question of Homer's reliability necessarily involves articulating a vision, however rudimentary, of who Homer was and what his intentions were. In the generally intentionalist interpretative world of antiquity, critics invariably assume a Homer in complete control of his text, and thus when Herodotus and Thucydides read Homer for 'hidden' historical evidence of the Trojan War, they cannot avoid assigning objectives to Homer (hinting at the truth, signaling to the reader) that collide with the poetic aims (epic appropriateness, exaggeration) that they had attributed to him earlier. Herodotus and Thucydides can maintain their equivocal stance toward Homer only because they choose not to fill out the portrait in detail, leaving their readers with a somewhat mysterious vision of the poet. In the end, rather than resolve the issue of Homer's reliability, Herodotus and Thucydides have only highlighted the challenges such an endeavor involves.

CHAPTER 3

Homer, the ideal historian

Strabo's *Geography*

One of the longest and most detailed ancient discussions of Homer's historical accuracy is found in the first book of Strabo of Amasia's *Geography*. The work, written in seventeen books around the beginning of the common era, is ostensibly a comprehensive description of the inhabited world.[1] But Homer, somewhat surprisingly, casts a long shadow over the text; Strabo quotes Homer over seven hundred times,[2] and the books on Greece (7–10) and the Troad (13) read for long stretches like a Homeric geographical commentary, featuring extensive textual exegeses of his poetry and often dispensing with any attempt to describe current or even post-Homeric conditions.[3] In these parts of his work, Strabo accepts Homer's fundamental accuracy without question and analyzes individual lines, phrases, and words of the poet down to the last detail for any information they might yield about the state of the world in heroic times. In tackling such problems, Strabo draws upon an impressive arsenal of interpretive techniques that speaks to his considerable familiarity with the intricacies of Homeric scholarship, as does the frequency with which he engages in spirited polemic with his Hellenistic predecessors.

The interest that Strabo shows in Homer – in identifying Homeric cities, regions, or peoples with their modern counterparts, making sense of the poet's topographical descriptions, or locating controversial sites (e.g., Pylos, Troy, and Ithaca)[4] – is, strictly speaking, nothing new; it is already in evidence among the early historical writers such as Hecataeus and Pherecydes

---

[1] On the *Geography*'s date and composition, see Clarke (1997); Dueck (1999); and Pothecary (2002).

[2] Cf. the index to Meineke (1866). For a full catalogue and brief discussion of Strabo's Homeric citations, see the useful study of Kahles (1976). On Strabo's use of poetry in general, see Dueck (2005).

[3] Prontera (1993), 387. Dueck (2000), 31–40 gives a good idea of the range and breadth of Strabo's Homeric interests; for more in-depth studies of Strabo's Homeric criticism regarding the Peloponnese and the Troad see Biraschi (1994) and (2000) respectively.

[4] On Homeric geography, see Bunbury (1883), 31–85; Dickie (1995).

and continues in Herodotus, Hellanicus, and Thucydides.[5] But as I mentioned in the introduction, the Hellenistic period witnessed an increase in the importance accorded such antiquarian inquiry, as both Homer and the heroic age begin to play an expanding role in the formation of various conceptions of Hellenistic Greek identities. In particular, the desire to demonstrate ties to any part of the Greek legendary tradition inspired a widespread interest in Homeric geography and a staggering amount of research on the topic: one only needs to think of the two massive second-century BCE commentaries often referred to in the *Geography* – that by Apollodorus of Athens on the Catalogue of Ships (in twelve books) and that by Demetrius of Scepsis on the Trojan Catalogue (in thirty books).[6] Strabo draws upon the vast increase in knowledge reflected in these and other works, and the *Geography* reflects the proliferation of learned discourse on Homer in the Hellenistic period, as well as the way in which history and the past pervaded the science of geography.[7]

In this chapter, I am primarily interested in exploring the theoretical and practical defense of Homer's historical and geographical knowledge that Strabo puts forward in the first book of the *Geography*. The discussion is technically a long reply to the second-century BCE polymath Eratosthenes of Cyrene (who had doubted Homer's accuracy in his own *Geography*),[8] but it also touches on the opinions of many other Hellenistic critics, geographers, and historians, like Posidonius, Polybius, and Crates of Mallus.[9] Strabo thus provides us with a valuable distillation, albeit from his particular perspective, of the centuries of previous thinking about the topic since the days of Herodotus and Thucydides. But Strabo's own ambitious attempt to tackle the problem that I outlined in the last chapter – reconciling Homer's competing roles as poet and historian – is the only substantial example to survive from that period of over four hundred years. Strabo not only develops and expands the implicit understanding of Homer in

[5] Prontera (1993), 387–9. E.g., Hecat. *FGrH* 1 F 75, 199; Hdt. 4.177, 7.70; Pherecyd. *FGrH* 3 F 136–44. Thucydides identifies Corcyra as Scheria at 1.25.4; cf. 3.88.1 on Aeolus and the Lipari islands; 4.24.5 on Scylla and Charybdis at the Strait of Messina; and 6.2.1 on Cyclops and Laestrygonians in Sicily.
[6] Prontera (1993). For Apollodorus' Περὶ τοῦ τῶν νεῶν καταλόγου (*FGrH* 244 F 154–207) see Niese (1877) and Pfeiffer (1968), 257–61; for Demetrius' commentary, Gaede (1880) and Pfeiffer (1968), 249–51.
[7] On Strabo and time, see Clarke (1999), 245–93.
[8] Strabo's defense of Homer (1.1.1–10; 1.2) is part of the critique of his predecessors that comprises the first two books of the *Geography* (the so-called *Prolegomena*). Strabo, however, focuses primarily on Eratosthenes' *Geography*: first his ideas on Homer (1.2) and then the first book in 1.3, the second in 1.4, and the third in 2.1. Strabo then moves on to Posidonius (2.2) and Polybius (2.3–4). For an overview, see Aujac (1969), 4–11.
[9] On Crates' Homeric scholarship, F 1–77 Broggiato.

Herodotus and Thucydides by outlining a portrait of the poet as a committed geographer and historian, but also tries to reconstruct the 'fictionalizing' method by which Homer transformed 'actual' places into 'myths' for use in his poetry.[10] And while Herodotus and Thucydides examined relatively 'realistic' Homeric episodes, Strabo centers his discussion around the fantastic wanderings of Odysseus, thus embroiling himself in thorny debates about the purpose and interpretation of Homeric myths.[11]

In fact one of the virtues of Strabo's account is its willingness to confront the difficult questions that arise from the belief that Homer was a historian. Ancient scholars of heroic society (like Aristotle and Aristarchus) or historians (like Strabo's contemporary Dionysius of Halicarnassus), avoid the quagmire into which Strabo wades by simply assuming that Homer, although a poet, could be relied upon as an accurate witness of the heroic age, without pursuing the matter any further. While Strabo takes this fact for granted in the main body of the *Geography*, he devotes much of his so-called *Prolegomena* (the first two books) to a head-on confrontation with the problems inherent in such a position. Strabo goes so far as to envisage Homer as a 'real' person, explore his motivations, and reconstruct his creative process, and one of my goals in this chapter is to demonstrate how his model of Homer embodies the contradictions at the heart of efforts to reconcile the 'wise,' authoritative, and canonical poet with the diligent and industrious historian who accurately describes the events and geography of the heroic world.

In fact, Strabo plays a pivotal role in this book because he subscribes, albeit in slightly exaggerated form, to the sort of adulation of the heroic age and apologetic conception of Homer as historian to which the Second Sophistic authors after him are responding.[12] Included as targets of their critiques are not only Strabo's reverent portrait of Homer and his complicated theory of Homer's 'mythification' of history, but also his attempts to link his defense of Homer with his conception of Greece and being Greek vis-à-vis the Roman Empire. At the end of the chapter, I thus shift the focus away from Strabo's 'Homeric poetics' and set his ideas about Homer in the context of his thinking about the heroic past, Greek tradition, and Greek identity at the advent of the Roman Empire.

[10] Strabo on Homer in *Geog.* 1.2: Neumann (1886); Floratos (1972); Schenkeveld (1976); Biraschi (1984), (1988), (2005); Meijering (1987), 5–7, 10–11, 58–62; Romm (1992), 183–94.

[11] This subject-matter sets the *Prolegomena* apart from the bulk of Strabo's inquiries in the remaining books of the *Geography*, where he only occasionally addresses theoretical issues of myth or poetic invention.

[12] Although there was probably no direct influence, since the *Geography* seems not to have been read much in the centuries after its composition: see Engels (1999), 383–8; Dueck (2000), 151–2.

HOMER'S KNOWLEDGE

On the face of it, the dispute over Homer's geographical accuracy that Strabo plunges into hinges on a single, fundamental issue: Homer's knowledge of places outside of the limited sphere of the Eastern Mediterranean.[13] Strabo's position in the debate is clear from the start, since he devotes part of his opening statements (1.1.3–11) to asserting and then demonstrating Homer's familiarity with the boundaries of the entire *oikoumenê*, or inhabited world.[14] The reason for this impromptu display, as we learn later, is that Homer's geographical knowledge had come under considerable assault from earlier geographers such as Apollodorus and Eratosthenes. Strabo outlines their critique in a passage from Book 7:

Apollodorus (*FGrH* 244 F 157) approves the declaration (ἐπαινεῖ... ἀπόφασιν) of Eratosthenes (F 1 A, 6), that although both Homer and others of ancient times (τοὺς ἄλλους τοὺς παλαιούς) knew places in Greece (τὰ μὲν Ἑλληνικὰ εἰδέναι), they had very *little experience* (πολλὴν ἔχειν ἀπειρίαν) of those that were far away, since they were *inexperienced* (ἀπείρους) either in making long journeys by land or voyages by sea. And in support of this Apollodorus says that Homer calls Aulis "rocky" (*Il.* 2.496) (and so it is), and Eteonus "place of many ridges" (*Il.* 2.497), and Thisbe "haunt of doves" (*Il.* 2.502), and Haliartus "grassy" (*Il.* 2.503), but, he says, neither Homer nor the others knew (εἰδέναι) the places that were far away. (7.3.6)

The critics thus acknowledge that Homer's descriptions of Greece and Asia Minor are reliable, but insist that those of "far away" places are not. The individual cases are discussed throughout section 1.2: for example, Eratosthenes claims that Homer was unaware of the name of the Nile, the fact that it has several mouths (1.2.22), the distance of the island Pharos from the mainland (23), and the isthmus between the Egyptian Sea and the Arabian Gulf (24); Apollodorus accuses Homer of being ignorant of the Scythians, the Paphlagonian seaboard, Arabia, and the multiple rivers flowing into the Black Sea; Demetrius of Scepsis says that Homer knew nothing about Jason's voyage (38).

Strabo contends that Homer does "know" (οἶδε) "the remote ends (τὰ ἔσχατα) of the *oikoumenê* and what surrounds it (τὰ κύκλῳ), as well as the regions around the Mediterranean Sea" (1.1.10). Even though Homer does

---

[13] Schenkeveld (1976), 53–5.

[14] See Aujac (1966), 20–6 for a succinct overview of this section. Many of the discussions here are relatively abbreviated versions of the in-depth defenses of Homeric geographical knowledge that will appear in 1.2: e.g., the Ethiopians divided in two, the tides, the location of the Cimmerians in Homer, the identity of the Erembians, the question of Iberia, etc.

not mention Iberia, the Cimmerian Bosporus, the Ister river, and the head-land of Italy, he nevertheless 'knows' of their existence. Strabo's (not always convincing) demonstrations of this knowledge plumb the depths of philo-logical ingenuity (cf. his complicated proof in 1.1.6 that Homer "knows" [οἶδεν] both the arctic circle and that "it touches the most northerly point of the horizon") and their intricacy shows how far matters have progressed from the days of Herodotus and Thucydides.

Confronted by such a tenaciously apologetic attitude, it would be under-standable if one were to group Strabo among those critics who saw Homer as the fountain of all knowledge – an idea usually attributed to Hellenis-tic Stoicism, but that has its roots in the Classical and Archaic periods and is probably best embodied in Ps.-Plutarch's *On Homer*, an Impe-rial text.[15] But Strabo's defense of Homer rests not on a priori assertions of Homer's wisdom and encyclopedic knowledge, but on a conception of the poet as a dedicated historian, similar to the image implicit in Herodotus. In fact, as we shall see, Strabo's Homer shares some features with that of Herodotus, in that he 'knows' the truth, but only reveals that knowledge by 'hinting' at it (1.1.3: Homer "names some of the coun-tries, but he *hints* at others with signs (τὰ δὲ ὑπηνίττετο τεκμηρίοις τισί)." While Strabo shares this logic and language of 'hinting' and 'signs' with the didactic and allegorical interpreters of Homer,[16] the motiva-tions behind Homer's activity stem from the vivid portrait of Homer as researcher, historian, and poet that Strabo sketches right at the begin-ning of his work and fills in little by little throughout the first book of the *Geography*.

The ideal historian-geographer

Strabo lays out his portrait of Homer in the first few paragraphs of the *Geography*. Homer, he says, was the first of an illustrious line of geographer-philosophers; indeed he was "the founder of geography" (ἀρχηγέτην εἶναι τῆς γεωγραφικῆς ἐμπειρίας: 1.1.2). The ideal geographer must have "examined both human and divine affairs," and "investigated the art of life" in order to possess the πολυμάθεια (wide learning) necessary to prac-tice geography and properly achieve the ὠφέλεια ποικίλη (multifaceted

---

[15] See Koster (1974), 143–51, on the ancient debate on the purpose of poetry and Hillgruber (1994), 1: 5–35, on the idea of Homer as the source of all knowledge; cf. Russell (1981), 84–98.

[16] Similarities that I observed in Herodotus as well (Ch. 2: 00–0).

utility) that is its goal (1.1.1).[17] That Homer is a worthy exemplar of these qualities is then emphasized in 1.1.2:

[Homer] has surpassed everyone, ancient and modern, not only in the excellence of his poetry, but also, I might say, *in his experience of all that pertains to public life*. And from this experience, he *eagerly strove to learn about and transmit* to those who came after him, not only as many events as possible, but also facts pertaining to places, both on an individual basis and with regard to the entire inhabited land and sea. Otherwise, *he would not have reached its farthest borders*, going around it in his description.

...ὃς οὐ μόνον τῇ κατὰ τὴν ποίησιν ἀρετῇ πάντας ὑπερβέβληται τοὺς πάλαι καὶ τοὺς ὕστερον, ἀλλὰ σχεδόν τι καὶ τῇ κατὰ τὸν βίον ἐμπειρίᾳ τὸν πολιτικόν, ἀφ' ἧς οὐ μόνον περὶ τὰς πράξεις ἐσπούδασεν ἐκεῖνος ὅπως ὅτι πλείστας γνοίη καὶ παραδώσει τοῖς ὕστερον ἐσομένοις, ἀλλὰ καὶ τὰ περὶ τοὺς τόπους τούς τε καθ' ἕκαστα καὶ τοὺς κατὰ σύμπασαν τὴν οἰκουμένην γῆν τε καὶ θάλατταν· οὐ γὰρ ἂν μέχρι τῶν ἐσχάτων αὐτῆς περάτων ἀφίκετο τῇ μνήμῃ κύκλῳ περιιών.

Homer is thus central to Strabo's objectives in the *Prolegomena*, not only as the founder of geography, but also as an embodiment of the qualities and attitude that the ideal geographer ought to possess. Hence the emphasis on Homer's "experience" (ἐμπειρία) (to be contrasted with the geographical inexperience (ἀπειρία) that Apollodorus had accused the poet of in the passage quoted earlier), and on his eagerness to learn about places, to pass on this knowledge, and to travel in pursuit of it.[18] These virtues also sound very much like those praised in historians – no surprise given the overlap in the two professions ever since the days of Hecataeus and Herodotus – and should remind us that for Strabo the qualities necessary to conduct historiographical and geographical enquiry are virtually identical.[19]

Homer's dedication to historico-geographical inquiry is stressed throughout Book 1 of the *Geography*: Strabo speaks of Homer's "zealous curiosity" (φιλοπραγμοσύνης: 1.1.10), his "love of learning" and "love of travel" (τὸ φιλείδημον; τὸ φιλέκδημον: 1.2.29), and emphasizes both his geographical *and* historical interests at 1.2.13:

[17] Strabo's notion of 'philosophy': Biraschi (1984), 131–6; French (1994), 123–30; Engels (1999), 40–4. On the appeal to philosophy in technical treatise introductions, see Dihle (1986).

[18] Strabo's assertion that Homer traveled widely seems intended to correct Eratosthenes, who had said that the 'ancients' had not sailed very far from the Aegean (1.3.2 = F I B, 8).

[19] On the importance of travel and inquiry for historians, see Marincola (1997), 148–51; Schepens (2006). Strabo himself wrote history (now lost) before geography, and one of his most influential models, Polybius, similarly treated both topics. As I have argued elsewhere (Kim [2007], 370–3), Polybius also treats Homer (implicitly) as a historian, and Strabo's image of Homer and the ideal geographer embody many of the traits Polybius insists upon in a historian.

For we do not demand (ζητοῦμεν) that the poet has *inquired* accurately into each particular (ἀκριβῶς ἕκαστα πυθέσθαι), nor do we demand precision from him (παρ᾽ ἐκείνου ... τὸ ἀκριβές); but we should not go so far as to suppose that he composed his poems (ῥαψῳδεῖν) without having *inquired* at all (μηδὲν πεπυσμένον) about where or how the wandering [of Odysseus] occurred (μήθ᾽ ὅπου μήθ᾽ ὅπως γεγένηται).

Homer's investigative efforts are further highlighted by Strabo's repeated use of the verb πυνθάνομαι, "inquire" or "learn from inquiry," when discussing the poet, whom he imagines as investigating local tradition, listening to obscure legends, and recording his findings for posterity: e.g., 1.1.4 on the wealth of Iberia (πεπυσμένος), or 1.2.30 on the silting of the Nile (πεπύσθαι). Homer is the first geographer not only because of what he knows, but because of the effort he expended to acquire that knowledge.

An excellent example of this vision of Homer as inquirer is found in Strabo's lengthy discussion of the two sets of Ethiopians (Αἰθίοπας τοὶ διχθὰ δεδαίαται) mentioned at *Od.* 1.24–5: "some at the setting of Hyperion, some at his rising" (οἱ μὲν δυσομένου Ὑπερίονος οἱ δ᾽ ἀνιόντος). The problem of identifying these mysterious western and eastern Ethiopians had exercised the ingenuity of many ancient critics.[20] Aristarchus, as Strabo tells us, simply concluded that "Homer, not knowing this [the location of Ethiopia] ... falsely reported things that are not true about these areas" (τοῦτο δὲ ἀγνοοῦντα τὸν ποιητήν ... καταψεύσασθαι τῶν τόπων τὰ μὴ ὄντα: 1.2.24). Others, however, tried harder to make sense of Homer's words. Strabo offers at least six possible solutions: three of his own (including his favorite – the Ethiopians are split in two by the Red Sea: 1.2.27–8), a typically wild interpretation by Crates, and others by Posidonius and the fourth-century historian Ephorus of Cyme. Of these, Ephorus' and the second of those proposed by Strabo interest me here.[21]

At 1.2.26 Strabo suggests that, until Homer's time, anyone who had attempted to circumnavigate the African continent, whether starting from the Pillars of Hercules or the Red Sea, was always forced to turn back for one reason or another. This left the erroneous impression that a land mass of some sort, like an isthmus, made a circumnavigation impossible (even though, as Strabo points out, this was not in fact the case). Since these travelers, whether they had originally left from the east or the west, noted that the last people they had contact with were Ethiopians, "Homer also

[20] The lines were well known in antiquity; cf. Ramin (1979), 73–80; Nadeau (1970) on Virgil, Lucan, Statius, and Juvenal's use of the interpretative tradition.

[21] Posidonius' solution appears later in 2.3.7–8. For a concise summary of the various positions outlined by Strabo, see Kidd (1990), 268–73.

was led by such a report (ὑπὸ τοιαύτης ἀκοῆς ἀχθείς) into dividing the Ethiopians into two groups, placing one group in the east and the other in the west, since it was not known whether the people in between them really existed or not" (1.2.26). Ephorus, on the other hand, "conjectured" (τεκμαίρεται) that Homer spoke of the "Ethiopians divided in two" on the basis of a Tartessian report "that Ethiopians went through Libya all the way to Dyris [the Atlas mountains in Morocco], and that some remained there, while others occupied the sea-coast" (*FGrH* 70 F 128). Strabo adds that "it is not unreasonable (ἄλογον) to believe that Homer had also encountered (ἐντυχεῖν)" this story of how some Ethiopians had ended up on the west coast of the African continent (1.2.26).

What Strabo and Ephorus' explanations of the twin Ethiopias share is their stress on how Homer gained his knowledge about the Ethiopians, even granting, as Strabo does, that it was incorrect. In one the information is characterized as a "report" (ἀκοή), in the other as a *logos* that he had "encountered" (ἐντυχεῖν [or perhaps "read"?]). Neither critic expects Homer to have access to firsthand information about the Ethiopians; in fact Strabo himself, in the so-called second introduction at 2.5.11, argues that secondhand information (ἀκοή) is more important for knowledge than eyewitness testimony.[22] But both historicize Homer as a person living at a particular place and time and envision him basing his poetic geography on reports from faraway places that he believed were accurate. In short, they imagine him as a historian much like themselves.

This envisioning of Homer in one's own image was already present *in nuce* in Herodotus and Thucydides, who implicitly treat Homer as a historian (albeit with some conflicting poetic aims). Herodotus had also emphasized Homer's inquiring nature, suggesting that Homer had learned of the story of Helen in Egypt through *inquiry*: Ὅμηρος τὸν λόγον τοῦτον πυθέσθαι (Hdt. 2.116.1). And the linking of Homer and travel can be found in the Homeric biographical tradition, where it is often suggested that the variety of the poems' content (especially of the *Odyssey*) was due to Homer's experiences on his travels. Only in the Ps.-Herodotean *Life* (7), however, is it specified that Homer "inquired into and learned" (ἐξιστορῆσαι καὶ πυθέσθαι) a particular *logos* – in this case the story of Odysseus, obtained during a stay on Ithaca. Strabo has taken something that had been suggested

---

[22] "He who claims that only eyewitnesses (τοὺς ἰδόντας) have knowledge (εἰδέναι) destroys the criterion of hearing (ἀναιρεῖ τὸ τῆς ἀκοῆς κριτήριον), which is much more important than sight for knowledge (ἥτις πρὸς ἐπιστήμην ὀφθαλμοῦ πολὺ κρείττων ἐστί)" (2.5.11). The sentiment is at odds with Polybius' well-known emphasis on autopsy and participation: Engels (1999), 157–65.

here and there in the tradition and made it the centerpiece of his vision of Homer.

Like his predecessors, Strabo retains this view of Homer as a historian even though he apparently thinks of him as born long after the Trojan War. For a writer as invested in proving Homer's historical accuracy as Strabo is, he is surprisingly reticent about establishing the age in which the poet lived. He mentions attempts by others to date Homer – during or after the Cimmerian invasion (1.2.9) and after the Ionian colonization (8.7.2) – but avoids saying whether he agrees with them or not. The only time Strabo specifically states that Homer lived well after the heroic period is at 10.4.15, when he draws a distinction between the time of the Trojan War and Homer's own time in order to solve the problem of why Crete is called "ninety-citied" (ἐνενηκοντάπολιν: *Od*. 19.174) at one time and "hundred-citied" at another (ἑκατόμπολιν: *Il*. 2.649).

The poet does not say that Crete had one hundred cities at the time of the Trojan War (κατὰ τὰ Τρωικά), but rather in his own time (κατ᾽ αὐτόν) (for he is speaking in his own person [ἐκ γὰρ τοῦ ἰδίου προσώπου λέγει]), although, if the statement was made by some person who was living at the time of the Trojan War, as is the case in the *Odyssey*, when Odysseus says "of the ninety cities," then it is proper to take it this way.[23]

But it is significant that this passing and imprecise reference to Homer's date is one of the few times Strabo addresses the question at all. Homer's distance from the events that he reports is used as an interpretative tool, to explain away inconsistencies and apparent errors, but not discussed with reference to his knowledge of the truth.

Despite this reticence to date Homer more specifically, Strabo is clearly *historicizing* the poet, and this suggests a very different attitude from that of ancient Homeric exegetes who posit Homer's words as a priori authoritative or 'scriptural,' whether in moral, scientific, or other terms. The Ethiopian example shows that Strabo hardly advocates Homer as an infallible geographical authority, and at 1.2.3 he explicitly criticizes those who try "to assign (περιποιεῖν) every art and all knowledge (πᾶν μάθημα καὶ πᾶσαν τέχνην) to Homer." Moreover, even though Strabo tries his best to square Homer's information with reality, he often acknowledges the limits of Homer's knowledge – he insists, against Posidonius, for example, that Homer did not know of India (2.3.8).[24] What matters is Homer's *character*,

---

[23] The interpretative technique here recalls that of Aristarchus (see, Ch 2., n. 21), in which a correspondence is drawn between what Homer mentions in his own voice and what was the case in the poet's own time.

[24] Kahles (1976), 200, provides other examples.

as a committed historian-geographer, who always did his best to ascertain the truth even if he may not always have been successful.

STRABO VS. ERATOSTHENES ON ODYSSEUS' WANDERINGS

It is with this conception of Homer as a dedicated historian-geographer in mind that I want to approach the defense of Homer's geographical accuracy that Strabo makes against the criticisms of the Alexandrian poet, philologist, and geographer Eratosthenes of Cyrene. Eratosthenes, as I have mentioned, maintained that much of Homer's geography was incorrect. But he had also connected this accusation with the more general claim, made programmatically near the beginning of his own geographical work, that poets "aim at entertainment not instruction" (στοχάζεσθαι ψυχαγωγίας, οὐ διδασκαλίας: 1.2.3 = F I A, 20).[25] The debate (which is perhaps the wrong term, given the century or so separating the two) has often been cast as a standoff between a subtle thinker (Eratosthenes) who understands the nature of fiction against an obstinate defender of Homer's universal wisdom (Strabo).[26] But their differences have less to do with the long-standing controversy over poetry's didactic claims than with the issue of Homer's geographical and historical accuracy – the point of contention here is how each critic conceives of the relation between the geography of Homer's poetic world and that of the actual world of the heroic age.[27] Eratosthenes' dismissal of Homer's 'instructional' intent is taken by Strabo as a direct assault on the portrait of Homer he holds so dear, which puts instruction at the very heart of Homer's geographical interests.[28]

---

[25] On Eratosthenes' *Geography* (fragments cited from Berger [1880]), see Pfeiffer (1968), 165–8, and Geus (2002).

[26] Rudolf Pfeiffer (1968: 154; 166–8), in an influential characterization, praised Eratosthenes' "fearless" and "scientific" declaration of poetic autonomy and dismissed Strabo as a "Stoic 'convert'" determined to defend Homer's universal wisdom at any cost. Compare similar comments in the standard handbooks on ancient literary criticism: Grube (1965), 128; Russell (1981), 42 and 95; Innes (1989), 272.

[27] Strabo obscures the discussion by initially proposing a Stoicizing and moralizing rebuttal to Eratosthenes that has little to do with his main argument. His arguments – that poetry is an elementary philosophy for the moral education of the young, that only the wise man can be a poet, that poets teach farming, rhetoric, and generalship, and that poets use myths to shape the thoughts of the masses – are not compatible with the thrust of his arguments in the bulk of the *Prolegomena* and indeed of the *Geography* as a whole. Unfortunately, Strabo's comments have distorted modern views of his position: de Lacy (1948) uncritically uses Strabo as evidence for Stoic poetics; Walbank (1979), 577, thinks that Strabo sees Homer as the "prototype of the Stoic σοφός"; Russell and Winterbottom (1970), 300, introduce their translation of 1.2.3–9 as "a statement of the Stoic position about the didactic value of poetry."

[28] Kim (2007).

I want first to clarify Eratosthenes' position, as far as it can be reconstructed from Strabo's polemic. Like Strabo, Eratosthenes also considered Homer a philosopher and the first geographer,[29] and admits a correspondence between Homeric depictions of the world and those in real life:

In the beginning, everyone *eagerly* paraded their *knowledge* of such things [i.e., geography] (φιλοτίμως ἔχειν εἰς τὸ μέσον φέρειν τὴν ὑπὲρ τῶν τοιούτων ἱστορίαν); certainly Homer made a place in his poetry (καταχωρίσαι εἰς τὴν ποίησιν) for as much as he had *learned* (ὅσα ἐπύθετο) about the Ethiopians and things in Egypt and Libya, and he proceeded *with great detail* (λίαν περιέργως ἐξενηνοχέναι) in regard to things in Greece and places nearby. (1.2.3 = F I A, 4)

As we see here, Eratosthenes is not only willing to concede that Homer included accurate geographical details in his poetry, but even seems to characterize Homer's capacity for inquiry (ἱστορίαν; ἐπύθετο) and industry (φιλοτίμως; περιέργως) as Strabo does, and in a similarly positive light. Eratosthenes and Strabo also agree that the events depicted by Homer actually happened, and that, in this case, Odysseus had wandered throughout the Western Mediterranean on his way back to Ithaca. For Eratosthenes, however, it was *Hesiod* who "learned by inquiry (πεπυσμένον) that the scene of Odysseus wanderings lay in the region of Sicily and Italy," while "Homer did not know (μήτε εἰδέναι) these places, nor did he wish to depict (ποιεῖν) the wandering in known locales" (1.2.14 = F I B, 3).[30] Eratosthenes thus believed that while some locales in Homer, like Ilium and Mt. Ida, were accurately described and "not invented" (οὐ πεπλασμένοις), others had no correspondence to real places and were completely fictional, like Geryon's home and especially the places where Odysseus traveled (1.2.12 = F I A, 12). He is thus not casting doubt on Odysseus' voyage, but on the accuracy of Homer's depiction of that voyage.[31]

So far, Eratosthenes' stance echoes other Hellenistic scholars who claimed that Homer invented names, places, and peoples that correlated neither with geographical nor historical reality. I mentioned above that Aristarchus

[29] Str. 1.1.1 = F I A, 1: "those who in earliest times ventured to treat [geography] were, in their way, philosophers – Homer, Anaximander, and Hecataeus – just as Eratosthenes has already said." Str. 1.1.11 = F I B, 5: "Eratosthenes declares that the first two successors of Homer [in geography] were Anaximander . . . and Hecataeus of Miletus."

[30] Similarly at 1.2.22 (= F I B, 1), Eratosthenes asserts that Hesiod knew the name of the Nile, while Homer did not, and contends that because Hesiod named the Homeric locales *and* the actual places that they were to be identified with, e.g., "Aetna, Ortygia . . . and Tyrrhenia," he was the first to know the true locations of Odysseus' journey.

[31] A distinction that is easy to blur; e.g., Schenkeveld (1976), 61, makes it sound as if Eratosthenes was casting doubt on the reality of Odysseus' wanderings as well as their location near Italy ("Eratosthenes, again, held that the wanderings are a myth"), rather than just on Homer's knowledge of that reality. For more on Homeric 'invention,' see below.

concluded that Homer had been "ignorant" of the Ethiopians and told things about them "that were not true," and that Apollodorus followed Eratosthenes, according to Strabo, in thinking that: "although [Homer] wanted to tell the truth (ὡς λέγειν μὲν τὰ ὄντα βουλομένου), he did not, but through his ignorance (κατ᾽ ἄγνοιαν) told things that were not true as if they were true" (τὰ μὴ ὄντα ὡς ὄντα: 1.2.35 = *FGrH* 244 F 157f). But Eratosthenes goes further than his colleagues by hypothetically reconstructing the process by which Homer decided to fictionalize the geography of the wanderings:[32]

Eratosthenes says that the poet wished to depict the wanderings of Odysseus in the west, but abandoned his plans (ἀποστῆναι δ᾽ ἀπὸ τῶν ὑποκειμένων) because he had not accurately learned some things (τὰ μὲν οὐκ ἀκριβῶς πεπυσμένον), nor even preferred to be accurate with respect to others (τὰ δὲ οὐδὲ προελόμενον οὕτως) but rather to develop each incident in the direction of the more awe-inspiring and fantastic (ἀλλ᾽ ἐπὶ τὸ δεινότερον καὶ τὸ τερατωδέστερον ἕκαστα ἐξάγειν). (1.2.19 = F I A, 14)

This claim particularly angers Strabo, and it is not hard to see why. Eratosthenes posits a Homer similar to that imagined by Strabo – a man interested in geography, investigating and inquiring about Odysseus' voyage – but claims that he not only did a poor job of obtaining information (οὐκ ἀκριβῶς πεπυσμένον), but at a certain point decided to drop historical accuracy altogether. Homer *knew* the wanderings took place in the west, but could not be bothered to determine the details. These accusations cut to the very heart of Strabo's exaltation of the poet's industrious character. Indeed, Eratosthenes casts further aspersions on the poet's motives by subsequently saying that Homer situated his most fantastic stories (τὰ πόρρω τερατολογεῖσθαι) in far-off places "because they were easier to lie about" (μᾶλλον διὰ τὸ εὐκατάψευστον: 1.2.19 = F I A, 14).[33]

The point of contention is not just Eratosthenes' claim that Homer invented in order to make his poetry "more awe-inspiring and fantastic" (ἐπὶ τὸ δεινότερον καὶ τὸ τερατωδέστερον) but his suggestion that Homer's poetic imperatives ('entertainment') overrode his historico-geographical concern for discovering and reporting the truth

---

[32] This skepticism is no doubt related to his belief that, historically, people of that period did not make long sea voyages, cf. 1.3.2. Strabo characteristically refutes Eratosthenes by citing the journeys of Dionysus, Heracles, Jason, Odysseus, and other heroes.

[33] Romm ([1992], 193) sees as the hallmark of Eratosthenes' criticism "to have charted the *Odyssey* on a literary rather than geographical map, gauging its veracity according to how far from *terra cognita* it travels."

('instruction').[34] Strabo himself grants Homer the freedom to invent – for instance he belittles those who claim that Odysseus' return to Ithaca, the massacre of the suitors, and the battle with the Ithacans all took place just as described (1.2.11). But invention and delight are subsidiary, not primary goals. Consider the following passage from a discussion of a sanctuary to Poseidon where Strabo claims Telemachus met the Pylians:

> It is indeed permissible for the poet also to invent things that are not true (πάρεστι μὲν γὰρ τῷ ποιητῇ καὶ πλάττειν τὰ μὴ ὄντα), but whenever it is possible to adapt his words to what is true and preserve his narrative (ὅταν δ᾽ ᾖ δυνατὸν ἐφαρμόττειν τοῖς οὖσι τὰ ἔπη καὶ σώζειν τὴν διήγησιν), it is more appropriate to abstain [from assuming that the poet invented things that are not true] (τὸ ἀπέχεσθαι προσήκει μᾶλλον).[35] (8.3.17)

Strabo insists upon a principle of interpretative charity. One must assume Homeric correctness, doing one's best to "preserve the narrative", and only attribute "invention" to Homer as a last resort.[36] This is why Strabo insists that Eratosthenes "understands well what Homer did, but not why he did it (τοῦτο μὲν αὐτὸ εὖ, τὸ δ᾽ οὐ χάριν τοῦτ᾽ ἐποίει κακῶς δεξάμενος); for it was not for the sake of nonsense, but utility (οὐ γὰρ φλυαρίας, ἀλλ᾽ ὠφελείας χάριν)" (1.2.19).

Eratosthenes and Strabo thus have different views on Homer's reliability, but the divide is not as stark as scholars have made it out to be.[37] Both believe

---

34 When Eratosthenes advises his readers "not to judge (κρίνειν) poems with reference to their thought (πρὸς τὴν διάνοιαν), nor to seek history from them (μηδ᾽ ἱστορίαν ἀπ᾽ αὐτῶν ζητεῖν)" (1.2.17 = F I A, 17) he does so because he believes that poets are not bound to the accuracy of their content and that the presentation of technical information, whether correct or not, is irrelevant to the judgment of Homer's qualities as a *poet* (cf. Arist. *Poetics* 25.1460b13–21; 30–2: correctness in poetry should not be judged by the standards of any other *technê*). Eratosthenes asks "what does it contribute to the excellence of a poet (πρὸς ἀρετὴν ποιητοῦ) to have experience (ἔμπειρον) of many places, generalship, farming, rhetoric or whatever it is that people have wanted to secure (περιποιεῖν) for him?" (1.2.3 = F I A, 21). Strabo's paraphrase of Eratosthenes at 1.2.12 (= F I A, 12) – "He declares that every poet is a fool and believes that their knowledge (ἐμπειρίαν) of places or *technai* does not lead to virtue (πρὸς ἀρετήν)" – shows clearly that he misunderstands what Eratosthenes means by ἀρετή (see Floratos [1972], 44, and Biraschi [1984], 139–43).

35 Following the translation proposed by Biraschi (1992); Jones (1917) and Baladié (1978) take Homer as the subject of the infinitives in the second clause, translating "whenever possible *he* should adapt . . . and preserve" and rendering τὸ ἀπέχεσθαι as "more appropriate [that he] abstain". Their translation makes Strabo's statement about what *Homer* should do, as opposed to Biraschi's, which emphasizes the task of the reader or interpreter. Biraschi's translation fits much better with Strabo's outlook on Homer, as we shall see. Radt, following Meineke (1866), transposes this passage to 8.3.17, but this does not affect my argument.

36 Note that this idea of poetic license concentrates on the poet's invention of things that are not real (τὰ μὴ ὄντα) as opposed to the invention of variant traditions; for the distinction, see Meijering (1987), 63–7.

37 So Grube (1965), 128, summarizes Eratosthenes' view: "critics should not waste their time establishing the truth of a poet's facts."

that Homer was the first geographer and that his work includes a wealth of important geographico-historical knowledge, occasionally elaborated for poetic purposes. The difference lies in their conception of Homer's own attitude toward this knowledge. While Strabo believed the poet's concern for geography trumped his poetic aims, Eratosthenes assumed it was the other way around. The issue of Odysseus' wanderings brings this difference into sharper focus. Like most ancient historians and geographers, Strabo and Eratosthenes agree that the historical Odysseus wandered through Sicily and Italy, but they disagree over how much of this voyage was known to Homer and depicted in his poetry. Eratosthenes reads the fantastic aspects of the wanderings as evidence of Homer's lack of interest in the historical reality of those events, and suggests that Homer purposefully placed the wanderings in far-off places to make it easier to fictionalize. To Strabo, such claims cast aspersions on Homer's dedication to conveying geographical information and suggest that the very man who founded geography was a less than ideal practitioner of the science. Eratosthenes makes no attempt to "preserve the narrative" but, to Strabo's mind, reads Homer uncharitably. In other words, the two geographers differ in their account of Homer's intentions with regard to the depiction of Odysseus' wanderings: Strabo asserts his *historical* objectives, Eratosthenes his *poetic, fictionalizing* ones. In this sense, Eratosthenes follows in the footsteps of the critics I examined in the last chapter: he tries to explain why Homer abandoned the 'truth' by appealing to Homer's *poetic* objectives. But his solution is more radical, positing Homer's wholescale rejection of reality and (perhaps more disconcerting to Strabo) his ignorance of that reality. Theirs is not so much a debate over poetry and its objectives in general, as one over Homer's character, his intentions, his knowledge, and the nature of his work.

Myth and history in Homer

By defending Homer's historical intentions in composing the Phaeacian Tales, Strabo has set himself a much more difficult interpretative task than Eratosthenes, who could (and did) simply dismiss them as pure poetic invention with no connection to reality. Indeed, the Homeric episodes discussed by ancient critics in the last chapter were all, generally speaking, 'realistic,' and thus did not present the sort of credibility problems that the narrative of Odysseus' travels did, with its clearly unhistorical monsters, magic, and metamorphoses. Strabo thus has to address the place of 'myths' and the 'fantastic' in Homer's historically oriented poetry. If Odysseus' voyage took place in the western Mediterranean, why did Homer, the archetypal geographer, not say so directly but instead set the wanderings in a fantastic, mythic setting? How is the critic meant to locate the 'truth' from Homer's fictions? In response, Strabo develops his own model of Homer's *poetic* objectives that tries to balance Homer's right to invent while retaining Strabo's faith in Homer's devotion to historical inquiry and the truth. Strabo's basic solution, that Homer's inventions, or myths, are all built around a basic truthful core, is a familiar one, but it is the nuances and detail he brings to it that are of interest.

Strabo acknowledges early on in the first book that Homeric poetry contains much that is fantastic. He insists, however, that Homer should not be criticized,

if he has interwoven some mythic material in among the things said historically and for instruction (εἰ μυθώδη τινὰ προσπέπλεκται τοῖς λεγομένοις ἱστορικῶς καὶ διδασκαλικῶς), for what Eratosthenes (F I A, 20) says is not true, that every poet aims at entertainment, not instruction (οὐδὲ γὰρ ἀληθές ἐστιν, ὅ φησιν Ἐρατοσθένης, ὅτι ποιητὴς πᾶς στοχάζεται ψυχαγωγίας, οὐ διδασκαλίας). (1.1.10)

Note how Strabo establishes a correspondence between Homer's use of historical subject-matter and Eratosthenes' concept of instruction (διδασκαλία), by glossing ἱστορικῶς with διδασκαλικῶς. When Strabo returns to this issue in 1.2.3, he formulates his modification of Eratosthenes' theory along the same lines. Given that Eratosthenes claimed (F I A, 4), as we saw above, that Homer presented accurate geographical information about Greece but filled places farther away full of "mythic fantasy" (τερατολογίας μυθικῆς), shouldn't we rather say, Strabo asks, that "every poet expresses only *some* things for the sake of entertainment and others for the sake of instruction (ποιητὴς πᾶς τὰ μὲν ψυχαγωγίας χάριν μόνον ἐκφέρει, τὰ δὲ διδασκαλίας: 1.2.3)?" For Strabo, some things, i.e., accurate facts, are included for instructive purposes, while others, i.e., myths and fantastic tales, are aimed at entertaining the listener. Eratosthenes' distinction between types of poetic *function* – entertainment and instruction – is now tied to two different kinds of poetic *content* – the mythic and sensational on the one hand and the historical and true on the other.

This formulation may seem self-evident, but it is by no means the only way to construe the relation between the two concepts. The claim that poetry had two objectives – one variously termed pleasure, delight, or entertainment (ἡδονή, τέρψις, ψυχαγωγία) and the other benefit, utility, instruction (ὠφέλεια, τὸ χρήσιμον, διδασκαλία) – is an old and durable one, best known perhaps from Horace's praise of the poet "who mixes the *useful* with the *pleasant, delighting* and *instructing* the reader in equal measure" (*qui miscuit* utile dulci | *lectorem* delectando pariterque monendo: *Ars P.* 343–4).[38] But precisely what "pleasure" or "utility" comprised could vary considerably from text to text (and indeed at times Strabo himself conceives of the terms in mutually contradictory ways, as I indicate below). Pleasure might arise from the verse form itself, from poetic style more broadly conceived, or as Strabo understands it here, from fantastic content; the benefit might derive from direct ethical maxims, technical instruction, or exemplary characters. A given critic could further refine or combine these categories or, as often, leave the definition of the two terms ambiguous.[39] Strabo's decision to conceive of poetry's balancing of pleasure and utility solely in terms of its content – entertaining myths and instructive facts – is thus one stance among many.

Strabo views Homer primarily through a historico-geographical lens, and in this light, one might ask how he integrates his model of poetry's dual purpose of entertaining and instructing with his portrait of Homer as a dedicated historian. After all, the same two objectives were often claimed for historiographical writing; as evidenced in the work of Polybius, Diodorus, and Dionysius.[40] One possible reply, then, to the question of why someone so interested in conveying the truth would introduce pleasurable, but false, myths into his narrative draws attention to the use of myth in historiography. If Homer weaves in myths into his otherwise historical works, he is, Strabo claims, only doing what other historians have done. So in 1.2.35, he argues that one should not accuse Homer of ignorance because he tells myths (μυθεύοντος), since it is obvious that they

---

[38] Cf. Hor. *Ars P.* 333–4 *aut prodesse volunt aut delectare poetae | aut simul et iucunda et idonea dicere vitae* (Aly [1957] attempts to draw a direct connection between Strabo and Horace). This sort of compromise solution no doubt derived from an attempt to answer Pl. *Resp.* 10.607d where Socrates issues the call to others to explain how poetry can be "not only *pleasant* but also *beneficial* for states and human life" (οὐ μόνον ἡδεῖα ἀλλὰ καὶ ὠφελίμη πρὸς τὰς πολιτείας καὶ τὸν βίον τὸν ἀνθρώπινον).

[39] For instance, according to Philodemus, Heraclides Ponticus (Phld. *Po.* 5, col. v.27 Mangoni) and Neoptolemus of Parium (Phld. *Po.* 5, col. xvi.9–15 Mangoni) each claimed that poetry delights and benefits its readers, but did not specify in what way it does so. Philodemus seems to have seen poetry's utility as arising both from its form and content. On this, see Asmis (1991), 149–51.

[40] I have argued elsewhere (Kim [2007]) that Eratosthenes' formulation and Strabo's modification have parallels in historiographical discussions about the purpose of history.

are not intended to be taken as truth.[41] After adducing several examples
from other poets, he continues:

[W]e do not pay attention to those who write in prose about many things in
the form of history (ἐν ἱστορίας σχήματι), even if they do not acknowledge
their myth-writing (ἐξομολογῶνται τὴν μυθογραφίαν). For it is immediately
clear that they willingly interweave myths, not out of ignorance of reality (μύθους
παραπλέκουσιν ἑκόντες, οὐκ ἀγνοίᾳ τῶν ὄντων), but because they fabricate
impossible things for the sake of enjoyment and fantasy (ἀλλὰ πλάσει τῶν
ἀδυνάτων τερατείας καὶ τέρψεως χάριν). But they seem to do so out of ignorance
(κατ' ἄγνοιαν), because they especially tell myths, in a plausible way, concerning
things that are obscure and unknown (πιθανῶς τὰ τοιαῦτα μυθεύουσι περὶ τῶν
ἀδήλων καὶ τῶν ἀγνοουμένων). Theopompus acknowledges this when he says
that he will mention myths in his histories (καὶ μύθους ἐν ταῖς ἱστορίαις ἐρεῖ);
[this is] better than what Herodotus, Ctesias, Hellanicus, and those writing *Indica*
[do].[42]

Like Homer, these historians "interweave" (παραπλέκουσιν; cf. 1.1.10
on Homer: προσπέπλεκται) myths into their histories, inventing for the
sake of delight. And note how closely the suggestion that historians tell
myths concerning things that are obscure and unknown parallels Eratosthenes' accusation that Homer set Odysseus' wanderings far away because
they would be easier to lie about. The criticism leveled against these historians is that they do not make it clear that their 'myths' are only for
enjoyment and not to be taken as reality; Theopompus gets some credit for
admitting that he will employ myths in his history as opposed to others that
try to pass their myths off as truth (by telling myths *plausibly*). This does
not mean, however, that they *believed* in the myths they tell. So Homer
may have included myths, but he did so for the pleasure of the reader, and
not out of ignorance of the truth.[43]

This anxiety over myths "in the form of history" is echoed elsewhere in
the *Geography*. For instance, in 11.6.3 Strabo accuses Herodotus, Ctesias,
and Hellanicus (three of the historians mentioned in the passage above) of
emulating writers of myth (μυθογράφους), telling of things that they had
neither seen nor heard from any reliable source "in the form of history"
(ἐν ἱστορίας σχήματι), and aiming only at "a pleasing and marvelous

---

[41] Cf. 1.2.30: "The μυθοποιίαι are not a sign of ignorance (οὐκ ἀγνοίας σημεῖον δήπου) . . . not even
    if the poets invent (οἱ ποιηταὶ πλάττουσιν) something, for these are not told in ignorance of
    places (οὐ γὰρ κατ' ἄγνοιαν τῶν τοπικῶν λέγεται) but for the sake of sweetness and pleasure
    (ἀλλ' ἡδονῆς καὶ τέρψεως χάριν)."

[42] On the common misinterpretation of this fragment of Theopompus (*FGrH* 115 F 381), see Biraschi
    (1996). Theopompus was often pilloried for his 'myths': e.g., Cic. *de leg.* 1.1.5.

[43] I discuss this passage in connection with the preface of Lucian's *True Stories* in Ch. 5: 148–9.

reception" (ἀκρόασιν ἡδεῖαν . . . καὶ θαυμαστήν). Elsewhere Strabo criticizes other historians (such as Ephorus at 9.3.12) for blending myth and
history[44] – and the accusation was common enough in historiographical circles ever since Thucydides' famous disparagement (1.21.1) of the τὸ
μυθῶδες of the logographers, who compose more for attractiveness than
truthfulness.[45] The strongest condemnation is directed at Hecataeus and
other "early historians" (οἱ ἀρχαῖοι συγγραφεῖς), who "say many things
that are not true (μὴ ὄντα), since they were accustomed to falsehood due to
their writing myths (συντεθραμμένοι τῷ ψεύδει διὰ τὰς μυθογραφίας)"
(8.3.9).

Thus Strabo's decision to defend Homer's use of myth on historiographical grounds is somewhat ambivalent; Homer's myths are obviously myths,
and not to be taken as history, nor as signs of his ignorance of the truth,
and this elevates him over historians who fail to distinguish their myths as
myths to their readers. But Strabo has a generally negative opinion of myths
in historiography; while he admits that some historians use myths for entertainment purposes, he seems to believe that the proper historian should
not. Strabo has explained that Homer's myths are aimed at pleasure, not
instruction, and that this follows standard historiographical practice, but
given Strabo's insistence on Homer's dedication to geographical instruction and historical utility, the use of myths by Homer at all is still suspect.
Moreover, accepting such a position draws him uncomfortably close to
Eratosthenes' theory of Homeric wholesale invention for entertainment.
As we shall see, there is little room in Strabo's model of Homer as ideal
geographer for purely pleasurable myths.

In 1.2.7 Strabo appears to advocate a very different position: that myth
itself plays a paideutic or instructional role in addition to entertaining,
which would render Homer's myths more palatable. But the incompati-
bility of this option with the position he advocated earlier in 1.2.3 – that
myths only entertain – leads to considerable confusion. He begins:

[Homer] tells myths more than those after him (καὶ μᾶλλόν γε τῶν
ὕστερον μυθολογεῖται), but he does not make everything fantastic (οὐ πάντα

---

[44] Cf. 1.3.23, where Strabo criticizes Eratosthenes for replying to those who are clearly "speaking
of invented and impossible things, some in the form of myth, others of history" (πεπλασμένα
καὶ ἀδύνατα λέγοντας τὰ μὲν ἐν μύθου σχήματι, τὰ δ᾽ ἱστορίας). See also 5.1.9 and Strabo's
remarks on his own practice at 11.5.3: "for our accounts of other peoples keep a distinction between
the mythical and the historical elements (τὸ μυθῶδες καὶ τὸ ἱστορικόν); for the things that are
ancient and false and monstrous are called myths (τὰ γὰρ παλαιὰ καὶ ψευδῆ καὶ τερατώδη μῦθοι
καλοῦνται), but history wishes for the truth (ἡ δ᾽ ἱστορία βούλεται τἀληθές), whether ancient or
recent, and contains no monstrous element (τὸ τερατῶδες), or else only rarely."
[45] On this issue, see Wardman (1960); Marincola (1997), 117–27.

τερατευόμενος), rather, he contributes to knowledge by allegorizing, elaborating, or popularizing (πρὸς ἐπιστήμην ἀλληγορῶν ἢ διασκευάζων ἢ δημαγωγῶν), especially with reference to the things concerning the wanderings of Odysseus.

On first glance, this contention seems similar to those made previously. Strabo denies that Homer only fantasizes (πάντα τερατευόμενος: i.e., aims only at entertainment),[46] arguing that he also looks to convey knowledge (πρὸς ἐπιστήμην: i.e., instruction). The difference now is that knowledge is passed on by "telling myths" (μυθολογεῖται), and "allegorizing, elaborating, or popularizing" rather than, as previously, by the accuracy of his narrative. In other words, Homer's myth-making is no longer directed at entertainment, but instruction, and "history" has dropped out of the picture altogether.

This new understanding of myths' function prevails in the speculative cultural history that Strabo offers in 1.2.8. Even before the poets, myths were used by cities "for utility" (τοῦ χρησίμου χάριν) to sway the masses, who do not listen to the reasoning of a philosopher and can only be drawn to piety and faith "by religious fear" (διὰ δεισιδαιμονίας), which "cannot exist without myth-making and fantasy (οὐκ ἄνευ μυθοποιίας καὶ τερατείας)." In a similar way, societies use myths and "the fantastic" (τὸ τερατῶδες), which can be both pleasing (ἡδύ) and frightening, to incite their members toward exemplary behavior or dissuade them from evil courses of action.[47] Thus "through poetry, every age of life could be ethically educated (σωφρονίζεσθαι)" (1.2.8). This digression is linked to earlier remarks that Strabo makes in 1.2.3 about poetry as a first philosophy; the Greek cities "educate [their children] through the poetic not for the sake of entertainment, but *ethical education*" (διὰ τῆς ποιητικῆς παιδεύουσιν οὐ ψυχαγωγίας χάριν . . . ἀλλὰ σωφρονισμοῦ: 1.2.3). Both discussions focus on the realm of moral instruction; myths and fantasy (τὸ τερατῶδες) are employed to control behavior and represent a primitive stage of moral philosophy. But like that passage, this one has little to do with Strabo's ideas about Homer qua geography and seems like a poor attempt to integrate into the discussion elements of a Stoic theory about the early stages of human civilization and the origin of myth.[48] In any case, none of the myths

---

[46] Strabo uses τερατ- words (e.g., τερατεία, τερατολογία, τὸ τερατῶδες, τερατεύομαι) virtually interchangeably with their corresponding μυθ- terms (μῦθος, μυθολογία, τὸ μυθῶδες, μυθολογέομαι). Cf. Sacks (1981), 162–70, on Polybius' frequent employment of τερατ- words.

[47] Cf. Arist. *Metaph.* 1074a38–b14 and especially Polyb. 6.56 on the Roman's use of δεισιδαιμονία "for the sake of the common people."

[48] Schenkeveld (1976), 56–7, notes the problem, but takes the moralizing position outlined here as Strabo's dominant belief.

mentioned by Strabo in 1.2.8 concerns Homer,[49] and Strabo never interprets a Homer passage in a manner compatible with these moralizing standards elsewhere in the *Geography*.[50] In his desire to defend Homeric myth as part of his vision of Homer as the ideal geographer, Strabo naturally wants to claim an instructive value for it, but in his fixation on 'education' and utility he has forgotten that his overarching method of reading Homeric poetry demands that any value he extracts from it is not ethical, but historical or geographical in nature.

Hidden in Strabo's detour into the origins of myth, however, is another possible answer to the question of why Homer used myths, one which fits more smoothly into his broader image of the poet. At the end of 1.2.8, after Strabo has explained that myth and poetry were used by the ancients in the aforementioned moralizing way, he adds that "now, a long time later, the writing of history and philosophy have come to the fore", that is, they have replaced poetry. In the last sentence of the paragraph he adds that "the first historians and natural scientists were also myth-writers" (καὶ οἱ πρῶτοι δὲ ἱστορικοὶ καὶ φυσικοὶ μυθογράφοι: 1.2.8). Since the entire preceding discussion of myths' origins had only mentioned philosophers and poets, Strabo's addition of historians here is odd, but it allows him to twist a fundamentally moralizing theory of instruction ever so slightly to fit into his historically oriented scheme.

With these two statements, Strabo implies that history and philosophy developed as separate disciplines after the onset of poetry as part of a gradual evolutionary process; he had stated earlier in 1.2.6 that the first historians – Cadmus, Pherecydes, Hecataeus and their followers – still wrote prose in a poetic manner ("imitating" it [μιμούμενοι]), but that with each successive stage, the poetic aspects of prose dropped out until it reached its present state.[51] Since prose did not yet exist in Homer's day, historical or philosophical writing could only be composed in poetic form, employing myths to ensure that the information, which, as we recall, Strabo imagines Homer to be so eager to transmit to his readers, would reach the widest possible audience ("poetry is more useful for the masses"

---

[49] Strabo mentions the labors of Heracles and Theseus, Lamia, Gorgo, the giant Ephialtes, and Mormolyce.

[50] Biraschi (1984), 152; (1988), 135. Contrast, e.g., the moralizing allegorical readings of the *Odyssey* in Heraclitus' *Homeric Problems* (60–75), on which Buffière (1956). Strabo's strongly Stoic discussion of myth, allegory, and theology in 10.3.23 also has nothing to do with Homer.

[51] 1.2.6: εἶτα ἐκείνην μιμούμενοι λύσαντες τὸ μέτρον, τἆλλα δὲ φυλάξαντες τὰ ποιητικὰ συνέγραψαν οἱ περὶ Κάδμον καὶ Φερεκύδη καὶ Ἑκαταῖον· εἶτα οἱ ὕστερον ἀφαιροῦντες ἀεί τι τῶν τοιούτων εἰς τὸ νῦν εἶδος κατήγαγον ὡς ἂν ἀπὸ ὕψους τινός. On the theory of the development of prose from poetry, cf. Varro (F 319 Funaioli); Plut. *De Pyth. or.* 24; Max. Tyr. *Or.* 4. Further discussion in Floratos (1972), 61–6; Schröder (1990), 53.

[ἡ δὲ ποιητικὴ δημωφελεστέρα: 1.2.8]). If even the first prose historians, writing long after him, still employed myths, then Homer, as a poet, had no other choice but to use myths. The result is that Homer's lines require interpretation and careful study, not because he was being purposefully obscure, but because he was a poet, and poets were bound to use myths in their work: as Strabo says elsewhere, Homer's statements "demand critical inquiry (σκέψεως δεῖται κριτικῆς), since he speaks poetically (ποιητικῶς)" (8.1.1).

To summarize my construal of Strabo's position so far: as an intrepid historian, Homer was dedicated to passing on his historical and geographical knowledge, but since he was a poet, and prose did not exist, he went with prevailing custom and also included myths in his work. This is why his use of myths can be excused, whereas that of later historians is not. These myths are for entertaining the listener, while the rest, the 'history,' is meant to educate them by revealing accurate historical and geographical knowledge. The Stoicizing view of myths as themselves possessing an instructive, educative objective, while understandably attractive, is irreconcilable with this model, even though Strabo tries his best to incorporate it. It is important, however, to highlight the influence of this long-standing idea of Homer as moral and technical 'instructor' upon Strabo's thinking, even as it stands diametrically opposed to his belief in Homer as a historian. By explicitly arguing for Homer's paideutic intentions on an *ethical* plane in order to defend Homer's commitment to history, Strabo inadvertently demonstrates how fundamentally at odds these two ways of thinking about Homer were.

ΠΡΟΣΜΥΘΕΥΕΣΘΑΙ: ADDING MYTHS TO THE TRUTH

Strabo has thus established and defended Homeric poetry's combination of myths and history in a manner consistent with his portrait of Homer as the ideal geographer. His next task is to lay out a method of *reading* Homer that can differentiate between the mythic and historical content of his poetry. This is essential because Strabo believes that much of what is geographically accurate in Homer has been dismissed as myth by critics who fail to understand how to read the poet correctly. Previous critics had developed the 'historical exegesis' that Strabo employs, but he goes one step further, outlining a theory of how Homer composed his epics in order to disentangle the poet's blend of myth and history in his work. In essence he is trying to reconstruct and thus unravel Homer's process of fictionalizing (or, in Strabo's parlance, "adding myths" to) a basically historical narrative universe – that is, Homer's method of composing historical fiction. Strabo's discussion, rambling over many pages, is probably the most in-depth attempt to grapple with this problem that survives from antiquity. It ultimately, perhaps inevitably, fails to produce a coherent picture of Homer's poetic process, but this failure only puts Strabo's presumptions and prejudices about Homer in greater relief, and demonstrates both how vital Homer's historical reliability was to Strabo's larger vision of heroic geography and how difficult it was to reconcile the clashing ideals of Homer as poet and Homer as historian.

The first crucial passage is 1.2.9, when Strabo returns to Homer after his moralizing excursus on poetry, myth and early man:

Since Homer directed his myths toward education, he was particularly concerned with the truth, but he also "inserted" (*Il.* 18.541, etc.) falsehood, affirming the former and using the latter to win over and outwit the masses. "As when some man pours gold over silver" (*Od.* 6.232; 23.159),[52] Homer added μῦθος to true events, sweetening and adorning his style, but looking to the same end as the historian and the one depicting reality. So for instance he took the Trojan War, which had actually occured, and adorned it by making myths; he did the same to the wanderings of Odysseus. It is not Homeric to tell idle fantasies without connecting them to anything true.

Ἅτε δὴ πρὸς τὸ παιδευτικὸν εἶδος τοὺς μύθους ἀναφέρων ὁ ποιητὴς ἐφρόντισε πολὺ μέρος τἀληθοῦς, «ἐν δ' ἐτίθει» καὶ ψεῦδος, τὸ μὲν ἀποδεχόμενος, τῷ δὲ δημαγωγῶν καὶ στρατηγῶν τὰ πλήθη. «ὡς δ' ὅτε τις χρυσὸν περιχεύεται ἀργύρῳ ἀνήρ», οὕτως ἐκεῖνος ταῖς ἀληθέσι περιπετείαις προσετίθει μῦθον, ἡδύνων καὶ κοσμῶν τὴν φράσιν, πρὸς δὲ τὸ αὐτὸ τέλος τῷ ἱστορικῷ καὶ τῷ τὰ ὄντα λέγοντι βλέπων. οὕτω δὴ τόν τε Ἰλιακὸν πόλεμον γεγονότα παραλαβὼν ἐκόσμησε ταῖς μυθοποιίαις καὶ τὴν Ὀδυσσέως πλάνην ὡσαύτως· ἐκ μηδενὸς δὲ ἀληθοῦς ἀνάπτειν κενὴν τερατολογίαν οὐχ Ὁμηρικόν.

We can first note, in light of my previous discussion, how the definition of myth's purpose shifts in the course of his argument. At first, Strabo reasserts his thesis of 1.2.7–8 that Homer's myths are aimed at both instruction (τὸ παιδευτικὸν εἶδος) *and* entertainment, repeating the participle δημαγωγῶν from 1.2.7. But in the following sentences myth's moralizing objectives have been forgotten; the purpose of Homer's myths is to make

[52] The simile describes Athena's beautification of Odysseus in front of Nausicaa: "Then Athena...made him look taller and more muscled and made his hair tumble down his head like hyacinth flowers" (*Od.* 6.229–31). Is Strabo reading this line of Homer programmatically and metapoetically and suggesting that Odysseus' true appearance is being sweetened and adorned by the addition of myth? The passage is alluded to and criticized at Philostr. *Her.* 15.

his style more pleasurable, and the μυθοποιίαι with which Homer adorns the Trojan War and Odysseus' voyage are imagined as decorative rather than instructive. In contrast, notions of 'truth,' 'reality,' and the 'historical' are re-introduced, and the last sentence underscores the privileging of the historical, truthful core over the "idle fantasies" (κενὴν τερατολογίαν) of the mythic ornaments. Strabo's initial position that myths themselves serve an ethically pedagogical purpose has no sooner been established than it is pushed aside; now, as previously, myths contain no intrinsic educational value and are simply decorative sweeteners (entertainment).[53]

But Strabo's neat separation of Homeric poetry into mythic entertainment and factual instruction also undergoes a subtle yet vital modification in this passage. In the first sentence, Homer "inserts" (ἐν δ' ἐτίθει) something false into the truth; this conforms to what we have seen previously, where 'myths' are considered as distinct entities from 'history.' But in the next sentence, Homer "adds" (προσετίθει) myth to true events, as one "pours gold over" (περιχεύεται) silver. Strabo thus first characterizes myths as false bits of information placed *alongside* true narrative elements but by the end of the passage conceives of them as accretions *atop* a truthful core.

The latter model permits him to maintain something that the former does not – that myths are not completely fantastic and false but are linked to the truth. Homer, in Strabo's eyes, does not mythify *ex nihilo*;[54] his inventions are always elaborations of something real: "Homer took his starting points from history" (ἔλαβεν οὖν παρὰ τῆς ἱστορίας τὰς ἀρχάς: 1.2.9). For example, Strabo explains that certain characters encountered by Odysseus were historical figures: "they say (φασι) that Aeolus ruled the islands around Lipara, and that certain inhospitable Cyclopes and Laestrygonians ruled the area of Etna and Leontini ... and that Charybdis and Scyllaeum were in the hands of pirates" (1.2.9).[55] Homer knew this, and "convinced that [the voyage] took place [around Sicily and Italy], he took the material as true and he elaborated it poetically (λαβὼν ἀληθῆ ταύτην

---

[53] Meijering (1987), 60, in summarizing this passage, conflates the two ideas of myth here without being aware of the contradiction.

[54] On this conception of lying, see Veyne (1988).

[55] Radt's (2002) emendation of φασι for the manuscripts' φησι (retained by Aujac and Lasserre [1969] but not Meineke [1966]), makes better sense of the sentence in ascribing the historical information to the tradition rather than to Homer himself (as the subject of φησι), as Biraschi (1988) does. The distinction is important because Biraschi uses this passage as evidence of Strabo's occasional failure to differentiate between what Homer himself says and what Homer is interpreted as having said – a discrepancy that disappears with Radt's reading. One might add against Biraschi that Strabo does not refer to these 'historical' interpretations elsewhere. Jones' (1917) Loeb translation retains φησι but understands "history" as the subject, matching the sense of Radt's rendering.

τὴν ὑπόθεσιν ποιητικῶς διεσκεύασε)" (1.2.11).[56] True historical "material" (ὑπόθεσις), therefore, underlies the fantastic, mythic "elaboration" (διασκευή) which has been added onto it. Thus one should not dismiss these stories as merely 'myths'.

On the other hand, Strabo warns readers not to go too far in the other direction and accept "the elaboration as history" (τὴν διασκευὴν ὡς ἱστορίαν).[57] After all, he clarifies, he too believes that Homer "is clearly writing of fantastic things" (ἐκείνου . . . τερατογραφοῦντος φανερῶς) when he mentions "Ocean, Hades, the cattle of Helios, stays with goddesses, metamorphoses, the great size (μεγέθη) of the Cyclopes and Laestrygonians, the form (μορφήν) of Scylla, sailing distances, and many other such things" (1.2.11).[58] Note how careful Strabo is not to condemn figures like the Cyclopes or Scylla as wholly false; he specifies that it is the enormous 'size' of the Cyclopes and the Laestrygonians, and the monstrous 'form' of Scylla that is fantastic, not their existence *per se*.[59]

Strabo even coins a term – προσμυθεύω – to describe the Homeric process of "adding myth":[60]

Since they [the μυθοποιοί], and Homer in particular, do not completely mythologize (οὐ πάντα μυθεύουσιν), but more often *add myths* (προσμυθεύουσι), the one inquiring after what myths the ancients added (τί οἱ παλαιοὶ προσμυθεύουσιν) does not ask whether the *added myths* (προσμυθευόμενα) were or are true, but rather inquires after the truth about those places or characters to which the *myths are added* (οἷς προσμυθεύεται τόποις ἢ προσώποις, περὶ ἐκείνων ζητεῖ τἀληθές). (1.2.19)

Only the true, instructive core (τἀληθές) of the Homeric account – the ἱστορία, τὰ γενόμενα, or τὰ ὄντα – is reliable, and not the pleasant

---

[56] Strabo's terminology here – ὑπόθεσις for history or the facts (cf. 1.2.19: ὑποκειμένων) and διασκευή for myth or fantasy (although cf. 1.1.10: διασκευάζων) – adheres to literary-critical vocabulary familiar from tragic and Homeric scholia. See Meijering (1987), 33–4, on the terms διασκευή and διασκευάζω in tragic scholia; 99–103 on the term ὑπόθεσις in ancient literary criticism.

[57] This is the "worse" (χεῖρον: 1.2.11) interpretation of the opinion that Homer placed Odysseus' travels near Sicily and Italy.

[58] Cf. 1.2.30: "Myths are certainly not a sign of ignorance" (αἱ δὲ μυθοποιίαι οὐκ ἀγνοίας σημεῖον δήπου) and 1.2.35 where Strabo, discussing identifications of Homer's Erembians, criticizes previous scholars for a certain "confusion of mythic and historical form" (σύγχυσίν . . . τινα τοῦ μυθικοῦ καὶ «τοῦ» ἱστορικοῦ σχήματος).

[59] Schenkeveld (1976), 62, fails to notice this and assumes that Strabo is saying that these figures were entirely Homeric fictions.

[60] Cf. 1.2.40 where the variant προσμυθοποιέω is used. See also 5.1.9 on Diomedes in Italy, 5.4.5 on Avernus, 6.1.10 on Croton, 10.2.24 on Acarnania. The only other ancient authors to use προσμυθεύω are Polybius (see next note, although this is in a paraphrase by Strabo and may not be a *verbatim* quotation), and Eustathius in his commentary on the *Odyssey*, which is dependent on Strabo in many places. In fact, the first section of Eustathius' preface to this work is strikingly similar to Strabo 1.2. See Valk (1971–87), vol. I, introduction, for Eustathius' use of Strabo, and Pontani (2000) for a translation and discussion of the preface to the *Odyssey* commentary.

and entertaining "added myths" (τὰ προσμυθευόμενα) – the πλάσμα, ψεῦδος, μυθοποιία, or τερατολογία. The interpreter has to reverse the poetic process and pare away the mythic elaborations and additions in order to discover the factual basis from which the poet began the creative process.[61]

The test case for Strabo's reading method is the notoriously difficult one of identifying the true historical base of Odysseus' wanderings, long the ultimate example of fantastic, incredible fiction. If Strabo can demonstrate that a true core lies at the heart of these stories and articulate precisely how Homer transformed that core into the mythic version that survives, he will have established a principle that will presumably hold for other instances less removed from reality. For assistance Strabo turns to Polybius, a predecessor who, in contrast to Eratosthenes, knows how to read Odysseus' wanderings correctly (ὀρθῶς ὑπονοεῖ τὰ περὶ τῆς πλάνης: 1.2.15).[62] Polybius shares (and indeed may be the source of) many of Strabo's views – he adheres to the "adding myth" (προσμεμυθεῦσθαι: 1.2.15) theory, defends Homer by attributing discrepancies to "changes" (μεταβολάς), and asserts that "total invention is not plausible nor Homeric" (τὸ δὲ πάντα πλάττειν οὐ πιθανὸν οὐδ' Ὁμηρικόν: 1.2.17).[63]

Polybius, Palaephatus, and historical exegesis

While the presence of fantastic elements in Homer's depiction of Odysseus' voyage had signaled wholesale invention to Eratosthenes, Polybius seems to have set up a system of correspondences between Homeric 'myths' and geographical locations in the region of Sicily and Italy by carefully noting possible real-life phenomena that might have been the inspiration

---

[61] Later writers expound similar theories that often match Strabo's explicitness, if not his abundance of illustrations and elaborations. Cf. Lactantius, *Div. instit.* 1.11.23–5: "The poets, then have not fabricated the exploits . . . but they added a certain color of poetic fancy to the deeds . . . men do not know what the measure of poetic license is, to what extent it is permissible to proceed in fictionizing, since the poet's function consists in this, that those things which were actually performed he may transfer . . . into other appearances by means of figurative language. But to feign the whole account which you relate – that is to be a fool and a liar instead of a poet."

[62] Walbank (1979) assigns all of 1.2.15–18 to Polybius (= 34.2.4–4.8). I suspect that Strabo's theory of "adding myth to truth" owes a great deal to Polybius, who had also criticized Eratosthenes' approach toward Odysseus' wanderings. Witness the similarity of phrasing in Polybius' protest against Eratosthenes to that of the Strabo passage just quoted: Polybius had asserted that Aeolus should not "be understood in the form of a myth (ἐν μύθου σχήματι ἀκούεσθαι), nor the whole of Odysseus' wandering, but little things have been added as myth (μικρὰ μὲν προσμεμυθεῦσθαι), just as in the Trojan War; but the entire thing has been set around Sicily by the poet (τῷ ποιητῇ πεποιῆσθαι)" (1.2.15).

[63] Cf. the interesting theory attributed to Polybius on "poetic license" (ποιητικὴν ἐξουσίαν) at 1.2.17, which consists of διάθεσις, μῦθος, and ἱστορία. Walbank (1979), 584–5, on Polyb. 34.4.1; Meijering (1987), 61–98, is an in-depth examination of the relation of this theory to Aristarchus' ideas about poetic license, the famous Sch. bT ad *Il.* 22.342–51, and the progymnasmata.

for Homer.[64] For instance, he identified Aeolus as "the man who taught navigators how to steer a course in the regions of the Strait of Messina, whose waters are subject to a constant ebb and flow and are difficult to navigate on account of the reverse currents" and for that reason had "been called lord of the winds."[65] Later in 6.2.10, Strabo reveals that Polybius came to this conclusion based on his knowledge of the weather-predicting methods practiced by the inhabitants of the Lipari Islands; by observing the behavior of the volcanoes there, it was possible to foretell what wind would blow as much as three days in advance.[66] As a result, "that which seems to have been the most mythical (τὸ μυθωδέστατον) thing said by the poet was not spoken foolishly (οὐ μάτην . . . λεχθέν), but he *hinted* at the truth (<u>αἰνιξαμένου</u> τὴν ἀλήθειαν) when he called Aeolus 'lord of the winds' (ταμίαν τῶν ἀνέμων [cf. *Od.* 10.21])." Similarly, Polybius presents a long disquisition on the effects of the Strait's current on tunny-fish and the method of hunting swordfish developed by Sicilian fisherman there, eventually drawing a parallel between these fishing methods and Homer's description of how Scylla attacks Odysseus' ship and men (*Od.* 12.95–6). "From such facts as these one may conjecture (εἰκάζοι) that Odysseus' wanderings took place near Sicily, inasmuch as Homer attributed (προσῆψε) to Scylla that sort of fish-hunting that is most characteristic of Scyllaeum."[67]

Such interpretations, presupposing that myths have at their core a kernel of truth recoverable through judicious analysis or correspondence with real-life phenomena, have a long and enduring history.[68] As I mentioned in the last chapter, Hecataeus inaugurated this rationalizing approach to mythic tradition, and nearly every historian who dealt with the distant past had it stored away in his arsenal ready for deployment. Félix Buffière coined the term "historical exegesis" to describe this kind of myth interpretation,

---

[64] As I mentioned above (n. 5), Western Mediterranean locations had been identified at least as far back as the fifth century. For a full listing of ancient identifications, see Ramin (1979), 121–37. Phillips (1953) goes through the traditions chronologically and attempts to postulate why the wanderings were located in the region of Italy and Sicily by the ancients.

[65] Polybius 34 2.5–10 = Strabo 1.2.15. Polybius offers a long Euhemerist justification for this identification as well. See Walbank (1974), 8; (1979), 579–80, for a brief discussion.

[66] = Polyb. 34.11.12–20; Walbank (1974), 9 for a full treatment of the matter.

[67] Polybius 34.2.12–3.8 = Strabo 1.2.15–16. Again, see Walbank (1974) for a full treatment that is much more lucid than the notes in his commentary (Walbank [1979], 582–3). There is some controversy over whether Polybius means to compare Scylla with the fishermen (Walbank) or with the swordfish (e.g., Pédech [1964], 584; Romm [1992], 190), which he mentions as hunting tunny-fish in the beginning of the passage. Perhaps the answer is both; Polybius could have thought that Homer had drawn both observations together into a composite figure.

[68] Veyne (1988) is the most accessible treatment of this mode of thought; Wipprecht (1902–8) is still useful.

to distinguish it from the various allegorical and moralizing approaches he surveys.[69] Buffière's prime examples were Strabo, Euhemerus, and the rationalizing mythographic tradition founded by Palaephatus, the shadowy fourth-century BCE author of *On Unbelievable Things*.[70]

While allegorists might construe the Sirens or Circe as personifications of passions, the Palaephatean interpreter sees them as actual historical figures. They were courtesans, the former particularly skilled in singing, the latter so attractive that people attributed it to 'magic.'[71] The supernatural elements are thus eliminated, but an explanation of how the myth arose is also provided; usually it is a simple matter of an exaggeration or a literalization of misunderstood figurative language. So Scylla was the name of a pirate boat that terrorized the area, which Odysseus evaded; through retellings, the ship became a female monster (Palaeph. 20). Sometimes, the results are strikingly similar to those of historians; Strabo also mentions that the Scyllaeum region was full of pirates, and Polybius' Aeolus is paralleled in Palaephatus' characterization of him as a metereologist familiar with wind patterns of the area, which led to his being called the "lord of the winds" (Palaeph. 17).[72]

But if Strabo and Polybius also envision a basic historical truth at the bottom of Homer's myths, their readings diverge in significant ways from Palaephatus and his followers. First of all, the mythographers tend to avoid Homer; Scylla and Aeolus are the only two Homeric myths treated by Palaephatus, and a similar reticence marks the rest of the tradition. Moreover, in the examples we do have, Homer himself plays almost no role.[73] The 'mythification' of history is not due to a conscious decision by a particular poet, but to a series of involuntary misunderstandings and exaggerations on the part of those who heard and transmitted the originally true stories. Compare this to Polybius, who emphasizes that it was Homer who invented the fantastic parts of Aeolus' depiction, based upon empirical observation of specific practices deriving from particular geographical regions. In other words, both the Palaephatean and the Polybian interpreter see their task as uncovering the truth by paring away mythic accretions, but

[69] Buffière (1956), 228–48: "l'exégèse historique."

[70] On Palaephatus, see Buffière (1956), 231–42, and Stern (1996).

[71] Heraclitus *Incred.* 14, 16 (on this work, which combines Palaephatean rationalizing with allegorical interpretation, see Stern [2003], who argues against the identification of this Heraclitus with the author of the *Homeric Problems*).

[72] Strabo's rationalizing readings in 1.2.9 do not correspond with his later interpretations of Scylla and Charybdis. For Aeolus, see Buffière (1956), 235–7. In the scholia, Aeolus becomes an astronomer who predicts the winds based on the observation of the stars.

[73] I am not convinced by Santoni (2002), who posits a greater interest in Homer on the part of Palaephatus than witnessed in the surviving text.

these accretions are seen by the former as products of a collective, unintentional transmission process, and by the latter as the result of an intentional
act of fabrication by a specific person – Homer – who nevertheless hints at
the truth in his descriptions.[74] The creative agency of the poet, as well as
his knowledge and experience, is thus central to Polybius' conception of the
interplay between myth and history in Homer. Moreover as we saw with
Herodotus and Thucydides, the recovery of the 'truth' underlying Homer's
poetry is imagined as engaging in a process encouraged by Homer himself –
the clues by which Polybius reconstructs the historical core are reconceived
of as 'hints' that Homer has left behind, indicating to his followers that he
did indeed know the truth.

For Strabo, however, Polybius' recovery of historical truth from Homer,
while correct in its basic presumptions and method, requires further elaboration. Polybius holds that Homer knew the truth and used it as the basis
of his poetry, but it is not always clear how much of the truth Homer knew.
For instance, while Strabo describes Polybius' detailed musings on Sicilian
swordfish, he never explains how Polybius envisaged Homer transforming this practice, observed at the Scyllaeum, into the story of Odysseus
and Scylla we read in the *Odyssey*. Homer's "attributing" (προσῆψε)
Scyllaean fish-hunting to Scylla is sufficient reason for Polybius to conclude
that Odysseus' wanderings took place near Sicily "according to Homer"
(κατὰ τὸν Ὅμηρον: 1.2.16). Polybius presumably surmised that Homer
had derived the name Scylla from Scyllaeum and her behavior from the
activity of Scyllaean fishermen. Several other questions, however, remain
unaddressed. Did the historical Odysseus sail through the Strait? And if
so, whom or what did he actually encounter at this location? Fishermen?
Pirates? How much, if any, of this did Homer know? Left unclear here is
the extent of the underlying 'history' or 'truth'; the episode of Scylla can be
localized at the Strait (and hence retain a connection to 'reality') without
necessarily committing to the fact that Odysseus wandered there in real
life, or that Homer knew the truth about Odysseus' voyage.

While Strabo does not provide any enlightenment at this juncture, there
are hints elsewhere in the *Geography* that he was not completely satisfied
with the ambiguities in the Polybian position. A key passage is 3.2.12–13,
where Strabo argues for Homer's knowledge of Iberia, despite its not being
mentioned by name in his poetry.[75]

---

[74] Strabo elsewhere can rationalize in the Palaphatean manner; e.g., when he reports that "they
conjecture that the myth [about the cattle of Geryon] was invented from this [i.e., the unusually fat
cattle found on an island near Gades]" (τεκμαίρονται δ᾽ ἐκ τούτου πεπλάσθαι τὸν μῦθον: 3.5.4).
[75] Cf. 1.1.4.

The poet, a man of many voices and much learning (πολύφωνός τις ὢν καὶ πολυΐστωρ), gives us grounds (ἀφορμάς) that even these regions were not unheard of (ἀνήκοος) by him, if one wished to conjecture (συλλογίζεσθαι) correctly from both of the things that are said about them – the worse, and the better and more truthful (ἄμεινον καὶ ἀληθέστερον).

Both the better and worse arguments support the view that Homer knew Iberia; but the fact that Strabo considers one "better" than the other allows us to isolate the aspects of Homer's knowledge that Strabo particularly values. The 'worse' argument (3.2.12) hinges on the similarity in name between Homer's Tartarus and the Iberian city of Tartessus. The reasoning is as follows: Tartessus was the westernmost settlement known in Homer's day. The west, as the poet says, is where "the sun's bright light" falls into Ocean, "drawing black night over earth, the grain-giver" (*Il.* 8.485). The poet connects the west with the night and darkness, and it would be natural that he would situate the underworld in such a location. Thus:

Homer, having heard (ἀκούοντα) about Tartessus, called the farthermost of the nether regions 'Tartarus' with a slight change of name (παρονομάσαι), and also added a myth (προσθεῖναι δὲ καὶ μῦθον), preserving the poetic (τὸ ποιητικὸν σώζοντα).

A skilled reader, reversing this process of Homeric mythification, "might *get a hint* of a memory of the regions around Tartessus from the mythical invention of Tartarus (ἀπὸ τῆς τοῦ Ταρτάρου μυθοποιίας αἰνίττοιτό τις ἂν τὴν τῶν τόπων μνήμην τῶν περὶ Ταρτησσόν)."[76]

The better argument (3.2.13) does not address the Tartarus-Tartessus similarity and instead claims that Homer placed the Isle of the Blessed and the Elysian Field in the west because of Iberia's fabled prosperity.[77] In contrast to the previous argument, however, there is a stronger emphasis on the effort Homer expended in order to learn about Iberia's wealth; he "learned about it through inquiry" (πυνθανόμενος), and "knew by

---

[76] Strabo's supporting examples, such as the transferral of the Cimmerians from the Bosporus to Hades on the basis of the coldness and darkness of both regions, operate on similar principles of similitude; Homer makes analogies "always introducing myths from certain historical facts" (ἀεὶ τοὺς μύθους ἀπό τινων ἱστοριῶν ἐνάγων: 3.2.12). The transferral of the Cimmerians is mentioned also at 1.2.9, where the verb used is μετήγαγεν. An alternative explanation given there is that Homer placed the Cimmerians near 'Hades' because, like all Ionians, Homer had a hatred for the Cimmerians, living as he did within recent memory of the Cimmerian invasion (Homer's knowledge of this event is demonstrated at 1.2.9). On the treatment of the Homeric Cimmerians in antiquity, see Ramin (1979), 127–30.

[77] That he believes in the better argument is confirmed by his reference to it in 1.1.4, where Homer "has learned of" (πεπυσμένος) Iberia's wealth.

inquiry" (ἱστορηκώς) of many expeditions to Iberia.[78] But there is another, even more significant difference: a direct connection to Odysseus' actual wanderings.

> Odysseus' expedition to Iberia, having actually occurred, had also been learned of by Homer (ἱστορηθεῖσα ὑπ' αὐτοῦ), and furnished a pretext. So he transferred the *Odyssey*, just like the *Iliad*, from real events into poetry and the mythical invention familiar to poets (ἀπὸ τῶν συμβάντων μεταγαγεῖν εἰς ποίησιν καὶ τὴν συνήθη τοῖς ποιηταῖς μυθοποιίαν). (3.2.13)

Both interpretations are acceptable inasmuch as they attribute knowledge of Iberia to Homer and stipulate that his placing of the fictional Tartarus, the Isle of the Blessed, and the Elysian Field in the west are due to the specific associations they have with characteristics of Iberia. Moreover, both adhere to the model Strabo has set up, in which Homer takes actual historical or geographical knowledge that he has obtained and uses it as the basis of his *muthopoiia*.

What differs is the level of knowledge attributed to Homer in each case. In the 'worse' interpretation Homer has heard only about the existence of the Iberian city Tartessus. Tartarus is thus not a complete invention of Homer and has a basis in real-life Iberia, but it is only the *name* (and the association of the west with darkness and the underworld) that provides the link. In the 'better' theory, however, Homer learns not only of Iberian wealth, but also of the expeditions to Iberia; the emphasis is on historical inquiry (ἱστορηθεῖσα; ἱστορηκώς; πυνθανόμενος). In addition, Homer has learned about and hence knows that Odysseus had wandered to Iberia *in reality*, which was why he situated Odysseus' journey to the underworld in the west. In the worse argument, Homer neither inquires as to whether Odysseus actually traveled to Iberia, nor obtains any evidence to connect Tartessus to Odysseus' wanderings.

There is thus much more at stake for Strabo than simply proving Homer's 'knowledge' of certain geographical locations and phenomena. Strabo is not satisfied with showing that mythic Homeric locations, such as the underworld or Aeolus' island, were based by Homer on 'real' places like Iberia and the Lipari Islands, but insists further that Homer was fully aware that Odysseus had traveled to these 'real' locations. Homer's knowledge thus extends beyond mere geographical matters (the location

---

[78] For instance, the expeditions of Heracles and the Phoenicians to Iberia "suggested" (ὑπέγραφεν: 3.2.13) to Homer that the people there were rich and led an easy life. Strabo offers more supporting arguments: the description of the Elysian Field matches that of Iberia, the Phoenicians were Homer's informants (μηνυτάς: 3.2.14).

and identity of places) to encompass historical ones as well (what important things happened in those places). For Strabo, it is unimaginable that Homer, so dedicated to historical inquiry, could have composed his narrative in any other way.

Reading Homer's mythic elaboration

The Iberia example demonstrates Strabo's strong investment in establishing Homer's awareness of the historical 'truth,' but it is rather less forthcoming about how he envisions Homer's creative process, that is, the elaboration of this 'truth' into mythic, poetic form. Strabo mentions only that Homer transforms the initial data that he has learned – that Odysseus traveled through Iberia, that Iberia is a wealthy, prosperous place – into a story about Odysseus' visit to the underworld in the far west, without much more detail.[79] Strabo is often vague about the transformation process, content to establish the firm connection of Homeric poetry to reality and thus assert Homer's knowledge of history. Occasionally, however, Strabo tries to elucidate the workings of Homer's 'mythifying' when the circumstances require it. As with the Iberia example, these often involve defending Homer from critics who used Homer's failure to explicitly refer to a geographical feature – the mouths of the Nile, Iberia, the Scythians – as an indication that he was not aware of it.[80]

Take Strabo's discussion of Menelaus' wanderings (1.2.30). One of the well-known criticisms leveled at Homer was that he had described the island of Pharos as "in the open sea" (πελαγίαν; cf. *Od.* 4.354: ἐνὶ πόντῳ) and a day's sail from the Egyptian coast, when in fact it lies much closer.[81] Another was his failure to mention the rising and silting of the Nile – an omission that led some to claim that he was ignorant of this important characteristic of the river.[82] In defending Homer from the first charge, Strabo

---

[79] Homer's technique can be reconstructed from Strabo's various scattered interpretations of different elements of Odysseus' trip to the underworld throughout the first book, but the point is that Strabo here does not dwell on Homer's mythic elaboration.

[80] Strabo's extensive demonstration of Homer's familiarity with the inhabited world at 1.1.3–11 is directed against accusations of this sort.

[81] The Pharos problem is first brought up in 1.2.23; for Strabo's interpretation there see Aujac (1966), 29–31, and Schenkeveld (1976), 60–1.

[82] Strabo's first line of defense is to assert that Homer's "silence is no sign of ignorance" (τὸ μὴ λέγειν οὐ τοῦ μὴ εἰδέναι σημεῖόν ἐστιν: 1.2.30), and that the poet "*knows* and expressly says what needs to be said, but *keeps silent* about what is totally obvious" (εἰδὼς καὶ λέγων ῥητῶς τὰ ῥητὰ καὶ σιγῶν τὰ λίαν ἐκφανῆ: 1.2.29). Homer did not feel it necessary to mention that the Nile has several mouths, since other rivers share this feature and his audience would have been aware of it in any case (1.2.30).

concedes that it is unlikely that Homer simply received bad information – the distance of Pharos from the mainland "would not have been circulated abroad falsified to such an extent" (οὐκ ἂν εἴη διατεθρυλημένη ἐπὶ τοσοῦτον ἐψευσμένως).[83] Homer himself must have exaggerated intentionally. Why? Strabo ingeniously maintains that it was due to Homer's knowledge of the rising and silting of the Nile, which "it was likely that he learned as a matter of common knowledge" (κοινότερον πεπύσθαι εἰκὸς ἦν). In a clever interpretative turn, Homer's erroneous description of Pharos actually demonstrates his knowledge of a phenomenon he never mentions:

> From [his knowledge of the Nile's silting], the poet concluded that (ἐξ ὧν συνθεὶς ὁ ποιητής) at the time of Menelaus' visit (κατὰ τὴν Μενελάου παρουσίαν) the island was more distant from the mainland than it was in his own times (τότε), and added, on his own initiative, a distance many times as great for the sake of the mythic (προσέθηκε παρ᾽ ἑαυτοῦ πολλαπλάσιον διάστημα τοῦ μυθώδους χάριν).[84]

All this is only discernible by the careful reader who knows how to differentiate myth from truth; Homer, Strabo reiterates after further argumentation, "confesses by a *hint* (δι᾽ ἐμφάσεως) that he does not mean 'in the open sea' literally (truthfully: πρὸς ἀλήθειαν), but as hyperbole or mythic invention (πρὸς ὑπερβολὴν καὶ μυθοποιίαν)" (1.2.30). We are left with a remarkable picture of Homer's poetic technique – as a committed historian he learns of Menelaus' visit to Pharos, but realizes that (when the silting of the Nile is taken into account) the island would have been farther from the coast in the distant past of Menelaus' day. He thus extends the distance to be more accurate, but then grossly exaggerates that distance not only to make the story more poetic and mythic, but also to somehow 'hint' that he knows the truth about the Nile's silting.[85]

Another example of the convoluted and tortuous reasoning Strabo employs in order to maintain a truth at the base of Homer's myths occurs at 1.2.36, in a discussion of Charybdis:

> Concerning the activity of Ocean [Homer] speaks in the form of a myth (ἐν μύθου σχήματι). For the poet must also aim at this. Charybdis is mythified

---

[83] Strabo vacillates between attributing this information to "common report" (ἡ κοινὴ φήμη) or "an informant" (ὁ . . . ἱστορῶν αὐτῷ) (1.2.30).

[84] Cf. 1.2.11 on Homer's "distances" (διαστήματα) as clear examples of τερατογραφία and 1.2.18, where Strabo criticizes Polybius' overly credulous acceptance of Homer's distances.

[85] Strabo also attributes the exaggeration to Homer's characterization of Menelaus as a boaster. Such sensitivity to the speaker of the verses in question is on display in the Charybdis discussion below as well; in Homeric scholarship, such solutions were known as ἐκ τοῦ προσώπου: "from the character." See below, 102, n. 42.

(μεμύθευται) by him from the ebbs and flows [of the tides]; it is by no means an invention (πλάσμα) of Homer, but has been elaborated (διεσκευασμένη) from the things reported (ἀπὸ τῶν ἱστορουμένων) about the Sicilian strait.

The connection between Ocean's tides, the Strait, and Charybdis depends upon Homer's description of Charybdis at *Od.* 12.105: "for three times a day she sends [the black water] forth, and three times she swallows it back again."[86] Strabo had already declared earlier at 1.1.7 that this line proved that Homer was aware of the Ocean's tides, and at 1.2.16 that it accurately described the behavior of the currents in the Strait of Messina. Here he links everything together in accord with his basic method of reading: Homer's Charybdis is not completely fabricated by Homer but is a myth, which means that it is an elaboration of something real, in this case the tidal flow of Ocean, which creates the dangerous currents in the Strait of Messina. Homer has not only made a Polybian-type observation of local phenomena, but also cleverly inserted proof of the poet's knowledge of its cause, i.e., the tides. Charybdis does double duty, demonstrating Homer's knowledge of Ocean's behavior and hinting at Odysseus' historical encounter with the dangerous currents of the Strait.

Normally, Strabo would be content to conclude here, having successfully identified the historical core of a Homeric myth and demonstrated Homer's knowledge of what had really happened. Here, however, a problem arises, which forces Strabo to venture once again into the murky waters of the elaborated, invented narrative. The difficulty with Strabo's argument is that Homer says that Charybdis spews out and swallows up water "three times" a day instead of "twice," which would be the more accurate way to refer to the ebb and flow of tides. Elsewhere Strabo cites Polybius' suggestion that scribal error was to blame (γραφικὸν . . . ἁμάρτημα: 1.2.16),[87] but here he tries another solution. He points out (1.2.36) that the speaker of the line in question is Circe, and attributes the use of "three times" instead of "two" to her desire to exaggerate the dangers (τραγῳδίας χάριν καὶ φόβου) of the journey. In support of this, Strabo observes that her subsequent claim that Charybdis was inescapable was also an exaggeration, judging from the fact that Odysseus *did* escape it.[88] In fact, Homer was fully aware of this, since he "is hinting" (ὑπαινίττεται) at the truth in the details of Odysseus'

---

[86] On the connection of tides to the theory of circumambient Ocean, see 1.1.7. For discussion, see Kidd (1990), 765–7 on Posidon. F 216; Buffière (1956), 223–5 is little more than a paraphrase of Strabo.

[87] Cf. 1.1.7: "a historical error or textual corruption" (τῆς ἱστορίας παραπεσόντος ἢ τῆς γραφῆς διημαρτημένης); on Polybius' view, see Walbank (1979), 584 = Polyb. 34.3.10–11.

[88] Romm (1992), 191.

escape from Charybdis, which "better suits (ἐφαρμόττοι) the assumption
that the refluent tide came in twice, rather than three times" (1.2.36).[89]

Strabo's reconstruction of Homer's activity is even more strained here
than in the Pharos discussion. Through Charybdis, Homer hints at his
knowledge that Odysseus traveled through the Strait of Messina *and* that
the tides are the cause of the dangerous waters there, but it turns out that it
is not Homer's explicit description of Charybdis that constitutes the hint
(since it is an inaccurate exaggeration of Circe), but rather the behavior of
Charybdis when Odysseus encounters it. Moreover, this behavior has to be
inferred by a very close reading of the text and an estimation of the time
that Odysseus spent hanging on the fig tree waiting for Charybdis to erupt
again. Strabo has ventured a long way from the traditional identification
of Charybdis with the Strait of Messina.

The problem with Strabo's explanation stems from his desire not just
to find correlations with 'reality' in Homeric poetry, but to maintain that
Homer intentionally established these correlations and tried to indicate his
knowledge to his readers. In this sense, his twisted interpretative logic recalls
the equally tendentious and implausible hypotheses found in Heraclitus'
Homeric Allegories or Ps.-Plutarch's *On Homer*, in which Homer is imagined
to enigmatically encrypt all sorts of information in poetic form. But Strabo's
view of Homer is actually more anomalous. Allegorists like Maximus of
Tyre or Heraclitus imagine Homer (if they imagine him at all) as some
sort of semi-divine, mystical proto-philosopher, which is at least consistent
with the enigmatic and convoluted manner in which they suppose him
to have hidden the truth in his poetry. Strabo's Homer uses a similarly
obfuscatory style of conveying and signaling the truth, but this method is
significantly at odds with his characterization as a historian dedicated to the
truth, engaged in the mundane activity of hearing reports and obtaining
his information by inquiry.

Indeed, for all Strabo's complex, ingenious theorizing, his Homer suffers
from the same kind of bi-polar disorder that was detected in the Homers of
Herodotus and Thucydides, an inability to reconcile the enigmatic, inventive poetic side of their personality with the side committed to learning and
communicating the historical truth. Strabo's Homer is basically built on the
same model as those I examined in the last chapter: he knows the truth,

---

[89] The argument depends on a close reading of *Od.* 12.433–7, where Odysseus describes how long he
clung to the tree waiting for pieces of his wrecked raft to be expelled from Charybdis; Strabo argues,
rather weakly, that the description suggests a twice-daily event. In addition, Odysseus' escape would
not seem "plausible" (οὐ πιθανήν) if Charybdis sucked water in three times a day, since Odysseus
would not have been able to drift far enough away before being drawn back toward the monster.

yet deviates from it for poetic reasons. Like Herodotus' Homer, he has 'learned' the truth and 'hints' at that truth in his poetry; like Thucydides, he exaggerates, yet is somehow still dedicated to giving future historians material to reconstruct the 'truth.' Strabo has taken seriously the basic idea of Homer as a historian that underlies the interpretative stances of his predecessors and worked through its implications, trying his best to concoct a vision of Homer that accounted for his knowledge of the truth as well as his choice to convey that truth in poetic form. The concept of the 'hint' that we saw all three critics employ in the last chapter to suture the gap between Homer's knowledge of the truth and his poetic imperative not to tell it is exploited again by Strabo, but is now stretched beyond its capacity. In fact by extrapolating a more general portrait of the poet from that suggested in his predecessors' restricted inquiries into Homer's historical accuracy, Strabo ends up unwittingly exposing the shaky foundations and irreconcilable forces that lie at the core of such assertions.

CONCLUSION: HOMER, GREEK TRADITION, AND ROME

Strabo's investment in the idea of Homer as a historian may have left him mired in interpretative difficulties, but his arguments demonstrate how thinking about Homer's relation to 'reality' could provide an impetus for imagining Homer as a person, as well as his activities, his motivations, and his objectives. And despite their incoherence, the results of Strabo's efforts retain a certain fascination: his vivid picture of an intrepid Homer, his vehement insistence on Homer's dedication to historical inquiry, his intricate demonstrations of Homer's knowledge, and finally the inordinate reverence he shows both for Homer and for heroic geography. I want to conclude this chapter with some observations on the motivating forces behind Strabo's vigorous defense of Homer as a geographer and the extensive, almost obsessive, Homeric discussions that follow later in his work.

Strabo explicitly states his reasons for spending so much time on Homer in two well-known passages from Book 8:

[I am] comparing current circumstances with the things mentioned by Homer (τά τε νῦν καὶ τὰ ὑφ' Ὁμήρου λεγόμενα); for it is necessary to do so because of the poet's *reputation and our having grown up with him* (διὰ τὴν τοῦ ποιητοῦ δόξαν καὶ συντροφίαν πρὸς ἡμᾶς), since each of us believes that a given statement is not correct until nothing conflicts with his accounts of these things, *so greatly are they trusted* (τοῖς οὕτω σφόδρα πιστευθεῖσι λόγοις). (8.3.3)

Perhaps I would not be examining ancient matters (τὰ παλαιά) at such length ... if there were not *a certain fame transmitted about them from the times of our childhood* (εἰ μή τις ἦν ἐκ παίδων ἡμῖν παραδεδομένη φήμη) ... It is the *most distinguished, the oldest, and the most experienced* men who are generally trusted (πιστεύονται ... οἱ ἐνδοξότατοί τε καὶ πρεσβύτατοι καὶ κατ᾽ ἐμπειρίαν πρῶτοι); and since it is Homer who has outstripped everyone in these qualities, it is necessary that I look closely at the things he has said and reconcile them with current circumstances ... (ἀνάγκη συνεπισκοπεῖν καὶ τὰ ὑπ᾽ ἐκείνου λεχθέντα καὶ συγκρούειν πρὸς τὰ νῦν). (8.3.23)

The reverential tone of these passages is reminiscent of the paeans to Homer I quoted in Chapter 1: in the first, to explain why Homer figures so large in his text, Strabo appeals to the 'trust' or 'faith' in Homer's words that stem from his fame, or *doxa*, and his central role in the early stages of education. In the second, that 'trust' is again due to Homer's fame, but also to his antiquity and his experience, or skill. Given this framework, it is easy to see why Dirk Schenkeveld suggested over thirty years ago that "by the dominant position of Homer's poetry in Greek life Strabo was conditioned to regard Homer as knowledgeable and trustworthy in matters of geography also."[90] Later scholars have noted individual factors contributing to this 'conditioning': Strabo's Stoic leanings, the influence of his teacher Aristodemus of Nysa (a noted Homeric critic), and the Homeric focus of previous geographical treatises.[91] But while Homer's prominent status in early Imperial intellectual life undoubtedly made a deep impression on Strabo, there is surely more to his devotion than such explanations can account for.

After all, one ought to keep in mind the context for Strabo's comments in the quoted passages; he is justifying his lengthy attempts to correlate places mentioned in Homer with modern topography, not just because the sites are Homeric, but because they are (to his mind) the *actual* locations of heroic historical activity. Strabo's privileging of Homer is thus closely linked to the importance of Hellenic tradition and the past in Strabo's conception of geography.[92] In fact, in the second passage quoted above (8.3.23), he speaks of "ancient matters" (τὰ παλαιά) in the same terms as he does of Homer, explaining that he spends so much time discussing them because of the "fame" (φήμη) that they have enjoyed since "our childhood" (ἐκ παίδων ἡμῖν; cf. 8.3.3 on Homer: δόξαν καὶ συντροφίαν πρὸς ἡμᾶς).

---

[90] Schenkeveld (1976), 63–4. [91] Dueck (2000), 38–40; Prontera (1993), 395.
[92] van Paassen (1957), 1–32; Biraschi (1988); Clarke (1999), 245–93 (esp. 248–51). Cf. 6.1.2: "The man who busies himself with the description of the earth must speak, not only of the facts of the present, but also sometimes of the facts of the past, especially when they are notable."

In Strabo's mind, Homer and the heroic age are inextricably linked; Homeric poetry, as a part of Greek tradition, or "ancient memory" (παλαιὰ μνήμη: 1.1.16), belongs as much to a given heroic locale as any topographical feature or material artefact, more so in fact, if like the Troad, it is "left in ruins and desolation" (13.1.1). Indeed, Strabo conceives of Homer's account as possessing a certain materiality: he claims that legendary tales become "a kind of natural attribute" (τρόπον τινὰ συμφυῆ) of certain places, one that bestows upon them "a certain distinction and fame" (ἐπιφάνειαν . . . τινὰ καὶ δόξαν: 2.5.17). Heroic legends, Strabo insists at 1.2.14, are not "the inventions (πλάσματα) of poets or historians but *traces* (ἴχνη) of events that have happened and people who have existed" (γεγενημένων . . . καὶ προσώπων καὶ πράξεων: 1.2.14).[93] Strabo's veneration of the world of the distant Greek past goes hand in hand with his devotion to Homer; for Strabo, separating the two is unthinkable, and to question one is to question the other as well.

Strabo's insistent apologetic remarks and lengthy discussions of the Homeric world are also closely connected to his attempts to make sense of the relatively recent extension of Roman dominion over the old Hellenistic world, and to construct a place for Greeks like himself, and Greek culture more generally, within it. On the one hand, as has often been noted, Strabo is exceptionally pro-Roman throughout the *Geography*.[94] But while he acknowledges and even praises Roman ascendancy in the political and military sphere, he also makes a significant effort to establish Greek primacy over Rome in other contexts. To do so, Strabo articulates a conception of Greekness that relies on the familiar claim of eminence in the *cultural* sphere (comprising art, literature, and scholarship), but also on the *chronological* precedence of Greek culture (based on its antiquity and distinguished history) in comparison to Rome.[95]

Is it a surprise, then, that Strabo's vision of Homer continually emphasizes the poet's possession of these pre-eminently 'Greek' values – *paideia* and antiquity? Because he invests Homer with the values he considers essential to being Greek, Strabo's defense of Homer is, in a sense, a defense of Hellenism. Within such a conception, Homer was not simply the oldest and therefore most trusted poet, but a crucial witness for the entire world of the heroic age, upon which Greek claims to superiority (at least in Strabo's

---

[93] Cf. 2.5.17: even when places no longer exist, people still desire to experience "the *traces* (ἴχνη) of such celebrated deeds."

[94] E.g., Lasserre (1982).

[95] Dueck (2000), 75–84. Strabo recognizes that Roman rule has enabled Greek culture to flourish (2.5.26).

mind) rested. It is therefore essential for Strabo that Homer be historically and geographically accurate, but also that he exemplify the same values that Strabo himself esteems as a scholar and educated member of the elite; Homer was not only correct, but *wanted* to be correct, and expended considerable effort and energy in learning the truth and conveying it to his readers.

By endowing Homer with the historiographical qualities he holds most dear, and figuring them as particularly Greek values, Strabo fashions a Homer in his own image, as he tries to reinstill a sense of the relevance and importance of the traditions of Greek culture and the Greek past for the nascent Roman Empire. As Anna Maria Biraschi has observed, "one can almost see a fear that limiting oneself to only 'physical' geography and describing only the present state of things would risk losing the historical connotations that through tradition have come to form an integral part of the very individuality of place; a fear that the new political order could forget preceding assets, different customs and institutions from which there was always something to receive and learn."[96] In hindsight, Strabo's worries were largely unfounded; by the second century CE, local historiography and antiquarianism would be blossoming, and the ancient Greek sites and Greek culture as a whole would undergo a significant revival, centered on a renewed appreciation of ancient tradition and the distant past. But at the time Strabo was writing his *Geography*, late in life, near the end of Augustus' reign or the beginning of Tiberius', he could not have anticipated the Second Sophistic renaissance. Strabo's emphasis on *paideia* and tradition as constituent elements of Greek identity, coupled with his desire to keep such 'ancient memory' alive for posterity, may not completely explain his overwhelming devotion to Homer, but it strongly suggests that the seemingly arcane, philological and antiquarian discussions of the poet that he indulges in ultimately derive from very real concerns about the place of being Greek in a changing world.[97]

---

[96] Biraschi (1988), 133 (my translation of the Italian).

[97] Gabba (1982), esp. 59–61, sees Strabo's return to Homer as part of a so-called 'classicistic revival' at Rome during the Augustan period, spearheaded by Dionysius of Halicarnassus. While there may be some similarities in the two authors' motivations and their privileging of ancient literature, there are starker differences: Dionysius concentrates on rhetorical style and Classical authors, while Strabo's interests are historico-geographical and focus primarily on Homer. Unlike Dionysius, Strabo is quite positive toward Hellenistic predecessors and colleagues, suggesting that his praise of Homer is not dependent on a denigration of 'recent' historians.

CHAPTER 4

Homer the liar

Dio Chrysostom's *Trojan Oration*

Only two generations or so separate Strabo from Dio of Prusa, also known as Chrysostom ('Golden-Mouth'), the itinerant orator and moralist of the late first century CE. It is therefore striking to encounter Dio demolishing Homer's authority and historical credentials as vigorously as Strabo had tried to establish them. The work in question is one of Dio's longest and most celebrated speeches, the *Trojan Oration* (Τρωϊκός, *Or.* 11): an anti-Homeric *tour de force* addressed to the citizens of the Roman Ilium of his own day (ἄνδρες Ἰλιεῖς: 4) that sets the record straight about the Trojan War. Among other things, Dio insists, on the alleged testimony of an Egyptian priest, that Helen was rightfully married to Paris, Hector killed Achilles, and Troy actually won the war. But the speech is not only an alternate history obtained from a more reliable source. Dio paradoxically proves these theses through a close analysis of the Homeric poems themselves, in a forceful attack on the improbabilities and contradictions of the *Iliad* and (to a lesser extent) the *Odyssey*. As he says, his objective is to expose Homer's lies (ψευδῆ), "refuting him from no other place than his own poetry" (οὐκ ἄλλοθέν ποθεν, ἀλλ᾽ ἐξ αὐτῆς τῆς ποιήσεως ἐλέγχων: 11) – a joking allusion to the interpretative maxim attributed to Aristarchus, 'to elucidate Homer from Homer' (Ὅμηρον ἐξ Ὁμήρου σαφηνίζειν).[1] As one might imagine, the implausibility and audacity of the premise, combined with the virtuosity with which Dio sees it through, helped make the *Trojan Oration* his most notorious work in antiquity, the Byzantine period, and early modern Europe.[2]

Although it bears some resemblance to famous Classical rhetorical show-pieces like Gorgias' and Isocrates' *Helen*, which similarly apply sophistic

---

[1] Montgomery (1901), 10. The phrase appears in Porph. ad *Il.* 297, 16 Schrader; cf. Sch. D ad *Il.* 5.385 and Eust. *Il.* 561, 28–30 (2.101.13–15) van der Valk). The authenticity and precise meaning of this maxim has been frequently discussed: see Pfeiffer (1968), 225–7; Schäublin (1977); and Porter (1992), 70–85.

[2] On the *Trojan's Nachleben*, see Desideri (1978), 502–3; Brancacci (1985), 275–88; and Swain (2000b), 18–20.

argumentation to the legendary heroic tradition, the *Trojan* differs from those works in its focus on Homer (conspicuously ignored by Gorgias and mentioned only once by Isocrates) and its engagement with the concerns and interpretative techniques of ancient Homeric scholarship.[3] Moreover, Dio's interest in Homer is chiefly historiographical in nature, and his intention to refute the poet's version and tell the true story of the Trojan War situates the *Trojan* squarely in the critical debate over Homer's historical accuracy that I have been tracing in this book.

But Dio's approach to the issue marks a significant break from that of the authors we have examined so far. Herodotus, Thucydides, and Strabo, whether defending or attacking Homer's account, undertake their analyses in earnest, as befits the genres in which they operate – history and geography. Some of their presumptions and arguments could be considered tendentious and problematic, but there is little doubt that they take the problem seriously. With Dio, however, his surprising claims of Trojan moral superiority and ultimate victory so completely up-end traditional views, and his claims of demonstrating their truth through Homer's poetry itself seem so outrageous, that it is hard not to question his sincerity. Did he really believe that Troy won the Trojan War? Or that Homer was a liar? And if not, then what was his purpose in arguing such a counter-intuitive case? There are indeed plenty of signs that Dio's denunciation of Homer is not entirely sincere. For example, nowhere else in his corpus, which is filled with references to Homer, does he refer to the so-called 'true' story of the Trojan War advocated here, nor does he ever accuse Homer of having misrepresented historical events.[4] In fact, Dio is generally an admirer of Homer, and frequently praises the ethical content of his poetry.[5] Dio's claim that he will use Homer's own words to prove that he was lying is reminiscent of the preposterous premises of the rhetorical school exercises and declamations that were vehicles for sophistic virtuosity. The story of his meeting with an anonymous Egyptian priest in an otherwise unknown Egyptian town, who happens to have access to records dating

---

[3] For Dio's knowledge of Homeric scholarship, see Montgomery (1901); Valgimigli (1912); Seeck (1990); and Vagnone (2003a).

[4] On Dio's use of Homer, see above all Valgimigli (1912), 1–45; Kindstrand (1973), 13–44 and 113–62; Desideri (1978), ch. vii; more summarily, Montgomery (1901); Drules (1998). Kindstrand (1973), 19–26, conveniently lists the majority of Dio's Homeric quotations, paraphrases and references; cf. Gangloff (2006b).

[5] Kindstrand (1973), 33 and 138–9, on the rarity of criticism directed against Homer, and Blomqvist (1989), 44 n. 29, on instances of praise for the poet (*Or.* 53 is the best-known example). On Dio's moralizing Homeric criticism: Affholder (1966–7); Kindstrand (1973), 125–6; Desideri (1978), 480–5; Blomqvist (1989), 43–6; Drules (1998), 74–5; Kim (2008).

back to Menelaus' visit, virtually advertises its artificiality, alluding both to Herodotus' encounter some five hundred years earlier and to the fictional discoveries of 'ancient' sources that littered the Hellenistic and Imperial literary landscape.

Viewed from this perspective, the *Trojan* can be seen as Dio's own sophistic tongue-in-cheek response to the problem of Homer's historical accuracy that earlier writers like Strabo had so earnestly tried, yet failed, to resolve. In this chapter, I show how Dio takes several of the methodological presumptions of his predecessors – Homer's knowledge of the historical truth, the presence of hints hidden in his poetry, his inquiring, honest character, his factually oriented intentions, etc. – and transforms them in order to fashion his own warped vision of the poet. In fact, although I doubt that Dio was familiar with the *Geography* or its author, he was certainly acquainted with the idea of Homer sketched out there, as a diligent, knowledgeable, and truthful historian, and it is instructive to read the *Trojan Oration* with Strabo's Homer hovering in the background. Like Strabo, Dio provides his own construction of Homer, and uses that image to 'read' Homer and make sense of his story; like him, too, there is a way in which Dio's Homer is created in his own image, as an itinerant orator. But Dio is also representative of the way that Second Sophistic authors, rather than attempt yet again to 'solve' the Homeric reliability dilemma, choose instead to comically refashion it in order to address a set of broader issues only touched upon in the earlier works. Dio's 'true' story of the Trojan War and his new portrait of Homer, I suggest, caricatures the idea of Homer as a historian advocated by critics like Strabo and raises trenchant questions about the impulses that motivate it – the exaltation of Homer and the heroic past, the significance of the Trojan War in defining Greekness, and the uncritical acceptance of canonical authority – a task that is helped, rather than hindered by the speech's exaggerated claims and ironic tone.

In what follows, I first address the way Dio frames his critique of Homer with an interrogation of the belief in the Greek heroic tradition and the authority granted to Homer, before turning to the detailed and innovative picture he paints of Homer as a liar and the bravura presentation of the 'true' story he sets forth in counterpoint to that of Homer. The conclusion of the chapter discusses how the end of the speech returns to the themes introduced at the beginning in a surprising defense of Homer that offers further reflections on the relationship between historical 'truth,' literary authority, and the reverence for the past in the Roman Empire.

BELIEF, LITERARY AUTHORITY, AND GREEK TRADITION

As adumbrated above, the question of belief is one raised by the *Trojan Oration* as a whole: should we believe it? Is Dio serious? A marker of the difficulty in reaching a firm answer is the extent to which 'belief' in the sincerity of Dio's *Trojan Oration* has fluctuated since its own day. From late antiquity to the Renaissance, it appears that the *Trojan* was taken quite seriously as an expression of Dio's genuine opinion of Homer and as compelling evidence of the untrustworthiness of the Homeric account.[6] But by the late nineteenth and early twentieth century, as readers began identifying the speech's ironies and insincerities (as listed above), a consensus had arisen that the *Trojan* was merely a *jeu d'esprit*, typical of the Second Sophistic, meant as an entertainment or rhetorical exercise with no serious intent whatsoever, and to be attributed to the juvenilia of a Dio still in his 'sophistic' phase.[7] Over the last forty years or so, the pendulum has swung again, with renewed scholarly efforts to locate a serious purpose in the speech; the *Trojan* has been judged an earnest intervention into contemporary literary critical debates, a Cynic polemic against ignorance and popular opinion, or a devastating parody of the excesses of Homeric criticism.[8]

The most controversial and influential theory, however, proposes that the speech's purpose is primarily political, as pro-Roman propaganda. Although the idea had been floated before, J. F. Kindstrand was the first to argue for it at length. He pointed to, among other things, Dio's repeated praise of the Trojans (read: Romans), his highlighting of Aeneas, a hero virtually ignored by other Greek authors (who "founded the greatest city of all" [πόλιν ᾤκισε τὴν μεγίστην πασῶν: 138]), and Dio's assertion, near the end of the oration, that the truth can now be told because "the situation has changed... for Greece is subject to others (ὑφ᾽ ἑτέροις) and so is Asia" (150).[9] The most forceful proponent of this position has been Paolo Desideri, who has made the *Trojan* the cornerstone of his vision of Dio's project and career as a large-scale attempt to intervene in the

---

[6] Blomqvist (1989), 116–17; Swain (2000b), 18–19.

[7] So von Arnim (1898), 169; Lemarchand (1926), 54–6; Jones (1978), 17: "his most sophistic [oration]." Cf. Anderson (1993), 175: "His contradictions of the poet [Homer] require little comment." On the theory of Dio's 'conversion' from sophist to philosopher following his exile (a notion promulgated by Dio himself), see Moles (1978) and the more nuanced view of Whitmarsh (2001), 158–60.

[8] Kindstrand (1973), 156; Szarmach (1978), 200–1; Seeck (1990). See Saïd (2000), 177–80, for an overview of scholarship on the *Trojan*.

[9] Kindstrand (1973), 160–1; as he mentions, previous scholars had noted, but not developed, the possibility that the speech contained pro-Roman sentiments.

social fabric of Greek political life under the Roman Empire.[10] The *Trojan*, on his view, communicates a fundamental message of harmony between Greek and Roman, a coming to terms with the changed world of the Roman peace. The tradition of East–West antagonism represented by the Trojan War, and by extension Homer, in Desideri's reading, is the major obstacle to such a message, and must thus be painstakingly and thoroughly overturned, which accounts for the lengthy detailed refutation undertaken by Dio.

On the face of it, Desideri's reading is plausible, given Dio's penchant for employing paradoxical theses and sophisticated interpretations of literary and mythical stories in service of a broader "message," and in some quarters, notably Italian scholarship, the *Trojan's* pro-Roman stance is virtually taken for granted.[11] But as critics have noted, Desideri and other advocates of the pro-Roman view place great weight on what after all is a relatively small stretch of text – a few paragraphs dealing with the aftermath of the war that twice allude to present political conditions in Dio's day without actually mentioning the words Rome or Romans.[12] A more significant objection, however, is that such a reading requires taking Dio's Homeric revision at face value, and ignores the obvious signals that Dio was not committed to his new version of the truth, as well as the undercurrents of irony running through the entire *Trojan Oration*. One might ask why in such a context Dio's references to Rome should be read as a sudden intrusion of sincerity, as a heartfelt appeal to end the outdated antagonisms and ideologies of the past.[13]

---

[10] Desideri (1978), 431–4, 496–503; (1991), 3886–7.

[11] Others sympathetic to Desideri, if not in complete agreement: Fornaro (2000); Torraca (2001), 245–52; Vagnone (2003a), 12–13; 19–20; (2007). Cf. Blomqvist (1989), esp. 166–7.

[12] Swain (1996), 210–11; Said (2000), 178–9. There is a parallel to Isocrates' *Helen*, which concludes with a brief reference to the Panhellenic benefits of the Trojan War; naturally, this too has led some scholars (e.g., Kennedy [1958]) to propose a 'political' reading of Isocrates' text.

[13] The question of the *Trojan's* purpose and seriousness is intertwined with that of its date, since as Jones (1978), 17, has noted, the tone of the speech "is the only indication of date." Although my analysis does not depend on a particular date, I offer here a brief summary of the possibilities. Those who dismiss the *Trojan* as mere sophistic cleverness, a rhetorical exercise, or juvenilia, assign it to Dio's pre-exilic, 'sophistic' phase (von Arnim [1898], 169; Lemarchand [1926], 54–6; Jones [1978], 17). Others place it late in his career, post-exile, for a variety of reasons: (1) the maturity and sophistication of the arguments; (2) its Cynic elements and affinities to the Diogenes speeches (Kindstrand (1973), 161); (3) its political pro-Roman stance (Kindstrand [1973], 161; Desideri [1978], who sees the *Trojan* as Trajanic in order to fit his model of Dio's development). Torraca (2001), 249, follows Desideri's characterization of the speech, but argues for an early Vespasianic date. Blomqvist (1989), 156–65, has perhaps the best arguments for an early dating, based on the unconscious moral code that underlies the piece, one that is starkly different to that of his later works (note, too, her trenchant criticism of Kindstrand's arguments for a late date, 164 n. 127, and her full bibliography on the issue, 117–20).

Nevertheless dismissing the work as mere entertainment is not a satisfactory option either; the *Trojan* is quite entertaining, but it is also a complex and virtuosic display of Dio's mastery of arguments and terminology from a wide array of discourses, such as historiography, rhetorical theory, Homeric criticism, mythography, and Platonic thought.[14] If Dio is not 'serious' in a traditional sense, he combines this erudition with humor and irony in an attempt to provoke audiences and readers, and challenge their assumptions. In the *Trojan* the target is less the individual implausibilities of Homeric poetry than the authority of Homer himself, as a repository of Hellenic tradition, as well as the unthinking reverence toward the poet shared by his audience (and indeed by Dio as well, at least in the rest of his corpus). In this sense the allusions to Rome and the present, as we shall see, are important but cannot be read as the 'point' of the entire speech, nor as simply an expression of pro-Roman ideology. Rather, they figure in the more general question that informs the whole work – that concerning the place of the heroic and Homeric past in the self-definition of Greeks living in the Roman Empire.[15]

HOMER, *DOXA*, AND BEING GREEK

The question confronting readers of the *Trojan* – whether to believe Dio or not – is reflected within the text in the frequent discussions of credibility, authority, and belief that Dio brings to bear on his assessment of Homer's historical honesty. While the greater part of the speech is dedicated to elucidating Homer's lies and revealing the real story, at pivotal moments in the text (the prologue [1–14], the peroration [145–54], and a transitional interlude [37–42]) Dio shifts the focus from Homer's production of falsehood to its *reception* and the culpability of audiences in fostering and facilitating his lies. Dio thus explicitly frames his investigation into Homer's accuracy in terms of belief and authority – whom one should believe, what is 'credible,' why people believe, etc.

The prologue, for example, sets up an opposition between the unquestioning belief in and reception of Homer's false account, and the hostile

---

[14] Kindstrand (1973), 141–62, is still the best study, supplemented by Szarmach (1978); Seeck (1990); Fuchs (1996); Saïd (2000), 176–86; Gangloff (2006a), 118–36, 291–3, 305–9; and especially Hunter (2009), whose interests most closely overlap with mine. Other recent work includes Blomqvist (1989), 115–68; Mestre (1990); Fornaro (2000) and (2002); the commentary of Vagnone (2003a); and Billault (2006). The source question lives on in some spheres: Ritoók (1995) revives the idea of Peripatetic influence and Jouan (2002) proposes Dio's dependence on Aeschylus' *Philoctetes*. I have not been able to consult Jouan (1966).

[15] See Gangloff (2006a), 282–309.

incredulity Dio will no doubt encounter despite presenting the 'truth.' Here the spotlight falls upon popular opinion, or δόξα, Dio's favorite object of derision (τὴν δόξαν: 3); as often in Dio it signifies *false* opinion or belief. The opening lines explain how and why *doxa* establishes itself as truth, setting up an opposition between the difficulty of teaching (διδάσκειν) people the bitter truth (τὸ . . . ἀληθὲς πικρόν) and the ease of deceiving (ἐξαπατᾶν) them with sweet lies (τὸ . . . ψεῦδος γλυκύ)" (1). "For how else," Dio exclaims, "could lies (τὰ ψευδῆ) so often prevail over truths (τῶν ἀληθῶν), unless they conquer them through pleasure (δι' ἡδονήν: 2)?" Over time, these lies are hardened into fact by their constant repetition in each successive generation. In the case of Homer, these lies taken as truth have now acquired canonical status, so that even the Trojans, for whom Homer "has nothing but insults, and untruthful ones at that (οὐκ ἀληθεῖς)," revere him and "teach their children his verses from the very beginning" (τοὺς παῖδας εὐθὺς ἐξ ἀρχῆς τὰ ἔπη διδάσκειν: 4). The Trojans, like most people, have been "corrupted by *doxa*" (ὑπὸ δόξης διεφθαρμένοι), and Dio realizes that his revelations will thus not be "pleasing" to them (πρὸς ἡδονήν: 6). In fact, he would not be surprised if the Trojans find "Homer, who has lied about the most serious things, more believable than himself, who is telling the truth" (πιστότερον . . . Ὅμηρον τὰ χαλεπώτατα ψευσάμενον . . . ἢ ἐμὲ τἀληθῆ λέγοντα: 4).

The prologue's basic stance accords well with Dionian Cynic-Stoic moralizing boilerplate: the polemic against *doxa*, the assumption of an unpopular position, the passionate denunciation of pleasure and falsehood.[16] But it also situates Dio firmly in the tradition of paradoxical rhetorical speeches on Trojan topics, particularly Gorgias' *Helen*, a work which similarly opposes received opinion and is interested in the relation of deception, belief, and *doxa*.[17] Gorgias asserts, for example, that the success of those who have "persuaded" others by "fabricating false speech" (ψευδῆ λόγον πλάσαντες) is due to the fact that most people retain "*doxa* as their soul's adviser" (τὴν δόξαν σύμβουλον τῇ ψυχῇ), which is, however, "slippery and unreliable" (11). The close links between lies, belief, and *doxa* are reiterated a bit later when he remarks that competition speeches "please and persuade (ἔτερψε καὶ ἔπειθε) large crowds because they are artfully written, not uttered truthfully (τέχνῃ γραφείς, οὐκ ἀληθείᾳ λεχθείς)," and that "a clever mind reveals that belief based on *doxa* is easily changed (ὡς εὐμετάβολον . . . τὴν τῆς δόξης πίστιν)" (13). In the opening of his

---

16 For the Cynic nature of this part of the discourse, see Kindstrand (1973), 145–56. On its connection to Platonic thought, see Gangloff (2006a), 124–36, and (less convincingly) Fornaro (2000).
17 On the games Gorgias plays in the *Encomium of Helen*, see Porter (1993), 273–83.

speech, Dio, like Gorgias, sets out to establish how deception functions and why it is so powerful, concentrating on the reception, rather than the production, of falsehoods (although Gorgias never mentions Homer or any other poet by name).

But it is also worth noting how Dio works within the basic conceptual fields used by Strabo and Eratosthenes. Homer, he implies, has avoided the difficult task of "teaching" (διδάσκειν: 1) his audience the truth (precisely the "instruction" (διδασκαλία) which Strabo saw as Homer's primary goal), and chosen the easy path: to "deceive" (ἐξαπατᾶν: 1) them with "pleasing" lies. As in Strabo these lies (Strabo calls them "myths") are not related to verse form, ornamentation, or moral principles, but are falsifications of the historical record, opposed to "the true things that happened" (τὰ ὄντα καὶ γενόμενα: 4). And in a clever twist, Dio takes Homer's canonical status (his *doxa*), which Strabo continually cites in order to justify his investigations and defenses (cf. 8.3.3: διὰ τὴν τοῦ ποιητοῦ δόξαν), as cause for suspicion rather than reassurance. Over time, Dio maintains, anything, even lies, can attain the status of truth – a far cry from Strabo's eulogies of Homer's antiquity and canonicity.

This concern for the relation of *doxa* not just to belief and persuasion, but also to questions of authority and canonicity marks Dio's divergence from Gorgias. On the one hand, their targets and purposes are different: Gorgias' comments about persuasive speech are meant to excuse Helen's susceptibility to persuasion by Paris, whereas Dio castigates the easy way in which audiences embrace Homer's persuasive lies. Gorgias is also interested in the immediate effect of speech upon *doxa*, while Dio extends his analysis of *doxa*'s influence over time – its repetition and transformation into tradition. In fact, Dio plays on the two different (yet interrelated) meanings of *doxa* here – opinion (one's own) and reputation (the opinion others have of one). Each incarnation of *doxa* comes under Dio's scrutiny in other works – *Orr.* 66 and 67 rail against 'popular opinion' while *Or.* 68 pillories the obsession with 'fame.' But in characterizing Homer's lies as first transformed into *doxa*, or popular opinion, and then cemented over time and accepted as the truth, Dio is suggesting that Homer's fame or reputation (which he mentions at 11: τῆς δόξης) is based on and linked to false popular belief (*doxa*). When Dio declares that by refuting Homer he will anger the Argives because he would be "obliterating and destroying their *doxa*" (τὴν ... δόξαν ... ἀφανίζων καὶ καθαίρων: 5), the slippage between the two definitions becomes apparent: Dio would be destroying the Argives' false 'belief' in their victory over Troy *and* the 'fame' of Argos which depends upon that belief. In this sense, Dio's attack on Homer could be seen as part of a wider exposé of the arbitrariness of authority and tradition as a whole.

In this light, the Trojan, or Ilian, audience is crucial to the effect of the speech. The paradoxical situation that Dio finds himself in – trying to convince the Trojans, who stubbornly support Homer, that their ancestors actually won the war – is a delicious irony, but it also serves to more vividly underline the power of *doxa* as well as the arbitrary nature of belief in the poetic and historical tradition. This is the case regardless of whether Dio actually delivered the oration at Troy; the important thing, as with so many of his speeches, is that he represents himself as doing so.[18] In this respect, the *Trojan* can be set alongside a host of other long speeches in which Dio attacks the beliefs and practices of the citizens to whom he is speaking: the statue re-naming practices of the Rhodians (*Or.* 31), the Alexandrians' love of spectacle entertainment (32), an unidentified disgusting practice of the Tarsians (33).[19] Such speeches inspire a certain admiration for his boldness tempered by incredulity – did Dio *really* stand up in front of these cities and so vigorously lambaste their inhabitants to their face? But such an effect is best produced if the speeches were delivered not to the putative addressees, but to other audiences, who could marvel at Dio's effrontery and take pleasure in imagining the consternation of the 'original' recipients.[20] In the case of the *Trojan*, Dio mentions within the speech itself (6) that he plans to present it "to others."[21]

The best example of a speech intended for two separate audiences is the *Borysthenitic Oration* (*Or.* 36) which is addressed to his fellow Prusans, but tells of his visit to Borysthenes (or Olbia) on the Black Sea and the speech he delivered there to its inhabitants.[22] The oration is also a good illustration of Dio's ability to take up an ironic stance toward the reverence for Homer and Hellenic tradition similar to that in the *Trojan*. While Dio admires the Borysthenites' Homeric qualities – their worship of Achilles (36.9; 13), their long hair (17) – he cannot help painting a slightly condescending picture

[18] There is very little in the speech that is specific to the Trojan setting; the references to local tombs and topography are generic, and even incorrect in one instance: Trachsel (2002). This corresponds to Dio's general avoidance of myths with only a local significance to his addressees: Gangloff (2006a), 282–4.

[19] Gangloff (2006a), 273–82.

[20] Cf. Whitmarsh (2001), 325–7, who argues that the *Kingship Orations* were not delivered to Trajan, but in an Eastern civic context (a different account in Swain [1996], 193–4).

[21] I am thus skeptical of the claim that, by addressing his Ilian audience as descendants of the Homeric Trojans, Dio is intervening on their behalf in the ancient debates about the location of Troy, which some, like Strabo, believed to lie elsewhere (see the long discussion at Str. 13.1.25–42 and Trachsel [2007]).

[22] Swain (1996), 83–5; Porter (2001), 85–90; Gangloff (2006a), 299–305.

of the inhabitants as zealous devotees of Homer (Ὁμήρου... ἐρασταί: 26), clinging to their primitive Greek culture despite being isolated on the hostile Scythian frontier:

And nearly all the Borysthenites are so passionate about Homer (περὶ τὸν ποιητὴν ἐσπουδάκασιν)... that they do not even want to hear about anybody other than Homer (ὥστε οὐδὲ ἀκούειν ὑπὲρ οὐδενὸς ἄλλου θέλουσιν ἢ Ὁμήρου). And although in general they no longer speak Greek clearly, because they live in the middle of barbarians, nevertheless nearly all of them know the *Iliad* by heart (τήν γε Ἰλιάδα ὀλίγου πάντες ἴσασιν ἀπὸ στόματος). (9)

As we have seen, Dio can be an ardent admirer of Homer when it suits his purposes, but here he questions, rather than embraces, the citizens' devotion.[23] He tells the young man Callistratus, a particularly committed follower of Homer (φιλόμηρον: 9), that a three-line epigram of Phocylides describing how a "small, well-ordered *polis* on a rock is greater than the deranged city of Nineveh" perhaps "is more useful" (μᾶλλον ὠφελεῖ: 13) to the small-town Borysthenites than the grandiose and long-winded *Iliad* and *Odyssey*. This sort of provocation is characteristic of Dio, an attempt to disrupt a complacent and uncritical audience by calling their core beliefs into question. His surprising dismissal of Homer fits into the broader exploration and questioning of Greek identity that runs through the speech; is the love of Homer enough to qualify the Borysthenites as 'Greek'? Or is it completely inappropriate for their semi-'barbaric' situation and station?

The question here, as in the *Trojan*, is the appropriateness and validity of Homer in the construction of Greekness, even if the context and Dio's overall goals in each speech are very different. In the *Borystheniticus*, Dio chooses to set the authority of another archaic poet, Phocylides, against Homer, but in the *Trojan*, it is Dio himself who has to take up the task, a latecomer to the game competing with the most revered and trusted opponent. No wonder he anticipates failure. But the vast gap, in time and authority, between Homer and Dio serves to highlight Dio's challenge to his audience: to consider *why* they believe the poet, and what his authority depends upon, other than his antiquity and reputation. The way that such issues of belief are intimately tied to questions of identity is brought out by Dio's attempts to cast his Ilian audience as direct descendants of the Trojans: "I expended considerable effort on behalf of your ancestors" (ὑπὲρ γὰρ τῶν ὑμετέρων προγόνων ἐσπούδακα: 5), he asserts at one point.

[23] A parallel attitude toward Homer is that of the young Alexander the Great in Dio's *Second Kingship Oration* (Or. 2), who "not only cannot bear to hear any poet recited except for Homer, but also to hear any meter except for the Homeric hexameter" (7).

The Ilians' ethnic 'Trojan' ancestry thus jars with their otherwise exemplary cultural 'Greekness,' represented by Dio as revolving around Homer, the center of their educational curriculum, and object of their reverence.

HOMER THE LIAR

If the *Trojan* is framed as an interrogation of belief, tradition, and authority, its test case is Homer, and a sustained and profound overturning of his account lies at the heart of the oration. Dio's main assertion is that "Homer was the boldest liar of all" (ἀνδρειότατος ἀνθρώπων ἦν πρὸς τὸ ψεῦδος Ὅμηρος: 23), and one of the pleasures of the speech arises from witnessing how Dio's withering assault on Homer's character and storytelling habits so cleverly dismantles the considerable authority of his opponent, considered by many to be a "divine and wise man" (θεῖον ἄνδρα καὶ σοφόν: 4).[24]

One way to mark Dio's originality here is by considering his idea of Homer's lies. As is well known, the labelling of poets as liars boasts a long and illustrious pedigree. When Dio accuses Homer of lying, deception, and pandering to his audience (with words such as ἀπατή, ἡδονή, ψεύδεσθαι, etc.), one is immediately reminded of the famous pronouncements of early Greek poetic criticism that identify deception, pleasure, and falsehood as somehow intrinsic and essential to poets and their work.[25] Hesiod's description of the Muses, who "know how to tell many lies similar to truth" (ἴδμεν ψεύδεα πολλὰ λέγειν ἐτύμοισιν ὁμοῖα), Solon's maxim that "poets speak many falsehoods" (πολλὰ ψεύδονται ἀοιδοί), and especially Plato's remarks on the falsehoods of the poets in the *Republic*.[26] Dio certainly knew his Plato well, but there is a significant difference between what he and Plato mean by the term "lie" or "falsehood," and hence, by extension, "truth." In *Republic* 2–3, Plato generally is concerned with improper depictions of the gods, or portrayals of heroes doing or saying things that he believes are *ethically* false. For Dio, Homer's falsehoods and deceptions are much more straightforward; he criticizes Homer not because poetry is an inadequate means for instilling the proper moral and religious standards essential for a well-run community, but because Homer has misrepresented how things actually happened. This is a crucial distinction, because Dio has sometimes been characterized as wholeheartedly taking over the Platonic

---

[24] On this section see Montgomery (1901), 10–11; (1902), 406–7.
[25] Valgimigli (1912), 37, sees a strong connection to Plato.
[26] Hes. *Theog.* 27–8; Sol. 29 West; Pl. *Resp.* 2.376e–3.398b. On lying and poetry in the Archaic and Classical periods see, e.g., Pratt (1993) and Finkelberg (1998).

attack on Homer.[27] But it also brings up a larger issue, which centers *on*
around the extent to which post-classical authors manipulated and re-
deployed language and concepts from the great masters of the past for their
own particular objectives. Even close contemporaries' use of terms such as
lies and truth could be radically different, and we have to be sensitive to
these discrepancies.

The potential for confusion is on display in Kindstrand's attempt to connect Dio's attack on Homer's lies in the *Trojan* with Plutarch's criticism of
poetic 'lies' in his *How the Young Man Should Listen to Poetry*.[28] Plutarch
warns that all poets lie, and that young students need to be able to differentiate between the true and false elements of poetry. To this end, Plutarch
separates poets' 'lies' into two types: some are intentional – "for the purpose
of giving pleasure and gratification" (16a) – while others are unintentional –
"the things which they do not fabricate, but think and believe in their own
hearts, and then impart to us in their false coloring" (16f). But both kinds
of lies have very little to do with Dio's Homeric 'lies.' Plutarch's intentional
lies are "mythical fabrications which have been created to please or astound
the hearer," such as the weighing of Achilles' and Hector's fates by Zeus,
which no one believes actually occurred. His unintentional lies are ethical
statements that poets utter "in accord with their opinion and belief, as
they . . . try to make us share their delusion and ignorance" (17b), and are
judged 'false' because they do not accord with Plutarch's philosophical,
theological, and moral beliefs. Despite their shared interest in Homer's
'lies,' Plutarch takes up the Strabonian definition of a fantastic tale and
the Platonic conception of ethical lies, while Dio, as I mentioned above, is
overwhelmingly interested in Homer's misrepresentation of what actually
happened during the Trojan War.

This historiographical focus is maintained throughout the entire speech,
but is especially apparent in the opening sections of Dio's critique (15–36).
Some scholars, like Kindstrand and more recently Sotera Fornaro, have
argued that Dio is basically portraying Homer as a bad historian in this
part of the oration, but that is only partially accurate.[29] Dio does, it
is true, deploy criticisms frequently used in historiographical attacks on
colleagues – poor use of sources, clumsy narrative arrangement – but he
combines these with arguments reminiscent of those deployed to subvert
the credibility of witnesses in forensic oratory. Dio is not only trying to

---

[27] Valgimigli (1912), 33–7.
[28] Kindstrand (1973), 158. On Plutarch's text, see Bréchet (1999) and Konstan (2004).
[29] Kindstrand (1973), 157–9, and Fornaro (2002).

show that Homer is a bad historian, but also constructing an image of Homer as an improvising lying witness.

The untrustworthy witness

It is hard to imagine a description of Homer that contrasts more with Strabo's vision of the truth-loving ideal geographer encountered in the last chapter than that offered by Dio. Like Strabo, Dio focuses on Homer's character and the motivations underlying the historical aspects of his poetry, but where Strabo sees a diligent traveler and inquirer, always concerned to locate what and where things happened, Dio paints a quite different picture, of a traveling beggar, forced *"by poverty"* (ὑπὸ πενίας) literally to sing for his supper, interested primarily in lying to *court the favor* of his hosts (ψεύσασθαι πρὸς χάριν τῶν διδόντων: 15) and telling stories pleasing to them (καθ᾽ ἡδονήν: 15).[30] In any case, Dio argues, no one today would accept a beggar as "a witness (μάρτυρα) for anything nor take their praise as true" (ἀληθεῖς: 15).[31] Dio's poverty-based dismissal of Homer's value as a witness comes straight out of the rhetorical handbooks:

We must slander the witness' character (δεῖ τὸν τρόπον τοῦ μάρτυρος δια-βάλλειν) if he is evil... another thing to consider is whether the witness (ὁ μάρτυς) is a friend of the man for whom he is giving evidence... or an enemy of the person against whom he is giving evidence, or *a poor man* (πένης); witnesses in these circumstances are suspected of giving false testimony (ὑποπτεύονται τὰ ψευδῆ μαρτυρεῖν), because of, respectively, *courting favor* (διὰ χάριν), revenge, and profit.[32]

This is the first in a series of allegations in which Dio applies criticisms culled from forensic oratory and historiography about witnesses and sources to aspects of Homer's life or poetry for comic effect. In other words, he takes

---

[30] Dio offers a more positive spin at *Or.* 47.5, where Homer is described as "not only a good poet, but also in a way a philosopher" who spent his life abroad, "and preferred to receive twenty-five drachmas by begging, and as if crazy (ὡς μαινόμενος), rather than reside at home."

[31] Dio also adds an argument (16) based on those who assume that Homer was crazy (μαινομένῳ), a reference to the divinely inspired Homer familiar from Plato's *Ion*, among other places. Like the beggar, such a Homer was hardly trustworthy. It should be noted that Dio is not impugning beggars *per se*; as Valgimigli (1912), 34, points out, Dio praises Diogenes on these same grounds in *Or.* 9.8, and during his exile took on the persona of the poor wanderer. Dio's argument is that people believe both that Homer was a beggar and that beggars tell lies, yet still contradictorily maintain that Homer told the truth.

[32] Anaximenes, *Rhet. ad Alex.* 1431b. This is probably the earliest example; the rest of the rhetorical tradition, Latin and Greek, is remarkably consistent, with the notable exception of Quintilian (*Inst.* 7.2.28ff.) who expands the discussion with what appears to be knowledge culled from personal experience. Cf. Cic. *Part. or.* 14.48–9.

the image of Homer as a historian or an eyewitness at face value, assessing it in the light of traditional information about the poet's life and poetry. How does the widely believed picture of Homer as beggar and madman square with his alleged historical accuracy? Or consider Dio's argument that Homer's praise of Odysseus, whom "he has represented as telling many lies" (πλεῖστα . . . πεποίηκε ψευδόμενον: 17), suggests that the poet himself condones, and even recommends, lying. The line of reasoning hearkens back to Plato, *Resp.* 1 (334a10–b2), where Socrates suggests that Homer's fondness for Odysseus' grandfather Autolycus, whom the poet describes as "surpassing all men in thievery" (*Od.* 19.395–6), indicates that Homer viewed "the just person as a sort of thief." Other critics went further and inferred details about Homer's (and other authors') prejudices and predilections from the characters and events depicted in their work.[33] For instance, the early third-century BCE historian Timaeus of Tauromenium sees in the constant feasting of Homer's heroes an indication that the poet was a glutton (γαστρίμαργον: Polyb. 12.24.2), and an anonymous Cynic treatise from the early Imperial period accuses Homer of being "a woman-lover" (φιλογύνης) because in his poetry (a) several men die for the sake of women, (b) the passions of women (Helen, Penelope) are foregrounded, and (c) all Odysseus ever does of his own free will is live with women.[34]

Dio's cleverest intervention, however, is without a doubt his treatment of the Homeric gods, which had long been considered the most egregious example of the poet's lies. Dio sidesteps the old debate (οὐ λέγω, πρότερον εἰρημένα πολλοῖς: 18) over Homer's allegedly impious and unflattering depiction of the gods by trenchantly pointing out what both critics and allegorically minded defenders have in common – the belief that Homer's *literal* description of the gods is false.[35]

Virtually everyone, even those who especially praise Homer, agrees that he does not say anything true (μηθὲν ἀληθές) about the gods, and they try to defend him by claiming that, when he says such things, he is not intending them [literally], but is allegorizing and employing metaphors (οὐ φρονῶν ταῦτ᾽ ἔλεγεν, ἀλλ᾽ αἰνιττόμενος καὶ μεταφέρων: 17).

For Dio, the most famous of Homer's 'lies' – his depictions of the gods – serves primarily as an a fortiori argument establishing his penchant for lying: if he dares to lie about the gods, "what, then, prevents him from having spoken in the same way about humans?" (18). But with a

---

[33] Luce (1989), 21–2.   [34] For this text, see Kakridis (1974).

[35] Cf. 19: "Leaving aside, then, the terrible and inappropriate things he seems to have represented (πεποιηκέναι) concerning the gods . . . "

characteristic twist, Dio also approaches the issue from a forensic and historiographical angle, asking where Homer obtained the information he used for his detailed accounts of the gods' activities and even verbatim conversations.[36] Indeed, Homer reports not only the words spoken by the gods in public (ἐν κοινῷ), but also those said to each other privately (ἰδίᾳ), such as in their domestic squabbles, which, Dio reminds his audience, even mere mortals manage to keep secret (19). This lack of explanation cannot be attributed to ignorance; Homer was perfectly aware of proper historiographical procedure regarding the attribution of sources:

Homer has depicted Odysseus correcting [a potential error] of this sort in order that he [Homer] might not appear immodest in narrating the gods' conversations about him [Odysseus]. Odysseus says that he heard about them from Calypso and that she learned them *by inquiry*; but concerning himself Homer has not said anything like this, namely, that he *learned of* the conversations from some god. (20)

καὶ τὸν Ὀδυσσέα πεποίηκεν ἐπανορθούμενον τὸ τοιοῦτο, μὴ δόξῃ ἀλαζών διηγούμενος τοὺς παρὰ τοῖς θεοῖς γενομένους ὑπὲρ αὐτοῦ λόγους. ἔφη γὰρ ἀκοῦσαι τῆς Καλυψοῦς, ἐκείνην δὲ παρὰ τοῦ πυθέσθαι· περὶ αὐτοῦ δὲ οὐδὲν τοιοῦτον εἴρηκεν ὅτι πύθοιτο παρὰ θεοῦ τινος.[37]

Homer, then, is aware of the need to justify how one obtained certain types of privileged information (note the use of the historiographically marked verb πυνθάνομαι), but openly ignores this responsibility. For Dio, this isn't simply an oversight; rather, it illustrates "the degree to which Homer regarded people with contempt and was completely unconcerned whether or not he appeared to say anything true" (καὶ οὐθὲν αὐτῷ ἔμελεν, εἰ δόξει μηθὲν λέγειν ἀληθές: 21). The "finishing touch" (τόν κολοφῶνα σχεδόν: 22) is Homer's presumption in explaining the differences between divine and human language, such as when he differentiates between the names Xanthus and Scamander, the bird called χαλκίς by the gods and κύμινδις by humans, and a place near Troy which humans call βατίεια and the gods call Σῆμα Μυρίνης.[38] The same three examples are cited in Plato's

36 Fornaro (2002), 553–4.
37 I follow Cohoon (1932) and Vagnone (2003a) in understanding Homer, rather than Odysseus, as the subject of εἴρηκεν. For discussion, see Vagnone (2000), 107–9.
38 In 23b, the divine word μῶλυ is mentioned as another example. The same list appears in Dio, *Or.* 10.23–4; Dio's rough contemporary Ptolemy the Quail also discusses "double appellations" in Homer (Phot. *Bibl.* 149b33–8). The argument in 22–3 is repeated in a variant form in 22b–23b; the double redaction most likely reflects the fact that the speech existed in multiple versions (although see Vagnone (2000), 109–13). von Arnim (1898) devotes much of his discussion of the *Trojan* to this question (esp. 183–204), justifying his decision to bracket large chunks of the speech in his (1893) edition. Kindstrand (1973), 142–3, justly criticizes the excesses of von Arnim; Lemarchand (1926), 35–56, (on which see n. 59 below) and Szarmach (1978), 196–7, attribute the frequent repetitions to the need to remind the audience of the extremely long and complicated argument. Vagnone (2003a) *passim* restores many of the passages deemed by von Arnim to be interpolations.

Cratylus (391d) in a discussion about the correctness of names; here Dio asks how Homer possibly could have learned divine vocabulary. Homer acts as if he held some privileged access to the gods' language, and was accustomed "not only to mix other Greek dialects together – sometimes Aeolicizing, sometimes Doricizing, sometimes Ionicizing – but even to speak Zeus-dialect" (διαστὶ διαλέγεσθαι: 23).

This absurdist insistence on assessing Homer's presentation of the proper channels of obtaining information about the gods seems aimed at the ubiquitous use of the poet as 'witness' or testimony, which Dio referred to in passing above. Dio acknowledges the claim, and then proceeds to attack Homer's credibility with a straight face, following the guidelines of forensic rhetoric. The early first-century BCE handbook known as the *Rhetorica ad Herennium*, for instance, lists nearly every method of attacking witnesses' credibility employed by Dio against Homer:

Against witnesses (*contra testes*): their base manner of living (*vitae turpitudinem*); the contradictory character of their testimony (*testimoniorum inconstantiam*); if we contend that what they allege to have happened either could not have happened, or did not happen (*si aut fieri non potuisse dicemus aut non factum esse quod dicant*), or that they could not have known it (*aut scire illos non potuisse*), or that it is partiality that inspires their words and inferences (*aut cupide dicere et argumentari*). (2.6.9)

For Dio, all of his criticisms point in one direction: Homer had the capacity, the motive, and the character to lie, he lied about the gods, and he did not even bother to disguise his lies by accounting for his sources. In a way, Dio exposes the inherent ridiculousness of the idea that Homer was a historian, or even a reliable source, by taking it 'seriously' and submitting the poet to the same sort of scrutiny awarded to that of historians or witnesses in court. This assessment of Homer and his work by standards taken from other fields, like historiography and rhetoric, is sustained throughout the speech and accounts for much of its comic incongruity. But Dio takes the conceit much farther. While Dio's attack in 15–23 had established the unreliability of Homer's testimony on the basis of his lying character, in the following section, paragraphs 24–36, he shows that the text itself can prove that Homer was a liar – by demonstrating that Homer tells his story in the same way that liars tell theirs. This conception of Homer's narrative as the record of a long, extemporaneous fabrication is the linchpin of Dio's argument, and he constructs it through a deft combination of Homeric criticism, rhetorical strictures, and a healthy dose of audacity.

Poetic virtues, rhetorical flaws, and narrative blushes (24–36)

Dio's argument assumes the following about liars – when they tell false stories, they mix up the order of the events (a) so that they can confuse the listener and hide their lies in this fashion, and (b) because they shy away from directly speaking about the most important matters that they are misrepresenting; this second reason also accounts for why liars often say they heard these stories from other people.[39] Homer, he claims, can be demonstrated to have been guilty of each of these strategies.

When Homer tried to tell of the war that occurred between the Greeks and the Trojans, *he did not begin right at the beginning*, but at random (οὐκ εὐθὺς ἤρξατο ἀπὸ τῆς ἀρχῆς, ἀλλ᾽ ὅθεν ἔτυχεν). Virtually all liars do this in order to escape detection, entwining and entangling [their account], and being reluctant to tell anything *in sequence* (ἐμπλέκοντες καὶ περιπλέκοντες καὶ οὐθὲν βουλόμενοι λέγειν ἐφεξῆς); otherwise they are exposed by the events themselves. One can observe this happening in the courts as well as among other men who artfully lie. Those who want to show what actually occurred (τὰ γενόμενα), however, narrate [their accounts] just as they happened– the first thing first, the second thing second and so on, *in sequence* (ἐφεξῆς). This is one reason why Homer did not begin his poem in the "natural" way (κατὰ φύσιν). (24–5)

Homer also employed a convoluted narrative sequence, according to Dio, because he "had no confidence . . . and was unable to speak readily" (οὐ γὰρ ἐθάρρει . . . οὐδὲ ἐδύνατο εἰπεῖν ἑτοίμως: 26) about the events involving Helen and Paris and the outcome of the war itself.

Because he intended to obscure the beginning and end as much as possible and to produce the opposite opinion about them, he did not dare to mention either the beginning or the end openly (ἐκ τοῦ εὐθέος) . . . and if he does mention them somewhere, [he does so] briefly and incidentally (παρέργως καὶ βραχέως) and is clearly uncomfortable. (25–6)

Dio again connects this behavior with the practices of liars:

It also usually happens to liars that they tell some parts of the story and linger over them, but they mention whatever they especially want to conceal (κρύψαι θέλωσιν) without preparation, when their audience is not paying attention, setting it not in its proper place, but in the manner in which it might best escape notice. They do this also because lying makes them ashamed and hesitant to go on, especially concerning the most important matters. (26)

---

[39] See Hesk (2000), ch. 4 (esp. 231–41) on methods of lie detection in fourth-century BCE Attic oratory, e.g., Aeschin. *In Ctes.* 98–9.

Homer's failure to directly relate the abduction of Helen or the fall of Troy is an indication, to Dio, that it was in regard to precisely these points that Homer had the most to hide; not only did Homer downplay these events in order to confuse, but also because he "flinched and weakened since he knew that he was telling the reverse of the truth and falsifying the essential part of his subject" (ὑποκατεκλίνετο καὶ ἡττᾶτο, ὅτι ᾔδει τἀναντία λέγων τοῖς οὖσι καὶ τὸ κεφάλαιον αὐτὸ τοῦ πράγματος ψευδόμενος: 27).[40] Dio goes on to enumerate a few other important events which Homer alludes to but does not directly describe (or even ignores) and concludes from this evidence:

So for these reasons, one has to acknowledge either that Homer was so ignorant and such a poor judge of the events (ἀγνώμονα Ὅμηρον καὶ φαῦλον κριτὴν τῶν πραγμάτων) that he chose the lesser and more trivial and left the most important and serious to others, or that he was unable, as I have mentioned, to resolutely maintain his lies, and that in these [lies] his poetry itself exhibits the events whose actual course he wanted to conceal (δὲ ἐν τούτοις ἐπιδεικνύναι τὴν ποίησιν ἃ ἐβούλετο κρύψαι ὅπως γέγονεν). (33)[41]

Finally, Dio notes Homer's propensity to have his characters narrate lies that, due to their importance, he cannot bring himself to tell in his own voice.[42] In the *Odyssey*, for example, Homer has no problem narrating events, Dio claims, that are clearly true, such as those in Ithaca. But "he did not dare to mention the greatest of his lies . . . these he has represented Odysseus as narrating to Alcinous' court" (τὸν Ὀδυσσέα ἐποίησε διηγούμενον τοῖς περὶ τὸν Ἀλκίνοον: 34), and he has Demodocus recite the (to Dio) false stories of the Trojan Horse and the sack of Troy "in a song of only a few lines" (ἐν ᾠδῇ δι' ὀλίγων ἐπῶν).[43]

---

[40] If Homer had begun with Helen's seizure, "all the readers of his poem (οἱ τῇ ποιήσει ἐντυγχάνοντες) would have expressed outrage together and he would have been assured of a more enthusiastic and well-disposed audience (τὸν ἀκροατήν: 28)." "What greater or more awe-inspiring subject could he have chosen" than the capture of Troy? (29). Cf. the similar criticisms of Thucydides at Dion. Hal. *Pomp.* 10.

[41] On the frequent mistranslation of the last part of this sentence (e.g., Cohoon [1932]: "to bolster up his falsehoods *and show his poetic genius in handling* those incidents") see Vagnone (2003b), 140–1.

[42] As Montgomery (1902), 407 n. 1, notes: "Dio's perversion of the well-known λύσις ἐκ τοῦ προσώπου." The 'solution from the character' (see Dachs [1913] and Nünlist [2009], 116–34) entailed explaining a problematic line by taking into account the context-specific intentions of the character who spoke the words in question. Strabo's claim that Homer's description of Charybdis as spewing forth water 'three times' a day should be attributed to Circe's desire to exaggerate its danger is a good example (Ch. 3: 79–80).

[43] On the Phaeacian tales, see Ch. 5: 151–5 and Ch. 6: 178, 202. [Plut.] *Vit. Hom.* 162 makes the opposite claim, that Odysseus' travails seem *more* credible because they are told by the person

What is so clever about Dio's characterization of Homer as a liar is that each of his accusations criticizes as deceptive an element of Homer's narrative strategy that was traditionally singled out for praise in Homeric scholarship.[44] Dio was not the only one to wonder at Homer's choice of starting point; compare the very first scholium to the *Iliad* – "It is asked (ζητεῖται) why the poet began from the final [events of the war] and not from the first?" – which offers the standard explanation that nothing worth recounting occurred during the first nine years of the war.[45] The scholiast, however, points to this ploy as evidence of Homer's skill: "they say that taking up the final events and narrating the remaining things from the beginning is a *poetic virtue*" (λέγουσι δὲ καὶ ἀρετὴν εἶναι ποιητικὴν τὸ τῶν τελευταίων ἐπιλαμβάνεσθαι καὶ περὶ τῶν λοιπῶν ἀνέκαθεν διηγεῖσθαι: Sch. bT ad *Il.* 1.1b).[46] The scholia also defend Homer's failure to narrate important events such as the abduction of Helen and the death of Achilles as another marker of poetic skill, emphasizing Homer's decision to adopt an inverted style of narration (ἐξ ἀναστροφῆς) and contrasting this to "narration in order" (ἡ κατὰ τάξιν διήγησις) which is specified as "*historiographical* and removed from poetic elevation" (συγγραφικὸν καὶ τῆς ποιητικῆς ἄπο σεμνότητος: Sch. bT ad *Il.* 2.494–877).[47] Like Dio, other Homeric critics (such as Ps.-Longinus in *On the Sublime*) noted that the poet chose to embed stories about the end of the war within narratives voiced by his characters, particularly in the *Odyssey* – e.g., Menelaus' story of Helen and the Trojan Horse, Demodocus' song about the Sack of Troy.[48] To Ps.-Longinus and others, Homer's incorporation of material spanning

who had experienced them (ἃ καὶ δεινότερα καὶ πιθανώτερα ἔμελλε φαίνεσθαι ὑπὸ αὐτοῦ τοῦ παθόντος λεγόμενα).

[44] So Montgomery (1901), 407 n. 2; Valgimigli (1912), 38–9; and Hunter (2009), 52–3.

[45] Sch. bT ad *Il.* 1.1b: "We say that the battles before were sporadic and not [fought] over the greatest cities; for since Achilles was present, the Trojans never went out of the gates, and the Greeks spent nine years virtually idle, diverted to neighboring villages. It was not necessary for him to write about these things, since there was no material for a story (περὶ ὧν ἀναγκαῖον αὐτῷ γράφειν οὐκ ἦν, μὴ παρούσης ὕλης τῷ λόγῳ)." As we will see in the next chapter (Ch. 5: 163–4), Lucian gets to ask Homer the question directly in his *True Stories*.

[46] Porph. ad *Il.* 12.127 claims that "to begin from the later things, go back to the beginning, and then connect these to the later things again" (ἐκ τῶν ὕστερον ἀρξάμενον ἀναδραμεῖν εἰς τὰ πρῶτα καὶ πάλιν συνάψαι ταῦτα τοῖς ὑστέροις) is also Homer's "customary method of exposition (καὶ ἔστι συνήθης ὁ τρόπος τῆς ἑρμηνείας τῷ ποιητῇ)" for minor episodes.

[47] Cf. Sch. bT ad *Il.* 11.671–761 and the discussion in Heath (1989), 115–16. [Plut.]. *Vit. Hom.* 162 similarly praises Homer's *oikonomia* in selecting his starting point, as well as his choice to concisely narrate what happened earlier in the war at various other places in his poem.

[48] Ps.-Longinus calls the Odyssey "nothing other than the epilogue (ἐπίλογος) to the *Iliad*" because "Homer has clearly composed the plot of the *Odyssey* second . . . especially from the insertion of the leftovers of Iliadic events into the *Odyssey* as 'episodes' (δῆλος . . . συντεθεικὼς ταύτην δευτέραν τὴν ὑπόθεσιν, ἀτὰρ δὴ κἀκ τοῦ λείψανα τῶν Ἰλιακῶν παθημάτων διὰ τῆς Ὀδυσσείας ὡς ἐπεισόδιά τινα προσεπεισφέρειν: 9.12). Cf. Sch. bT ad *Il.* 24.804a: Homer "has beautifully distributed the

many years into the restricted temporal frame of the *Iliad* and *Odyssey* is an elegant solution to a poetic difficulty; to Dio it is just further evidence of Homer's obfuscatory attitude toward the truth.

In sum, Dio treats what Homeric scholars praised as poetic virtues as evidence that he was a liar. He maps Homer's narrative choices onto the behavior of liars by incongruously holding Homer's poetry (just as he had done earlier) to rhetorical and historiographical, rather than poetic standards – as transgressions of the "narrative virtues" (ἀρεταὶ τῆς διηγήσεως, or *virtutes narrationis*) repeatedly discussed in ancient rhetorical treatises, and comprising clarity, concision, and credibility (σαφήνεια, συντομία, πιθανότης).[49] Dio's accusations against Homer – confusing the order of the events, neglecting to tell them in proper sequence, failing to mention the most important parts of the story, such as the beginning and the end, and choosing to concentrate on insignificant and improbable episodes rather than those central to his story – are precisely the sorts of compositional practices the treatises emphasize as obstructing a narrative's achievement of "clarity of events" (σαφήνεια ἀπὸ τῶν πραγμάτων).

For instance, one text insists that clarity will only be achieved "if we do not set out [the events] in a transposed order, but state *first the things that were done first* and arrange the remaining ones *in sequence* (ἐὰν μὴ ὑπερβατῶς αὐτὰ δηλῶμεν, ἀλλὰ τὰ πρῶτα πραχθέντα... πρῶτα λέγωμεν, τὰ δὲ λοιπὰ ἐφεξῆς τάττωμεν: Anaximenes, *Rhet. Alex.* 1438a28–34).[50] Others note that "narration becomes unclear by the omission of what ought necessarily to have been mentioned" (ἀσαφὴς δὲ γίνεται διήγησις παρὰ τὴν ἔλλειψιν ὧν ἐχρῆν ἀναγκαίως μνήμην ποιήσασθαι: Theon, *Prog.* 81) and that concision will be achieved "if you hurry over what is trivial and less essential, but speak sufficiently of important matters" (εἰ παραθέοις μὲν τὰ μικρὰ καὶ ἧττον ἀναγκαῖα, λέγοις δὲ ἱκανῶς τὰ μεγάλα: Luc. *Hist. conscr.* 56). Lucian's *How to Write History*, which

---

remaining things (καλῶς δὲ ἐταμιεύσατο τὰ λοιπά) into the *Odyssey* ... the events left over (τὰ λείψανα) [from the *Iliad*] which Odysseus, Nestor, Menelaus, and Demodocus the bard narrate."

[49] So Theon, *Prog.* 79. Cf. *Rhet. Her.* 1.14: *brevitas, diluciditas, verisimilitudo*; Cic. *Inv. rhet.* 1.28: *brevis, aperta, probabilis.* Cf. Hor., *Ars P.* 146–50; Meijering (1987), 146–8.

[50] Comparable is Luc. *Hist. Conscr.* 55: "for only when he has completed the first section will he introduce the second one, touching it and linked to it as in a chain" (τὸ πρῶτον ἐξεργασάμενος ἐπάξει τὸ δεύτερον ἐχόμενον αὐτοῦ καὶ ἁλύσεως τρόπον συνηρμοσμένον). Cf. Theon, *Prog.* 80: "one should also guard against confusing the times and order of events ... for nothing else confuses the thought more than this" (φυλακτέον δὲ καὶ τὸ μὴ συγχεῖν τούς χρόνους καὶ τὴν τάξιν τῶν πραγμάτων... οὐδὲν γὰρ ἧττον τῶν ἄλλων καὶ τοῦτο συγχεῖ τὴν διάνοιαν).

is deeply indebted to the prescriptive template of the rhetorical treatises, provides perhaps the best description of the poor treatment of subject-matter:

[Bad historians] omit or treat cursorily important and noteworthy events (οἳ τὰ μεγάλα μὲν τῶν πεπραγμένων καὶ ἀξιομνημόνευτα παραλείπουσιν ἢ παραθέουσιν) but through amateurism, lack of taste, and ignorance of what to say and what to pass over in silence (ὑπὸ δὲ ἰδιωτείας καὶ ἀπειροκαλίας καὶ ἀγνοίας τῶν λεκτέων ἢ σιωπητέων), very carefully and laboriously linger over descriptions of the most unimportant things (τὰ μικρότατα πάνυ λιπαρῶς καὶ φιλοπόνως ἑρμηνεύουσιν ἐμβραδύνοντες). (27)

Indeed, as this example illustrates, the narrative qualities valued in rhetorical theory were nearly identical to those valued in historiography, and our best parallels for Dio's criticism come from discussions of the proper method of arrangement, or τάξις, of historical narratives.[51] Polybius urges that the διήγησις needs to be easy to follow and clear (τό εὐπαρακολούθητον καὶ σαφῆ), and Dionysius of Halicarnassus criticizes Thucydides' division of his narrative into summers and winters because of the confusion this caused the reader.[52] Much as Dio criticized Homer's endpoint, Dionysius finds fault with that chosen by Thucydides: "it would have been better, having narrated everything, to have made the end of the history extremely wondrous and especially gratifying to this audience" (κρεῖττον δὲ ἦν διεξελθόντα πάντα τελευτὴν ποιήσασθαι τῆς ἱστορίας τὴν θαυμασιωτάτην καὶ μάλιστα τοῖς ἀκούουσι κεχαρισμένην: *Pomp.* 3.10).[53]

But Dio makes a striking departure from these historiographical and rhetorical critiques when he claims not just that Homer has poorly arranged his material, but that these errors are the direct result of his attempts to misrepresent the truth.[54] Not even Lucian suggests, in a treatise specifically on historical writing, that a historian's poor arrangement has any

[51] Fornaro (2002), 557–8; Hunter (2009), 55. On arrangement (τάξις), see Meijering (1987), 138–43, and on its application to historiography, Heath (1989), 71–87.
[52] Polyb. 5.31.4; Dion. Hal. *Pomp.* 3.13 (ἀσαφὴς καὶ δυσπαρακολούθητος); cf. *Thuc.* 9 and Theon, *Prog.* 80 Spengel. For more citations, see Avenarius (1956), 119–30 on τάχος and τὸ σαφές.
[53] Of course, Thucydides did not *choose* to end his history where he did, since it is incomplete, breaking off in the middle of a sentence. The parallels with historiographical practice, it should be remarked, are again the result of the influence of rhetorical principles of critiquing and composing narrative. Dionysius' historiographical treatises are overwhelmingly rhetorical, as many disappointed modern readers can attest. If Dio is criticizing Homer in the same way as Dionysius criticizes Thucydides, it is on the basis of his compositional decisions, not his adherence to the truth.
[54] This part of my argument marks my most significant divergence from that of Fornaro (2002).

relation to the historian's knowledge of the truth, and no rhetorician is worried that a narrative's lack of clarity is a deliberate attempt to mislead his audience. Dio's originality lies in positing a causal relationship between narrative choices and the observable behavior of liars, who "do not speak in a loud voice . . . some of them whisper and speak unclearly (βατταρίζουσι καὶ ἀσαφῶς λέγουσιν), while others speak with the proviso that they do not know anything themselves, but that they have heard it from someone else (οἱ δὲ οὐχ ὡς αὐτοί τι εἰδότες, ἀλλ' ὡς ἑτέρων ἀκούσαντες)" (27). Compare Dio's remarks with the following passage from Cicero's *De partitione oratoria* on the involuntary physical gestures and speech patterns that constitute signs of guilt:

Subsequent indications of something that is past (*consequentia quaedam signa praeteriti*), the traces and imprint of a previous action (*quasi impressa facti vestigia*); these indeed are most powerful in exciting suspicion, and are silent evidence of guilt (*quasi tacita sunt criminum testimonia*) . . . for instance a weapon, a footprint, blood; the discovery of some article that looks as if it had been taken away or snatched from the victim; *an inconsistent answer, hesitation, stammering (ut responsum inconstanter, ut haesitatum, ut titubatum) . . . looking pale, trembling (ut pallor, ut tremor);* a writing or a sealed document or deposition. For these are the kind of things that whether part of the affair itself or even as prior or subsequent occurences render the charge suspicious. (33.114)

Alongside material evidence (what we would call 'clues') of a crime, Cicero includes evidence based on the behavioral response of the guilty party; both types are "the traces and imprint of a previous action."[55] In the *Rhetorica ad Herennium* signs based on behavior have their own category (2.5.8):

Consecutio is when the signs which usually attend guilt or innocence are investigated (*consecutio est cum quaeritur quae signa nocentis et innocentis consequi soleant*). The prosecutor will, if possible, say that his adversary, when come upon, blushed, went pale, faltered, spoke uncertainly, collapsed, or made some offer (*erubuisse, expalluisse, titubasse, inconstanter locutum esse, concidisse, pollicitum esse aliquid*) – signs of a guilty conscience (*quae signa conscientiae sint*).

Although Dio cannot claim to have observed Homer engaged in any of this 'guilty behavior,' he interprets Homer's obfuscating narrative decisions as textual equivalents of these examples of unease. A conspicuous failure to narrate vital portions of a story in the correct order, and then to give

---

[55] The proper use of signs, and arguments from signs, or clues, or evidence, constituted a fundamental portion of rhetorical training. See Manetti (1993).

them only a cursory treatment are the narrative analogues of "blushes," the textual manifestations of "faltering speech."

This parallelism between how liars construct their lies and the composition of a narrative can only be valid if Dio imagines the text of the *Iliad* to be a written manifestation of what was originally an oral performance of a spoken lie, and furthermore a performance which was spontaneous and *ex tempore*. He explains:

> It seems to me that [Homer] *had not prearranged these things from the beginning*, since they had never occurred; but *as his poem went along*, and he saw that people would readily believe anything, he regarded them with contempt and was also ingratiating himself to the Greeks and the sons of Atreus, by mixing everything up and turning events to their opposite. (35)

> δοκεῖ δέ μοι μηδὲ προθέσθαι ταῦτα τὴν ἀρχήν, ἅτε οὐ γενόμενα, προϊούσης δὲ τῆς ποιήσεως, ἐπεὶ ἑώρα τοὺς ἀνθρώπους ῥαδίως πάντα πειθομένους, καταφρονήσας αὐτῶν καὶ ἅμα χαριζόμενος τοῖς Ἕλλησι καὶ τοῖς Ἀτρείδαις πάντα συγχέαι καὶ μεταστῆσαι τὰ πράγματα εἰς τοὐναντίον.

As proof of this assertion, Dio quotes the first five lines of the *Iliad* and explains that at this point Homer had implied that the things mentioned here – the wrath of Achilles, the sufferings and deaths of the Greeks, etc. – would constitute the primary subjects of his poem. But in this preface, Dio notes, Homer neglects to mention "his later transformation of events, the death of Hector... and the final capture of Troy. Perhaps he had not yet intended to turn everything upside down" (ἀναστρέφειν ἅπαντα: 36).[56]

In other words, the fact that Homer's initial remarks make no mention of the (in Dio's eyes) false stories of Hector's death or Troy's defeat suggests that he was initially prepared to tell the truth; only as he continued did his intentions and practice change. This conception of Homer and his narrative is essential to Dio's strategy for impugning Homer's reliability. Dio envisions a fluid, rather than static, notion of Homer's narration; it is not a composition, revised, corrected, set down, but a narrative act, in which Homer has to make up things on the spot, cover up past mistakes, and finally gives up, "unsure of how to continue his poem and displeased at his own lies" (οὐκ ἔχων ὅτι χρήσηται τῇ ποιήσει καὶ τοῖς ψεύσμασι δυσχεραίνων: 109). From here, Dio can not only interrogate these texts as the utterances of a Homer who had the means and motive to lie, but also grant the narratives a progressive character and approach them as a process

---

[56] Note the different twist given here to the ἐξ ἀναστροφῆς of the scholia. Further remarks in Hunter (2009), 54; on the various treatments of the term in the scholia, see Nünlist (2009), 89–92.

inseparable from the context in which they were produced. The narrative itself can shed light on Homer, because it can be seen in the same way as a witness testifying in court who has to invent and distort at a moment's notice.[57]

In fact, the comical effect of this whole section depends upon the fact that Dio has consistently, skillfully, and carefully taken the idea of Homer's reliability as a witness or storyteller 'seriously,' producing this surprising portrait of Homer as extemporaneous liar by rigorously holding up his person and narrative to forensic and historiographical critiques. Dio's reconstruction of the original performance context of the *Iliad* is the final step in this process, transforming the Homeric epics from the carefully polished poems conceived by the Alexandrian critics into the products of a kind of oral improvisatory composition. But rather than participating within a culture of oral poetry that renews itself with every performance and retelling, as moderns posit, Dio's Homer engages in a one-time, spur-of-the-moment, unplanned improvisation in order to conceal the truth.

The 'authority' of the Egyptian priest (37–42)

Dio has thus accomplished the task he set out for himself – dismantling Homer's authority – and cleared a space for his new 'true' version of events. But at this juncture, almost a third of the way into the speech, Dio belatedly reveals that his authority, and his 'truth,' derives from an external source, an account told to him by an Egyptian priest.

I, therefore, shall give the account as I learned it (ἐπυθόμην) from a very old man in Onuphis, one of the Egyptian priests, who often ridiculed the Greeks because they knew nothing true about most things (τῶν Ἑλλήνων καταγελῶντος ὡς οὐθὲν εἰδότων ἀληθὲς περὶ τῶν πλείστων). He used as his best evidence of this, the fact that they were persuaded (εἰσι πεπεισμένοι) both that Troy was conquered by Agamemnon and that Helen fell in love with Paris while she was living with Menelaus; so thoroughly persuaded were they and so deceived (ἐξαπατηθέντες) by a single man that every [Greek] has sworn [to its truth]. (37)

Dio's revelation comes as something of a surprise; he never mentions this source in his initial attempts to convince his audience of his trustworthiness, and the description of his informant is curiously vague: the priest is unnamed, resides in an obscure Egyptian city (the name of which is

---

[57] Seeck (1990), 106, hypothesizes that Dio's critical acumen developed from courtroom experience: "Tactical observations sharpen the look for the technical tricks of opponents; one pays attention to traces where the real truth shines through."

only a modern conjecture),[58] and indeed vanishes altogether by the end of the speech, as his voice and Dio's own merge into one.[59] The 'barbarian' sage who dispenses ancient wisdom while disparaging Greek ignorance and immaturity is a well-worn topos by this time, and Dio enjoys deploying it elsewhere to destabilize easy attitudes toward Hellenic tradition and identity.[60] The *Borysthenitic Oration* again provides a good example – when asked by the Borysthenites to deliver a Platonic speech on the cosmic city, Dio perversely offers them a 'Zoroastrian' myth told by Persian Magi (*Or.* 36.39–41). The Magi, like the Egyptian priest in the *Trojan*, criticize the Greeks for their "youth and weak memory" (49), and "expound their myth not with much persuasion [as poets do], but completely truthfully" (ἐξηγοῦνται δὲ τὸν μῦθον οὐχ... μετὰ πολλῆς πειθοῦς, ἀλλὰ μάλα αὐθαδῶς: 42). One can only imagine the bewilderment with which the Borysthenites greeted this speech, not to mention Dio's Prusan audience, but it is clear that his ironic appeal to 'barbarian' wisdom is an intentional and carefully cultivated challenge to received notions of Greek identity and cultural authority.[61]

In the case of the *Trojan* the same logic is in play, as Dio's Egyptian ridicules the Greeks for their gullibility and contrasts them to the Egyptians, who love truth so much that they have banned poetry, which they see as a vehicle for deceit. The dependence on a non-Greek source is complicated

---

[58] Morelius emended the incomprehensible ὄνυχι of the manuscripts to Ὀνούφι, which corresponds to an Egyptian *nomos* (Ὀνουφίτης) mentioned in passing by Herodotus in a list (2.166) but with no details (such as location) provided. If this is the correct reading, Dio has certainly chosen (intentionally?) a very little known locale for his encounter.

[59] Ostensibly, the bulk of the *Trojan* is supposed to be a report by Dio of his conversation with the priest, but the distinction between the two is maintained only for a short while; Dio refers to the priest in the third person at 54 and 57 and the first person asides at 61 and 68 (ὡς ἔφην; ὡς ἐγώ λέγω) are clearly spoken by the priest, but after 68 there is no way of determining whether the use of the first person, e.g., at 110 and 116, is to be referred to Dio or the priest until 124, when the phrase οὐ μόνον οἱ Ἕλληνες, ἀλλὰ καὶ ὑμεῖς makes it apparent that Dio is addressing the Trojans. The prevailing opinion is best expressed by Seeck (1990), 98, who sees the priest as a fictional *Hilfskonstruktion* on par with the Doric priestess of *Or.* 1. Fuchs (1996), 133, adds that Dio's failure to maintain the fiction of the priest is another self-conscious marker of the text's fictionality. Lemarchand (1926), 35–56, even tries to show that the present speech is an amalgam of two different versions – one in which Dio uses the device of the Egyptian priest and another in which he speaks throughout in his own voice. Vagnone (2003b), 139–40, believes that Dio begins speaking at 70, but even he admits that this is just a guess. One should note, however, that the Loeb translation of Cohoon (1932) often falsely gives the impression that Dio explicitly refers to the Egyptian priest throughout his speech; on this see Vagnone (2003a) at 76, 91, 93, 96.

[60] See the insightful discussion of Gangloff (2006a), 88–97, comparing the framing of the *Trojan* with that of the 'myths' in the *First Kingship Oration* (*Or.* 1), *Charidemus* (30), the *Alexandrian Oration* (32), and the *Borysthenitic Oration* (36), and the more general remarks of Gangloff (2007).

[61] See Moles (1995), 100–2; Swain (1996), 83–5; and especially Porter (2001), 85–90.

further by the obvious intertextual allusions to the Homeric revisionist tradition. On the one hand, the priest repeats many of Dio's complaints from the prologue: the Greeks have been "persuaded and deceived" by Homer and thus "consider as true (ἀληθῆ νομίζουσι) whatever they hear someone saying pleasingly (ἡδέως)" (42). He also seems suspiciously well versed in Greek tradition; one of his arguments notes the unresolved contradiction in the Greek belief in both Homer's account *and* that of Stesichorus' *Palinode*, which claimed that Helen had never left Sparta (not to mention other versions in which Paris takes Helen to Egypt). The priest's story will not agree with either poet, but his mention of Stesichorus is surely no accident; it inscribes the new 'truth' into the venerable tradition of Homeric historical revisionism by referencing its 'founding father.'[62]

It would also hardly escape a learned listener that Dio's tale of his encounter with an Egyptian priest, who ridicules Greek ignorance and provides the true story of the Trojan War, is an unmistakable allusion to Herodotus' excursus on Helen in Egypt. Herodotus, too, had appealed to Egyptian priestly records to authorize his new version of the Trojan War story and judged it favorably in contrast to Homer's account. The original source of those records was Menelaus; in Dio, the priest mentions that "Menelaus had come to visit them and told them everything just as it had happened (διηγήσασθαι ἅπαντα ὡς ἐγένετο: 38)." Moreover, the idea of rewriting Trojan history from new 'sources' had been taken up in the Hellenistic period by the mythographer Dionysius Scytobrachion[63] and the historian Hegesianax of Alexandria Troas, who circulated his *Troica* under the pseudonym of Cephalon of Gergis.[64] Similar examples of citing non-existent works and forging ancient documents are, of course, rife in the Imperial period,[65] and I will treat those more fully in the chapters to come, but for now it is enough to note that from a fairly early point, appeals to such kinds of evidence raised rather than answered questions of authenticity. To posit these kind of sources was akin to declaring the fictionality of one's work, and it is safe to say that by the time Dio offered his own variant of this topos in the *Trojan Oration*, a claim of access to

---

[62] Cf. the interesting reading of Wright (2005), 96–9.

[63] Dionysius' 'source' was the so-called *Phrygian Poem* of Thymoetes, a grandson of Priam's father Laomedon. See Rusten (1980).

[64] Or perhaps 'Cephalion of Gergitha,' depending on the source (*FGrH* 45 T 7). The surviving fragments of Hegesianax's *Troica* (F 1–10) concern pre- and post-Homeric events (Dardanus, Paris and Oenone, Aeneas' travels) and there is thus no indication that Hegesianax used 'Cephalon' to contradict Homer's account. Many scholars seem convinced that Cephalon was conceived of as, if not a participant in the war, at least contemporary with it, but I cannot see any evidence of this in the fragments or testimonia.

[65] Speyer (1970); Hansen (2003); and Ní Mheallaigh (2008).

Egyptian records could hardly be taken as anything other than a winking nod to Herodotus and the 'discovered source' tradition.[66]

In fact, other aspects of Dio's story of his encounter seem to undermine, rather than vouch for the authority and authenticity of his account. Consider the priest's curious description of the transmission of Egyptian records:

[The priest] said that all previous history had been recorded among the Egyptians, some in the temples, some on certain pillars, and that some of these were remembered only by a few, since the pillars had been destroyed, while many of the things that had been inscribed on the pillars were unknown due to the indifference and ignorance of those who came later. (38)

ἔφη δὲ πᾶσαν τὴν πρότερον ἱστορίαν γεγράφθαι παρ᾽ αὐτοῖς, τὴν μὲν ἐν τοῖς ἱεροῖς, τὴν δ᾽ ἐν στήλαις τισί, τὰ δὲ μνημονεύεσθαι μόνον ὑπ᾽ ὀλίγων, τῶν στηλῶν διαφθαρεισῶν, πολλὰ δὲ καὶ ἀγνοεῖσθαι τῶν ἐν ταῖς στήλαις γεγραμμένων διὰ τὴν ἀμαθίαν τε καὶ ἀμέλειαν τῶν ἐπιγιγνομένων.

The idea that written records extending much farther back than Greek memory existed, stored in Egyptian temples, points to the influence of the story of Atlantis told in Plato's *Timaeus* (20d–26a) and *Critias*.[67] According to Critias, Solon had learned the tale from Egyptian priests at Saïs who told him that all notable events that have ever happened "have been inscribed and preserved from antiquity here in the temples" (πάντα γεγραμμένα ἐκ παλαιοῦ τῇδ᾽ ἐστὶν ἐν τοῖς ἱεροῖς καὶ σεσωσμένα: 23a4–5). Other similarities to Dio's tale are evident: the Saite priests also ridicule the Greeks as young and ignorant, and Plato continually emphasizes the truth of the ancient narrative: e.g., Critias begins by declaring that the story is "completely true" (παντάπασί γε μὴν ἀληθοῦς: 20d8) while Socrates (ironically?) notes that "it is not an invented story but a true account" (τό τε μὴ πλασθέντα μῦθον ἀλλ᾽ ἀληθινὸν λόγον: 26e4–5). Dio's priest's explanation of the tenuous transmission of the information inscribed on the pillars[68] also roughly parallels the extraordinary lengths taken by Plato in the *Timaeus* to account for how Critias learned of a story no one had ever heard before. Apparently Solon told the story to Dropides, Critias'

---

[66] See Fuchs (1996), 134–5, on Dio's use of the Egyptian priest as a signal of the fictionality of his account.

[67] First noted, I believe, by Lemarchand (1926), 35; see Saïd (2000), 176–7.

[68] Dio's inscribed pillars recall the "golden pillar" (στήλην . . . χρυσῆν) that Euhemerus of Messene (third century BCE) claims to have found in a temple of Zeus on the island of Panchaea, on which the deeds of Uranus, Cronus, and Zeus "had been inscribed in Panchaean letters (γεγραμμένας . . . τοῖς Παγχαίοις γράμμασιν: Diod. Sic. 6.1.1).

great-grandfather, who told it to Critias' grandfather, who in turn told it, when he was ninety, to the ten-year-old Critias; the detailed circumstances of Critias' hearing of the story for the first time are also set out at length, as are the efforts he undertook to remember the story at the present moment, many years later.[69]

But while Critias' ostensible purpose in specifying each step of transmission and remembrance is to engender credibility in his narrative (even if it sometimes has precisely the opposite effect), in Dio, the priest's comments on the destruction of the pillars and the inability to read the inscriptions seem intended to cast doubt on the authenticity of the Egyptian account. In fact, far from owing their survival to the permanence of writing, the Egyptian records are "remembered" and thus passed down orally, a process which seems suspiciously similar to the process disparaged by Dio in the opening of the speech, whereby *doxa* is repeated by generation after generation among the Greeks. It seems as if Dio has gone out of his way to remind his audience of the precarious 'authority' on which his *own* account rests, and thus to destabilize the contrast he had just established between Homer's old lie and his new truth.

REFUTING HOMER: CREDIBILITY AND HOMERIC PROBLEMS

Dio's story about the Egyptian priest stands at the conclusion of the 'destructive' first part of the *Trojan* (1–42), in which he attacks Homer as a liar, and introduces the longer 'constructive' portion (43–154), which is ostensibly a record of Dio's conversation with the priest, although as I pointed out above, the dialogue gradually reverts to a Dionian monologue by the end of the oration. The two (unequal) halves of the speech are closely connected in that Dio's critique of Homer as an oral improvisatory performer in the first part plays an essential role in the second, where he presents the new, true story of the war. Dio as we recall, has promised to "refute Homer from his own poetry," and it turns out that his model of Homeric composition will allow him to simultaneously reject the traditional version and discover traces of his new 'true' account in the Homeric text.

[69] Moreover, in the *Critias*, there appears a seemingly contradictory anecdote about Critias' possession of Solon's original manuscripts, which Critias had studied in his youth (113a–b). As this example illustrates, the 'discovery' of ancient sources for previously unknown narratives of the mythic and heroic eras has a long history – we might also think of the inscribed bronze tablets allegedly unearthed by the fifth-century BCE mythographer Acusilaus of Argos from his father's yard (*FGrH* 2 T 1).

To accomplish this, Dio eschews a continuous exposition of the true story in favor of an alternating series of narrative and argumentative passages. He informs his audience that his own interventions will be supplementary – "I will therefore try to repeat what I heard from [the priest], adding the reasons for which the things he told me seem to me to have been true" (προστιθεὶς ἐξ ὧν ἐδόκει μοι ἀληθῆ τὰ λεγόμενα: 43) – although in the beginning it is often the priest himself who pauses to point out the implausibility of the Homeric version.[70] These periodic interruptions, arguing for the likelihood of the Egyptian narrative by impugning that of the Homeric one, permit us to examine how the process of criticizing Homer is intimately connected with imagining an alternative. In keeping with Dio's criticisms of Homer's decision to start *in medias res*, the priest follows the more 'natural' procedure and begins at the beginning; the opening section (43–78) takes us through the events leading up to the Greek forces' arrival at Troy and is followed by the part of the war covered by the *Iliad* (79–110), and an account of the final year of the war (111–24). After a brief pause (125–9) in which he recapitulates the improbabilites of the Homeric version, Dio concludes by summarizing the post-war period: the fleeing of the Greeks back home and the triumphant colonizing missions sent out by Troy (130–44).

This stretch of the speech is extremely long, and it is easy to lose track of Dio's 'true' story in the relentless barrage of criticisms and corrections of Homer. I devote the next two sections of this chapter to examining the technique Dio employs to recover this true story of the Trojan War by a careful reading of Homer's poetry. I first focus on Dio's treatment of the causes of the war, showing how he uses the skills honed in rhetorical exercises not only to refute the version adopted by Homer, but to offer a 'true' story that does so in the most elegant and economical manner possible. Part of this process involves reading Homer's text as the transcript of an improvisational narrative, and in the following section I analyze in some detail how Dio adapts this method to incorporate and 'explain away' a slew of well-known Homeric problems when he turns to the events related in the *Iliad*. Dio's recovery of 'what really happened' advertises its debts to Herodotus' famous alternative history of Helen while going far beyond it; Dio takes Herodotus' claim that Homer leaves 'hints' of the truth in his 'false' narrative and transforms it into an ingenious method of extracting the true story from the false account of a slippery, deceitful liar.

---

70 As I mention below in n. 83, apart from my summary of 43–70, I refer to Dio throughout as the architect of the argument.

The marriage of Paris and Helen

Dio's treatment of the alleged cause of the Trojan War, Paris' abduction of Helen, is a good example of his revisionist methods, particularly his use of Homer's 'mistakes' to support the 'true' story that Dio reveals. The beginning of the priest's account holds, more or less, to the version familiar to Greek tradition. Tyndareus, the king of Sparta, had four children – Clytemnestra, Helen, Castor, and Polydeuces. Helen, widely famed for her beauty, was kidnapped while still a girl by Theseus, the king of Athens. Her brothers immediately went after her, sacked Athens, and recovered Helen, keeping Theseus' mother Aethra as punishment for the crime (44). Later, Agamemnon, the ruler of Argos, married Clytemnestra in order to cement an alliance with Sparta (46).

At this point, the changes begin. Agamemnon wanted his brother Menelaus to marry Helen, but this suit was contested by other Greeks as well as foreigners. Among these was Paris, who impressed Tyndareus and his family with his wealth, beauty, and the power of his father, among other things (48–50). Against the objections of Agamemnon, Tyndareus accepted Paris' offer, and so "After winning over her parents and brothers, Paris took Helen lawfully and led her home with pride and joy" (53). Agamemnon, however, saw this new Trojan-Spartan alliance as a threat and stirred up the animosity toward Paris which lingered among the other Greek suitors, who, spurred on by this newfound hatred (and also by their hope of plunder), sent an embassy to Troy to demand the return of Helen while they amassed their forces (62–3). The Trojans, on the other hand, expressed outrage at this clear breach of contract, and, suspecting correctly that the charge was simply a pretext for war, prepared for the coming attack (64–6).

The psychological and naturalistic realism of this lengthy revisionist account (from which I have omitted much of the detail) is reminiscent of the Persians' revisionist story of Helen's seizure in Herodotus 1.1–5, Thucydides' reworking of Trojan and Greek motivations in his *Archaeology*, and other 'rationalizing' attempts to bring the legendary tradition back into the fold of credibility. Here the priest juxtaposes the verisimilitude of his account to the absurdities of the traditional version in several long digressions (54–61, 65–70). For instance, the priest asks Dio to "consider the silliness (τὴν εὐήθειαν) of the opposite version; does it seem possible (δυνατόν) to you that someone fell in love with a woman he had never seen? . . . To account for this absurdity (τὴν ἀλογίαν) they made up that myth (συνέπλασαν τόν . . . μῦθον) about Aphrodite, which is even more nonsensical (ἀποπληκτότερον: 54)." This emphasis on

verisimilitude dominates Dio's critique of Homer, which is filled with
the type of petty insistence on continuity and consistency that characterize
the concerns found in the Homeric scholia. But Dio seems here to be
reveling in the inconsistencies of the mythic tradition and taking the practice to ludicrous extremes. A harbinger of this occurs back in paragraphs
11–14, when Dio holds up the Judgement of Paris (an non-Homeric story,
it should be pointed out) to standards of verisimilitude in a manner that
looks forward to Lucian's practice in his *Dialogues of the Gods*: why would
Hera have even entered a beauty contest with Aphrodite? Why did they
value the opinion of a shepherd from Ida? Why after having entrusted the
decision to Paris was Hera so angry at the decision?

In a similar way, the priest demonstrates that his account is "much more
believable" (πολύ . . . πιστότερον: 68) by summarizing the traditional version and comically emphasizing its implausibilities:

[It is not credible] . . . that Paris fell in love with a woman he didn't know and
that his father allowed him to sail on such an enterprise, even though, according
to the story, Troy had recently been taken by the Greeks and Priam's father,
Laomedon, slain; and that afterwards in spite of the war and their countless
hardships the Trojans refused to surrender Helen either when Paris was living or
after he died, although they had no hope for safety, that Helen gave her affection to
a stranger with whom she had probably never come in contact at all and shamefully
abandoned her fatherland, relatives, and husband to come to a people who hated
her, that no one should have nipped all these doings in the bud, or sought to
catch her while she was hurrying to the sea, and on foot too, or pursued after she
had embarked, and that the mother of Theseus, an old lady, who certainly hated
Helen, should have accompanied her on the journey. (68–9)

The incessant insistence on probability on display here recalls both the
eikos-arguments of the historians, like Herodotus, Thucydides, and their
descendants, but also the literary-critical dictates of Aristotle's *Poetics* and
the carping complaints concerning Homeric poetry's lack of verisimilitude attributed to anti-Homeric critics like the notorious Zoïlus of
Amphipolis.[71] "None of these things," the priest concludes in an Aristotelian vein, "are probable or even possible" (τούτων οὐθὲν εἰκὸς οὐδὲ
δυνατόν: 70).[72]

---

[71] Billault (2006), 7–8, on the frequent use of εἰκός in this section of Dio's text. On Zoïlus, nicknamed *Homeromastix*, or, the "scourge of Homer" (*FGrH* 71), see Gärtner (1978).
[72] These are most likely the priest's words, not Dio's. See Vagnone (2003b), 139–40. For some remarks on Dio's use of 'probable' vocabulary (τὸ εἰκός, τὸ πιθανόν) see Ritoók (1995), although he overemphasizes the debt to Aristotle. Cf. Montgomery (1902), 405, who considers the whole *Trojan* as an "application of Aristotle's theory of τὸ εἰκός and τὸ ἀναγκαῖον as laid down in *Rhetoric* 1.2.14–15."

Refutation and Homer: Or. 60 Nessus

Dio's procedure in these interludes, in which the illogicalities of the Homeric account are specified point by point in order to call its credibility into question, bears a striking resemblance to the rhetorical exercise of ἀνασκευή, or refutation. This was defined as "an overturning of a given event" (ἀνατροπὴ τοῦ προτεθέντος πράγματος) and was accomplished by arguing from the narrative's unclarity (ἐκ τοῦ ἀσαφοῦς), implausibility (ἐκ τοῦ ἀπιθάνου), impossibility (ἐκ τοῦ ἀδυνάτου), inconsistency (ἐκ τοῦ ἀνακολούθου), and inappropriateness (ἐκ τοῦ ἀπρεποῦς).[73] The similarity has often been remarked upon; the *Trojan* is "the ultimate extravagance of *anaskeuê*," in the words of one scholar,[74] and Eustathius had already described the oration in these terms in the twelfth century: "It is clear that the Ilians boasted that their city had not been completely destroyed; from this Dio strove to *refute* [the standard view of] Trojan events" (ὅθεν καὶ ὁ Δίων ἐπηγωνίσατο ἀνασκευάσαι τὰ Τρωικά).[75] The subtitle of the *Trojan Oration*, "That Troy was not conquered" (ὑπὲρ τοῦ Ἴλιον μὴ ἁλῶναι), even sounds like the title of a refutation, and stories of the heroic age were particularly well suited as subjects which were required to be "open to argument on either side" and not "completely false (πάνυ ψευδῆ) like myths" [Hermog.] *Prog.* 5 Rabe (9 Spengel).

The question of whether the *Trojan* is or is not a 'refutation' in the official sense of the term seems beside the point, important only to those still arguing for the speech's sophistic leanings. The refutation, after all, was one of the *progymnasmata*, preliminary exercises designed to teach budding orators how to compose speeches, and none of our surviving examples are comparable, either in scope, size, or content with the *Trojan*.[76] Moreover,

---

[73] [Hermog.] *Prog.* 5 Rabe (11 Spengel). Cf. the definitions of *anaskeuê* in Theon, *Prog.* 93–6 Spengel; Aphth. *Prog.* 10 Rabe; Nicol. *Prog.* 29–33 Felten. On these rhetorical exercises, or *progymnasmata*, see Bonner (1977), 250–76; Patillon and Bolognesi (1997), i–cxiv; and Webb (2001); translations in Kennedy (2003).

[74] Anderson (1993), 50. Cf. Jones (1978), 17, and Jouan (2002), 409–10. Kroll (1915) first proposed the parallel; Mesk (1920–1) made a more thorough comparison. del Cerro Calderón (1997) and Bolonyai (2001) do not add a great deal to the discussion.

[75] Eust. *Il.* 460, 7 (1.727.11 van der Valk). Desideri (1978), 519–20 n. 46, and others take this passage as an indication that the *Trojan* was responding to existing revisionist thought about the outcome of the war among the Ilians themselves. Szarmach (1978), 197–8, believes, however, that Eustathius simply inferred this fact from the *Trojan* itself.

[76] Kindstrand (1973), 154–5, argues that the terms for which Mesk had so painstakingly found parallels were just as common in the Homeric scholia, and not necessarily integrally connected to the refutation. He also insists that the *Trojan* is not simply reducible to a school exercise, a point that Szarmach (1978), 198–9 elaborates by showing how in other speeches Dio characteristically takes the exercises as a rough starting point and guide and then moves from that foundation to a much more complex and expansive whole. Cf. Desideri (1978), 518–20 n. 46.

as Kindstrand has noted, it is hard to differentiate rhetorical refutations of Homeric subjects from scholarly criticisms of Homer since refutations often are nothing more than a catalog of the problems or censures familiar from the Homeric scholia, cast in expanded and stylistically developed form. As I have already suggested, the list of criteria on the basis of which one could argue for or against a narrative's truth is remarkably parallel with those used in the scholia and Homeric problem-literature to attack and defend Homer. The series of terms enumerated above as refutation criteria recalls, for instance, the five types of 'censures' (τὰ ἐπιτιμήματα) Aristotle lists in *Poetics* 25 – "impossible, irrational, harmful, contradictory, or against the correctness of the art" (ἢ γὰρ ὡς ἀδύνατα ἢ ὡς ἄλογα ἢ ὡς βλαβερὰ ἢ ὡς ὑπεναντία ἢ ὡς παρὰ τὴν ὀρθότητα τὴν κατὰ τέχνην: 1461b22–4). It is obvious that the two discourses are closely linked, and this was perhaps inevitable, given the fact that the scholia themselves, particularly those represented by bT, overwhelmingly view Homer through the terminology and concepts of rhetorical theory.[77]

A more useful way to consider the matter is to examine how Dio adapts the basic principles of the refutation in his individual attacks on Homeric episodes, such as the one under consideration here. Dio is not simply refuting the traditional story; he uses this refutation to justify and create a more compelling alternative. Before turning back to Dio's revisionist tale of Paris and Helen, it will be instructive to take a look at Dio's procedure of constructive refutation at work in *Or. 60, Nessus, or, Deianeira*.[78] There, he similarly examines a heroic myth according to probabilistic criteria – "if we consider how the affair happened and how it was *likely* to have happened" (ἄνπερ λογιζώμεθα ὡς ἐγένετο καὶ εἰκὸς ἦν γενέσθαι τὸ πρᾶγμα: 3) – and criticizes the traditional version of events – "does it seem plausible (πιθανόν) to you that the centaur would try to rape Deianeira while Heracles was watching, armed with a bow?" (3).[79] Like the composers of refutations, Dio points out problems with the story, relying on concepts

[77] For a succinct account of the bT scholia's 'rhetorical' approach to Homer, see Schmidt (2002); cf. Meijering (1987), 223–5. As to the subject matter of confirmations and refutations, Theon's examples (Medea's murder of her children, the crimes of the lesser Ajax: *Prog.* 94–5 Spengel) and the model exercises of the fourth-century CE orator Libanius (on which see Gibson (2009)), which focus on episodes from the Trojan War, are a better guide than the 'myths' involving divine or fantastic events refuted and confirmed in [Hermog.] *Prog.* 5 Rabe (9 Spengel) and Aphth. *Prog.* 10–16 Rabe. Such stories – Narcissus, Arion and the dolphin, Apollo and Daphne – seem easier to refute than confirm and do not conform to the requirement of being legitimately open to debate.

[78] On *Or. 60* see Höistad (1948), 54–6; Blomqvist (1989), 183–6; Desideri (1978), 491–3 (he notes its similarity with the *Trojan* at 432); Gangloff (2006a), 106–8.

[79] The dialogue is framed as Dio's attempt "to solve the *aporia*" (λῦσαι ταύτην τὴν ἀπορίαν: 1) of his student, who, knowing Dio well, pleads that he not simply proceed in his usual manner, paradoxically overturning *doxa*. Dio of course insists that if the interlocutor wants the correct reconstruction of events, it will necessarily be against popular opinion (2).

of psychological probability, likelihood, and narrative consistency. But to simply refute the traditional tale or even to substitute another in its place would not be as effective as showing how the story has been improperly read, and how it could be rendered more satisfactory.

In this case, Dio realizes that one simple alteration can cut the Gordian knot of interpretative difficulties: Nessus, rather than seizing Deianeira, was simply *talking* to her, advising, in his nefarious way, how she might best gain control over Heracles (4). Nessus urged her to soften Heracles' wild behavior and get him to spend more time at home, knowing that, "when Heracles changed his life and his behavior (ἄσκησις), he would be easy to handle and weak" (5). Heracles, suspecting Nessus was up to no good, killed him, but Deianeira took the centaur's words to heart (6). When Heracles' behavior grew more and more unacceptable (e.g., bringing home Iole from Oechalia), Deianeira put Nessus' plan into action and managed to get Heracles to exchange his lion's skin for regular clothing, and adopt a more sedentary and domestic lifestyle (8). Eventually, disgusted at the weakness and softness of his life and body, Heracles committed suicide by immolation.[80] "By Zeus," Dio's stunned interlocutor declares at the end of the tale, "your account does not seem bad at all, nor implausible" (οὐδαμῶς φαῦλος οὐδὲ ἀπίθανος: 9).

The student's astonishment is directed at how Dio's new version not only ends with a flourish, conveying a moralizing message dear to his Cynic heart, but also eliminates the problems and maintains plausibility.[81] By replacing the act of seizure with that of conversation, Dio can retain the basic form and elements of the rest of the narrative – Heracles' killing of Nessus, Deianeira's jealousy, Heracles' suicide – while eliminating everything suspicious about the story (note the elegance with which Dio turns the poisoned shirt into a metaphor for domestication). The story has not so much been refuted, or shown to be false, as it has been re-read and reconfigured by employing the principles and presuppositions of the ἀνασκευή.[82]

---

[80] Dio elsewhere (e.g., *Or.* 77/78.44) holds to the more traditional version of Heracles' death. On Dio's treatment of Heracles, a favorite of the Cynics, see Höistad (1948), 50–60.

[81] Desideri (1978), 493: "the type of moral teaching which this revision aims to provide . . . corresponds perfectly to the entire thematic of the Diogenic discourses [*Orr.* 8–10]: the exaltation of a life lived according to nature, and the denunciation of a life based on luxury and pleasures."

[82] This is, as Desideri (1978), ch. vii, has well argued, an essential aspect of Dio's reading of myths. The last paragraphs of *Nessus* amount to a methodological statement of this practice. The student judges Dio among those philosophers who "reveal any myth or story they get hold of, by dragging and fashioning it according to their own purpose, as useful and appropriate for philosophy" (ὁποῖον ἂν μῦθον ἢ λόγον ἕλκοντες καὶ πλάττοντες κατὰ τὴν αὐτῶν διάνοιαν ὠφέλιμον καὶ φιλοσοφίᾳ

Aethra, Helen, and the Dioscuri

In the *Trojan*, Dio proceeds in similar fashion on more complicated terrain, deploying similar principles, but drawing on Homeric and historiographical scholarship as well.[83] As I noted above, Homer's version is ridiculed for its multiple improbabilities, but as in *Nessus*, a single alteration brilliantly and economically explains away the difficulties. Dio's assertion that Paris *married* Helen rather than kidnapping her casts the whole story in a new light, making sense of what had seemed unlikely. To observe this process in more detail, let us look at one well-documented example of such a transformation. One of Dio's arguments runs: "how likely (εἰκός) was it . . . that Aethra, Theseus' mother and a prisoner, would sail away with Helen?" (59). Dio refers here to *Iliad* 3.144, where one of Helen's maidservants is called "Aethra, the daughter of Pittheus," a name and patronymic identical to that of Theseus' mother. The coincidence was puzzling to the scholiasts as well. "If he is speaking of Theseus' mother then this must be athetized (ἀθετητέον), for it is implausible (ἀπίθανον) that a servant of Helen was such an old woman."[84] But for others, Homer's identification was correct, and constituted indirect evidence that the poet knew of the tradition of Helen's kidnapping by Theseus. Aethra was captured by the Dioscuri when they rescued Helen, and became her servant, accompanying her new mistress to Troy.[85]

As we have seen, Dio's version agrees with this interpretation, detailing the Dioscuri's campaign against Theseus and their concomitant capture of Aethra. In his reference to Aethra as Helen's servant, Dio thus relies on a fact gleaned from Homeric poetry. He then uses this fact to cast doubt on a central pillar of Homer's story, Paris' rape of Helen, pointing to the

---

πρέποντα ἀπέδειξαν: 9). Note, however, that while Dio expresses these sentiments in regard to myth criticism, he never applies such drastic measures to Homer.

[83] From this point on, I will dispense with references to the priest and assume that all of the argumentation and content are Dio's. As I mention above in n. 59, there is no clear indication after paragraph 68 of whether the speaker is the priest or Dio.

[84] Sch. A ad *Il.* 3.144. It continues: ἦν οὐκ ἐκποιεῖ ζῆν διὰ τὸ μῆκος τοῦ χρόνου. The rather unsatisfactory answer in the scholia relies on homonymy: this Aethra, daughter of Pittheus, is not the mother of Theseus, but should be identified as some other Aethra, daughter of some other Pittheus. Cf. Eust. *Il.* ad 3.144: "But if it is a homonymy (ὁμωνυμία), just as in many other places, it can remain (δύναται μένειν); for there are some other homonyms (ὁμώνυμοί) in the *Iliad*." Normally homonymys involve only a single name, e.g., the two different men named Adrastus at *Il.* 2.572 and 2.830. An example of how homonymy could be used in conjunction with rationalizing myth-criticism can be found in Plut. *Thes.* 31: Theseus and Pirithous travel to the land of "Aidoneus, the king of the Molossians, who called his wife Phersephone, his daughter Core, and his dog Cerberus."

[85] Plut. *Thes.* 34.

unlikelihood that "the mother of Theseus, an old lady, who certainly hated Helen, would have accompanied her on the journey" (69). Rather than conclude that Homer's story is completely false, Dio shows how Aethra's presence at Troy is no longer a problem when seen in the light of his new version of events, and in fact offers it incidental support.[86] "For it was reasonable (εὔλογον) that Aethra had come with Helen... this is not evidence (σημεῖον) of a rape, but rather of a marriage" (61). Once we accept Dio's claim that Paris and Helen were legitimately married, details of Homer's 'false' account that had seemed puzzling and problematic become smoothly reintegrated as 'true' components of Dio's new narrative.

The best example of Dio's technique of using Homer as a witness against himself occurs in his treatment of Helen's brothers, Castor and Polydeuces (70–2). Their absence from the Trojan campaign is one of the well-known oddities of the Homeric account, given their close relationship with Helen as well as their famed martial skills. The only time they are mentioned in the *Iliad* is in a passage from the *teichoskopia* episode in Book 3, when Helen, at Priam's request, is identifying the Greek heroes to the king. As she is doing this, she wonders aloud about her siblings: "yet nowhere can I see those two" (*Il.* 3.236) and seems genuinely puzzled as to where they might be. Homer informs the reader, however, that in actuality "the teeming earth lay already upon them ‖ away in Lakedaimon" (*Il.* 3.243–4).

Two elements of this passage struck commentators as "implausible" (ἀπίθανον) or "irrational" (ἄλογον) (aside from Priam's inability to recognize the Greek heroes after nine years).[87] First, how could Helen not have known anything about her brothers' whereabouts? Second, why did it suddenly pop into her head at that moment to wonder about them, as if it hadn't occurred to her before? To these, Dio adds that an acceptance of Homer's explanation breeds more inconsistencies. Even if the Dioscuri were dead, Helen's ignorance of that fact means that her brothers were still alive when she left Troy; "so why did they wait ten years for Agamemnon as he spent time gathering an army, rather than immediately pursue their

---

[86] In contrast, Dio's use of *Il.* 5.640–2 on Heracles' sack of Troy under Laomedon (56–8) is more straightforward; he simply points to its implausibilities in order to emphasize how Homer says nothing true. Cf. Str. 13.1.32: "And it appears that the poet, in what he says about Heracles, represents the city as small, if it is true that 'with only six ships and fewer men he sacked the city of Ilium' (*Il.* 5.641)."

[87] The problem was an old one; Aristotle tried his hand at solving it (F 147 Rose [371 Gigon]) and Heraclides Ponticus' solution also survives (the Greeks were scattered for years in small battles, so no one noticed: F 172 Wehrli). Porphyry has recourse to the Aristotelian ethnographic ἔτι καὶ νῦν argument: "still even now" barbarians are loathe to deliver bad news to their rulers. Cf. Zenodotus' suggestion that the Dioscuri had been left behind in Greece as "administrators": διοικηταί (Sch. T ad *Il.* 3.236; Eust. *Il.* 1.645 van der Valk).

sister?" (71). That, after all, is what they did when Helen was stolen by Theseus.[88] For Dio of course, the solution is right at hand; what better reason for their absence than that they did not actually go on the expedition? If Helen and Paris were married with their blessing, the brothers obviously would not have supported a military mission against their new in-laws. Thus Dio again deploys Homer against Homer; a fact derived from a Homeric line – the Dioscuri's absence from Troy – becomes evidence of the improbability of Homer's account. When inserted into Dio's alternative narrative, the improbability disappears, and thus functions as another bit of supporting evidence for the 'truth' of Dio's account.

This time, however, Dio adds a further bit of ingenuity. Even if we accept Dio's explanation for the Dioscuri's absence, the problem of Helen's ignorance of their whereabouts remains. Dio could and does point to this as a Homeric lie, but he also explains how the lie came about, attributing it to Homer's poor skill at extemporaneous narration: "Homer, concealing this error (ταύτην δὲ τὴν ἄγνοιαν κρύπτων Ὅμηρος),[89] has represented Helen as surprised (πεποίηκε θαυμάζουσαν τὴν Ἑλένην); then he defends himself (ἀπελογήσατο), saying that [the Dioscuri] had died earlier" (71).[90] Dio reads the lines in Homer as if they were a virtual transcript of Homer's orally performed narrative; Helen's surprise mirrors the poet's own realization at this point in his own 'lying' tale that the Dioscuri's absence from the campaign cannot be readily explained. Homer's authorial intrusion informing the audience of the Dioscuri's death is read as a hasty and belated attempt to patch over the inconsistency, a mistake stemming from the necessities of the moment.[91]

Paradoxically, the egregiousness of Homer's error, his virtual advertising of his inability to create a smooth, probable narrative, is yet one more proof of Dio's version of the truth. The narrative 'blushes,' the clumsy attempts to patch up errors that slip out, are hints embedded in the narrative that Homer was lying, but they also allow Dio to pinpoint the specific lies,

---

[88] In fact, Dio muses, the same could be said for Helen's father, Tyndareus, who would have been likely (εἰκός: 72) to have come on the campaign if his own daughter had been stolen from Sparta.

[89] I follow Vagnone (2003a), who retains the manuscript's ἄγνοιαν (von Arnim (1893) prints Emperius' conjecture ἀλογίαν). There is little difference in meaning; Vagnone (2003b), 140, follows Giangrande (2000), 250, in pointing out that here ἄγνοια means, not 'ignorance' but 'mistake.'

[90] The scholia, on the other hand, *praise* Homer for this device: "the poet clearly sets it up beforehand, wishing to speak of their absence" (δῆλον οὖν ὅτι προοικονομεῖ ὁ ποιητής, βουλόμενος εἰπεῖν τὴν ἀφάνειαν αὐτῶν: Sch. bT ad *Il.* 3.236a).

[91] Dio has (inadvertently?) perverted Aristotle's praise of Homer's ability to eliminate problems with his poetic qualities (τοῖς ἄλλοις ἀγαθοῖς ὁ ποιητὴς ἀφανίζει ἡδύνων τὸ ἄτοπον: *Poet.* 24.1460b1–2). Valgimigli (1912), 42, sees a parallel between Dio's strategy and Aristotle's remarks at *Poet.* 24.1460a20–7 on Homer's teaching other poets the correct way to lie.

and to show how his new revisionist history 'solves' the problems that
Homer's ineptitude created, restoring the seamlessness and plausibility
of the narrative. This sort of interpretation is what gives the Trojan its
originality, its audacity, and much of its humor. Dio's revelation that Paris
and Helen were legitimately married is not only an original riff on the
old question of the cause of the Trojan War, but its ingenuity stems from
Dio's demonstration that many of the 'problems' with the episode fall away
once it is accepted. On his model of Homer as extemporaneous liar, the
'problems' can be read as *failures* on Homer's part to properly synchronize
his lie – that Paris stole Helen – with the reality of events. In other words
the passages that fit poorly into Homer's narrative are problematic precisely
because they are *true* (according to Dio's version). That Dio can actually
point to a section of Homer's poetry where the shoddy improvisation has
left its mark, where he lets the truth slip out by accident and then clumsily
patches it up, is another testament to the care with which he makes his case.

SIGNS OF THE TRUTH: DIO ON THE *ILIAD*

Dio's treatment of the pre-Iliadic Trojan War narrative is radically revisionist – by claiming that Paris married Helen legitimately, it eliminates the
alleged justification for Greek aggression, and squarely lays the blame for
the war onto the Greeks. Despite this major alteration, the so-called new
version agrees substantially in other respects with the traditional account.
In fact, as we have just seen, Dio goes so far as to use evidence from
Homer's narrative in support of his own version. Homeric details such as
the Trojan's refusal to surrender Helen, the presence of Aethra at Troy as
Helen's servant, and the Dioscuri's absence from Troy are treated as true
elements of a fundamentally false story. Their truth, paradoxically, arises
from their incongruity with the main stream of Homer's narrative, which
Dio has asserted is a lie.

Dio's new vision of Helen and the causes of the Trojan War is quite
original – his Helen goes to Troy but the trip is fully justified, the Greeks
attack Troy on account of her, but are in the wrong – but its hetero-
doxy sets it in a long tradition, linked to Gorgias' and Isocrates' *Helen*,
which deflected culpability away from Helen, or to Stesichorus' *Palinode*,
Herodotus' *Histories*, and Euripides' *Helen*, which offered a radical departure from Homer's story by contending that Helen never went to Troy at
all.[92] Of these, however, Dio's debt to Herodotus is the most considerable.

---

[92] On the tradition of Helen in Egypt, see Austin (1994).

The similarity lies not only in their Trojan sympathies, nor that both Dio and Herodotus attribute their revisionist accounts to Egyptian priests, who are themselves dependent on records dating back to Menelaus' visit.[93] Rather, Dio's method of reading is strikingly parallel *mutatis mutandis* to that employed by Herodotus and could be read as a parody of or homage to its principles. The Egyptian priests whom Herodotus interviewed insisted that Paris had never brought Helen to Troy, since she had been rescued by the Egyptian king during a layover in that country and remained there until the war was over. For Herodotus, this story seemed convincing because its adoption explained away a serious implausibility in Homer's account: the Trojan unwillingness, even with their losses mounting, to return Helen to the Greeks and bring an end to hostilities. Homer, in Herodotus' view, knew the truth, but told the false version because he thought it more fitting for epic poetry. What is so interesting about this last assertion is that Herodotus assumes a priori that Homer was aware of the real story (no explanation is given as to how the poet might have learned it) and then goes to some length to prove that he could find traces of that true story hidden in Homer's poetry.

Dio too, despite asserting that Homer was *not* an eyewitness, or even a contemporary of the Trojan War, takes it for granted that Homer knew what actually happened, but consciously chose to ignore or distort it. Herodotus' insistence on Homer's knowledge of the Egyptian account is understandable to some degree, given his general view of the poet as an authoritative source of Greek culture and tradition. But Dio's criticism of Homer's narrative practice and his attacks on Homer's credibility – his failure to list sources, his bias, his love of lying – as well as his general picture of the *Iliad* as the written record of an oral off-the-cuff performance, made up on the spot, marked by textual manifestations of the poet's continuous catering to the desires and reactions of his audience, hardly explains why such a person would ever have known the truth in the first place. Such an incongruity suggests that Dio was quite consciously adopting the 'Homer knows the truth' presumption common to both Herodotus and Thucydides, despite their criticisms of the poet's accuracy. Moreover, like Herodotus, and to a lesser extent Thucydides, Dio declares that he can find hints and traces of the truth embedded within Homer's verses. The example concerning Helen's wondering about her brothers showed how Dio could get at the truth by identifying problems arising from Homer's hasty and imperfect improvisation.

---

[93] See above, 108–12. On the *Trojan* and Herodotus, see Hunter (2009), 48–50.

The next sections (79–110) of the *Trojan Oration*, which treat episodes from the *Iliad*, shine an even brighter spotlight on this aspect of Dio's project. Here Dio transforms the lines of argumentation used to such effect in the critique of Homer's character (15–36) into presupposed modes of accounting for and extracting the truth from Homer's narrative performance in an exaggerated interpretive variant of the 'hinting Homer' discussed in the two previous chapters of this book. Dio offers a running point-by-point comparison of his version with the *Iliad*, constantly switching back and forth from a narration of his new 'true' episode to a demonstration of precisely *how* we can witness Homer maliciously distorting or reluctantly acknowledging this truth. The 'facts' cannot ever be entirely effaced; their traces, however faint, are visible to the careful observer, and properly read, allow that observer to recover the facts themselves. In this fashion, Dio's narrative, though diametrically opposed to Homer's, remains entirely parasitic upon it. His procedure allows us to see exactly how he imagines the relation between truth and lies in the *Iliad*, and how he is able to produce the true story from a hostile, deceptive witness.

After a brief section (74–8) on the first nine years of the War, which treats some episodes mentioned in passing by Homer, such as Protesilaus' death and burial, Achilles' killing of Troilus (78), and the building of the Achaean Wall (76),[94] Dio begins his analysis of the *Iliad*. Here the opening events of the *Iliad* – the plague among the Greek forces and the quarrel between Achilles and Agamemnon – are, far from being false, employed as evidence for Dio's new truth that the Trojans had been winning the war (79).[95] As a further piece of evidence, he points to the curious and disastrous 'test' of the Greek forces by Agamemnon in *Iliad* 2.1–210 – another favorite of the commentators – which revealed the widespread desire among the Greek troops to return home (80). Dio has not simply asserted that things were going badly for the Greeks, but inferred and supported it from the testimony of the very witness whose credibility he has recently condemned. This is possible because, as Dio claims, "until this point, Homer was clearly not disdainful (καταφρονῶν) of people, but held to the truth (ἔχεσθαι τἀληθοῦς) in some fashion, except for the events concerning the kidnapping [of Helen]" (81).

---

[94] On Dio's treatment of this notorious problem, see Caiazza (2001).

[95] "Since the Achaeans were faring badly in the war, and nothing was turning out as they had hoped ... disease and famine bore down upon them, and *stasis* was arising between their leaders – the sort of thing which usually happens to the unsuccessful side, not those who are winning" (79).

Dio's main point is to prove that Hector killed Achilles and that the Trojans defeated the Greeks; as part of his thesis he holds that the Trojans decisively took the upper hand in the fighting in the ninth year of the war, foreshadowing their eventual defeat of the Greeks. Homer roughly agrees with this, although he attributes the Trojans' gains to Achilles' withdrawal and Zeus' will and concludes his story rather differently. As a result of this confluence, Dio has to concede that Homer "speaks of true things (τἀληθῆ λέγει) – the defeat and rout of the Achaeans, the glorious deads of Hector, and the masses of the dead – just as he had promised (ὥσπερ ὑπέσχετο ἐρεῖν)" (83). I have already pointed out, in the arguments about Paris, Helen and the Dioscuri, Dio's tendency to retain much of the Homeric narrative, and moreover, to use his poetic statements as evidence of the truth, whether understood as slips of the tongue or inadvertent remarks. But here the practice seems particularly problematic. Given the fact that Homer is biased for the Greeks and against the Trojans, why would he portray the Trojans as having the upper hand (at least until Achilles' return to battle)? The problem for Dio then, is not, paradoxically, to counter Homer, but to explain why an egregious liar like the poet would have told the truth.

Irrepressible truth

In order to do so, Dio imagines a Homer not only in possession of the truth, but unable to keep it repressed within himself; despite his best efforts, the true story keeps leaking out, escaping his control. Dio repeatedly emphasizes this incontinence as the reason why Homer often tells the truth: "Homer agrees with" Agamemnon's 'testing' of the Greeks, despite its unflattering implications, "since he could not conceal the whole truth" (οὐδὲ γὰρ ἐδύνατο πάντα τἀληθῆ ἀποκρύψασθαι: 80). Similar phrasing recurs in the descriptions of the fighting in *Il.* 9–10; "Homer cannot conceal (ἀποκρύψαι: 84) Hector's deeds" as he conquers and pursues the enemy to their ships; "he does not want to speak of these things so vividly, but since they are true, he cannot stop himself once he has started" (ταῦτα γὰρ οὐ βουλόμενος εἰπεῖν οὕτως ἐναργῶς ὅμως ἐπεὶ ἀληθῆ ἦν, ἀρξάμενος αὐτῶν οὐ δύναται ἀποστῆναι: 85). The next day's events (from *Il.* 11 on) also find Homer overwhelmed by truth's compelling power – "he is clearly describing things that are true and that have happened, impelled forward by the events themselves" (καὶ ταῦτα μὲν λέγων δῆλός ἐστιν ὅτι ἀληθῆ λέγει καὶ τὰ γενόμενα ὑπ' αὐτῶν τῶν πραγμάτων προαγόμενος: 86).

Homer, despite his best intentions, is not able to "conceal" (ἀποκρύψαι) the truth, and once some of it makes its way to the surface, he is led forward by the inexorable pull of the facts. Dio's model of the *Iliad* as spontaneous narrative thus allows him to identify, not only the lies in the text, but the truth as well. For Dio, Homer knows what really happened, and since he is fashioning his story on the spot, it would naturally be easier to relate the truth than to fabricate. After all the truth, as every good critic and rhetorician knew, possesses a certain plausibility and consistency by virtue of its having actually occurred. As Strabo, reporting Polybius, puts it: "to tell idle fantasies without connecting them to anything true is not Homeric (ἐκ μηδενὸς δὲ ἀληθοῦς ἀνάπτειν κενὴν τερατολογίαν οὐχ Ὁμηρικόν). For it happens, as is likely, that someone would lie more plausibly if he were to mix in something of the truth itself" (ὡς πιθανώτερον ἂν οὕτω τις ψεύδοιτο, εἰ καταμίσγοι τι καὶ αὐτῶν τῶν ἀληθινῶν: 1.2.9 = Polyb. 34.2.1–3). In Dio's perverse adaptation of such truisms, even telling the truth is characteristic of a liar.

Another sign that these involuntarily uttered portions of Homer's narrative are 'true' is their *lack* of fantastic and improbable elements. In Dio's eyes, Homer's descriptions of Hector's activities – his defeat of various Greek warriors, his crossing of the trench, the siege of the naval station, the defeat of Ajax atop the wall, the firing of the ships – are noticeably bereft of the "incredible" (ἀπίθανον) because they are depicting "true events, similar to things that have actually happened" (πράγματα ἀληθῆ καὶ ὅμοια γεγονόσι: 90)." In contrast, when Homer describes the exploits of the Achaeans – Ajax's defeat of Hector, Diomedes of Aeneas – naturalism and sense seem to disappear; "it is clear to everyone that he is lying" (πᾶσι φανερὸς ὅτι ψεύδεται: 86). Because the Trojans had won all these combats in reality, Homer had no true Greek success stories at his disposal. Such tales of valor were, however, what his Greek audience wanted to hear, and he was thus forced to make them up on the spot. Aside from the aforementioned instances of Aphrodite's rescue of Aeneas and Diomedes' woundings of Ares and Aphrodite, Menelaus' victory over Paris is deemed "ridiculous" (νίκην γελοίαν: 82) and Ajax's duel with Hector declared "false" (ψευδής), especially "the silly ending" (πάνυ εὐήθης ἡ διάλυσις: 83) where they exchange gifts.[96] Dio concludes:

---

[96] It should come as no surprise that Dio has selected as indications of these lies episodes that were the basis of well-known Homeric 'problems.' For specific references to the scholia, see Montgomery (1902), 409–12, and the relevant notes of Vagnone (2003a).

In all these episodes he is clearly well disposed (εὔνους) to [the Achaeans] and eager to marvel at them (θαυμάζειν), but not having anything true (ἀληθές) to say, he falls into impossible (ἀδύνατα) and impious deeds through his *aporia* – something that all who contradict the truth (τῇ ἀληθείᾳ μάχονται) usually experience. (87)

Once again, Dio is comparing Homer's narrative practice with that of liars. In sections 15–36 he had concentrated on their propensity to mix up the order of events or to eschew responsibility for truth by attributing particularly incredible stories to other people. Here, Dio attributes the inclusion of such absurd episodes to Homer's deficiencies in improvisation. They result from Homer's *aporia* (πολλῆς ἀπορίας μεστός: 86; διὰ τὴν ἀπορίαν: 87), which itself arises from the confluence of a desire to praise with a lack of material. Conversely, when he is describing Hector's glorious deeds, "he is not at such a loss (οὐ . . . ἀπορεῖ) for something great and marvelous to say because, I believe, he is narrating what actually happened" (τὰ γενόμενα διηγούμενος: 88). As with all liars, the fabulous nature of certain descriptions functions as a sign of their author's *aporia*, and hence of their status as fabrications, while the consistency and plausibility of others guarantees their truth. We are back to the *virtutes narrationis* again, only this time the main concern is plausibility, πιθανότης; Dio reads any implausible episode or compositional flaw as a sign of the *aporia* that descends upon a liar when he is forced to fabricate on the spur of the moment. But of course, the episodes that Dio homes in on were precisely those that caused Homeric critics such consternation because of their fantastic or implausible nature: heroes wounding gods, goddesses whisking off heroes from battle, etc.

Homeric aporia: Dio on the death of Achilles

The centerpiece of Dio's argument concerns the 'true' story of Patroclus, Achilles, and Hector (93–110). Here the entire arsenal of demonstration is on display – a brilliant substitution that forces a radical reinterpretation of the episode, the identification of implausibilities and well-known problems as evidence of botched cover-up operations, Dio's insistent adherence to much of Homer's allegedly false narrative (attributed to Homer's inability to completely stifle the 'truth'), and the simultaneous refutation of Homer and use of his material as supporting testimony. Dio's pivotal contention is that it actually was Achilles, not Patroclus pretending to be Achilles, who was fighting in *Iliad* 13–17, and that hence it was also Achilles, rather than Patroclus, whom Hector killed. Dio's earlier changes to Homer's story were directed against the margins of the *Iliad*. His claim that Paris had married Helen corrected an incident that Homer had only mentioned indirectly (Paris' kidnapping of Helen) and that lay outside the chronological scope of his poem. Likewise, Dio's assertion that Homer had tried to disguise the fact that the Trojans had the upper hand in the ninth year of fighting only accuses the poet of some misdirection and prejudicial treatment. Even Dio's subsequent claim that Troy won the war deals with offstage, that is post-Iliadic, events, although it uses the *Odyssey* for much of its evidence. But to declare that Hector killed Achilles rather than the other way round is to attack the very heart of the *Iliad*. To go further and declare that one can prove this from the text itself . . . is, well, very Dionian.

Aware of the enormity of this correction, Dio nonchalantly attributes it to Homer's improvisational sensitivity to his audience; at this point, "Homer had no more concern for the truth but . . . simply overturned all the events and turned them to their opposite, having contempt for people because he saw how easily they believed everything else" (Ὅμηρος οὐδὲν ἔτι τἀληθοῦς ἐφρόντισεν, ἀλλ᾽ . . . πάντα τὰ πράγματα ἁπλῶς ἀνέτρεψε καὶ μετέστησεν εἰς τοὐναντίον, καταπεφρονηκὼς μὲν τῶν ἀνθρώπων, ὅτι καὶ τἆλλα ἑώρα πάνυ ῥᾳδίως πειθομένους αὐτούς: 92). This assertion of Homeric disdain for his audience is essential to Dio's vision of the latter part of the *Iliad*.

But in telling his story, Homer still mostly adhered to the truth, as all liars do. Dio explains that when Achilles had beaten back the Trojan forces (part of Hector's strategem of a planned retreat aimed at tiring Achilles), Hector engaged him in battle, slew him, and gained possession of his arms, "just as Homer has told it" (ὡς καὶ τοῦτο Ὅμηρος εἴρηκε: 96). After the two Ajaxes had dragged Achilles' body back to the ships, Hector put on Achilles' armor and pressed on in pursuit to the sea, "just as Homer admits" (ὡς ὁμολογεῖ ταῦτα Ὅμηρος: 97). In the *Iliad*, of course, Hector kills, not Achilles, but Patroclus in Achilles' armor. Dio first reads the poet's substitution of Patroclus for Achilles as a sign of Homer's inability to fabricate wholesale; because he "was not able to conceal the truth" (οὐκ ἔχων ὅπως κρύψῃ τἀληθές: 97), Homer described the episode largely as it happened, changing only the identity of the slain man in order to rob Hector of his glory. The absurdity of the Homeric version is then demonstrated at length by Dio, in another ἀνασκευή marshaling the familiar arguments from psychological and narrative probability. How could Achilles have sat idly by while Hector was firing the ships? How could he have let Patroclus, a hero much his inferior, go out in his stead? What sort of advice was it for the latter to avoid Hector, since "it wasn't up to Patroclus to choose the man with whom he would fight?" (98). All of these problems, however, disappear if we accept the more likely, and more economical, alternative: rather than imagine that someone else put on Achilles' armor, beat back the Trojans, and then was killed by Hector, isn't it easier to assume that Achilles himself did these things? Homer's story simply does not make sense; rather, as Dio asserts later, again in Aristotelian fashion: "what happened was something that could have happened" (ἀλλὰ τὸ γενόμενον δυνατὸν γενέσθαι: 139).

Instead, Homer decided simply to suppress Achilles' death at Hector's hands, and make the opposite statement, that Hector was killed by Achilles. The entire ending of the *Iliad*, which details this event and its aftermath, is, to Dio, a complete mess of improbabilities:

Finally, Homer brings out Achilles (who was already dead) and depicts him fighting. Since his arms were not there but in the possession of Hector (for this one true fact slipped by [Homer's] notice [ἕν τι τῶν ἀληθῶν ῥηθέν]), he says that Thetis brought the arms made by Hephaestus from heaven, letting Achilles in this way ridiculously (γελοίως) rout the Trojans single-handed, and ignoring all the other Achaeans as if no one else was there. And having dared to lie once about this, he distorts everything (ἅπαξ δὲ τολμήσας τοῦτο ψεύσασθαι πάντα συνέχεε). At this point he represents the gods fighting with one another, virtually acknowledging his utter disregard for the truth (σχεδὸν ὁμολογῶν ὅτι οὐδὲν αὐτῷ μέλει ἀληθείας). Moreover, he recounts Achilles' heroic deeds quite feebly and implausibly (πάνυ δὲ ἀσθενῶς καὶ ἀπιθάνως). At one point the hero is fighting with a river,[97] at another he is threatening Apollo and pursuing him – from all these things, one can see Homer's virtual *aporia* (ἀπορίαν). For he is not so implausible or unpleasant in the true episodes (οὐ γάρ ἐστιν ἐν τοῖς ἀληθέσιν οὕτως ἀπίθανος οὐδὲ ἀηδής). (106–7)

The scene where Achilles finally kills Hector is similarly ridiculed – Hector circles the city in flight when he could have entered it, Achilles is unable to catch him despite being the swiftest of men, all of the Achaeans are standing around as if watching a show, without helping, and Athena intervenes pretending to be Deïphobus. Homer, according to Dio, has completely abandoned any confluence with the truth at this point,[98] since, in focusing on Achilles, who was already dead, he had given up any pretence of maintaining plausibility. Everything else is told "ridiculously" (γελοίως), "feebly and implausibly" (ἀσθενῶς καὶ ἀπιθάνως), with "utter disregard for

---

[97] Achilles' battle with the river Scamander was a notorious problem in ancient criticism: Hellanicus of Lesbos (*FGrH* 4 F 28) had already rationalized it in the fifth century BCE; cf. Philostratus' treatment in *Heroicus* 48 (below Ch. 6: 203).

[98] Although there is one element of truth that has worked its way into this narrative – Achilles' lack of weapons and armor – since it has carried over from the Patroclus episode.

the truth" (οὐδὲν αὐτῷ μέλει ἀληθείας); full-scale invention and fantasy have taken its place, and the whole episode is evidence of the poet's *aporia*. After this, Homer had nowhere else to go, because he "could not bear (ὑπέμεινεν) to depict Achilles, who had died some time ago, being killed again, or the defeated and routed being victorious, or the city that had prevailed being sacked" (110).

When he reached this point, Homer gave up (εἰς τοῦτο δὲ προελθὼν ἀπεῖπε λοιπόν), not knowing how to continue his work and being dissatisfied with his lies (οὐκ ἔχων ὅ τι χρήσηται τῇ ποιήσει καὶ τοῖς ψεύσμασι δυσχεραίνων). (109)

As noted earlier, this strange stopping point raised Dio's suspicions of Homer's veracity – what of the death of Achilles, the capture of Troy, Memnon's arrival, the battle with the Amazons? But if the question of why the *Iliad* begins where it does, in the ninth year of the war, was answered with an eye to Homer's avoidance of his most egregious lies, that of the poem's ending is attributed simply to Homer's becoming entangled in his own web of lies, unable to keep his falsehoods consistent, and weary of constructing the completely false narrative now required.[99] The lie, which had started with the poet's attempt to excuse the Greeks' unjustified military aggression by assigning the blame to Paris, has now mushroomed to such an extent that Homer does not have the heart (or the skill?) to continue. Homer is not even a *good* liar.

Dio's innovation in the *Trojan Oration* lies in his decision to read Homer's text as the written transcription of an oral, improvisatory, testimonial narrative. By envisioning Homer in this way, he is able to make a series of equations between narrative decisions and the obfuscatory and deceptive practices of liars, exploiting and erasing the differences between poetic, literary storytelling, with its concern for entertainment and a straightforward rhetorical *narratio* presenting the facts of a case or a clear account of historical events.[100] In the process, he accounts for and solves some of the most puzzling inconsistencies and Homeric problems, and displays a deep and detailed knowledge of the poem's structure, biases, and compositional tendencies. Most importantly he is consistently entertaining and persuasive. This last point should be underlined, because whatever one might think

---

[99] Cf. Menecrates of Nysa (Sch. bT ad *Il.* 24.804), who said that "the poet was silent about the events after [the death of] Hector, because he perceived his weakness and his inability to adequately treat them" (αἰσθόμενον ἑαυτοῦ ἀσθενείας τὸν ποιητὴν καὶ τοῦ μὴ ὁμοίως δύνασθαι φράζειν σιωπῆσαι τὰ μεθ᾽ Ἕκτορα).

[100] Seeck (1990), 106, sees Dio's "insights into the difficult structural problems of the *Iliad*" as a highlight of the speech.

of Dio's level of seriousness in composing and delivering this speech, there can be no denying that his arguments demonstrate a keen understanding of Homer; indeed his method of inquiry is remarkably similar to much subsequent Homeric scholarship. Olivieri called Dio a Lachmann *avant la lettre*, and G. A. Seeck has pointed out how close Dio's methods (if not presuppositions) are to the Analysts of the nineteenth and early twentieth centuries.[101]

But Dio also shows his familiarity with the presumptions and tendencies of historical critics of Homer, and one can make out amidst the dense argumentation and rhetorical sleight of hand a sustained exploitation and parodic deformation of the image of Homer as dedicated historian seen in Strabo, the faith in Homer's knowledge of the truth that is a cornerstone of the tradition, and the claim that Homer 'hints' at the truth. In contrast, Dio's Homer only tells the truth involuntarily, or because he cannot invent quickly enough, is concerned to flatter his Greek audience, and is guilty of clumsy cover-ups of his errors. The way in which the improvisatory liar model so smoothly incorporates historiographical, rhetorical, and literary-critical critiques of Homeric accuracy and verisimilitude demonstrates that Dio is less interested in answering the question of whether Homer knew the truth than in illustrating its inherent unanswerability and engaging in an incisive play with the tradition of debating Homer's historical credentials.

THE DEFENSE OF HOMER

Dio's claims about Homer's character and improvisatory lies can also be viewed in light of the questions he raised at the outset of the *Trojan*: why do we believe Homer, and what is at stake in this belief? What is the nature of Homer's authority? Dio has proven that Homer had lied, and shown how the *Iliad* makes better sense when seen as an improvised attempt to tell a false story. But so far, there have only been hints as to *why* Homer lied; in particular Dio accuses him of wishing "to court the favor of (χαριζόμενος: 35) the Greeks and the sons of Atreus." Homer knew the 'truth' but was willfully misrepresenting, distorting, or omitting it in order to show the Greeks in the best possible light. The idea is a familiar one: Homer's philhellenic bias is frequently commented upon in the scholia,

---

[101] Olivieri (1898), 593: "The critical method continuously adopted by Dio . . . is that which Niebuhr and Schnegle initiated in the study of Roman history . . . at its base it is that which Lachmann and his followers introduced into Homeric studies." Cf. Desideri (1978), 502–3, on D'Aubignac's use of Dio in the seventeenth century.

although there it tends to be viewed positively.[102] But Dio's performance model allows him to situate Homer at a particular time and place, and hence to add a historicized and political element to the creation of the *Iliad* and the idea that the poet was "courting the favor" of the Greeks.

The kind of accusation of favoritism made by Dio against Homer was the primary method used by ancient historians to cast doubt on the reliability of their predecessors. This is why so many historians begin their works by trumpeting their lack of bias – *sine ira et studio* in Tacitus' famous formulation – which seems to have been considered sufficient to guarantee the truth of one's account.[103] In *How to Write History*, Lucian even illustrates the prevalence of this view with reference to Homer:

Some people today are inclined to believe Homer, although most of what he has written about Achilles smacks of myths, taking as great evidence for the demonstration of its truth only the fact that he did not write about a living person; for they cannot find any reason why he would have lied. (40)

Ὁμήρῳ γοῦν, καίτοι πρὸς τὸ μυθῶδες τὰ πλεῖστα συγγεγραφότι ὑπὲρ τοῦ Ἀχιλλέως, ἤδη καὶ πιστεύειν τινὲς ὑπάγονται, μόνον τοῦτο εἰς ἀπόδειξιν τῆς ἀληθείας μέγα τεκμήριον τιθέμενοι ὅτι μὴ περὶ ζῶντος ἔγραφεν· οὐ γὰρ εὑρίσκουσιν οὗτινος ἕνεκα ἐψεύδατ' ἄν.

For Lucian, the fact that Homer wrote well after Achilles' death, rather than bringing up doubts about his detailed knowledge of Achilles' exploits, paradoxically bolsters confidence in his account, because it removes the possibility of currying the great hero's favor. Dio spins a variation on this historiographical commonplace: Homer is guilty of favoritism despite living well after the Trojan War. Rather than 'courting the favor' of the Greeks who are portrayed in his poetry, Homer is flattering his audience, the Greeks of his own time. His mention of the "sons of Atreus" might suggest otherwise, but is revealed as an oversight when Dio addresses the issue in more detail later in the speech:

Since there were no other poets or historians in whose work the truth could be read, Homer was the first who set himself to writing about these events, although he composed [his account] *many generations later*, when those who knew [the truth] had perished along with their descendants, and only an obscure and weak tradition still survived, as is natural with very ancient events. Moreover, he intended to narrate his epics to the uncultured masses and so *exaggerated* the deeds of the Greeks, that even those knowing [the truth] were not able to refute him. (92)

---

[102] Cf. Desideri (1978), 466 n. 7, and the interesting modern debate between Valk (1953) and Kakridis (1971).
[103] Luce (1989).

οὐκ ὄντων δὲ ἑτέρων ποιητῶν οὐδὲ συγγραφέων, παρ᾽ οἷς ἐλέγετο τἀληθές, ἀλλ᾽ αὐτὸς πρῶτος ἐπιθέμενος ὑπὲρ τούτων γράφειν, γενεαῖς δὲ ὕστερον
ξυνθεὶς πολλαῖς, τῶν εἰδότων αὐτὰ ἠφανισμένων καὶ τῶν ἐξ ἐκείνων [ἔτι],
ἀμαυρᾶς δὲ καὶ ἀσθενοῦς ἔτι φήμης ἀπολειπομένης, ὡς εἰκὸς περὶ τῶν σφόδρα παλαιῶν, ἔτι δὲ πρὸς τοὺς πολλοὺς καὶ ἰδιώτας μέλλων διηγεῖσθαι τὰ
ἔπη, καὶ ταῦτα βελτίω ποιῶν τὰ τῶν Ἑλλήνων, ὡς μηδὲ τούς γιγνώσκοντας
ἐξελέγχειν.

In Dio's eyes, Homer's improvisational lie was so successful despite all
of its implausibilities that he did not even feel compelled to revise it when
he wrote it down for posterity. Here Dio has turned Homer's exalted
status as the 'first' poet, understood chronologically, against him: there
were no other writers to reveal his lies. He has also modified a traditional
historiographical boast to the same end – the lack of predecessors and
obscurity of his subject matter, rather than testifying to his singularity and
rigor, now are construed as enabling Homer to lie about the war that much
more easily.[104]

For Dio, Homer's exaggeration of Greek achievements in order to win
support among his Greek audience provides both evidence of his bias
and an explanation for the subsequent acceptance of his account as true;
indeed, Dio complains that Homer's account soon became authoritative
since subsequent writers "were deceived" (ἐξηπατημένοι) and "the lie
prevailed" (τοῦ ψεύδους ἰσχύοντος: 110). The ideas expressed here hearken
back to the diatribe against the intransigent power of *doxa*, deception, and
falsehood with which the oration began, and to which Dio returns later in
his peroration, once again rebuking those "who, because of an old *doxa*, are
not persuaded (μὴ πείθεται . . . ὑπὸ τῆς παλαιᾶς δόξης)," and accusing
them of "being unable either to leave deception (ἀπάτης) behind or to
differentiate lies from the truth" (144; cf. 124–5).

In the prologue, however, Dio's examples of lies accepted as true had been
fantastical stories of poetry and myth, but in the conclusion his focus shifts
to historical 'facts' of the Archaic and Classical periods: the dating of the
battle of Plataea before that of Salamis, the conviction that Harmodius and
Aristogeiton were tyrannicides, and the existence of a Spartan Scirite band.
The last two examples are clear allusions to Thucydides 1.20 (Dio names
Thucydides as the source of the second), and in fact, the entire argument
made here is a virtual paraphrase of Thucydides' famous complaints about
uncritical belief in the past. Compare Dio's outburst:

---

[104] For the point about historians, see Vagnone (2003a), 151.

The fact that something has been believed (τὸ πιστεύεσθαι) for a long time by foolish people is not a strong argument nor that the lies (τὰ ψευδῆ) were being told among those of former times (παρὰ τοῖς πρότερον) . . . For the masses do not know anything accurately (οὐ γὰρ ἴσασιν οἱ πολλοὶ τὸ ἀκριβές). They only listen to rumor, even when they are contemporary with the time in question, and the second and third generations are entirely unfamiliar (ἄπειροι) [with the events] and easily accept (παραδέχονται) whatever anyone says. (145–6)

with Thucydides 1.20:

People are inclined to accept (δέχονται) all stories of ancient times in an uncritical way . . . The rest of the Greeks, too, make many incorrect assumptions (οὐκ ὀρθῶς οἴονται) not only about the dimly remembered past, but also about contemporary history . . . Most people, in fact, will not take trouble in finding out the truth (ἡ ζήτησις τῆς ἀληθείας), but are much more inclined to accept the first story they hear.

As has long been recognized, Thucydides' diatribe is aimed primarily at Herodotus, in whose work both alleged errors – about the Spartan band and the tyrannicides – occur, and Dio is casting his battle with Homer as a historiographical dispute on similar lines, seeing himself as an analog to the meticulously precise Thucydides, who corrects his careless predecessor's errors and 'lies.' It is therefore somewhat curious that Dio's own accuracy in reporting these 'historical' lies taken for truth leaves something to be desired. There is no evidence that anyone in antiquity believed that the battle of Plataea took place before the battle of Salamis, and even if this was a position held by some deluded minority, it is surely a strange example to head a list of 'common' historical misperceptions. More seriously, Dio's reference to Thucydides illustrates that he is a victim of the very "lack of accurate knowledge" that he so vigorously decries – in 1.20.3 Thucydides denies the existence of the *Pitanate* band, not the Scirite, which is a legitimate Spartan band mentioned elsewhere in his *Histories*. Could Dio have unwittingly committed such an egregious error and thus made himself the target of a delicious irony – alluding to Thucydides in support of his diatribe against those who uncritically accept false stories, but then failing to accurately recall a fact that Thucydides had specifically cited as something that everybody gets wrong? Or is the irony the intended effect, a means of calling into question the very nature of claims to authority? Is Dio really more trustworthy than Homer? In his attempt to cast suspicion on the unquestioning belief in Homer, Dio has planted some seeds of doubt as to his own historiographical reliability and credibility, and these will only grow as the *Trojan* nears its conclusion.

Defending Homer

Dio's turn toward Classical historical examples and away from those of legendary tradition, however, indicates that he is expanding his critique of the power of tradition and the past beyond the heroic age, a change that is significant in assessing the unexpected 'political' defense of Homer that he introduces right at the end of the speech. Dio had hinted way back in paragraph 11 that he had no wish "to quarrel with Homer," but his audience could be excused for thinking otherwise after listening to the lengthy assault that followed. At the conclusion of the speech, however, Dio suddenly wants to "defend" (ἀπολογήσασθαι) Homer. His lies, it turns out, "had some *benefit* for the Greeks of those times" (ὠφέλειάν τινα εἶχε τοῖς τότε Ἕλλησιν); war between Greece and Asia was looming, and Homer assured the Greeks of their earlier 'victory' in order to avoid alarming them and creating a widespread panic. "Thus," Dio says, "we can pardon one who, being Greek (Ἕλληνα ὄντα), used every means to *benefit* his countrymen (τοὺς ἑαυτοῦ... ὠφελεῖν)" (147).[105] This stunning revelation is important on several levels.

First of all, it is another example of the way Dio cleverly tweaks the standard terminology and concepts of Homeric literary criticism to serve his portrait of Homer as improvisatory liar. As I discussed in the last chapter, it was a truism of ancient literary critics that the primary objective of poetry (and many other genres besides) was "benefit" or "utility" (ὠφέλεια). A natural defense against those charging Homer as a liar was to excuse his 'falsehoods' about the gods, let's say, as somehow 'useful' or 'beneficial,' whether by construing them as allegories that revealed a 'truth' about the world, or by claiming that they taught a 'useful' moral lesson. Strabo, as I showed, repeatedly gets entangled in his attempts to demonstrate that Homer's 'myths' are aimed at 'utility' (as moral exempla) in addition to entertainment. But at various points in his discussion of the topic, Strabo refers to the *political* utility of 'myths' and 'falsehoods': he defines poetry as "*beneficial* for the people" (δημωφελεστέρα: 1.2.8), describes Homer as using the "false" (ψεῦδος) for "popularizing and leading the masses" (δημαγωγῶν καὶ στρατηγῶν τὰ πλήθη: 1.2.9; cf. δημαγωγῶν: 1.2.7), and acknowledges the use of myths "in the social and political scheme of life" (εἰς τὸ κοινωνικὸν καὶ τὸ πολιτικὸν τοῦ βίου σχῆμα: 1.2.8). While the nature of the political use of myth is not always clear, Strabo seems to be

---

[105] Cf. 149: "If Homer did this too, then he may be excused" (εἰ δὴ καὶ Ὅμηρος ἐποίει τοῦτο, συγγιγνώσκειν ἄξιον).

talking about employing myths in order to deter the populace from, or spur them to emulate some kind of behavior (εἰς προτροπήν, εἰς ἀποτροπήν: 1.2.8). Strabo's theory, and others like it, are aimed at explaining away the parts of Homeric poetry that are, as I mentioned above, primarily fantastic, supernatural stories embedded in larger narratives, but when Dio seizes upon this sort of thinking, substituting Homer's entire epic-long 'historical' lie for Strabo's 'myths,' he nonchalantly gives political utility as the reason for Homer's falsification of *history*, which of course fits smoothly with his portrait of the poet as an improvisatory calculating liar.[106]

Secondly and more significantly, Dio's revelation that Homer had composed his poems extemporaneously due to the political exigencies of a particular moment in history is in its own way a much more subversive claim (even though it is being made in Homer's defense) than his direct assaults on Homer's inconsistencies and veracity, which, after all, others had been impugning for centuries. Dio situates Homer in mainland Greece some time after the Trojan War, associating him less with the glories of the heroic age than with the banalities of an anonymous epigonal era. Rather than an epic memorial to the past aimed at posterity, Dio sees Homeric poetry as a momentary opportunistic creation. The grand irony is that this ramshackle account, composed on the spot, has over time ossified into historical truth, so revered and believed that *Dio*, who, countless generations later, is similarly traveling around and explaining to Imperial audiences the story of what 'really' happened, will be taken for a liar. In a twist on Plato's famous expulsion of Homer from his ideal city for the 'lies' he tells about the gods and heroes (*Resp.* 2.398a), Dio claims that he will be expelled for claiming that Homer's lies are *not* true (τὸν δὲ εἰπόντα ὡς οὐ γέγονεν οὐδὲν αὐτῶν ἐκβάλλουσιν: 9).

The relativity of historical truth encapsulated in Dio's 'defense' of Homer also raises questions about the role that fiction and falsehood play in the construction of civic and national identities. This is brilliantly illustrated by Dio's example of the 'truth' believed by the Persians – that they actually won the Persian Wars and conquered Greece. After their defeat at Plataea in 479 BCE, Dio informs his audience, the Persians had pursued a similar policy as the Greeks of Homer's day, spreading the false story that they had won a great victory over the Greeks in order to prevent the masses from panicking in fear that the Greeks would invade Persia (149). This neat

---

[106] Both Strabo and Dio's conceptions of 'useful' lies probably ultimately derive from the popular view that lies were acceptable if they were considered 'useful,' that is, for helping friends or harming enemies; cf. Luc. *Philops.* 2: "lying for utility" is excusable, as opposed to those who lie for no reason; on which Fuchs (1996), 129, and below Ch. 5: 149–50.

parallel, exactly reversing the situation in Dio's account where Greeks are defeated in the East, but tell everyone back home that they had won, is yet again typical of his wit. But it is significant that the Persians too, like the Greeks and the Trojans, *still believe* in the 'false' account; Dio himself has heard the story recently from "some Mede" (149). The amusing situation that Dio has laid out, in which Imperial Greeks believe, after a thousand years, that they won the Trojan War when in fact they lost it, while Imperial Persians believe they conquered Greece five hundred years ago, when in fact they did nothing of the sort, conjures up a world of false beliefs and hollow traditions, where both historical 'truth' and the investment in that history as a source of ethnic pride are exposed as unstable and contingent.

Dio's comments on Rome should be read in this context. The reason that Dio can set the record straight now, after so many centuries, is because "the situation has changed" (ἀλλ' οὐδέν ἔστιν ἔτι τοιοῦτον: 150) and there is no longer any fear of Asia ever invading Greece; "for Greece is subject to others and so is Asia" (ἥ τε γὰρ Ἑλλὰς ὑφ' ἑτέροις ἐστὶν ἥ τε Ἀσία: 150). As I mentioned at the beginning of the chapter, this allusion to Rome has been understood by some scholars either as Dio's suggestion that the extension of Roman rule has rendered the old antagonisms between East and West irrelevant or as a coded reference to the pro-Roman aims of Dio's elevation of the Trojans. But seen against Dio's characterization of 'truth' as primarily a matter of political expediency, his comments on Rome seem laced with cynicism rather than praise. Is Dio's new 'truth' of Trojan victory not simply another 'useful lie' told for the benefit of those who happen to be in power, flattering the Romans either by praising their Trojan ancestors or by acknowledging the benefits of the Roman rule that has finally allowed Dio to tell the 'real' story? Is there any more reason to 'believe' Dio's alternative history than Homer's original propagandistic version, or the Persians' revisionist account of the Persian Wars?

Support for such suspicions is found in the frequent signals, noted throughout this chapter, that Dio gives of the fictitious nature of his truth. Late in the speech, as I mentioned above, Dio relates that Homer "composed [his account] many generations later [than the war], when those who knew [the truth] had perished along with their descendants, and only an obscure and weak tradition still survived, as is natural with very ancient events" (92). But Dio himself had argued in the prologue that the Trojans will disbelieve him "just because I was born many years later than Homer" (4). It turns out, then, that neither Homer nor Dio have any real access to the truth; even the Egyptian records on which Dio depends have been ravaged by time: "some of these records were remembered only by a few, since the pillars had been destroyed, while many of the things that had been inscribed on the pillars were unknown due to the indifference and ignorance of those who came later" (38). It is striking how much emphasis Dio places on the obscurity of the past and the tenuous transmission of knowledge about that past; he even illustrates the difficulties involved by naming the wrong Spartan band from Thucydides while lambasting people for failing to "know anything accurately." So, too, in the speech itself, the 'source' for Dio's material, the priest, fades away, abandoned by the end — as if Dio himself had forgotten the origin of his 'true' story.

Conclusion

Strabo's straightforward attempt to tackle the problem of Homer's reliability ends up in confusion and *aporia*. Dio's solution is to parodically expose the unexamined assumptions and blindnesses inherent in the idea of Homer as historian, by 'taking seriously' the claims of the poet's desire for historical accuracy and submitting his text to a ruthless analysis on those grounds. Dio's resulting portrait of Homer as an improvising liar inventing on the spot to please his listeners, forces his audience in the end to reconsider what *they* think about Homer, and why. It is thus essential that Dio construct the arguments of his *jeu d'esprit* so carefully, because the more persuasive they are, the more he is able to subvert the assuredness with which his audience unquestioningly believes in the tradition represented by Homer.

But the *Trojan Oration* is not just a clever and ingenious reinterpretation of the idea of Homer as historian; it also targets the ideological investment in the heroic past that underpins such characterizations. Dio shows not only that Homer was a liar, but also that his lies were motivated by the desire to protect 'Greece' in the wake of a catastrophic defeat by 'barbarians,' thus mocking the process through which ethnic identity is asserted by appeals to the glories of the past. Far from being merely a witness and recorder of the illustrious deeds of Greek heroes so central to the Imperial Greek sense of self-definition, Homer is actively participatory in the construction of Greekness in his own time. But he does so by fabricating a *false* narrative of the past and instilling in his countrymen a false sense of pride in being Greek, when in fact there was nothing to be proud of at all, only an unjust war followed by an inglorious defeat. If even Homer, the first and most revered narrator of 'history,' is already manipulating the past, why should any tradition about the distant past command belief? Dio thoroughly dismantles Homer's accuracy, trustworthiness, and character, but he also reveals, in the guise of defending the poet's decision to lie, the contingency, not only of Homer's account, but of his own as well. Talking about the heroic past, Dio suggests, is always a matter of fictionalizing, of telling stories, of constructing, rather than just reflecting, the 'truth.'

CHAPTER 5

Homer on the island

Lucian's *True Stories*

Dio's *Trojan Oration* is part of the wider development in the Imperial period that I sketched out in Chapter 1, in which Homer and his poetry become the object of fervent literary experimentation. Dio's exploration of the intersections of tradition, authority, truth, and lies takes on additional significance when seen in the light of the activity of Ptolemy the Quail, Dictys of Crete, and Dares of Phrygia, who present invented narratives similarly purporting to provide the 'true' stories behind Homer.[1] Within this intellectual milieu, it would be natural to turn our attention to the satirist Lucian of Samosata, active in the second half of the second century CE and probably the Imperial writer who most explicitly and memorably addresses the issues of history, fiction, truth, lying, and storytelling in his work.[2] He is also one of our best sources for the classicizing tendencies of the Second Sophistic, as one of its most skilled practitioners and most vicious satirists; a self-styled 'Syrian' who writes in a near-flawless Attic Greek as he mocks the conceits and hypocrisies of contemporary intellectuals, particularly those who parade their *paideia*, or 'learning,' without actually possessing it.[3]

Homer, naturally, is an essential element of Lucian's repertory, both as a source of quotations and examples, but also as the object of his ridicule.[4] On the face of it, Lucian is much more critical of the poet than Dio is (outside of the *Trojan*). Much of this opprobium, however, is directed at

[1] I discuss these authors more fully in Ch. 1: 00–0 and Ch. 6: 178–81, 186–7.
[2] Useful recent studies of Lucian include Branham (1989); Camerotto (1998); and Whitmarsh (2001), ch. 5. See also the collections of Billault (1994) and Bartley (2009), the historically oriented study of Jones (1986), and the older, more comprehensive treatments of Bompaire (1956) and Hall (1981). On Lucian and Dio, see Pernot (1994).
[3] E.g., *The Ignorant Book-Collector* (*Ind.*), *The Master of Rhetoric* (*Rh. Pr.*), *Lexiphanes* (*Lex.*), *Hermotimus* (*Herm.*), *The Mistaken Critic* (*Pseudol.*), *How to Write History*, etc. See Hall (1981), 252–309; Jones (1986), 101–16; and Swain (1996), 45–9. On the general slipperiness of Lucian's play with identity, see Goldhill (2002), 60–93.
[4] On Lucian's use of Homer and citations of his poetry: Householder (1941), 18–30, and Bouquiaux-Simon (1968). On his attitude toward Homer: Camerotto (1998), 175–90.

Homer's depiction of the gods, whose incongruities are sent up in several of his works, including the large-scale collections *Dialogues of the Gods* and *Marine Dialogues*.[5] When he criticizes Homer explicitly, Lucian takes the standard Platonic line of censuring the morally questionable deeds the poet attributed to the gods – their battles with each other, adulteries, assaults, kidnappings, sibling marriages, etc. (*Menippus* 3; *Zeus, the Tragic Actor* 39) – or challenges (much as Dio did) Homer's supposed knowledge of divine affairs (*Twice Accused* 1; *Icaromenippus* 11). In contrast, he seems less interested in scrutinizing Homer's representation of the heroes or their correspondence with (historical) 'reality.' Only a few of the *Dialogues of the Dead* are devoted to Homeric heroes, and his one foray into the 'revisionist' branch of Homeric historical criticism amounts to a single paragraph in *The Rooster* (17: I discuss this further in the next chapter).

The one work where Lucian addresses the complex interweaving of Homer, the heroes, truth, and fiction in any sustained manner is the *True Stories* (Ἀληθῆ διηγήματα),[6] and the current chapter is devoted to teasing out his position(s) from this seemingly straightforward yet maddeningly difficult text.[7] A tongue-in-cheek parody of travel and ethnographic literature (and much else besides), it relates a series of fantastic adventures that Lucian claims to have experienced, including a voyage to the moon, six months spent trapped inside a whale, visits to the Islands of Dreams and Lamps, and encounters with odd creatures such as the Pumpkin-pirates, Horse-vultures, and men who float on their backs and attach sails to their enormous penises. The *True Stories* is probably Lucian's best-known and most influential work, important both as an example of the interest among Imperial authors in self-conscious experiments with fictional creation[8] and

---

[5] Branham (1989), 127–77, is the standard treatment.

[6] The Latin title, *Verae historiae* (or alternatively *Vera historia*), has given rise to a number of variations in English: *A True History, True History, True Histories*. While the Latin *historia* can refer to either a "history" or a "story"/"narrative," the Greek *diêgêma* is simply a "story" and I thus use *True Stories*. For citations, I use the abbreviation formed from the Latin title (*VH*) as set out in *LSJ*. I follow the same procedure in referring to the rest of Lucian's works: in the main body of my text I use the English title (translated from the Greek), while for citations, I use *LSJ*'s Latin abbreviation: e.g., *How to Write History* vs. *Hist. Conscr.*

[7] On Lucian's elusive maneuvers in the preface of the *VH*, see Whitmarsh (2006).

[8] E.g., Bowersock (1994), ch. 1; Swain (1994), 178; Anderson (1996). There are significant affinities with Antonius Diogenes' contemporary *The Wonders Beyond Thule* (lost, but summarized in Phot. *Bibl.* 166), which similarly parades its fictionality while maintaining its 'historical' authority (Swain [1992]; Ní Mheallaigh [2008]), and seems to have parodied at least in part the excesses of traveler's tales and ethnographic treatises (Romm [1992], 205–11). The question of a more direct relationship between Lucian and Antonius Diogenes is discussed (with mostly negative conclusions) by Anderson (1976), 1–7; Hall (1981), 342–6; and Morgan (1985); Anderson (1996), 556–8, and Möllendorff (2000), 104–9 are more circumspect. There are some resemblances to Iamblichus' lost *A Babylonian Tale* (Phot. *Bibl.* 94) as well.

as the forerunner of classic satirical fantasies like Swift's *Gulliver's Travels* or the *Adventures of Baron Münchausen*.[9]

In the preface to the *True Stories* Lucian famously invites his readers to identify the numerous parodic allusions he makes throughout the work to unnamed "poets, historians, and philosophers" (1.2); scholars, spurred on by these encouraging remarks, have been hunting for such hidden targets ever since.[10] Lucian also singles out several individual inspirations by name:[11] Ctesias of Cnidus, the early fourth-century BCE author of an Indian ethnography (*Indica*) filled with marvelous descriptions of animals, peoples, and customs, and Iambulus (second or first century BCE), who wrote a fantastic account of his travels to, among other places, the Ethiopian Island of the Sun.[12] Later on in the *True Stories*, Lucian sees Ctesias being punished for his lies along with Herodotus on the Island of the Wicked and it is natural to see the "father of history" as another of Lucian's professed models. But the literary predecessor who looms largest over the *True Stories* is undoubtedly Homer, as Lucian himself indicates when he claims that "the founder and teacher of this sort of foolishness is Homer's Odysseus" (ἀρχηγὸς... καὶ διδάσκαλος τῆς τοιαύτης βωμολοχίας ὁ τοῦ Ὁμήρου Ὀδυσσεύς: 1.4).

The *True Stories'* profound engagement with Homer manifests itself in a variety of ways.[13] The *Odyssey*, that foundational narrative of travel and adventure, provides the chief intertext for Lucian's work; the sea-journey to strange lands that structures the work is modeled on Odysseus' wanderings, and in that sense parallels are unavoidable: storms, islands with odd inhabitants, monsters, etc.[14] Lucian has been seen as a 'new Odysseus': his ship is equipped with fifty rowers and a steersman,[15] just as in the

---

[9] For the *Nachleben* of the *True Stories*, see Robinson (1979), 129–44.

[10] Stengel (1911); Hall (1981), 339–54; Georgiadou and Larmour (1998), 22–44; Möllendorff (2000).

[11] Due to a lacuna in the manuscripts, the relation of these named authors to the authors Lucian says that he will *not* name is unclear. Most editors take Ctesias and Iambulus as examples of Lucianic targets, but some scholars, like Romm (1992), 212 n. 86, see them as literary models, not to be included among the parodied writers (against this view, see Möllendorff (2000), 31 n. 3). Ctesias and Iambulus' works, however, *are* parodied in the *True Stories*, and it is probably best to assume that they are grouped among Lucian's satirical targets yet singled out also as models and inspiration for the work as a whole.

[12] Ctesias' *Indica* is summarized by Photius (*Bibl.* 72, 49b39–50a4); fragments in *FGrH* 688. Iambulus' work is only known from Diod. Sic. 2.55–61.

[13] Bompaire (1958), 659 n. 2; Mal-Maeder (1992); Camerotto (1998); Zeitlin (2001), 242–7; Georgiadou and Larmour (1998), 23–4 (n. 70 on some examples of echoes of *Od.* 7–12); and Möllendorff (2000), 69–72, 92–5, etc.

[14] Cf. Andreani (1998) on the allusions to Homer in the shipwreck scenes of the *True Stories*; Bornmann (1994) on the Lamp-land episode at *VH* 1.29; Scarcella (1988) on Lucian's 'Homeric' use of numbers.

[15] Danek (2000).

Odyssey, and the double role of Odysseus as traveler and as (lying) narrator of his own travels is similarly assumed by Lucian.[16] The Homeric allusions are most conspicuous in the long portion of Book 2 (5–35) detailing Lucian and his companions' six-month stay on the Island of the Blessed, the afterlife residence of the Homeric heroes and other famous figures. The location recalls Homer's Elysian Field, where Proteus prophesies Menelaus will be taken after death (*Od.* 4.561–9), and the episode as a whole looks to Odysseus' encounter with the ghosts of the underworld in the *Nekuia* (*Od.* 11). Lucian finds himself side by side with Homeric heroes, such as Achilles, Agamemnon, and Ajax, witnesses Homeric episodes (the rape of Helen, athletic games) as they recur in comic form, and even literalizes his 'new Odysseus' role by delivering a letter to Calypso on Ogygia for Odysseus.[17] In fact, Lucian meets Homer on the Island, interviews him, receives a new poem of his to deliver to the world of the living, and is memorialized upon his departure with an inscribed epigram penned by the poet. These multiple and rather bewildering levels of interaction between Lucian, Homer, Homeric characters, and Homeric poetry have been the focus of numerous studies interested in Lucian's play with ideas of authorship, narrative, and fictionality, most significantly by Danielle van Mal-Maeder,[18] who elegantly demonstrates how the *True Stories* functions simultaneously as a parody of and homage to Homer.[19]

It is not my concern in this chapter to rehearse this oft-treated material, nor to add to the catalog of Lucian's possible allusions to Homeric poetry. Rather, my interest lies in the way that Lucian's *True Stories* can be seen as his own exploration, albeit in predominantly fictional form, of the complicated relations between truth and lies, history and myth, and Homer and historiography that preoccupy Dio, Strabo, and their predecessors. To this end, I focus first on Lucian's treatment of Homer in the preface of the *True Stories*, where Lucian inscribes his own work into the debate over Homer, credibility, historical veracity, and deception, while articulating a significantly different view of Homer's 'lies' and the idea of fiction than the other authors examined so far. Lucian also addresses these issues in the *True Stories'* narrative proper, by staging a face-to-face encounter with Homer and the heroes on the Island of the Blessed, and I read this episode as Lucian's literary response to the question of Homer's relation to history.

---

[16] Bompaire (1958), 669–72 (cf. [1988], 38); Mal-Maeder (1992), 127–8.
[17] Zeitlin (2001), 245.
[18] Mal-Maeder (1992); see also Bompaire (1988) and Briand (2005).
[19] Cf. Camerotto (1998), 141–70, who shows how this attitude applies to the use of Homer in Lucian's corpus as a whole.

LYING, HISTORIOGRAPHY, AND POETRY IN *TRUE STORIES* I.1–4

The preface to the *True Stories* outlines Lucian's ostensible rationale for composing the work, situating it firmly in the tradition, broadly conceived, of historiographical writing. The genesis of the *True Stories*, Lucian informs us, arose out of the desire to emulate such authors as Ctesias, who wrote about things "that he had neither seen himself nor heard from anybody else who was telling the truth," Iambulus, who "wrote of many strange things, having invented a lie that was apparent to everyone," and others who purport "to write down their wanderings and travels (συνέγραψαν... πλάνας τε καὶ ἀποδημίας), telling of (ἱστοροῦντες) giant creatures, savage peoples, and strange lifestyles" (1.3). Not wanting to be left out, Lucian too has decided to try his hand at telling similar things, even though he has never experienced anything remarkable (οὐδὲν γὰρ ἐπεπόνθειν ἀξιόλογον). What amazed him, however, was not that these writers lied (τοῦ ψεύσασθαι), but that they thought that nobody would notice (ἐνόμιζον λήσειν οὐκ ἀληθῆ συγγράφοντες: 1.4). In contrast, Lucian's intentions are unambiguous:

I turned *to lying*, but in a much more reasonable way than the others. For I will say one *true* thing – that I *lie*... I write, then, about things I have neither *seen* nor *experienced* nor *learned* from others: things, moreover, that *do not exist* at all and absolutely *could not have occurred*. My readers, therefore, should definitely *not believe* these things. (1.4)

ἐπὶ τὸ ψεῦδος ἐτραπόμην πολὺ τῶν ἄλλων εὐγνωμονέστερον· κἂν ἓν γὰρ δὴ τοῦτο ἀληθεύσω λέγων ὅτι ψεύδομαι [...] γράφω τοίνυν περὶ ὧν μήτε εἶδον μήτε ἔπαθον μήτε παρ' ἄλλων ἐπυθόμην, ἔτι δὲ μήτε ὅλως ὄντων μήτε τὴν ἀρχὴν γενέσθαι δυναμένων. διὸ δεῖ τοὺς ἐντυγχάνοντας μηδαμῶς πιστεύειν αὐτοῖς.

This paragraph, which concludes the preface, is a justly famous example of the self-conscious and paradoxical wit that pervades the whole text. Claims of autopsy, experience, and inquiry geared toward instilling readers' belief had been *de rigueur* in historiographical prefaces since Herodotus and Thucydides, but the ubiquity of such claims and the incredible material they frequently authorized had rendered their validity increasingly suspect.[20] False avowals of autopsy were a particular pet peeve of Lucian, to judge from *The Lover of Lies*, in which he ridicules otherwise distinguished

---

[20] See Marincola (1997), 63–86 on eyewitness claims in ancient historiography. On Imperial Greek 'fictional' eyewitness narratives, see the brief but useful survey of Maeder (1991), 23–31 (an article primarily treating Achilles Tatius).

men who tell unbelievable stories about their firsthand experiences with magic and the supernatural, and from the derision he showers upon 'bad' historians in *How to Write History*, who make egregious errors describing things that they have allegedly 'seen' themselves or 'heard' from a reliable source (e.g., 24, 25, 29).[21] Lucian's "more reasonable" (εὐγνωμονέστερον) ploy in the *True Stories* is to turn the standard declarations of experience and eyewitnessing on their head, denying any authority to his work on these grounds, and inverting the historian's familiar plea for the trust of his audience into a request that his readers *not* believe his stories (μηδαμῶς πιστεύειν).[22]

While these sort of broader historiographical tropes come under Lucian's satirical fire, he takes particular aim, as the preface makes clear, at a certain type of historiographical content: his work "hints in a not un-comedic manner" (οὐκ ἀκωμῳδήτως ᾔνικται) at certain ancient writers "who have written many *fantastic and mythic* things" (πολλὰ τεράστια καὶ μυθώδη συγγεγραφότων: 1.2) – tales of exotic peoples, monstrous creatures, and bizarre customs. In fact, much of the humor of the *True Stories* arises from the disconnect between the narrative's fabulous content and the style and persona of the narrator (also named Lucian [2.28]), who relates all of the outrageous events he observes and experiences in a dry, just-the-facts manner characteristic of (purportedly) impartial, sober ancient historiographical accounts.[23] As he says in the preface, his readers will be attracted to the way he tells "all sorts of lies in a *plausible* and *truthful* fashion" (ψεύσματα ποικίλα πιθανῶς τε καὶ ἐναλήθως). Lucian's adventures may be so exaggerated and fantastic that no one could be expected to swallow them as having actually occurred (and in fact he acknowledges that they have not), but he goes out of his way to pepper his narrative with comments and mannerisms that are typically employed in historical literature to give assurance of credibility. For instance he is hyper-precise with numbers and measurements, scrupulous in informing the reader exactly what he did and did not personally witness, and internally consistent and rational in his description of ridiculous and impossible events.

In this light, Lucian's expressed models, Ctesias' *Indica* and the work of Iambulus, are entirely fitting, since both authors, like Lucian, report strange and unbelievable things from far-off places that they claim either to have

---

[21] Georgiadou and Larmour (1994) on the links between *VH* and *Hist. Conscr.*

[22] Bompaire (1958), 672–3; Georgiadou and Larmour (1994), 1486–7; (1998), 58–9.

[23] Often noted: Bompaire (1958), 658–73; Fusillo (1988); Mal-Maeder (1992); Georgiadou and Larmour (1994) 1491–500. Saïd examines Lucian's parodic use of the first-person 'reporter' narrative in general (1993), 255–62, and of a wide range of historiographical techniques (1994).

seen for themselves, or at least to have heard from a reliable source. The two, however, represent different subsets of 'historical' writing: Ctesias' *Indica* is basically an ethnographic collection of marvels, similar to the relevant sections of Herodotus' Egyptian *logos* in Book 2 of his *Histories*,[24] while Iambulus' work more closely resembles the *True Stories* – a first-person narrative of one's own travels and adventures, in which exotic wonders are detailed as they were witnessed on the course of one's journey.[25] Moreover, Lucian intimates that Iambulus' narrative somehow signaled its fictionality – "he fabricated a lie recognized by everyone" (γνώριμον μὲν ἅπασι ὁ ψεῦδος πλασάμενος: 1.3) – suggesting a further affinity between the work and Lucian's own admittedly false account.[26]

Strabo and Lucian

Lucian's views on the fabulous 'lies' told by travelers and ethnographers are quite similar to those expressed by Strabo in his *Geography* regarding the 'myths' he attributes to the same two groups of writers (as well as to historians). Although various points of contact between the arguments and terminology of Lucian and Strabo have occasionally been noted, few scholars have properly conveyed the extent of the similarities.[27] While the parallels are probably not due to Lucian's direct knowledge of Strabo's text (although this is hard to prove conclusively), they highlight the important fact that Lucian has chosen to frame and justify his narrative within the same historico-geographical discourse employed by 'serious' authors like Strabo.[28] The one point, however, on which they significantly disagree concerns Homer, and more specifically, how Homer fits into their model of 'lying' storytellers, a disagreement all the more striking in light of the basic compatibility of their other arguments. As I hope to show a bit

---

[24] Bigwood (1989) and Romm (1992), 85–94.

[25] On Iambulus, see Ferguson (1975), 125–9, and Winston (1976); Holzberg (1996), 621–8, sets his work within the history of ancient prose fiction.

[26] This possibly explains why Ctesias, but not Iambulus, is seen suffering on the Island of the Wicked (*VH* 2.31).

[27] Romm (1992), ch. 5, treats the Strabonian material and adds some brief remarks on Lucian's *True Stories* (211–14); Möllendorff (2000), 38–44, concentrates on the opening of the preface and Lucian's transformation of Strabo's idea of *psuchagogia* in the definition of Lucian's project in the *True Stories*. My discussion of Strabo and Lucian is greatly indebted to Ní Mheallaigh (2005); the published version of this material is highly anticipated.

[28] Strabo's *Geography* does not seem to have been widely read under the Empire: the first two references are in the late second century CE, although a possible parallel in Dionysius Periegetes would push that back to the reign of Hadrian. As Möllendorff (2000), 38 n. 23, says, it is thus not impossible that Lucian might have had knowledge of Strabo. For Strabo's ancient reception, see Engels (1999), 383–9; Dueck (2000), 151–2.

later, this divergence is reflected in Lucian's singular vision of Homer and Homeric poetry as it plays out in the narrative portion of the *True Stories*.

For now, however, I want to concentrate on the correspondence between the two writers. The most obvious is that they both attack, in similar terms, the same kinds of 'lying' works – ethnographies of India and first-person accounts of far-flung travels by sea. Although Strabo does not mention Iambulus, he is familiar with two other Hellenistic writers who produced 'true' accounts of their voyages into uncharted waters: Euhemerus of Messene, whose *Sacred Inscription* told of his journey to the island of Panchaea, where he learned that the Olympian gods were merely famous men of ancient times who had been deified;[29] and Antiphanes of Berga, whose stories about his travels to the far North were so fantastic and outrageous that "Bergaean" (Βεργαῖος) became a byword for patently false storytelling.[30] Strabo characterizes Antiphanes and Euhemerus in much the same way as Lucian sees Iambulus, as writers of fictions whose marvels, though ostensibly 'true,' were not to be taken seriously: the "lies" (ψευσμάτων) of Antiphanes and Euhemerus, Strabo explains, "can be forgiven, just like those of entertainers who strive to amaze" (τοῖς θαυματοποιοῖς: Str. 2.3.5).

Strabo is less charitable to other explorers whose works, in his view, were just as false, yet managed to deceive geographers like Eratosthenes or Posidonius into believing they were true. Two celebrated explorers bear the brunt of his disdain: Pytheas of Massilia, who professed to have traveled to Thule in the far north (Str. 1.4.3; 2.4.1–2) and Eudoxus of Cyzicus, who claimed to have circumnavigated Libya and sailed to India (2.3.4–5). Pytheas comes in for Strabo's harshest criticism: he calls him "the worst of liars" (ψευδίστατος: 1.4.3) and declares that "anyone who has lied (ἔψευσται) so greatly about places that are known, would hardly be able to tell the truth (ἀληθεύειν) about those that are unknown" (1.4.3). To complicate matters, Strabo even includes Pytheas along with Antiphanes and Euhemerus among the "entertainers" of 2.3.5, as if his lies were so obvious that he must have intended them to be taken as fiction. Eudoxus, too, is tarred with the same brush; Strabo refers to his work as "the 'Bergaean' narrative" (τὸ . . . Βεργαῖον διήγημα: 2.3.5) which was either "invented" (πεπλασμένον) or "taken as true from those who had invented it" (ἄλλων

---

[29] Cf. Ch. 4: 111 n. 68. On Euhemerus, see Ferguson (1975), 102–10; Holzberg (1996), 621–8; Winiarczyk (2002). Diodorus is our primary source for Euhemerus and Iambulus.

[30] On Antiphanes: Romm (1992), 196–202 (197: "the term 'Bergaean' can virtually be translated as 'purely fictional'"). According to Strabo, Eratosthenes had called Euhemerus a "Bergaean" (Βεργαῖον: 2.4.2).

πλασάντων πιστευθέν). In other words, Strabo, like Lucian, demarcates evidently fictional travel narratives (those of Antiphanes and Euhemerus), which are not deceptive, from other 'lying' accounts that try to pass themselves off as true (those of Pytheas and Eudoxus).

Writers on India constitute another untrustworthy lot – nearly all of them, Strabo says, are "liars" (ψευδολόγοι: 2.1.9), who tell of men that sleep in their ears, ants that dig for gold, and Pans with wedge-shaped heads.[31] At 1.2.35, Strabo groups "writers of *Indica*" along with Hellanicus, Theopompus, and the usual suspects, Ctesias and Herodotus, among those who "intentionally weave myths" (μύθους παραπλέκουσιν ἑκόντες) into their histories and "fabricate impossible things for the sake of *fantasy* and *enjoyment*" (πλάσει τῶν ἀδυνάτων τερατείας καὶ τέρψεως χάριν: cf. *VH* 1.2: τεράστια καὶ μυθώδη). And at 11.6.3 Strabo incorporates into this model a concern, reminiscent of Lucian's, for feigned autopsy and investigation, accusing Herodotus, Ctesias, and Hellanicus of emulating writers of myth (τοὺς μυθογράφους), "relating, in the form of history (ἐν ἱστορίας σχήματι), things that they had neither *seen* for themselves nor *heard* (εἶδον μηδὲ ἤκουσαν)" from any reliable source and aiming only at "a pleasing and marvelous reception" (ἀκρόασιν ἡδεῖαν . . . καὶ θαυμαστήν).[32] Strabo's elaboration of these ideas even foreshadows Lucian's descriptions of his own practice in the *True Stories*: the historians in 1.2.35 not only include myths, but, like Lucian they "tell them in a *plausible* way" (πιθανῶς . . . μυθεύουσι; cf. *VH* 1.2: ψεύσματα . . . πιθανῶς), and Strabo's subsequent comment that Theopompus, at least, openly acknowledged that he would be including myths in his history recalls Lucian's prefatory admission that his narrative contains nothing true.[33]

Strabo's targets, like Lucian's, are not travelers' tales and ethnographies *per se*, but the sort of 'myths' that are characteristic of those genres and that remain problematic even when they occur in more properly historical works, like those of Herodotus or Theopompus. From the examples that both Lucian and Strabo offer, the 'myths' and 'lies' in question are fantastic and unbelievable tales (of "giant creatures, savage peoples, and strange lifestyles" [*VH* 1.3]).[34] By way of contrast, in Dio's *Trojan Oration*, although

---

[31] Strabo's discussion: 11.5.5–6.4. Romm (1992), 99–103, shows how Strabo's skepticism of Indian marvels gradually diminishes throughout Book 15.

[32] Quoted above in Ch. 3: 62–4. Cf. *VH* 1.3 (quoted above at 144) on Ctesias, who wrote about "things that he had neither *seen* (εἶδεν) himself nor *heard* (ἤκουσεν) from anyone else."

[33] The difference being, of course, that Theopompus admits that *some* parts of his history will be 'mythic,' while Lucian emphasizes that *all* of his story will be false.

[34] This explains the preponderance in both the *Geography* and the *True Stories* of μυθ- and τερα- terms (mythic, fantastic) used as synonyms for 'lies' or 'falsehoods' (ψευδ-).

some 'false' episodes from the *Iliad*, such as Achilles' fight with the river Scamander, are considered 'lies' based on their 'fantastic' nature, the major 'lies' that Dio accuses Homer of telling (e.g., that Achilles killed Hector) are not *inherently* incredible, but simply verisimilar narratives that happen to be untrue. Strabo and Lucian, however, share a conception of 'lies' or 'myths' that emphasize the link between falsehood and the fantastic, and, moreover, employ similar examples and arguments to articulate this link: they condemn as liars writers who tell of the fabulous wonders they purport to have seen themselves or heard about from reliable witnesses; they consider works on India and explorers' accounts of their travels, along with the writings of Ctesias and Herodotus, as egregious examples of such practices; yet they are willing to excuse certain authors who indicate, either explicitly, or by some other less obvious means, that their lies are not meant to be taken seriously, but as part of fictional works.

How then do poetic (or Homeric) 'lies' fit into this scheme? In Strabo's discussions, he repeatedly refers to the idea that historians include myths for the sake of pleasing or delighting their audiences. As I showed in Chapter 3, this notion is closely tied to Strabo's views on myths in poetry, which are also aimed at a similar goal: "entertainment" (ψυχαγωγία: 1.1.10; 1.2.3, etc.).[35] In fact, the passage from Strabo (1.2.35) quoted above (on historians' use of myths) is deployed in order to defend the right of *poets*, like Homer, Hesiod, and Aeschylus, to "tell myths" (μυθεύοντος), and to argue that such myths cannot be taken as evidence of their authors' general lack of knowledge. Strabo's examples of such poetic myths – web-footed men, men who are half-dog, Pygmies, etc. – resemble the sort of fabulous exotic phenomena that he earlier listed as 'historical' myths (and in fact, the three listed above are found in the fragments of Ctesias' *Indica*). Strabo, then, appears to view the 'myths' used by poets and historians as essentially the same, as are the purposes for which they incorporate them into their work.

Lucian makes no specific mention of poets' lies in the preface to the *True Stories* (other than the reference to Homer's Odysseus, which I discuss below), but his thinking on the matter is set out clearly in *The Lover of Lies*, a text that also deals with lying stories and false claims of autopsy.[36] As in the

---

[35] Lucian is aware of the instruction-entertainment dichotomy; in fact at the beginning of the preface he applies it to the *True Stories* itself. The work, he says, will "not only provide unadorned entertainment (ψιλὴν . . . παρέξει τὴν ψυχαγωγίαν) but also display a cultured contemplation (θεωρίαν οὐκ ἄμουσον ἐπιδείξεται)" (1.2). See the long discussion of Möllendorff (2000), 38–46.

[36] On this passage, see Ní Mheallaigh (2005), 19–28; on fiction and the fantastic in *The Lover of Lies*, see Möllendorff (2006a).

True Stories, the primary concern is not lies per se but the deception entailed in passing them off as true. The two interlocutors, Tychiades and Philocles, thus begin the dialogue by systematically excluding from their discussion lies that are told for a legitimate purpose: lies for "utility" (τῆς χρείας ἕνεκα ψεύδονται: *Philops.* 1) such as those told by Odysseus to deceive his enemies, lies told to boost civic pride (local legends [τὰ μυθώδη: 4] touted by tour guides),[37] and the "fantastic little myths" (τεράστια μυθίδια: 2) of the poets (including Homer), which they use to create the "enjoyment" (τὸ ἐκ τοῦ μύθου τερπνόν) demanded by their audience (4).[38] By contrast, the "lovers of lies" (φιλοψευδεῖς: 2) who come under criticism are those who "take pleasure" (ἡδόμενοι: 1) in lying for no compelling reason and "delight in deceiving themselves and their associates" (χαίρουσιν αὐτούς τε καὶ τοὺς ἐντυγχάνοντας ἐξαπατῶντες: 2).[39] Tychiades' targets are contemporary intellectuals infatuated with fanciful tales of witchcraft and the supernatural, but he names the customary ancient 'liars', Ctesias and Herodotus, as their predecessors – further linking the preface of *The Lover of Lies* to that of the *True Stories*.

Poets' myths, then, are excused for the same reason as in Strabo – the need to provide "enjoyment" (τὸ . . . τερπνόν: 4) to their audience[40] (although it is significant that the historians, Ctesias and Herodotus, are not absolved on these grounds, as they are by Strabo).[41] It is no surprise either that Tychiades' examples of (excusable) poetic 'lies' are the poetic versions of the historians' implausible creatures and fantastic stories criticized by Strabo and Lucian in the *True Stories*; they center on monsters and divine myths – the castration of Uranus, the "tragic show in Hades," metamorphoses (e.g., Zeus, Callisto, etc.), Pegasi, Cyclopes, etc. (*Philops.* 2).[42]

---

[37] Cf. Dio's conception of lies believed by the Argives and Thebans in the *Trojan Oration* 7–10, and more generally, the conclusion to Ch. 4.

[38] Cf. *Zeus, the Tragic Actor* (*JTr.* 39), where Homer is acknowledged as a good poet, but hardly a "truthful witness." Rather than the truth, he cares only for bewitching his audience, enchanting them with meters and myths, and devising everything toward achieving pleasure.

[39] This is a clever shift in the agency of 'pleasure': rather than the audience 'enjoying' the lies, the liars themselves 'enjoy' deceiving their readers.

[40] Cf. Lucian's comment that Iambulus had written something "not unenjoyable" (οὐκ ἀτερπῆ: 1.3) despite it being patently false. Here the 'enjoyment,' however, seems to arise *despite* the falsity of the work, rather than *because* of it.

[41] Ctesias and Herodotus are initially grouped by Tychiades together with Homer and the poets as liars with no purpose, but in his response Philocles defends the poets on the grounds listed above. The historians, however, get no such defense and implicitly remain as the sole 'ancient' models for useless liars.

[42] Cf. Plutarch's 'intentional lies' of the poets as discussed in Ch. 4: 96.

Homer, Odysseus, and the Phaeacian tales

In the *True Stories'* preface, the same characterization of 'lies' as fantastic tales underpins Lucian's remarks on Homeric poetry, which stands atop the hierarchy of 'models' proposed there.[43] After listing Ctesias, Iambulus, and others who report their travels and the wonders they have seen, Lucian declares:

Homer's Odysseus (ὁ τοῦ Ὁμήρου Ὀδυσσεύς) is the founder and teacher of this kind of foolishness, who told stories to Alcinous and his court about winds kept in servitude, one-eyed men, cannibals, savage tribes, and even multi-headed beasts, and his companions' drug-induced metamorphoses; that man told many such fantastic tales (ἐτερατεύσατο) to the Phaeacians, those unsophisticated folk (ἰδιώτας ἀνθρώπους). (1.3)

It is interesting that Lucian does not refer to what modern readers probably think of as Odysseus' pre-eminent 'lies' – the 'Cretan' stories that he tells on Ithaca to Athena, Eumaeus, Penelope, and Laërtes[44] – but only episodes from the so-called Phaeacian tales, the narrative of Odysseus' adventures since Troy that he relates to the Phaeacians in *Odyssey* 9–12.[45] In other words, Odysseus is chosen as a precursor of the *True Stories'* narrator not only because he, like Ctesias and Iambulus, tells false things about his own adventures (which would apply just as well to his 'Cretan' tales), but also because the content of those 'lies' are fantastic and not merely untrue. Once again, this maps onto Strabo's position; his debate with Eratosthenes concerns the truthfulness of these same marvelous episodes: "Ocean, Hades, the cattle of Helios, stays with goddesses, metamorphoses, the great size of the Cyclopes and Laestrygonians, the form of Scylla, sailing distances, and many other such things" (*Str.* 1.2.11).

Strabo, of course, insists that there *is* truth lying at the bottom of these myths, while Lucian adopts the Eratosthenic opinion that they are completely false and invented. But Lucian also parts ways with both geographers

---

[43] As Möllendorff (2000), 55, observes, Homer's importance is reflected by the length of the text devoted to him relative to the others.

[44] E.g., Walcot (1977); Pratt (1993). On the ancient reception of the Cretan tales, see Grossardt (1998).

[45] Saraceno (1998), 413–14; her discussion is otherwise disappointing. For the modern debate about the 'truth' of the Phaeacian tales, see Most (1989) and Parry (1994); the difference to the modern reader is that the Homeric narrator gives no indication that the Phaeacian tales should be judged as untrue; on the contrary he seems to accept certain episodes such as that of Polyphemus as valid in other parts of the poem. The Cretan tales, on the other hand, while plausible, clash with Odysseus' story as the narrator has depicted it elsewhere.

Homer between history and fiction

by attributing the lies, not to Homer, but to Odysseus.[46] One might have
expected, given the issues under discussion – lying, fantastic myths, and
historiographical works – that *Homer* would be criticized for composing
the Phaeacian tales, or at least for representing Odysseus as telling them.
After all, for Dio, the fact that Homer has placed the Phaeacian tales, or
rather "the greatest of lies" (τὰ... μέγιστα τῶν ψευσμάτων: *Or.* 11.34),
into Odysseus' mouth rather than his own is a sign of Homer's mendacity, not that of Odysseus.[47] Moreover, Lucian's use of the designations
"founder and teacher" for Odysseus (ἀρχηγός... καὶ διδάσκαλος) recalls
the customary manner of speaking about *Homer's* 'didactic' qualities and
his role as 'founder' or 'originator' of any number of arts and sciences:
compare Strabo's declaration of Homer as the "founder" (ἀρχηγέτην:
1.1.2) of geography and his stress on the poet's concern for "instruction"
(διδασκαλία: e.g., 1.2.3).[48] The contrast with the arguments in *The Lover
of Lies* is also striking: there the same 'lies' mentioned in the *True Stories'*
preface, such as the journey to the underworld and the Cyclopes, are cred-
ited to Homer, while Odysseus is adduced as a liar not because of his tall
tales but on the basis of his ability to deceive his enemies – thinking perhaps
of his stratagems during the Trojan War, or the lies he uses to escape from
Polyphemus. It is worth noting that Lucian's departure from this tradition
in the *True Stories*, by transferring responsibility for the marvelous Phaeacian 'lies' away from Homer and onto Odysseus, is a somewhat unexpected
and therefore significant move.[49]

This is not to say that Lucian's focus on Odysseus rather than Homer
as 'author' of the Phaeacian tales does not make a certain amount of sense;
it better fits the immediate context, since Lucian is not criticizing false
stories per se, but those who pass them off as their own 'real' experiences. A
close parallel occurs in the beginning of Juvenal's fifteenth satire, where the
satirist similarly rails against the falsity of Odysseus' stories, the unreliability
of their first-person narrative, and the naïveté of the Phaeacians:

Ulysses, describing // a crime like that [i.e., cannibalism] to the astonished Alcinous as they sat over dinner, // elicited anger, or, in certain quarters possibly

[46] This is why Lucian cannot really be seen as navigating a middle ground between Eratosthenes and
Strabo, as Ní Mheallaigh (2005), 148–9, proposes, although she is right to point out the striking
similarities in thought that underlie all three authors' arguments.
[47] Cf. [Longin.] *Subl.* 9.13–14 where Homer is criticized for "the mythical and the incredible (κἂν τοῖς
μυθώδεσι καὶ ἀπίστοις)" episodes of the *Odyssey*: i.e., the Phaeacian tales.
[48] Hillgruber (1994), 5–35, on the ancient didactic view of Homer.
[49] Ní Mheallaigh (2005), 166: "So, with scrupulous precision in the proem, the author Lucian identifies
Homer's *narrator*, Odysseus, as the liar, without impugning the honesty of the author, Homer
himself."

laughter // as a spinner of lying yarns (*mendax aretalogus*): '... [Charybdis, Cyclopes, Laestrygonians, Scylla, Cyanean Rocks, Aeolus, Circe] // Does he take the folk of Phaeacia for such a witless lot?' // That would have been a fair response from a guest, still sober ... // for the Ithacan told that tale on his own; there was none to confirm it. (*Sat.* 15.13–26: tr. N. Rudd)

The slight but crucial difference between the two passages, however, is that Lucian does not just speak of Odysseus, as Juvenal does, but specifies that the Odysseus *of Homer* (ὁ τοῦ Ὁμήρου Ὀδυσσεύς) is the founder of such lying activity. Lucian uses the phrase "the X of Homer" or "the Homeric X" elsewhere of Homeric characters (and several times of Odysseus in particular), but it is usually just another way to introduce a Homeric quotation, a variant on the more verbose "as X says in Homer."[50] Here, however, the effect is to remove any lingering ambiguity as to Lucian's view of Odysseus' ontological status – he is not the historical hero, or a sort of composite literary figure, but the specific fictional character depicted in Homer's poetry.[51] The peculiarity of this decision becomes more pronounced when one considers that the other members of Lucian's list of liars are actual people, like Ctesias and Iambulus. Moreover, Lucian correlates Odysseus' fictional audience, the Phaeacians, with the modern readers of fantastic stories who are taken in by their authors' lies, furthering confusing the boundaries between fiction and reality.

An important observation to make here is that Lucian's use of "Homer's Odysseus" does not, as some scholars have assumed, condemn Homer as a liar, even if it does strongly hint at an intertextual affinity between the *True Stories* and the Phaeacian tales in Homer's *Odyssey*.[52] In fact, Lucian neither attacks nor defends Homer's reliability; by specifying that he is talking about the lies of Homer's Odysseus – that is, by treating Homer's character Odysseus as 'real' while simultaneously reminding us of his fictional status – Lucian succeeds in rendering the question of Homer's truth-telling or lying entirely moot. Lucian's disengagement of Odysseus from Homer's narrative and his subsequent placing of the hero onto the same ontological plane as Ctesias and Iambulus presupposes that Homer's creations have an independent existence, regardless of whether or not they are historically 'true.'

---

[50] Bouquiaux-Simon (1968), 44–5, 51.
[51] It may be significant that Lucian's other use of the phrase "the Odysseus of Homer" in *On Mourning* (*Luct.* 5) is also in reference to the narrative situation of the Phaeacian tales: the fact that Odysseus was able to tell of his trip to the Underworld proves that he did not drink from Lethe, the river of forgetfulness.
[52] E.g., Camerotto (1998), 175, on Homer as the target of *VH* 1.3.

The relation of Homeric fiction to reality is thus somewhat different from that formulated by Lucian with regard to his own narrative. At the end of the preface, Lucian declares that he will tell of impossible things, not say anything true, and indulge his "freedom to tell myths" (τῆς ἐν τῷ μυθολογεῖν ἐλευθερίας: 1.4). This frank admission of his forthcoming narrative's falsity is widely recognized as a humorous 'concretization' of the normally implicit fictional contract between author and reader, which carves out a space for storytelling that need not be assessed on the basis of its relation to 'reality.'[53] But Lucian's model (or target) of such fictional storytelling, as he states, is Homer's Odysseus, and the *True Stories* is an emulation of Odysseus' narration to the Phaeacians, not Homer's narrative of Odysseus.[54] In other words, Lucian defends his own work as fictional because it is openly filled with fantastic stories with no connection to reality, but he avoids making the same argument about Homer's poetry – that it is merely entertaining 'lies.' Nor does he assume its basic historical accuracy. Instead he focuses on Homeric poetry's power to fabricate a narrative (Odysseus' stay among the Phaeacians) that audiences (like Lucian himself) treat as 'real,' even as they acknowledge that it has been invented (by specifying 'of Homer').[55] The concept of fiction implicit in Lucian's comments on Homer, then, is subtler and more ambivalent than the one he explicitly formulates with reference to his own work, which advocates a more familiar ancient view of fiction as simply telling fantastic, impossible things that "do not exist at all and absolutely could not have occurred" and that his "readers should definitely *not believe*" (1.4).

This characterization of Homer and his poetry is a striking development in a preface that takes such pains to criticize people who tell false stories about things that never happened, and that displays such familiarity with previous complaints about 'myths,' 'lies,' and the authors who passed them off "in the form of history." Strabo, who adopted an initial position on the issue of poetic 'myths' similar to Lucian's, had also taken a curious next step, claiming a kernel of truth for (Homer's) Phaeacian tales, even though the thrust of his arguments about 'myths' should have more logically led to a defense excusing the tales as pure entertainments, included in Homer's 'history' for pleasure. But Lucian's response is perhaps even more radical – to write Homer out of this tradition entirely and make one of his characters,

---

[53] Fuchs (1993), 252, and Ní Mheallaigh (2005), 153.   [54] Camerotto (1998), 188–90.
[55] For a similar reading of Lucian's depiction of Plato and his 'republic' in the *True Stories* see Laird (2003).

rather than the poet, responsible for the 'lies' instead. These 'lies,' moreover, deceive the impressionable Phaeacians, that is, other characters in the poem, rather than the audience reading Homer. In other words, although Lucian employs arguments and examples familiar from and crucial to the debates concerning Homer's relation to historical reality, when he turns to Homer himself, he avoids the question entirely.[56]

This may seem like a lot of exegetical energy expended on a single turn of phrase, but as I have indicated, Homer and the *Odyssey* play major roles in the narrative portion of the *True Stories*, and for this reason any reference made to them in the preface takes on a much greater significance. What is more, I argue that these ideas about Homer, poetry, and 'reality' are fleshed out further in the main body of the *True Stories*, albeit in a more oblique fashion, given the fictional narrative form in which they are couched. In particular, Lucian's sensitivity to the relations between authors and characters expressed in the preface finds its fictional instantiation in the bewildering mélange of poets, historians, philosophers, heroes, and mythological characters that he encounters during his visit to the Island of the Blessed. The length of the episode (2.5–36, well over half of the second book) reflects its importance.[57] Lucian's visit to the Island suits the parodic objectives laid out in the preface, sending up not only Odysseus' wanderings (his encounter with the ghosts of the dead), but also the ethnographic descriptions of exotic societies and the visits to utopian islands common to travelers' tales and philosopher's treatises alike – e.g., Euhemerus' Panchaea, Iambulus' Island of the Sun, Plato's Atlantis, or Dionysius Scytobrachion's Hespera (occupied by Amazons).[58] But his account of the Island and its inhabitants, especially Homer and the Homeric heroes, strongly suggest that the heroic past on display in the *True Stories* is primarily seen in *literary* terms, and this prompts me to read the episode as an implicit expression

---

[56] There are only two hints of Homeric 'correction' in the *True Stories*, both poking fun at the practice: at 1.17, Lucian wonders whether the Homeric account of Zeus sending a rain of blood upon the death of Sarpedon (*Il.* 16.459) was perhaps to be explained by a previous battle in the sky such as Lucian witnessed. And in 2.32–3 he notes that there are *four* gates of dreams, rather than two, "as Homer said" (καθάπερ Ὅμηρος εἴρηκεν: 2.33) and that Homer "did not describe it very accurately" (οὐ πάνυ ἀκριβῶς συνέγραψεν: 2.32). The first 'rationalizes' Homer's marvelous account with an even more fantastic and unbelievable explanation, while the second 'corrects' Homer's description by claiming autopsy of an impossible sight – the gates of dreams.

[57] Thirty-two out of a total of forty-seven paragraphs; in addition to the stay on the Island of the Blessed, the episode includes Lucian's visits to the Island of the Wicked, the Island of Dreams, and Ogygia.

[58] On Hellenistic utopias, see Ferguson (1975), 122–9; Gabba (1981); and Hansen (2006). On Lucian's parody of island utopias in the *True Stories*, see Fauth (1979) and Nesselrath (1993).

of Lucian's thoughts on the 'truth' of Homer, his poetic fictions, and the heroic historical tradition.[59]

THE ISLAND OF THE BLESSED

Book 2 of the *True Stories* begins with Lucian and company's escape from the belly of a whale, where they have spent the last several months. After a few minor episodes, their ship approaches a single, flat island with beautiful rivers, meadows, forests, a strong flowery scent, and sweet breezes (2.5). Upon landing, a patrol brings them to the governor of the island, Rhadamanthus of Crete, one of the mythical judges of the dead, and Lucian quickly realizes that they have reached the Island of the Blessed, the heroic paradise of the Greek afterlife. While in line to see Rhadamanthus, they witness the judge handing down various decisions: he agrees to allow Ajax onto the Island once he has been cured of his madness, grants Menelaus possession of Helen over the claims of Theseus, and gives precedence in military achievements to Alexander over Hannibal (2.6–9). Lucian and his men, despite the fact that they are alive, are allowed to stay on the island for seven months (2.10).

An extensive description of the island follows that suggests numerous parallels with other literary utopias, from Homer's Scheria to Iambulus' Island of the Sun to the New Jerusalem in the *Apocalypse* of John – buildings of gold, emerald walls, vines bearing fruit twelve times a year, springs of wine, milk and perfume, an eternal springtime, etc. (2.11–13). The inhabitants are ghosts, but fully materialized; they never grow old and banquet in the Elysian Field, where the winds serve them, birds make the garlands, a light perfume sprinkles from the clouds, the glass trees produce wine-glasses that automatically fill with wine upon plucking, and two springs, of Laughter and Pleasure, run right near the tables (2.14). Lucian provides a long list of those present at the banquets (2.17–19), which mixes heroes of the Trojan War, kings, philosophers, and mythical figures in the manner already signaled by the account of Rhadamanthus' judgments: e.g., the two Cyruses, Hyacinth and Narcissus, Socrates, Nestor, Aesop, Epicurus, Achilles, etc. No Stoics are present, however, nor Academics, and no Plato, who was apparently off living in his own *Republic* (2.18). Homer is there of course, along with some lyric poets, as are nearly all of the heroes

---

[59] Lucian self-consciously and explicitly comments on his own literary practice in a number of works, such as *To the one who said "You are a Literary Prometheus"* (*Prom. Es*), *Zeuxis* (*Zeux.*), and *Twice Accused* (*Bis. Acc.*): Branham (1989), 38–43; Romm (1990); Whitmarsh (2001), 75–8; and Möllendorff (2006b).

whom he sings about, except for Locrian Ajax, who resides on the nearby Island of the Wicked with other evildoers like Phalaris, Busiris, Ctesias, and Herodotus (2.23; 31).

An encounter with cultural tradition

A large body of scholarship has exhaustively documented Lucian's possible sources for this episode, as well as allusions he might be making to other utopias and underworlds.[60] Much of this material is fascinating, but here I am more interested in the contours and peculiarities of the island as Lucian has portrayed it, regardless of its origins. An initial point is that the Island is occupied solely by illustrious figures from the Greek and Roman cultural canon; there is no chance here, it seems, of meeting deceased relatives or laymen as Odysseus does in the *Nekuia* (e.g., his mother Anticleia or his crewman Elpenor). This differentiates the Island from the more catholic underworlds, open to the famous and anonymous alike, that are depicted elsewhere by Lucian, such as those in *On Mourning* or *Menippus, or, the Oracle of the Dead*.[61] As a repository of famous Greeks and Hellenized barbarians, the Island is thus the ideal space in which Lucian can enact one of his favorite satirical ploys – juxtaposing famous figures either from vastly different time periods, cultural spheres, or both, for comic effect. So Lucian depicts philosophers (Socrates and Epicurus) reclining alongside mythical characters (Narcissus), monarchs (Cyrus the Great) next to poets (Homer and Arion) and Homeric heroes (Menelaus or Odysseus).[62] The resulting incongruities are the source of the fun, but also confirm what Bracht Branham holds for Lucianic satire in general: namely, that his "real subject . . . is the disconcerting babel of incompatible traditions that marks the post-classical form of Hellenic culture in the empire."[63] On the Island, however, Lucian seems less concerned with emphasizing the clash of viewpoints (as he often does elsewhere) than with marveling at the variety of the different strands of tradition that he brings together.

Such a dramatization of an allegedly 'true' face-to-face encounter with the Greek past is not unusual for a work of the Second Sophistic, which was fascinated by the possibility of accessing that past in a more direct manner than through books alone.[64] One recurring fantasy is that of

[60] Georgiadou and Larmour (1998), 182–200, and Möllendorff (2000), 286–9.
[61] On Lucian's use of the underworld motif, see Bompaire (1958), 365–78, and on his allusions to the *Nekuia* episode, Bouquiaux-Simon (1968), 247–70.
[62] Cf. Zeitlin (2001), 244.   [63] Branham (1989), 82.   [64] See Swain (1996), 79–87.

meeting 'primitives' who somehow preserve archaic culture: Dio's stay among the Borysthenites is an example (discussed in the last chapter), another is the anecdote told in Philostratus' *Lives of the Sophists* about Herodes Atticus' encounter with a wild man living on Mt. Cithaeron in Boeotia who spoke perfect Attic Greek.[65] Supernatural contact via dreams or ghosts was another way of bridging the present and past: Demosthenes appears to Aelius Aristides in a dream (*Or.* 50.19), as does Odysseus to the Egyptian priest Calasiris in Heliodorus' *An Ethiopian Tale* (5.22.3). The grammarian Apion claimed to have raised the ghost of Homer (see below, n. 81) while Philostratus, in the *Life of Apollonius* (4.11–16), tells us of the holy man's interview with the ghost of Achilles; the same author's *Heroicus* (which I consider in detail in the following chapter) features a vinedresser who is a close associate of the ghost of Protesilaus. And of course the idea of meeting the inhabitants of the underworld had good Classical precedent: e.g., Dionysus encounters Aeschylus and Euripides there in Aristophanes' *Frogs*, and Socrates expresses his pleasure at the prospect of commiserating with the shades of Ajax and Palamedes after his death (Pl. *Apol.* 41a–b).[66] Lucian spoofs such desires in *The Lover of Lies* (24), where one of the guests tells of a glimpse he once caught of the underworld: "I saw everything in Hades: Pyriphlegethon, the Lake, Cerberus, and the dead – so that I could even recognize some of them." He sees his father and many other souls "spending their time lying on the asphodel," but also Socrates (at least he conjectured it was him from his baldness and pot-belly).[67] These texts speak to, at varying levels of seriousness, the wish to gain closer and more personal access to the literary and historical past so revered in the Imperial period. In the *True Stories*, Lucian does these narratives one better; he fulfills the ultimate fantasy of the educated Imperial Greek, directly visiting and consorting for over six months with *all* of the illustrious figures of the Greek past (or at least all of the 'good' ones).

Despite the catholicism of the initial description of the Island's inhabitants, Lucian's sojourn there comes to have a distinctly Homeric flavor. Homer, as I have mentioned, is present, Odysseus is by his side, and the poet's songs are the main entertainment for the other symposium participants (ᾄδεται δὲ αὐτοῖς τὰ Ὁμήρου ἔπη μάλιστα: 2.15). The opening

[65] Philostr. *VS* 553–4. I discuss these encounters with the past in Ch. 6: 197–9.
[66] In the *VH*, Lucian depicts Socrates chatting with Nestor and Palamedes; see *Dialogues of the Dead* (*DMort.* 6[20]) and *Menippus* (*Nec.* 18) for other representations of Socrates in the underworld.
[67] The journey to the underworld is one of Lucian's favorite ways to enact his version of this theme: Micyllus journeys there in *The Downward Journey*, Menippus in *The Descent into Hades*.

scene thus plays on the thrill of juxtaposing poets and the subjects of whom they sing; the heroes find themselves in much the same situation as Odysseus on Scheria, as he listens to his own deeds sung by Demodocus. The close association between Homer and Odysseus had already been established in the preface where Lucian attributes the Phaeacian tales to the "Odysseus *of* Homer," that is, Homer's *character* Odysseus, as opposed to Odysseus the historical figure.[68] The placing of poet and creation on the same ontological level recurs throughout this episode: in addition to Homer and Odysseus, Lucian points out the presence of Stesichorus, who "had managed to make his peace with Helen" (ἤδη τῆς Ἑλένης αὐτῷ διηλλαγμένης: 2.15), alluding to the story of his blinding and subsequent recantation of his poem alleging that Helen had been at Troy. And later, the paradoxes made possible by the co-existence of poets and poetic characters are best exploited when Thersites brings a suit against Homer for defamation, which, however, Homer wins, with Odysseus acting as his lawyer (2.20).[69]

Such blurring of the levels between poets and their subjects is a characteristic method of Lucianic satire. Lucian's gods, for instance, are often comically aware of the debt they owe to Homer: Zeus is assumed to have read the poems of Homer and Hesiod (*Zeus Refuted* 1), quotes the *Iliad* (e.g., *Icaromenippus* 30), and insists that Hermes call the gods together using the words "with which Homer summoned us" (*Zeus, the Tragic Actor* 6). One of the jokes in *Zeus, the Tragic Actor* is that the gods are seated according to their literal worth, based on the material in which their most famous statues are cast – gold, bronze, marble, etc. Aphrodite, protesting her low rank due to Praxiteles' sculpting her in marble, claims that she is golden; to the skeptical Hermes she says "I will furnish a trustworthy witness to you (ἀξιόπιστόν σοι μάρτυρα), Homer, who calls me 'golden' up and down his poems" (10).[70] The same logic, treating Homer's verses as definitive, informs the only one of the *Dialogues of the Dead* in which Homer's name appears (30/25), an underworld beauty contest between Nireus and Thersites. Nireus cites Homer's line calling him "the most beautiful man who came to Troy" (*Il.* 2.672–3), and even urges the judge Menippus to "ask Homer what I was like when I was fighting with the Achaeans" (2). Even Thersites describes himself with the adjectives (φοξός and ψεδνός)

---

[68] Möllendorff (2000), 340.

[69] For a good account of the *True Stories'* vertiginous collapsing of the distinctions between authors, characters, and audiences, see Ní Mheallaigh (2005), 162–70.

[70] Branham (1989), 170: "the dialogue . . . insists on the reality of the gods as a product of the imagination." For another (humorous) interpretation of "golden Aphrodite" see Dio Chrys. *Or.* 6.17.

that Homer had used at *Il.* 2.219 (cf. *Menippus* 15). The impression one gets from the dialogue is not only that Nireus and Thersites are Homeric characters, defined and embodied by Homer's verses, but also that they are fully conscious of that fact.

As Branham has observed in his study of *Zeus, the Tragic Actor*, Lucian repeatedly portrays the failure of the gods to live up to their idealized Homeric image.[71] In this respect, Lucian's play with Homer's heroes is much more restrained; unlike his gods, they rarely step out of their established roles as laid out in Homeric narrative. For instance, the conversations in the *Dialogues* inspired by Homer are content to supplement the Homeric narrative without contradicting or mocking it: we simply learn Ajax's justification for his refusal to talk to Odysseus in the underworld (*DMort.* 23/29) and Achilles' defense of his famous words to the same hero (26/15). Likewise, in two other episodes, Polyphemus (*DMar.* 2) and the river Xanthus (*DMar.* 10/11) complain about the injuries they have suffered in Homer, at the hands of Odysseus and Achilles respectively.[72] There is little sense that these characters are anything other than those depicted by Homer; the pleasure of the dialogues arises from their 'filling in' and commenting on Homeric episodes rather than from any attempt at parody or burlesque.

Such a reluctance, if we can call it that, to experiment with Homeric characters in the same free and easy manner as he does with the gods is paralleled in Lucian's depictions of the heroes on the Island. In fact one gets the sense that for Lucian most of the Island's inhabitants are not so much historical individuals plucked from different points in the past, but stock characters of the Greek literary tradition, rising out of the pages of books. For instance, Lucian makes a point of emphasizing the inhabitants' ghost-like status, caught as they are in a strange state between life and death:

The people themselves have no bodies: they are intangible, without flesh; their only attributes are shape and form (μορφὴν δὲ καὶ ἰδέαν μόνην ἐμφαίνουσιν). Although devoid of body, they have position and movement, they think and speak. It is, in fact, as if it were a naked soul moving about, endowed with the semblance of a body; without touching them one would never be convinced that what one saw was incorporeal; they are like shadows, but upright and not dark. No one grew old (γηράσκει δὲ οὐδείς), but remained at the age he was when he came. (2.12)

---

[71] Branham (1989), 163–77.
[72] Cf. *Marine Dialogues* (*DMar.* 4), where Menelaus and Proteus discuss Proteus' metamorphosis into fire.

This ethnographic description owes much to Homer and Plato,[73] but the liminal existence of the island's inhabitants, wavering between corporeality and incorporeality, is also reminiscent of the hazy and dreamlike status of literary characters when one tries to 'corporealize' them, or bring them to life in the mind's eye. In this sense ghosts, as well as dream visions, which I earlier characterized as well suited to enable encounters with the past, are also an ideal metaphor with which one can depict the breaching of the boundary between literature and reality.[74]

Lucian also remarks that the inhabitants of the Island do not get older, but remain at the age at which they had come. On the one hand, this makes perfect sense – no one expects aging in paradise. But it also corresponds to the general timelessness that pervades the Island of the Blessed, a timelessness, oddly, which is one of the few aspects of Lucian's description for which scholars have not been able to locate a parallel in other sources:[75] there is no day or night, but it is always dawn, and spring is the only season; in other words, there is no natural way to gauge the passage of time.[76] This static existence on the part of the inhabitants, resistant to change and growth, parallels their situation as characters in canonized texts, who remain the same every time the text is read, never aging, never developing. The whole point of canonization, after all, and what gives literary tradition its power and strength, is the idea that 'great' texts provide stability and that their characters remain essentially the same.

The indistinct sense of time suggested by the description of the Island becomes even more pronounced when we note that Lucian's arrival coincides with judicial deliberations concerning heroes on the one hand (Ajax; Helen, Theseus, and Menelaus) and historical leaders on the other (Hannibal and Alexander) – figures who lived centuries apart. Why are these cases being decided now, in Lucian's own day? The same goes for the subsequent arrivals of Pythagoras and Empedocles (2.21). Taken as a whole, such temporal anomalies contribute to a sense of time out of balance, running in a

---

[73] On possible sources for Lucian's "Anatomy of Souls," see Möllendorff (2000), 328–35.

[74] Cf. Zeitlin (2001), 244–5: "The materialism of Lucian's exacting ethnographic detail acknowledges the paradox of the fantasy . . . The past lives on in this twilight state of being and non-being, in a reduction to essence of form and character that nevertheless is illuminated through vivid detail and the renewed activity of its actors." Dio compares Homer's description of the duel between Achilles and Hector "as if in a dream" (*Or.* 11.108), connects "incredible lies and dreams" (11.129) and says that "someone might rightly call Homer's poetry a dream" (11.129).

[75] Möllendorff (2000), 292.

[76] Lucian, however, is able to gauge the number of months that he has stayed on the island at *VH* 2.25, and refers to nightfall and midnight at 2.25–6. But this is because the events that occur depend on time, and point to an intrusion of the real world into this timeless paradise. Cf. Möllendorff (2000), 325, who emphasizes the contradictory nature of time on the island: static at times, at others quite rapid.

non-linear fashion, and even, one suspects, caught in a constant loop, in which events are repeated over and over again.

Lucian describes each of the characters on the Island as engaged in the characteristic behavior for which they are known from literary tradition: Ajax is mad, Aesop is a buffoon, Pythagoras foregoes beans, Socrates protests celibacy but cannot keep his hands off Hyacinth and Narcissus, etc.[77] The inhabitants of the island are condemned to continuously repeat their roles over and over; they are frozen in time, just as no matter how many times one reads Homer, the same things happen, the characters do the same things they did before. In this sense the Island represents Greek tradition by means of the cultural shorthand Lucian uses throughout his corpus – caricatures and representatives of certain fixed traditions and roles which can be manipulated ever so slightly for his own purposes.[78] But when combined with the inhabitants' ghostly nature and the pervasive timelessness on the Island, the stereotyping strongly suggests that Lucian is underlining the fact that the Island is the resting place, not for the 'real' illustrious figures of the Greek past, but those figures as they were typecast in the world of Greek *paideia*. When Lucian places Homer and Odysseus, for example, together at table, he is playing on the thrill of juxtaposing the poet with the character he has invented, not with the 'real' historical figure on which that character was based. This accords with Lucian's implicit characterization of Homeric poetry in the preface, a world that lies beyond questions of truth, lies, and history. The Island is very much an instantiation of the Greek *literary* tradition – to steal a phrase from Bompaire, it is "the dream of a librarian."[79]

The interview with Homer

Lucian's conversation with Homer (2.20), which is the first event he records following his initial description of the Island ("two or three days had not yet passed"), exemplifies this privileging of the literary over the historical, of fiction over reality.[80] In one sense, Lucian's Homeric 'encounter' is characteristic of the Second Sophistic preoccupations I outlined above; meeting Homer himself must have been the desire of many a second-century

---

[77] The only exception seems to be Diogenes, who has renounced his Cynicism and now indulges in dancing, women, and wine (2.18).

[78] This is, of course, the position taken by Bompaire (1958), 161–237.

[79] Applied by Bompaire (1958), 672, ("rêve de bibliothécaire") to the Cinyras and Helen episode, discussed below.

[80] On this episode, Jones (1986), 54–5; Georgiadou and Larmour (1998), 200–3; Möllendorff (2000), 367–73; Nesselrath (2002); Ní Mheallaigh (2009).

pepaideumenos.[81] But in other accounts, the objective is often to *bypass* Homer and obtain the 'real' story from a better source – the ghost of Protesilaus or Achilles, Egyptian priests, recently unearthed Trojan war diaries, etc. Lucian, however, chooses to interrogate Homer, the chronicler of the Trojan War, rather than those who took part in it (and who are, after all, also available for conversation on the Island). And although he mentions that he spoke with Homer multiple times and asked him about many things, the only questions and answers he reveals to his readers are centered on Homer's biography or the composition of his poetry, and scrupulously avoid any discussion of the *content* of Homer's poetry.

Thus he asks Homer "whether the verses athetized [by the Alexandrian critics] had been written by him (εἰσὶ γεγραμμένοι)," "whether he had written (ἔγραψεν) the *Odyssey* before the *Iliad*, as many asserted" and "why he had composed the beginning [of his poem] starting from [the word] 'anger' (τί δή ποτε ἀπὸ τῆς μήνιδος τὴν ἀρχὴν ἐποιήσατο)."[82] The questions are firmly focused on Homer's poetic activity and reflect topics popular in Imperial intellectual discussions; athetized lines are often mentioned in Athenaeus' *Deipnosophists* and Plutarch's *Table-Talk*, the question of which poem had temporal priority is famously treated in Ps.-Longinus' *On the Sublime* (9.11–13) and dismissed as pointless by Seneca (*Brev. Vit.* 13.2), and a series of explanations of Homer's choice to begin the *Iliad* with an inauspicious word – μῆνις – can be found in the Homeric scholia to the first lines of the *Iliad*.[83]

Homer's answers are brief and to the point.[84] He asserts that all of the contested lines are genuine (ἔφασκε πάντας αὐτοῦ εἶναι), explains that he began the *Iliad* with "the anger" because that is just what popped into his head (οὕτως ἐπελθεῖν αὐτῷ μηδὲν ἐπιτηδεύσαντι), and denies writing the *Odyssey* first (ἠρνεῖτο: thus agreeing with Ps.-Longinus in the passage

---

[81] An interesting, and possibly unique, parallel to Lucian's interview is found in the work of Pliny the Elder (*HN* 30.18), who relays, with a healthy dose of skepticism, a story told by Apion, a grammarian and Homeric critic of the first century CE. Apion claims to have raised Homer from the dead and asked him about his origins (parents and native land), "but," Pliny reveals, "he says that he does not dare to reveal the response he received." Apion's teasing reticence can be compared to Homer's own in Philostratus' *Heroicus* (44) and is surely poking fun at the desire for origins and the investment in ancestry that surrounded the discourse about Homer in the Imperial period. For more on the question of Homer's origins, see below, pp. 164–8.

[82] That Lucian means 'began his poem with the word μῆνις' and not 'began his poem with the episode of Achilles' anger' is suggested by the discussion of the question in the scholia to *Iliad* 1.1.

[83] Ní Mheallaigh (2009) notes also that these questions, like the other one about Homer's birthplace, are focused on origins and priority: which poem came first, which lines were originally in the poem, the first word in the *Iliad*.

[84] Cf. Zeitlin (2001), 246–7: "For an epic poet, Homer seems to be a man of few words."

referred to above). Armed with his new 'truths', Lucian condemns Homeric scholarship as a waste of time: "I accused the grammarians Zenodotus, Aristarchus, and their students of [promoting] a great deal of nonsense (πολλὴν τὴν ψυχρολογίαν)." In this respect, Lucian indulges in the Second Sophistic fantasy of discovering a pure and uncorrupted representative of the past, in this case Homer before his work had been mutilated by scholars and subjected to all sorts of fanciful interpretation. The joke here is that the sort of questions about Homer that Lucian asks are pointless and uninformative; Lucian only asks them to demonstrate their uselessness and seems delighted when Homer proves him right. Common sense about Homer, rather than learned scholarship, is correct: every verse in the epics is genuine, the *Iliad* naturally preceded the *Odyssey* just as the Trojan War happened before the Returns, and no significance is attached to Homer's choice of first word. Lucian implies that any attempt to gain insight into Homer's poetry by investigating his motivations or poetic decisions is bound to be fruitless.

If Homer's responses to Lucian's poetically oriented inquiries were predictably deflating, his biographical revelations are considerably more surprising. First of all, Lucian can "see" for himself that Homer is *not* blind (ὅτι μὲν γὰρ οὐδὲ τυφλὸς ἦν . . . αὐτίκα ἠπιστάμην· ἑώρα γάρ); second, when asked about his origins, Homer discloses that he was originally a Babylonian named Tigranes (εἶναι . . . ἔλεγεν βαβυλώνιος, καὶ . . . Τιγράνης καλεῖσθαι). Lucian does not, however, elaborate much on either of these two new pieces of information; he provides no reason for why Homer was thought to have been blind, and offers only a brief explanation of how the Babylonian Tigranes 'became' the Greek Homer: he was held as a hostage (*homêros*) by the Greeks (ὁμηρεύσας παρὰ τοῖς Ἕλλησιν) and thus took the name of 'Homer.' The question of Homer's native land was an old one: the competition between various cities to claim the poet as one of their own dates back to the Classical period, and inspired all sorts of speculation, serious and otherwise.[85] The controversy has even reached the underworld: when Lucian informs Homer that "this was still now being debated among us" (παρ' ἡμῖν εἰσέτι νῦν ζητεῖσθαι), the poet replies "that he was not ignorant of the fact that some believed he was Chian, some Smyrnaean, and many Colophonian."[86]

---

[85] Numerous examples in the various *Lives* of Homer collected in West (2003) and the epigrams treating Homer's birthplace (*Anth. Pal.* 16.292–9). On the epigrams, see Skiadas (1965); on early accounts of Homer's origins, Graziosi (2002), ch. 2; for references in the Imperial period, Jones (1986), 55 n. 45, with bibliography.

[86] The three most famous claimants: cf. *Certam.* 2, *Anth. Pal.* 16.296 (Antipater), and [Plut.] *Vit. Hom.* 11.2, etc. In the Ps.-Herodotean *Life* (*Vit. Hom.* 2 West) the conflict is resolved by having

In the Hellenistic and Imperial periods, the legendary indeterminacy of Homer's origins inspired ever more outlandish solutions, which looked beyond the Greek world to 'barbarian' locales such as Egypt, Syria, and even Rome.[87] But while the etymological explanation of Homer's name as derived from "hostage" is paralleled elsewhere,[88] Lucian's claim of Babylonian origin (along with the name Tigranes) seems to be an innovation.[89] The increasing geographical diversity of Homer's alleged birthplaces speaks, of course, to the spread of Greek *paideia* in the Hellenistic and Imperial worlds, and it is not hard to read Lucian's description of Homer's passage from Babylon to Greece alongside these others as a comment on the theoretical fluidity of Greek identity in the Imperial period. Homer's biography reflects Lucian's own journey from Syria and his assimilation into Greek culture;[90] Lucian is boldly asserting the originary foreignness of that most Greek of poets, but perhaps also implying that Homer, like Lucian, has been so successful at 'being Greek' that any trace of his 'Eastern' origins has been erased.

Lucian's laconic treatment of the information, however, suggests that there is something more to his choice of Babylonian origin than first strikes the eye. Ancient scholars who proclaim Homer's link with a particular city, region, or nation often rely on positing a correspondence between customs or objects mentioned in his poetry and those actually practiced or used by the group to which Homer allegedly belongs. For instance, in his *Life of Homer*, Ps.-Herodotus argues that Homer was Aeolian on the basis of a passage in which Homer mentions five-pronged forks (πεμπώβολα: *Il.* 1.463), a utensil unique to the Aeolians (other Greeks use *three*-pronged

Homer conceived in Cyme (2), born in Smyrna (3), blinded in Colophon (7–8), and composing the *Iliad* and *Odyssey* in Chios (26–8). Many other cities and regions claimed Homer: Athens, Ios, Thessaly, Salamis, etc.

[87] For a good overview, see Heath (1998). Homer's Egyptian origin: e.g., *Vit. Hom.* 7 West (*Vita Romana*) 2; *Vit. Hom.* 9 West (*Vita Scoraliensis* II) 2; Heliod. *Aeth.* 2.34 and 3.12–15. Syrian origin: Ath. 4.157b (Meleager of Gadara). Roman origin: Aristodemus of Nysa (*Vit. Hom.* 7 West [*Vita Romana*] 2). *Vit. Hom.* 6 West (*Suda* o 251) 2 lists Egyptian, Italian, Lucanian, and Roman among the proposed ethnicities.

[88] Homer as hostage: *Vit. Hom.* 1 West (*Certamen*) 3 (Homer's father a hostage), *Vit. Hom.* 5 West (*Procl. Chr.*) 3, *Vit. Hom.* 6 West (*Suda* o 251 3).

[89] Zenodotus of Mallus (not to be confused with the Alexandrian Homeric critic Zenodotus of Ephesus) had called Homer a Chaldaean (Sch. AT ad *Il.* 23.79b). Chaldaeans were Babylonians, so some have seen this as a parallel for Lucian's attribution (e.g., Ollier [1962]). Zenodotus, however, probably uses 'Chaldaean' as a synonym for 'astrologer,' which is the issue under discussion in the scholium. Bornmann's theory (1994: 66–7) that Lucian is (comically) literalizing Zenodotus' interpretation by calling Homer a Babylonian is ingenious but seems a bit strained. On the name Tigranes, see Möllendorff (2000), 368–9.

[90] Thus Nesselrath (2002), 155, and Matteuzzi (2000–02), 50 n. 7, who argues that in Lucian's time terms such as Syrian, Assyrian, Babylonian, and Chaldaean were virtually interchangeable.

forks; moreover the Aeolian word for 'five' is πέμπε, rather than πέντε).[91]
The same logic was deployed to argue for 'barbarian' descent: Aristodemus
of Nysa, who was a teacher of Strabo, bases his claim that Homer was
a Roman on Homeric depictions of the game of *pessoi* (*Od.* 1.107) and
the habit of rising when a superior arrives, "customs that are still even
now preserved among the Romans."[92] In other words, the assertion of
an unorthodox origin for Homer was often dependent upon the type
of Homeric historical interpretation that I discussed at the beginning of
Chapter 2, in which his poetry is presumed to accurately reflect aspects of
heroic society. In this variation, Homer is still considered a faithful reporter,
but the cultural practices or items he describes, rather than deriving from
the heroes, belong instead to Homer's own culture, and his inclusion of
them, wittingly or no, in his narrative provides the evidence from which
the clever scholar can infer the poet's 'true' origins.

This rather tendentious interpretative method, along with the often
transparently self-serving motivations behind its employment, became an
easy target for satire.[93] The Hellenistic Syrian poet Meleager of Gadara, for
instance, observed that "Homer represented (ποιῆσαι) the Greeks abstain-
ing from fish despite their abundance in the Hellespont, because he was
Syrian."[94] By Meleager's time the centuries-old problem of the Homeric
heroes' aversion to eating fish had become something of a literary critical
cliché, used to demonstrate, among other things, the heroes' moral superiority (Plato, Plutarch), Homer's refusal to depict the heroes engaged in
'vulgar' activities (Aristarchus), and the separate authorship of the *Iliad*
and the *Odyssey* (the 'Separatists').[95] Meleager's simple appeal to another
well-known 'fact,' the *Syrian* abstention from fish, humorously 'solves' the
notorious problem of fish-eating and at the same time reveals Homer's
'true' ethnic identity, which turns out to match that of Meleager himself. A
similarly dubious construction of Homer as a fellow countryman occurs in

---

[91] *Vit. Hom.* 2 West (Ps.-Hdt.) 37. A second argument points to Homer's failure to mention the loin in
the same sacrifice scene (at *Il.* 1.459–61) as further evidence, since the Aeolians are the only Greeks
not to burn the loin in their sacrificial rites.

[92] *Vit. Hom.* 7 West (*Vita Romana*) 2. On Aristodemus, see Dubuisson (1987) and Heath (1998).

[93] Ps.-Herodotus argues for Homer's Aeolian origins because he believes that Homer was born in
the Aeolian city of Cyme; the idea was probably pioneered by the fourth-century BCE historian
Ephorus, who was from Cyme (*FGrH* 70 F 1 = [Plut.] *Vit. Hom.* I.2; II.2). Aristodemus likewise
had good political reasons for positing a Roman Homer; see the articles listed in the previous note.

[94] Meleager of Gadara *apud* Ath. 4.45 (157b). The Syrian abstinence from fish was well known to the
Greeks; for details, Lightfoot (2003), 65–72.

[95] Pl. *Resp.* 404b–c; Plut. *Quaest. conv.* 4.4 (*Mor.* 668f); Aristarchus and the 'Separatists' (Χωρίζοντες):
Sch. A ad *Il.* 16.747a. See Schmidt (1976), 182–7, and Heath (2000) on the ancient debate over the
heroes' aversion to fish.

Heliodorus' *An Ethiopian Tale*, where the Egyptian priest Calasiris demonstrates Homer's Egyptian-ness by an outlandish interpretation of *Il.* 1.200
that depends upon positing the poet's familiarity with arcane Egyptian lore
concerning the gods' particular mode of moving through the air.[96] In these
examples, the historicizing argument based on ethnically specific customs
discovered in Homer's poetry has been joined to a self-conscious ethnically
based appropriation of Homer himself.

Lucian too, as I argued earlier, is claiming Homer as a countryman (for
'Babylonian,' read 'Syrian')[97] and therefore following, or alluding to, the
well-known practice of fashioning Homer in one's own image. But it is
striking that in Lucian's account, unlike in the examples I just mentioned,
the revelation of Homer's unexpected origins is not dependent upon, nor
does it illuminate anything in his poetry – no Homeric 'problem' is wittily resolved, nor is any Babylonian 'custom' adduced from his verses as
supporting evidence for the ethnic claim. In fact, one suspects that this
silence is not just due to the narrator Lucian's characteristic terseness, but
rather underscores a larger point about the author Lucian's attitude toward
critics who appeal to biographical and historical information to interpret
Homeric poetry.[98] Babylon, after all, is never mentioned by Homer, and
this fact convinced even Strabo that Homer must have not been familiar
with the city or its inhabitants.[99] Does the joke then depend upon the fact
that there was no connection at all between Homer and the Babylonians?
Homer was born Babylonian but no trace of that heritage remains; in
fact it would have remained unknown had not Homer revealed it himself. Knowing Homer's identity reveals nothing about Homer's poetry
at all.

In a way, this is Lucian's response not only to the biographical critics of
Homer, who are exposed as being just as deluded as Homeric philologists,
but also to the very idea of basing one's interpretation of Homeric poetry

---

[96] Heliod. *Aeth.* 3.13. Calasiris' subsequent narrative (3.14) of Homer's hybrid parentage, illegitimacy,
exile, and hidden identity (based on an even more fanciful etymology of 'Homer' as *ho mēros*,
"the thigh"), is clearly meant to reflect Calasiris' own biography and the themes of the novel as a
whole. See Winkler (1982), 102–3, and especially Whitmarsh (1998), 104–7. According to the *Vita
Romana* (*Vit. Hom.* 7 West) 2, others in antiquity claimed Homer's Egyptian roots based on a
different custom: Homer portrays heroes kissing one another, "which is a custom practiced among
the Egyptians."

[97] Lucian, however, refers to himself in his corpus only as 'Syrian' or 'Assyrian', and never as Babylonian
or Chaldaean (for a full list, see Swain [1996], 299 n. 5).

[98] The argument that follows owes much to Ní Mheallaigh (2009).

[99] Heath (1998). Str. 15.3.23: "Homer, at any rate, knows neither of the empire of the Syrians nor of
that of the Medes; for otherwise, since he names Egyptian Thebes and mentions the wealth there
and in Phoenicia, he would not have passed by in silence that in Babylon and Ninus and Ecbatana."

on a particular vision of the poet and his intentions. Strabo constructs his Homer as a diligent and intrepid historian to ground his inquiry into the historical and geographical underpinnings of his poetry. While Dio's portrait of Homer as an improvisatory liar mocks this sort of exercise by exaggerating it to a point just short of absurdity, Lucian implicitly severs any causal relation between Homer's life and the 'meaning' of his poetry. Furthermore, Lucian's interview with Homer questions the investment in ethnicity and descent that often fueled inquiry into Homer and the heroic age, by revealing first that the father of Greek culture was not even originally Greek, but then implying that this foreign ancestry has left no impression on his poetry, for better or for worse. In the same vein, Lucian makes it clear that resolving the questions about which poem came first, or whether verses are genuine, or why the first word of the *Iliad* is 'anger' also have little effect on one's understanding of the poems. Homer's 'true' origin offers no insight into his poetry, nor does knowing anything about his poetic motivations – all we need is the poetry itself, i.e., the fictional world that he has constructed.

Repetition and literary self-reflection

The conversation with Homer, then, has not really revealed any new truths about the poet or his poetry, but confirmed a view of Homeric poetry as occupying a space cut off to the outside world, upon which nothing – no information about Homer's life, his motivations, or historical 'reality' – can intrude. The failure to learn anything new about Homer and his poetry is in keeping with the general sense of inertia evoked by the island's timelessness and the unchanging nature of its inhabitants, whose existence as ghosts, as we have seen, resemble their literary lives. The rest of the stay on the Island continues in this fashion, as Lucian stages a series of repetitions and reconfigurations of Homeric events that nevertheless resist straying too far from their literary models. So, for instance, while Lucian includes some 'new' variations in his description of the so-called Thanatousia, or Games of the Dead (2.22) (Odysseus loses to a 'modern' wrestler and Epeius draws with a 'modern' boxer), they are moderate revisions to what remains a parodic reflection of the funeral games for the dead Patroclus in the *Iliad* (23.257–897).[100] And if he innovates by holding a poetic contest between

---

[100] On this episode, see Mal-Maeder (1992), 138–9, who notes the incongruity between Lucian's 'ethnographic' voice and the heroic content in this episode; the estrangement that results from looking at Greek heroic athletics as if it were alien is analyzed by König (2005), 75–80. Cf. Robert (1980), 427–32.

Homer and Hesiod during these games, the result repeats that found in the literary tradition; as in the *Contest*, "Hesiod defeated Homer, even though the latter was far superior."

The two major episodes that conclude Lucian's stay on the Island – Cinyras and Helen's attempted escape and Odysseus' letter to Calypso – are perhaps the most famous examples of his parodic transformations of epic. The two stories are linked, since the first Iliadic episode leads to Lucian's departure from the island and ushers the beginning of his own *Odyssey* home. They have also received the lion's share of critics' interest.[101] Mal-Maeder usefully classifies these scenes as two different types of Lucianic intervention in the Homeric tradition; if the second Rape of Helen functions as a parodic repetition of the cause of the War, occurring before the *Iliad*, the Calypso scene is a continuation of Homer beyond the *Odyssey*.[102] She, like many other critics, emphasizes the creative aspects of these episodes, foregrounding the pleasure Lucian takes in travesty-ing and supplementing Homer; Bompaire calls these interventions "the two most seductive moments" in the whole work.[103] But while Lucian's play with Homeric tradition is undoubtedly amusing, the tenor of the tales, and especially their outcomes, seems also to respect the strict literary boundaries that Lucian has drawn in his treatment of the heroes on the Island.

Take the comical replay of the Rape of Helen. Six months into Lucian's stay on the Island, one of his companions, a strapping lad named Cinyras, who had been flirting with Helen for a while already, conspires with her to run off together to one of the nearby islands (2.25). When their departure is noticed, Rhadamanthus outfits a ship with fifty heroes who give chase, catch them just before they have left territorial waters, and bring them back for punishment. Helen is embarrassed and repentant; the kidnappers are bound by their genitals and sentenced to the Island of the Wicked. Unfortunately for Lucian, because part of his crew was involved in the crime, he is forced to take leave of the island immediately (2.26). The Helen scene is a burlesque; history, or in this case literature, repeating itself as 'low' farce. Bompaire, however, emphasizes its revisionist nature; the Helen episode "is not a reconsition of the past, it is the past and myth invading the present with an irresistible vigor . . . A dream on the fringes of Homer and of the epic cycle." Perhaps. But what is the result of this dream? Helen runs off again but eventually returns repentant to take her

[101] Möllendorff (2000), 452–7.   [102] Mal-Maeder (1992), 140–4; cf. Zeitlin (2001), 245.
[103] Bompaire (1958), 671–2.

rightful place by Menelaus' side, just as before. Cinyras' intervention raises
the possibility of a new outcome for Helen, but by the end of the episode
she remains in the same position as before.

Thersites' suit against Homer, which I mentioned previously, also opens
up fascinating possibilities for alternate storylines, but Lucian again quickly
closes them off by arranging for Thersites' defeat and the restoration of
the status quo.[104] In the Lucianic model, Thersites *cannot* win, because if
he did, a gap would have arisen between his representation in Homer and
his *real* actions, whereas the ruling conceit in the *True Stories* is that the
figures encountered on the Island of the Blessed are literary characters. The
joke is that Thersites, unlike his namesake in the *Dialogues of the Dead*
referred to above, does not realize that his existence depends solely upon
Homer, and he is thus doomed to lose a case in which the poet is accused
of libel. On the Island, Helen too cannot escape, but simply replays her
unfulfilled adulterous desires over and over again. In fact, it seems as if
Lucian is calling attention to the fixed nature of the Homeric poetic world,
by depicting its characters, like Thersites and Helen, attempting to resist
their representations and 'escape' the narratives that define them, either by
physically leaving the Island, like Helen, or forcing the 'creator' of the story
to change it via a lawsuit. The fact that they both fail suggests that there is
no easy way out of this closed literary world.

What makes Lucian's portrayal of the heroes even more unusual is
that other ancient stories that juxtapose poets and their subjects tend
to do so in order to exploit the difference between poetry and 'reality,'
usually by confronting the poet with the 'real' person or object he has
portrayed in his poetry. The most famous case is that of Stesichorus and
Helen, where the poet is punished by the heroine's ghost because he had
sung what was not 'true' about her, and only regains his sight when he
recants and admits the 'truth.' An interesting variant of this story, told by
Lucian's rough contemporary Pausanias, reveals how Stesichorus learned
of Helen's displeasure: a contemporary of the poet, Leonomus of Croton,
had visited Leuke (the 'White Island' sacred to Achilles) and reported that
he had seen Achilles, both Ajaxes, Patroclus, and Antilochus living there.[105]
Helen resided with Achilles, and told Leonomus to tell Stesichorus that
her anger had caused his blindness. Leonomus delivered the message and

---

[104] Libanius' *Encomium of Thersites* (Foerster, vol. VIII: 243–51) is a good counter-example; Thersites
is sympathetically portrayed as a noble-born, truth-loving hero and defended by careful attention
to the inconcinnities of the Homeric account. See Gibson (2009), 229–37 for a translation and a
list of other ancient treatments of Thersites.

[105] All heroes who had died at Troy.

Stesichorus immediately composed the *Palinode* and recovered his sight.[106]
The resemblance to Lucian's encounter is fairly clear – a visit by a living
man to an island where the ghosts of heroes reside – but the point of
Pausanias' story is entirely different.[107] The emphasis is on the *gap* between
poetry and reality; what Leonomus learns on Leuke is that Stesichorus'
story was not true, and that the 'real' Helen was quite different from
her poetic depiction. On the Island, however, Stesichorus and Helen get
along harmoniously (Lucian refers to their quarrel, but only to note its
resolution), and the peaceful co-habitation of Homer and his heroes (aside
from Thersites) erases any sense of such a gap between poetic depiction
and heroic character.

The episode involving Odysseus' letter to Calypso similarly treats the
desire of a hero to break out of the literary world of the Island, although
in this case, Lucian never reveals (or perhaps never learns of) the outcome.
When Lucian is about to leave the Island, Odysseus surreptitiously slips
him a letter to deliver to Calypso, whose island is nearby (2.29). After
passing by the Island of the Wicked and spending a month on the Island of
Dreams, Lucian reaches Ogygia, Calypso's island.[108] Before he sees Calypso,
he reads Odysseus' letter:

Dear Calypso, I want to inform you that I . . . [a précis of his post-Calypso exploits
from the *Odyssey* follows, ending with his massacre of the suitors]. Then I was
killed by Telegonus, my son by Circe, and I am currently on the Island of the
Blessed, regretting terribly that I left behind my life with you and the immortality
you proposed to me. So if I have the opportunity, I will escape and return to you.
Odysseus. (2.35)

Lucian comes to the cave, which is "just as Homer had described it",
and finds Calypso working wool. She reads the letter, cries, and then
questions Lucian about Odysseus and especially Penelope: "what she looked
like and whether she was faithful as Odysseus used, long ago, to boast."
In his customary deadpan manner, Lucian concludes: "We gave her the
sort of answers we thought would make her happy" (καὶ ἡμεῖς τοιαῦτα
ἀπεκρινάμεθα, ἐξ ὧν εἰκάζομεν εὐφρανεῖσθαι αὐτήν: 2.36).

---

[106] Paus. 3.19.11–13. The story is far older; it dates back at least as far as the Hellenistic mythographer
Conon (*Narr.* 18 = *FGrH* 26 F 1.18)

[107] Möllendorff (2000), 342–3, sees Lucian's Island of the Blessed as a parody of traditions that depict
the island of Leuke as the haunt of Achilles and other heroes. For Philostratus' variation on this
motif, see Ch. 6: 212–13.

[108] In a way, Lucian takes on the role of Odysseus when he visits Calypso on his behalf, although the
natural Homeric parallel for Lucian, as Stengel (1911: 83) pointed out long ago, is probably Hermes
rather than Odysseus.

The episode is fashioned around a familiar 'problem' that vexed commentators – "why did Odysseus not accept Calypso's offer of immortality?"[109] – a decision that Lucian's Odysseus has now come to regret. Here we could legitimately speak of a sequel, or, in Froma Zeitlin's words, a reconceptualization of "the very ideological basis of the epic, its investment in marital fidelity and embrace of mortality as the human condition in favour of the all too human desire to live forever" (2001: 246). But Zeitlin also recognizes that "Lucian cannot go as far as to arrange for this reunion" although she fails to explain what might be preventing him. After all, isn't this sort of free invention precisely what Lucian arrogates for himself in his preface by acknowledging the falsity of all that is to come? But the self-imposed limits of the episode are in line with the rest of the stories that take place on the Island: like Helen and Thersites, Odysseus longs to write a new chapter to his story, but the best he can do is write a letter expressing these yearnings.

In a way, Lucian too is incorporated into the literary world of the Island that he visits. It has often been noted that the longer he stays, the more Lucian becomes involved in the events and characters on the Island. At first simply ethnographic observer and interviewer, he sees his companion Cinyras intrude directly into the life of the Islanders, and then, just when he is leaving, begins being treated *as* a hero by Rhadamanthus, who assures Lucian that he will return one day and even points out the chair and couch that will be his. His role as ersatz Odysseus on the visit to Calypso is foreshadowed by Rhadamanthus' description of the neighboring islands to Lucian upon his departure (2.27–8) – an obvious allusion to Circe's similar account told to Odysseus in *Odyssey* 12. The moment, however, when Lucian 'becomes' one of the literary characters on the Island occurs a little earlier, in another encounter with Homer.

When Lucian discovers that he has to leave the Island, he asks Homer to compose a two-verse epigram for him, which he then inscribes on a block of beryl near the harbor: "Lucian, dear to the blessed gods, saw // everything here and went back to his own native land" (2.28). Despite its brevity, the epigram, and especially Lucian's choice to inscribe it, plays with notions of literary attribution and naming: upon reading the stele, one would probably assume that Lucian himself had composed it, since there is no indication of Homer's authorship. On the one hand this is entirely fitting for the poet who famously never mentions his name in his poetry. But as Simon Goldhill has observed, it surely can be no coincidence that this is one of only three times in his entire corpus that Lucian refers to

---

[109] Sch. ad *Od.* 23.337.

himself by his own name, rather than by a pseudonym or other 'mask.'[110] In fact, it is only when Lucian records this epigram of Homer that the reader of the *True Stories* realizes that the as-yet-unnamed I-narrator of the *True Stories* is identical with, or at least has the same name as, its author. But it also represents the moment when the Lucianic narrator (and thus the Lucianic author as well?) is literally inscribed into Homer's poetic world, when he becomes a 'character,' like the other heroes, of his own (admittedly brief) Homeric narrative. In this sense his departure from the Island and his journey home have already been narrated by Homer ("and went back to his own native land"), and Lucian has been enclosed in the poet's literary universe.[111]

Conclusion: beyond history

The reworked Homeric episodes thus conform to the general parameters of Lucian's characterization of the Island as a whole. Lucian indulges in the thrill of entering the world of Greek *paideia*, meeting and conversing with the most famous figures of the literary and cultural canon. His experiences on the Island, however, seem marked less by novelty and the acquisition of knowledge than by a sense of déjà vu; what Lucian learns from his visit is that Homer and the heroes are more or less just as they appear in poetry and literature. One could argue that this is the whole joke of the *True Stories* – Lucian goes to the moon, lives inside of a whale, and visits the afterlife but always retains his unperturbed demeanor, remarkably unaffected by his adventures. The failure to deliver the tantalizing bits of new information for which the reader is eager is also part of the tease: just as Apion raised the ghost of Homer but could not reveal what he was told about the poet's origins, Lucian relates that Homer has given him a new epic about a battle between the heroes and escapees from the Island of the Wicked (2.24), only to disclose that he has lost it and can only remember the (ridiculous) first line: 'Now tell me, Muse, of the fight of the dead heroes' (Νῦν δέ μοι ἔννεπε, Μοῦσα, μάχην νεκύων ἡρώων).[112] So, too, Lucian reports his interview with Homer, but precious little information is revealed, and certainly nothing that provides any insight into his poetry.

---

[110] Goldhill (2002), 65.

[111] On the temporal complexity of the epigram, in which Lucian's future is narrated as already having occurred, see Ní Mheallaigh (2009).

[112] "When I was leaving [the island], Homer gave me the text (τὰ βιβλία) to take to the people of our world, but we lost it later along with everything else" (2.24).

Seen from another perspective, however, Lucian's depiction of the Island as a literary world of Greek *paideia*, and his reluctance to 'change' Homeric stories too much, is an implicit expression of his views upon the proper way to think about Homer in Imperial Greece. Lucian addresses Homer's status as a historian of the heroic age, so important to writers like Strabo, not by parodying or denying Homer's authority in the historical arena, but by ignoring it completely and refusing to grant 'history' any place in the self-contained literary world of the Island of the Blessed. This is particularly significant given that Lucian frames the *True Stories* itself as a response to his consternation at the inabilities of audiences to differentiate history and fiction, and conducts his discussion of this issue in the preface within the same conceptual framework of myth and history that Strabo uses in his *Geography*. On the other hand, Lucian also refrains from representing the poet as many of his contemporaries do, as a divinely inspired genius, font of philosophical wisdom, or venerable moral instructor. Instead Lucian suggests, through his descriptions of Homer's characters in the *True Stories*, his encounters with Homer himself, and his characterization of the poet's fictions in the preface, that Homer's legacy to the Imperial world resides not in his role as cultural icon, ambassador of Hellenism, or historiographical recorder of the glorious deeds of the Greek heroic age, but in his capacity as a storyteller, a creator of fictions that have become so powerful that they possess a certain reality of their own, even though they are acknowledged as invented. The proper response to Homeric fiction is thus to focus on the creative power it possesses to invent its *own* reality rather than engage in the fruitless enterprise of seeking the 'history' or 'truth' that underlies the poetry. The visions of Cinyras punished for trying to elope with Helen, Thersites losing his case against Homer, and Odysseus pining for a new end to his tale all illustrate Lucian's point about the integrity of Homer's fictional world, so powerful that its heroic protagonists cannot escape its boundaries. Lucian's utter denial of history's utility to an understanding of Homeric poetry is the most uncompromising, and perhaps most radical Imperial response to the question of reconciling Homer's twin roles as poet and historian.

CHAPTER 6

Ghosts at Troy

Philostratus' *Heroicus*

Philostratus' *Heroicus*, written at some point after 217 CE, probably in the early 220s, is the chronologically latest text devoted to assessing Homer's historiographical qualities that I examine in this book, and perhaps the most curious and innovative as well.[1] Framed as a contemporary dialogue between a Phoenician merchant and a Greek vine dresser in the Thracian Chersonese, it includes stories of present-day heroic epiphanies as well as an alternate history of the Trojan War, both deriving from information that the vine dresser has obtained directly from the ghost of Protesilaus, the first Greek soldier killed at Troy. Despite the acknowledged access to an 'eyewitness' source, much of the dialogue explores the history of the Trojan War and its heroes in counterpoint to Homer's account, frequently referencing the poet and his narrative. Philostratus presents this material in a far from linear fashion; the text is packed full of digressions (on giant skeletons, Amazons, athletes, etc.), and relates its new version of the Trojan War piecemeal through descriptions of individual heroes.[2]

If one steps back and takes the *Heroicus* in with an eye to its overarching structure, one can detect at least a modicum of organization. The medium-length dialogue (92 pages [128–219] in Kayser's *editio minor*)[3] begins with a leisurely introduction in which the two interlocutors meet, converse, and settle on the main topic of their conversation – Homer, the heroes, and the Trojan War – subjects that the vine dresser knows well, based on his friendship with Protesilaus' ghost (1–7). After a rather long excursus in which giant skeleton discoveries are used to combat the Phoenician's

---

[1] On the date, see Jones (2001), and Grossardt (2006), 16–19. For a lucid introduction to Philostratus and his work, see Bowie (2009); exhaustive discussion in de Lannoy (1997).

[2] Billault (2000), 126–36, gives an excellent general account of the *Heroicus*.

[3] I use de Lannoy's (1977) numbering system of chapter and sentence for its convenience, but refer to Kayser's (1870–1) page numbers (K) when discussing the relative length of individual sections of the text because the length of de Lannoy's chapters vary widely: compare ch. 33 on Palamedes (eight pages in Kayser) with ch. 36 (six lines).

skepticism about the heroes' size (8), the vine dresser then relates his encounters with Protesilaus as well as tales of other heroes' ghosts (9–22), particularly those who died at Troy – Ajax, Hector, Achilles, Patroclus, and Palamedes. The pace is unhurried: this first part accounts for nearly a third of the whole text (1–22; 128–55 Kayser). After this description of the heroes' activity in the *present*, the long central portion of the text (23–52.2; 155–206 K) describes their deeds in the *past*: the Mysian expedition omitted by Homer (23), an excursus on Homer's poetry (24–5), a central catalog of heroes (26–42) highlighted by an eight-page treatment of Palamedes (33; 177–84 K), another excursus on Homer (43–4), and finally an account of Achilles' life (45–52). Achilles' activities after his death – as cult hero, erstwhile poet, fighter of Amazons, and companion of Helen on the island of Leuke in the Black Sea – occupy the rest of the text (53–7: 207–18 K), save for a brief conclusion (58: 219 K) that returns us to the dialogue frame. The text thus moves symmetrically from the present to the past and back again: the conversation of the interlocutors and current stories of heroic ghosts open and conclude the text, bookending the central discussion of the past – Mysia, Homer, the heroes, and Achilles.[4]

Even this perfunctory summary illustrates the variety of the *Heroicus'* content and its complex temporal frame. Its literary form – a fictional dialogue featuring two anonymous conversationalists – also sets it apart from the other works we have examined in this book, whose authors (e.g., Herodotus, Thucydides, Dio, and Strabo) address their audience directly, investigating and passing judgment upon Homer's reliability in their own voice. The one exception is Lucian, but even he opens his work with a preface addressing his readers and explaining, however tongue-in-cheek, his intentions and motivations. Philostratus, however, is completely absent from the *Heroicus*, even as a narrator, rendering it that much more difficult to identify his voice.[5] To be sure, Dio and Lucian have their own methods of confounding efforts to locate their 'true' opinions, but Philostratus' choice of a dialogue, with no preface or opening narrative frame, sets the reader adrift from the start. To complicate matters, much of the dialogue is actually the vine dresser's report of the opinions and knowledge of Protesilaus' ghost, the authoritative 'source' at the heart of the text (who never appears or speaks directly); this mediation of the truth raises more

---

[4] For different outlines of the structure: Mantero (1966), 11–12; Beschorner (1999), 210–15; Grossardt (2006), 51–5. We should note that accounts of the past, positioned at the heart of the dialogue, take up nearly 60 percent of the text.

[5] On the dialogue form, see Hodkinson (2007), 6–7; Whitmarsh (2009), 207–9.

questions about Philostratus' position vis-à-vis the views expressed in his work.

The precise tone of the *Heroicus* is also difficult to pin down, hovering uneasily as it does between piety and parody, and as we shall see, this tension lies at the heart of modern interpretative disagreements over the text's meaning and purpose. To some degree this ambivalence of tone is closely related to its split subject matter – stories of heroic activity in the here and now juxtaposed with corrections and supplements of Homer's account of the heroic past. Philostratus' interweaving of contemporary religious discourse on heroic immortality and epiphany with the playful and somewhat disreputable critical enterprise of revising Homer leaves the text delicately poised between two incongruent forces – the solemnity of religious discourse and belief lends its weight to the hoary topic of Homeric revision, but by the same token, the literariness and untrustworthiness of Homeric revision calls that solemnity into question. Philostratus links one Second Sophistic fantasy – the literal revitalization of the Hellenic past and its religious energies – with another – discovering the truth about Homer and the Trojan War. In a way, one could even see the *Heroicus* as a combination of Dio's relentless interrogation of Homer's account as history in the *Trojan Oration* and Lucian's exploitation of the desire to meet and question the dead in the *True Stories*. The result is a singular text that manages to incorporate moments of great sublimity and a healthy dose of the absurd, and that fittingly stands as the capstone to centuries of thinking about Homer's reliability.

THE *HEROICUS* AND THE 'TRUE' STORY OF THE TROJAN WAR

For all of its quirks, the *Heroicus* is firmly situated in the tradition of texts devoted to the investigation of the Homeric past. Although stories of modern heroic epiphanies predominate at the beginning, the majority of the dialogue is taken up by the correction and supplementation of Homer's account of the heroes. Philostratus was surely well aware of his predecessors; his 'source' Protesilaus, at any rate, seems quite familiar with the chief criticisms of Homer's historical veracity. In an excursus on Protesilaus' views on the poet (25.10–13), we learn that the hero, in an evident nod to Herodotus, "blames" (μέμφεται) Homer for bringing Helen to Troy even though he "clearly knew" (σαφῶς γινώσκων) that she was in Egypt; he even rehearses several of his predecessor's εἰκός-arguments in support of the claim (25.10–11).[6] Protesilaus' subsequent insistence that the duel between Menelaus and Paris "must be eliminated" (ἐξῃρήσθω: 25.12) accords with Dio's opinion on the subject in the *Trojan Oration* (cf. *Or.* 11.83) while his criticism of how Homer "after [the death of] Hector leapt from the story [of the Trojan War] (ἀποπηδᾷ τοῦ λόγου μετὰ τὸν Ἕκτορα: 25.13)" and rushed ahead to the *Odyssey* echoes Dio's complaint (*Or.* 11.34) about the poet's failure to narrate the end of the war. Similarly both find fault with the decision to "cut off from the story" (ἀποτεμὼν τοῦ λόγου: 25.13) post-Iliadic episodes such as the Trojan Horse and the Sack of Troy and insert them piecemeal into "the songs of Demodocus and Phemius" in the *Odyssey*. Protesilaus also follows a long line of critics (Eratosthenes, Dio, Lucian, etc.) in dismissing the Phaeacian tales as pure fiction: the Cyclopes, Circe, Laestrygonians, etc., were all invented (ἐπενοήθη; ἀνετυπώθησαν; ἐξεποιήθη: *Her.* 25.13), and Calypso and Nausicaa never fell in love with Odysseus.[7]

This explicit nod to the anti-Homeric tradition reflects an extensive and detailed familiarity with Homeric criticism that runs through the entire *Heroicus*, one which I will be emphasizing throughout this chapter. But for now, I want to point out that this familiarity surely went hand in hand with the knowledge that proposing to contest Homer's account of the war had become, by Philostratus' time, virtually a declaration of non-serious intent. As the passage just referred to suggests, Philostratus was almost certainly acquainted with one of the most notorious examples, Dio's *Trojan Oration*.[8] And even if he had not read Lucian's *True Stories* and *The Rooster*, or Ptolemy the Quail's deliberately ludicrous *Paradoxical History*, he is clearly working in the same general milieu. For instance, many of the topics brought up by Philostratus in the *Heroicus* are also treated (albeit quite differently) by Ptolemy: among others, the divinity of Achilles' horses (Phot. *Bibl.* 190, 150b7–10), the *moly* (149b39–42), the coupling of Helen and Achilles in the afterlife (149a18–20), the enmity between Agamemnon and Palamedes (150b38–151a4), and Odysseus' mysterious death from the

---

[6] (1) Even if another woman had caused the mess (i.e., she herself wasn't guilty), Helen would have been ashamed at the accusation and not made herself visible; (2) Hector would have given her back to Menelaus; (3) Priam would not have indulged Paris, especially since many of his sons had died; (4) the Trojan women would have killed her, since she was the cause of their men's deaths; (5) perhaps she herself would have deserted back to Menelaus to escape the hatred of the Trojans.

[7] Protesilaus attributes many of Homer's faults to his desire to "gratify" or favor Helen, Achilles, and especially Odysseus. See below, 208–11.

[8] Philostratus includes Dio in his *Lives of the Sophists* (I.7; 487–8) and features him as a character in his *Life of Apollonius* (5.31–40). On the parallels between the *Heroicus* and the *Trojan Oration*, see Grentrup (1914), 44–6; Grossardt (2006), 70. Is it a coincidence that the title of Philostratus' work – ΗΡѠΙΚΟΣ – is only one letter removed from Dio's ΤΡѠΙΚΟΣ?

sea (150a12–19).[9] And Philostratus' revelation of Protesilaus' ghost as the 'source' for his new vision of the heroic, pre-Homeric past links him to a characteristic trope of Imperial Homeric revision: the discovery of pre-Homeric testimony. Aside from Dio's Egyptian priestly records and Lucian's reincarnated rooster, we hear, from Ptolemy and other sources, of several other Trojan War narratives pre-dating Homer: some in verse composed by Trojan War participants (Dares, assistant to Hector; and Corinnus of Ilium, follower of Palamedes) and others in prose by women (Helen, daughter of Musaeus; the aptly named Phantasia of Memphis).[10] Although it is not certain that any of these actually existed, the possibility of their existence was clearly something that gripped the Imperial imagination.[11]

Two such works that did exist, and with which the *Heroicus* has the most in common, were the so-called 'Troy Romances,'[12] which purported to be war diaries written by participants in the Trojan War, the Greek soldier Dictys of Crete (*Ephemeris belli Troiani*) and the Trojan ally Dares of Phrygia (*Acta diurna belli Troiani* or *De excidio Troiae historia*).[13] The extant versions are in Latin and belong (probably) to the fourth and fifth centuries CE respectively, but papyrus fragments of Dictys' *Ephemeris* in Greek dating to the early third century CE suggest that the work was originally written in Greek sometime before 200 CE and after the thirteenth year of Nero's reign (66 CE, the time of the text's alleged 'discovery' according to the *Ephemeris'*

---

[9] Note also that, according to Photius, Ptolemy treated the death of Protesilaus in his first book (Phot. *Bibl.* 190, 146b17–18; cf. 147a29–30 on Dardanus, the *mnêmôn* of Protesilaus); for more on Ptolemy, see Ch. 1, 18–21.

[10] Dares: Phot. *Bibl.* 190, 147a26–9. Helen: 149b22–6; Phantasia: 151a38–b5; Corinnus: *Suda* s.v. Κόριννος (κ 2091). Aelian (*VH* 11.2) also claims to know of a pre-Homeric *Phrygian Iliad* written by a Dares, which "is still to this day preserved"; he also mentions a pre-Homeric epic by Oroebantius of Troezen, although it is unclear whether this dealt with the Trojan War. While it is tempting to identify the putative author of the *Acta diurna* with one or both of the Dares' mentioned by Ptolemy and Aelian, the fact that the works of the two latter are in verse, rather than prose, suggests a more complicated relationship. In fact, Ptolemy by 'inventing' his Dares, might, as Cameron ([2006]: 148–9) proposes, have provided the inspiration for the *Acta diurna*. For a full discussion, see Beschorner (1992), 231–5.

[11] Cameron (2006), 147–50. Ptolemy's 'source' for Dares is Antipater of Acanthus, who is almost certainly an invention.

[12] There are fragments of a third 'eyewitness' Troy Romance attributed to (an otherwise unknown) Sisyphus of Cos (*FGrH* 50 F 1–3), a companion of Teucer, embedded in John Malalas' sixth-century CE *Chronographia*. While we have no idea when Sisyphus' account was written, Malalas mentions him and Dictys in the same sentence and was clearly using both texts as his primary sources (that Malalas used Sisyphus directly rather than at secondhand is suggested by his quotation of a speech by Teucer); it is thus tempting to situate Sisyphus in the second or third centuries CE, roughly contemporary with our other Trojan fictions. On Sisyphus, see Griffin (1908), 332–4, and Cameron (2006), 149–50.

[13] On the Troy Romances, see Merkle (1996); on Dictys: Merkle (1989) and (1994); on Dares: Beschorner (1992).

preface). Although there is no similar hard evidence for Dares' *Acta diurna*, many suspect that it also has an earlier Greek counterpart dating from roughly the same period.[14] Both works thus probably pre-date Philostratus, and it has been argued that the *Heroicus* directly responds to Dictys' *Ephemeris* in at least two places: Protesilaus' comment that writing did not yet exist before the Trojan War (23.11) undermines the very premise of a war journal, while his revelation that Idomeneus (whom Dictys allegedly served under) had not even taken part in the expedition (30.1) attacks the legitimacy of Dictys' participant status.[15] This is hardly conclusive evidence,[16] but regardless of whether or not one accepts Philostratus' awareness of Dictys' work, it is undeniable that the *Heroicus*' 'new' version of the Trojan War displays some general affinities with the Troy Romances. All three works treat the whole of the Trojan Cycle, supplementing the *Iliad* with accounts of, for example, the Mysian expedition, Palamedes, and the love of Polyxena and Achilles (although each author treats these stories quite differently at the level of detail).[17] More significantly, the worldview that permeates their narratives is characteristic of the romance rather than heroic epic: the gods are absent, fantastic and implausible elements are rationalized, the ethical landscape is rendered more clear-cut by eliminating moral lapses in some characters and accentuating them in others, and the enmities between East and West, Greek and Trojan, are heightened. Another point of convergence is the common appeal to a previously unknown 'source' for the new information purveyed in the works. If Philostratus depends upon the testimony of a hero's ghost, the Troy Romances purport to be the translations of recently 'discovered' written sources.[18] This recalls Herodotus and Dio, of course, but now the new information, rather than being reported at secondhand, is presented directly to the reader in its 'original' and 'authentic' ancient form (albeit translated), accompanied only by a brief editorial preface in which the circumstances of discovery and translation are

---

[14] On questions of date and the possible existence of a Greek original, see Beschorner (1992), 231–43, and Pavano (1998).

[15] Noted by Huhn and Bethe (1917); Mantero (1966). For discussion, see Grentrup (1914), 46–52; Merkle (1989), 254–9; Grossardt (2006), 71–2.

[16] The assertion about the lack of writing before the Trojan War need not be a veiled undermining of Dictys' premise; the origins of writing had been a topic of interest at least since Herodotus (5.58) and the specific question of whether Homer's heroes were aware of writing exercised a number of ancient Homeric critics (for details, see Schmidt [1976], 213–14). The pointed absence of Idomeneus seems the stronger case, but see the doubts of Grossardt (2006), 72.

[17] Grossardt (2006), 71, with specific references.

[18] As is typical of such forgeries, the authors are not heroes themselves (in fact, they are never mentioned in the *Iliad* – the Dares, priest of Hephaestus, of *Il.* 5.9 is clearly a different person), but are instead conceived of as their secretaries or companions: Idomeneus (Dictys), Antenor (Dares). The texts thus seem to be told from a more objective, observational perspective than that of the heroes themselves, while still maintaining their authors' participant status.

detailed.[19] Such an interest in pseudo-documentarism and authenticating devices is, of course, quite common in Imperial literature and links the Troy Romances with the Greek novels and other narrative fiction: one thinks of the buried cypress tablets unearthed by Alexander that preserve the story told in Antonius Diogenes' *The Wonders beyond Thule* (Phot. *Bibl.* 166, 111b), the painting that depicts the adventures of Daphnis and Chloe at the beginning of Longus' novel, and even, perhaps, of the memoirs of Damis that Philostratus claims as the primary source of his *Life of Apollonius of Tyana* (*VA* 1.3).[20]

In such an environment, Philostratus must have been aware that an attempt to propose yet another 'true story' of the Trojan War was akin to throwing one's hat into a very crowded ring,[21] and it is hard to imagine that he expected *his* new version, vouched for by *his* new source, Protesilaus' ghost, to be taken as anything but a self-conscious, knowing addition to a genre littered with forgeries, parodies, and literary fictions. The peculiarities of the *Heroicus* – its fictional dialogue form, its secondary focus on heroic epiphanies and cult, its oblique manner of correcting Homer – are signs that Philostratus was both cognizant of his latecomer status and actively trying to say something new about the topic. In what follows, I address the myriad ways in which Philostratus comments on, parodies, and transforms his predecessors' concerns about Homer's reliability and intentions, with a particular focus on the portrayal of the *Heroicus'* two competing 'sources': Protesilaus' ghost and Homer himself.

A meeting of Homeric critics

The opening scenes of the *Heroicus* enact a conversation between a Phoenician merchant and a Greek vine dresser as they make their way to the latter's vineyard in the Thracian Chersonese.[22] The atmosphere is replete with intertextual reference; Dio's *Euboean Oration* (*Or.* 7, a text known to Philostratus: *VS* 487) springs immediately to mind – an initial chance meeting on the beach, a walk to a pleasant location accompanied by conversation, rustic living at harmony with nature.[23] And once the two have

---

[19] The two prefaces to Dictys tell slightly different versions of an elaborate story of how the manuscript, written in Phoenician and buried in Dictys' tomb, was discovered and translated in the time of Nero, while the briefer preface to the Latin version of Dares, purporting to be a letter from Cornelius Nepos to Sallust, relates a more mundane tale of discovery in a library.

[20] On the Imperial vogue for 'pseudo-documentarism' see Speyer (1970); Merkle (1989), 73–80; Hansen (2003); and Ní Mheallaigh (2008).

[21] Beschorner (1999), 219–21, and more comprehensively, Grossardt (2006), 55–74.

[22] For an excellent reading of the opening of the *Heroicus*, see Hodkinson (2007), 6–23.

[23] Anderson (1986), 241–2, who points to Lucian's *Charon* and Longus' *Daphnis and Chloe* as well; Reuter (1932) gives a good account of the idealizing portrait of rustic life portrayed by Dio in the *Euboean Oration*.

entered the vineyard to pursue their conversation (3.3–5.4), there is a clear
nod to the famous opening of Plato's *Phaedrus* so frequently imitated in
Imperial literature.[24] Homer is also never far from the reader's mind. After
all, the Phoenician's encounter with the vine dresser is also a variation on
Odyssey 14, where the sea-faring traveler Odysseus is taken in by the rustic
local Eumaeus.[25] When the vine dresser's dog gives a friendly, fawning
welcome to the visitor (2.1), it is hard not to think of the parallel behavior
of Eumaeus' dogs to Telemachus in *Od.* 16.4, and the contrastingly hostile
greeting Odysseus gets from them in *Od.* 14.29–38.[26]

Owen Hodkinson has noted how this initial intertextual overload is
"teasing the reader, hinting at several genres misleadingly . . . the allusions
to multiple traditions themselves tell the reader to be on the alert for
disguises and deceptive appearances in the remainder of the text."[27] And
both Hodkinson and Whitmarsh have remarked on the unusual emphasis
placed on disguise and mistaken identity (another Odyssean trope) in the
opening of the *Heroicus*: in the dialogue's first line the vine dresser mistakes
the Phoenician for an Ionian because of his clothing, and the vine dresser
himself later reveals (4.6) that he is not the rustic fellow he appears to
be, but an urban *pepaideumenos* recently converted to country life.[28] But
surely the most surprising revelation for the reader is that the *Heroicus'*
three major characters – the Phoenician merchant, the kindly vine dresser,
and the ghost of Protesilaus – turn out to be erudite, learned students of
Homeric poetry. The encounter exemplifies the way that Homer functions
as a universal 'language' under the Empire that transcends ethnicity or
national identity; the Phoenician merchant and the Thracian vine dresser
may come from different cultures and walks of life, but they quickly find
a common ground in Homer and the heroic past, one shared also, as we
shall see, by the ghost of a long-dead hero.

Within a few lines of their encounter, the Phoenician and vine dresser,
despite their differing origins, both show off their knowledge of Homer,
skillfully trading Homeric tags: the vine dresser refers to Phoenicians by the
Homeric description "nibblers" (τρῶκται: *Her.* 1.3; cf. *Od.* 14.289, 15.416)
and the Phoenician's mention of Maron's wine from *Odyssey* 9 is matched
by the vine dresser's reference to the Cyclopes' proverbial easy life from the

[24] Grossardt (2006) notes the frequent verbal echoes (s.v. 3, 5); Martin (2002) on the parallels with
   the beginning of Achilles Tatius' *Leucippe and Cleitophon*; Trapp (1990) on the popularity of the
   Phaedrus; and Hodkinson (2007) on broader connections between the *Heroicus* and the *Phaedrus*.
[25] Anderson (1986), 249–50; Grossardt (2006), 49–50.
[26] The language most closely parallels the dogs' response to Athena at *Od.* 16.162–3.
[27] Hodkinson (2007), 14.   [28] Whitmarsh (2001), 103–5; (2004).

same book (*Her.* 1.4). The initial hint of familiarity with Homeric poetry is picked up again in chapter 6, after the vine dresser reveals that he is a close acquaintance of Protesilaus' ghost (2.6–11), and the intrigued Phoenician asks him to tell what he has learned about the heroes of the Trojan War (5.5). In an elaborate simile, the vine dresser reassures his guest that he will not be disappointed, likening the Phoenician and Protesilaus to Odysseus and Hermes in their meeting on Circe's island in *Odyssey* 10:

For just as Hermes, or one of his wise representatives, met Odysseus when he was wandering far from his ship and offered conversation and help (ἐς κοινωνίαν λόγου τε καὶ σπουδῆς ἀφίκετο) (for this is how one ought to understand the *moly* [τουτὶ γὰρ ἡγεῖσθαι προσήκει τὸ μῶλυ]), so Protesilaus will fill you up with *historia* (ἱστορίας) through me and make you wiser and more pleased (6.1).[29]

The vine dresser raises the level of Homeric reference by displaying his knowledge not only of the *Odyssey*, but of its critical interpretation. The identity of the *moly* (an obscure root of some sort) given by Hermes to Odysseus (*Od.* 10.305) was a famous conundrum in antiquity, an especial favorite of allegorical critics who liked to interpret it as an abstract *logos*, or rationality, that allowed Odysseus to withstand the charms of Circe.[30] The vine dresser's identification of *moly* as conversation and knowledge appears to be unparalleled, and his explicit gloss makes sure the Phoenician does not miss his clever hermeneutic intervention.[31]

The Phoenician responds to this gratuitous display of learning by disclosing that he too has more than a casual interest in Homer; upon his arrival in the Chersonese, he had dreamt that he was reading the Homeric Catalogue of Ships (ἔδοξα τὰ Ὁμήρου ἔπη ἀναγινώσκειν, ἐν οἷς τὸν κατάλογον τῶν Ἀχαιῶν φράζει: 6.3) and inviting the heroes on board his own vessel. When he bumped into the vine dresser he had been wandering on the beach, seeking a sign to explain the dream (βουληθεὶς δὲ ξυμβόλῳ περὶ τοῦ ἐνυπνίου χρήσασθαι: 6.5). He now realizes that it should be taken more literally than he had thought; rather than portending a long,

---

[29] Translations of the *Heroicus* are my own. The only English translation, Maclean and Aitken (2001), is unreliable; Grossardt (2006) notes its frequent misconstruals of the Greek in his commentary (e.g., 377, s.v. 6.7; 503, s.v. 25.12; 520, s.v. 26.12; 637, s.v. 38.3, 672, s.v. 45.7; there are many more). In this passage, for instance, Maclean and Aitken translate "the subject was probably the *moly*"; that is, that the 'conversation' was *about* the *moly*, rather than that the conversation *was* the *moly* (cf. Grossardt [2006], 373).

[30] Heraclit. *All.* 73.13. Sometimes Hermes is taken to symbolize the *logos*, as in [Plut.] *Vit. Hom.* 126.2. Ptolemy the Quail, in typically absurd fashion, says that it grew from the blood of a Giant that Helios killed on Circe's island. The fight was a 'struggle' or 'toil' (μῶλος), hence the name (Phot. *Bibl.* 190, 149b39–50a1). Cf. discussion in Buffière (1956), 292, 512, and Grossardt (2006), 373.

[31] A possible, but very oblique, parallel in Xen. *Mem.* 1.3.7.

slow return voyage, it foretells how he, with the help of the vine dresser, will indeed 'collect' the heroes, or at least stories about them (συλλεξαμένους τὸν περὶ αὐτῶν λόγον: 6.6), onto the metaphorical ship of his mind. The dream, in which the Phoenician imagines himself reading Homer on the one hand and encountering the 'real' heroes on the other, can also be seen as a straightforward expression of the Phoenician's desires: to compare what he has *read* to the 'reality' it represents, or, put another way, whether Homer's heroes correspond to their real-life counterparts. When the vine dresser reveals his close association with Protesilaus, the Phoenician can scarcely believe his good fortune and expresses his eagerness to learn "whether Protesilaus knows something about the events of the Trojan War similar to the poets or unknown to them" (εἴ τι παραπλήσιον τοῖς ποιηταῖς ἢ διηγνοημένον αὐτοῖς περὶ τῶν Τρωικῶν οἶδεν: 7.1). The Phoenician thus belongs to the long line of Homeric readers, such as Thucydides and Strabo, inquiring into the relationship between epic poetry and heroic history.

Like them, the Phoenician is interested primarily in what *really* happened and puts a premium on truth and accuracy. Consider his plea to the vine dresser at 7.7: "you must report these things soundly and just as you heard them" (ὑγιῶς γάρ που ἀπαγγελεῖς αὐτὰ καὶ ὡς ἤκουσας).[32] His ensuing comments consolidate the picture of the Phoenician as an aspiring Thucydidean:[33] he regards legendary tales with skepticism (φημὶ γὰρ ἀπίστως διακεῖσθαι πρὸς τὰ μυθώδη; cf. ἀπίστως ἐπὶ τὸ μυθῶδες: Th. 1.21.1) due to the unreliability of their sources, complaining, "I have never met anyone who has seen these things themselves. Rather one man says that he has heard these things from someone else, another simply that he believes them, and a third is excited by a poet" (οὐδενί πω ἑωρακότι αὐτὰ ξυγγέγονα, ἀλλ᾽ ὁ μὲν ἑτέρου ἀκηκοέναι φησίν, ὁ δὲ οἴεσθαι, τὸν δὲ ποιητὴς ἐπαίρει: 7.9). He may have believed in myths as a child, but "when I became a young man, I believed that I ought not to *accept* these things *uncritically*" (οὐκ ἀβασανίστως ᾠήθην χρῆναι προσδέχεσθαι ταῦτα: 7.10) – another unmistakable allusion to Thucydides: "People *accept* from each other everything that they hear about past events equally *uncritically*" (οἱ γὰρ ἄνθρωποι τὰς ἀκοὰς τῶν προγεγενημένων... ὁμοίως ἀβασανίστως παρ᾽ ἀλλήλων δέχονται: 1.20.1). By the seventh chapter, then, the Phoenician and the vine dresser have disclosed their shared interest in Homeric poetry and also strongly suggested that their ensuing

---

[32] Note the vine dresser's reassurance that Protesilaus is "a truth-loving hero" (φιλαλήθη ἥρωα: 7.8).

[33] Grossardt (2006), 383–4, s.v. 7.9.

conversation will focus on the evaluation of Homer's fidelity to the 'truth' underlying his poetry.

There is a hint of irony in Philostratus' presentation of the Phoenician's professed Thucydidean skepticism, given his earlier remarks attesting to his belief in signs and dreams, as well as his general excitement at the prospect of hearing the vine dresser's tales (5.5–6). But his hardcore skeptical historiographical attitude had already been subjected to some mockery in the exchange immediately preceding his declarations of skepticism, in which the vine dresser reveals Protesilaus' credentials as a source. The vision of Protesilaus sketched out here is essential to an understanding of the purposes and tone of the *Heroicus* and it is thus worth examining in detail.

The Phoenician tempers his enthusiasm when he realizes that Protesilaus is hardly the best witness of the war, and he politely points this out to the vine dresser:

By "events of the Trojan War" (Τρωικά) I refer to the gathering of the forces at Aulis and whether each hero was as noble, brave, and wise as they are said to be [by the poets]. For how could he tell of the war which happened concerning Troy (τὸν γὰρ πόλεμον, ὃς περὶ τῇ Τροίᾳ ἐγένετο, πῶς ἂν διηγοῖτο) given that he did not fight to the end and in fact was the first of the entire Greek force to die, on the very landing [at Troy], as it is called? (7.2).

In properly scrupulous fashion, the Phoenician acknowledges that he can only expect a partial story, restricted to events prior to Protesilaus' untimely early demise. His mistake, however, is in assuming that Protesilaus' authority stems from his status as participant and eyewitness. Indeed the privileging of eyewitness testimony is a cornerstone of the Phoenician's skeptical position: he disbelieves because "I have never met anyone who has *seen* these things" (7.9, quoted above). But it turns out that Protesilaus' knowledge derives not from his presence at the events, but from his powers as a heroic ghost. The vine dresser blithely assures the Phoenician that for heroes, death is only the soul's beginning of life, and if anything they know *more* about human affairs once they have died (7.3). Protesilaus thus "sings of many Trojan War-events that occurred after his own death" (καὶ πολλὰ μὲν ᾄδει Τρωικὰ μεθ᾽ ἑαυτὸν γενόμενα: 7.6). The Phoenician's historiographically informed question, which had seemed so sensible, is dismissed by the vine dresser as "silly" or "naïve" (εὔηθης: 7.3).

It is hard not to see this riposte as an example of Philostratus adding his own twist to the well-worn Homeric revisionist device of 'discovering' an eyewitness source more reliable than the poet. We have seen in previous chapters how Lucian repeatedly parodies the reliance on such claims in historiography, ethnography, and travel literature, and how Dio knowingly adopts Herodotus' dependence upon the age and authority of Egyptian priestly records ultimately deriving from Menelaus. But the Troy Romances, which purport to be the sources themselves, probably best embody the kind of claims that Philostratus had in mind. Like the Phoenician, Dictys of Crete (writing "in Phoenician letters" no less) places great importance on first-hand knowledge and accuracy; at 1.13, he states that "the account that follows, based as it is on my own observations, will meet, I hope, the highest critical standards," and in his so-called *sphragis* near the end of his work he reiterates: "Everything I have written about the war between the Greeks and the barbarians, in which I took a very active part, is based on first-hand knowledge" (5.17).[34] Dictys also matches the Phoenician's scrupulousness about accounting for the channels of information, taking care to explain how he learned about things that he could *not* have witnessed himself: "what I have told about Antenor and his kingdom was learned on inquiry from others" (5.17); "as to what happened earlier at Troy, I have tried to make my report as accurate as possible, Ulysses being my source" (1.13). The other Troy romancer, Dares, also assures his readers of his eyewitness status and identifies his other sources of information: "Dares the Phrygian, who wrote this history, says that he did military service until the capture of Troy and saw the people listed below either during times of truce or while he was fighting. As for Castor and Pollux, he learned from the Trojans what they were like and how they looked (12).[35]

The Phoenician's concerns, then, are precisely those anticipated and pre-empted by the Troy Romances; it is as if the Phoenician, familiar with the premises of these texts, is trying to show the vine dresser that he knows the rules of the 'authentication' game.[36] The joke, however, is on the Phoenician – the very thing, i.e., his premature death, that makes Protesilaus a poor eyewitness in the Phoenician's eyes is precisely what makes him so knowledgeable from the vine dresser's perspective. By dying and acquiring ghostly powers, Protesilaus, who did not even participate in the Trojan War, witnesses more of it than he would have had he been alive

---

[34] Translations of Dictys and Dares from Frazer (1966).

[35] Cf. 44: "So much and no more Dares the Phrygian put into writing, for, as a faithful follower of Antenor, he stayed on at Troy."

[36] Bowie (1994), 185–6, suggests a more direct correspondence.

and fighting. The choice of Protesilaus as the heroic ghost at the center of the *Heroicus* is appropriate for a number of reasons, such as the tradition of his resurrection,[37] but Philostratus also seems to have selected him because his status as least likely source for the Trojan War in the eyes of the skeptical Phoenician permits a spectacular upending of the presumptions about eyewitness testimony that characterize Homeric revision.

The scene is worth comparing to a chapter (17) of Lucian's *The Rooster* (*Gall.*), that parodies the same issue in a more familiar way.[38] *The Rooster* is a dialogue staged between a rich miser, Micyllus, and his rooster, who, much to his master's surprise, reveals that he is the reincarnation of the Trojan Euphorbus (as well as Pythagoras, Aspasia, Crates the Cynic, and others). The encounter is reminiscent of that presented in the *Heroicus*: a dialogue featuring a hero who claims superior knowledge to Homer on the basis of his own participant status, and an interlocutor eager to discover the 'truth.' Much like the Phoenician, Micyllus' initial thought is to test the veracity of Homer: "Tell me first about things at Troy (τὰ ἐν Ἰλίῳ). Were they as Homer said?" (τοιαῦτα ἦν οἷά φησιν Ὅμηρος γενέσθαι αὐτά;). The difference is that the rooster's 'revisions' are, in Lucianic fashion, deflating rather than radically revisionist; there was nothing extraordinary (ὑπερφυές) in those days – "Ajax was not as large, nor Helen as pretty as people think." But another source of humor is the rooster's insistence on adhering to the restricted knowledge standards of eyewitness testimony. To buttress his claim that Helen was nearly as old as Hecuba, he first argues from mythical chronology, dating her kidnapping by Theseus as contemporary with Heracles, who had sacked Troy before the rooster's (i.e., Euphorbus') time.[39] But he then offers better evidence, based on eyewitness testimony, explaining that his own father Panthous, who as a boy had seen Heracles, "told him these things" (διηγεῖτο . . . ταῦτα). And when Micyllus asks about Achilles and whether he too lived up to his later reputation, the rooster pleads ignorance: "I am unable to speak accurately (ἀκριβῶς) about affairs among the Greeks; how could I, being an enemy?" The incongruously naturalistic treatment of an inherently fantastic and absurd character – in this case a talking rooster who participated in the Trojan War – is a typical Lucianic technique, often deployed, as we have seen, in his *True Stories*.[40] One could compare Dio's insistence on holding Homer

[37] Maclean and Aitken (2001), l–lx; Whitmarsh (2004), (2009).
[38] On *The Rooster*, see Bompaire (1958), 178–80; on its Homeric references, Bouquiaux-Simon (1968), 117–18, 170–1.
[39] The question of Helen's age was a vexed one in Homeric scholarship: cf. Sch. T ad *Il.* 24.765a1 and Porphyry on *Il.* 24.765.
[40] See above, Ch. 5: 145.

himself to similarly rigorous standards in the *Trojan Oration* (19–21), when he demands to know how the poet was informed of private conversations between gods. By now, however, this is an old joke; rather than poke fun at the 'how did he know?' convention by yet again applying its strictures to inappropriate situations, Philostratus reverses Lucian's strategy; in *The Rooster*, Micyllus' error is to think that a reincarnated rooster's knowledge of the past was unlimited, in the *Heroicus* the Phoenician makes the mistake of thinking that ghosts are subject to the same strictures as mortals.

PROTESILAUS, HOMERIC SCHOLAR

The self-conscious and sophistic take on Homeric revision suggested by this exchange between the Phoenician and the vine dresser informs the latter's subsequent description of Protesilaus. One of the most surprising revelations about the hero is that he "knows" (οἶδεν) not only the truth about the Trojan War, but also "all of Homeric poetry" (τὰ Ὁμήρου πάντα: 7.6). Moreover, he is no casual reader, but the best and most meticulous: "whom can you name of those intensely *examining* Homer who has read Homer's poetry as Protesilaus has read and understood it?" (τὰ γοῦν Ὁμήρου ποιήματα τίνα φήσεις οὕτως ἀνεγνωκέναι τῶν σφόδρα βασανιζόντων Ὅμηρον, ὡς ἀνέγνωκέ τε ὁ Πρωτεσίλεως καὶ διορᾷ αὐτά: 7.4).[41] Just like the Phoenician and the vine dresser, then, Protesilaus too is revealed as a serious, hyper-skeptical Homeric critic – the vine dresser's description of the hero as one of Homer's "examiners" (τῶν βασανιζόντων) is picked up later by the Phoenician (βασανίζειν: 25.1) and looks ahead to the latter's self-characterization of his own attitude toward myth (οὐκ ἀβασανίστως: 7.10).

Protesilaus thus was not only contemporary with (and an omniscient ghostly witness of) the events that Homer depicted, but is also a careful reader of the poet. On the one hand, assigning this dual role to the hero allows Philostratus to 'solve' a problem encountered by previous revisionist texts in balancing their dependence on 'eyewitness testimony' with their concern to correct Homer. The Troy Romances' claims to be more truthful and accurate than the Homeric poems, for example, rests on their pose as genuine *pre*-Homeric documents. The Latin preface to Dares' work makes it clear that the text's superiority to Homer, stemming from the contemporaneity of its author with the War, was its primary claim to fame:

---

[41] Cf. Philostr. *VA* 5.14.3: "the poet leaves it to the judicious reader to *examine* whether his story has happened" (καὶ ὁ μὲν ποιητὴς εἰπὼν τὸν ἑαυτοῦ λόγον καταλείπει τῷ ὑγιαίνοντι ἀκροατῇ βασανίζειν αὐτόν, εἰ ἐγένετο).

Thus my readers can know exactly what happened according to this account and judge for themselves *whether Dares the Phrygian or Homer wrote the more truthfully* – Dares, who lived and fought at the time the Greeks stormed Troy, or Homer, who was born long after the War was over.[42]

The passage also unintentionally calls attention to a potential difficulty common to the creators of such texts: without such an intervention on the part of an editor or commentator the very name of Homer, much less his version of events, cannot be mentioned, even though competing with Homer is the *raison d'être* of the work. The Troy Romance authors must maintain the pretence of writing *before* Homer, and so cannot openly critique the poet, leaving any modifications and corrections to be inferred by the reader.[43] Herodotus and Dio, on the other hand, are able to assess Homer's accuracy in counterpoint to the accounts told to them by their Egyptian priestly sources. But the layers of transmission separating the historian and orator from the original eyewitness source of the information – Menelaus – are so numerous that their accounts fail to convey any sense of the immediacy and thrill that the *ipsissima verba* of allegedly 'original' testimony provides. Philostratus manages to cut through all of these difficulties by collapsing the two roles – source and critic – into one figure; even if his testimony is mediated by the vine dresser, Protesilaus' ghost is not only thoroughly informed about events before *and* after his own death, but also happens to be up on his Homer as well.

To further highlight the significance of this innovation, we might compare the interview with Achilles' ghost in Philostratus' *Life of Apollonius of Tyana* (4.16), an episode that seems like an embryonic version of the more extended interaction between the vine dresser and Protesilaus in the *Heroicus*.[44] In Book 4, Apollonius visits the Troad, and after "filling himself up with the ancient stories (ἀρχαιολογίας: 4.11.1)" and visiting the tombs of the heroes in standard touristic fashion, he decides to spend the night alone on the burial mound of Achilles. He is rewarded with an awe-inspiring epiphany: there is an earthquake, and a beautiful youth issues

---

[42] The Latin preface, of course, would not have been part of the Greek Dares, and if there was, as is likely, a Greek preface, it might not have made the comparison between Dares and Homer as explicit. Nevertheless, it still draws attention to one of the drawbacks of the Troy Romances.

[43] See my remarks in Ch. 1: 18.

[44] On Apollonius' interview with Achilles' ghost (*VA* 4.16), see Solmsen (1940); Zeitlin (2001), 247–55; and Grossardt (2009), who sees the influence of Lucian's interview with Homer in the *True Stories*, the emperor Caracalla's visit to Achilles' tomb in 214 CE, and the tradition (preserved in *Vit. Hom.* 7 West [*Vita Romana*] 5) of Homer's encounter with the ghost of Achilles at the hero's tomb (see below, 209 n. 88). On the entire episode (4.11–16), with a particular emphasis on its ironies and intertextual play, see Schirren (2005), 297–305, and Gyselinck and Demoen (2009), 114–17.

forth from the barrow, growing rapidly larger until he towers almost twenty
feet high (4.16.2). The detail matches the interest shown in the *Heroicus*
in the heroes' giant stature, and the ensuing interview reveals even more
striking parallels. Achilles asks Apollonius to persuade the Thessalians to
renew their long-neglected offerings to his tomb (4.16.3); in something of
a sequel, Protesilaus will explain in the *Heroicus* (53.18–23) how Achilles'
anger with the Thessalians for their continued neglect eventually led to
their destruction. The answers to four of the five questions Apollonius
asks Achilles (4.16.4–6) are repeated (and expanded upon) in the *Heroicus*:
Helen was not at Troy as Homer said but in Egypt (*Her.* 25.10–12); the
Nereids mentioned by Homer did indeed sing dirges over his tomb, but the
Muses have never come there (*Her.* 51.7); Polyxena did die over Achilles'
grave, but by her own hand (*Her.* 51.2–6); and Palamedes was ignored by
Homer purposefully, so he would not have to record Odysseus' shameful
role in Palamedes' murder (*Her.* 24.2).[45] Achilles shares Protesilaus' outrage
over Palamedes' unjust demise, and even enjoins Apollonius to seek out
the hero's neglected tomb on Lesbos (4.16.6; cf. 4.13.2–3). There is thus a
sense in which the *Heroicus* can be seen as an expansion of and a working
through of the ideas expressed briefly in this episode of *Apollonius*.[46] And
like the Phoenician, Apollonius is fixated on evaluating Homer's accuracy:
every question but one asks Achilles to confirm or deny Homer's version
and mentions Homer by name (or in one case, 'poets', but Homer is clearly
meant).[47] Furthermore, Apollonius 'corrects' Homer as well, when he tells
his audience that he did not use the method enshrined in the *Nekuia* scene
of the *Odyssey* to raise Achilles' ghost, but rather a prayer used by the
Indians to invoke their heroes (4.16.1).

---

[45] The fifth answer is that there were indeed as many heroes as suggested in Homer's poetry (4.16.5).
This statement is at least not contradicted in the *Heroicus*, and the sentiment is in keeping with the
Heroicus' general mood.

[46] Solmsen (1940); I find this more likely than the possibility that the *VA* is a condensation of ideas
already worked out at length in the *Heroicus* (broached, but dismissed also by Grossardt [2009],
91). The *terminus post quem* for both the *Heroicus* and the *Life of Apollonius of Tyana* is probably
217 CE (for different reasons: Jones [2001], 142–3), but there is no consensus on the relative dating
of the two works. On the numerous parallels between them, see Grossardt (2006), 14–17.

[47] Grossardt (2009), 80–91, argues that Apollonius' interview with Homer, like that of Lucian in the
True Stories, is concerned with philological, rather than historical, issues. Grossardt's argument,
however, only applies to Apollonius' first question (on Achilles' burial), which refers to a Homeric
passage (*Od.* 24.35–97) whose authenticity was questioned in antiquity by Aristarchus and others
(Sch. ad *Od.* 24.1; Garbrah [1977]). None of the other questions (on Polyxena's sacrifice and Helen's
and Palamedes' presence at Troy) are particularly 'philological' in nature, and the fact that they
were also debated by literary critics only proves that ancient Homeric scholars pondered 'historical'
questions. If, as Grossardt believes (and I am with him), Philostratus is parodying the desire to seek
the 'true' story of the Trojan War here, as he is in the *Heroicus*, much of the satirical bite is lost if
the questions are seen as merely philological ones.

But if the link between heroes and Homer as competing sources of truth is common to both works, Philostratus takes things much farther in the *Heroicus*. Achilles' information in the *Apollonius* primarily stems from autopsy (he does speak about two events after his death, but they both occur at his tomb), and while he seems to know some details of Homeric poetry involving his burial (*Od.* 24.43–92), he does not display anywhere near the familiarity with Homer attributed to Protesilaus.[48] It is significant, however, that even in the *Apollonius* episode there is something faintly ridiculous in the idea of mixing Homeric criticism with heroic *sunousiai*. Aside from Apollonius' curious 'correction' of Homer's method of raising the dead, one cannot help feeling that an incongruous note is struck when Apollonius decides to ask Achilles, who has just made an awe-inspiring entrance and issued several weighty commands, a series of pedantic questions about Homer. Is it unreasonable to detect a hint of exasperation in Achilles' response to Apollonius' request for an interview: "I understand; it's obvious that you are going to ask me about events at Troy" (ξυνίημι . . . δῆλος γὰρ εἶ περὶ τῶν Τρωικῶν ἐρωτήσων: 4.16.4)? Rather than pull back and downplay this tension, Philostratus draws it out more vigorously in the *Heroicus*, not only by having Protesilaus provide far more information about the Trojan War, but also by laying great emphasis on the amusing idea that Protesilaus, as a hero-scholar, has spent his time reading Homer closely.

Protesilaus is again a somewhat unexpected candidate for such a role: as one of the heroes whom Homer mentions least, it is surprising that he should be so interested in reading and "examining" his poetry. Then again, he *has* to closely scrutinize the poems to locate the meager handful of verses allotted to him by Homer:

Although he doesn't praise all of Homeric poetry, he praises the verses spoken about him by Homer (τὰ ἔπη τὰ ἐς αὐτὸν Ὁμήρῳ εἰρημένα ἐπαινεῖ), who called his wife "[cheek-]torn on both sides" (ἀμφίδρυφον), his house "half-complete" (ἡμιτελῆ), the ship on which he sailed "much-combatted" (περιμάχητον) – and him warlike (πολεμικόν). (12.3)

On the one hand, this speaks to Protesilaus' detailed knowledge of Homeric poetry (one that will be on ample display throughout the dialogue); he refers to *Il.* 2.700–1 where his wife is called ἀμφιδρυφής and

---

[48] Apollonius' questions are aimed at determining Homer's accuracy, but Achilles draws on his own knowledge to answer them without showing any awareness of the details of Homer's account, other than those implied by Apollonius in phrasing his questions.

his house ἡμιτελής⁴⁹ and *Il.* 2.698 and 708, where he is called "warlike" (although the word used by Homer is ἀρήιος rather than πολεμικός). But there is also something comical about how well Protesilaus knows these few lines, the only appearance he makes in Homer, and it highlights the irony that the best critic and most enthusiastic reader of Homer is a hero who barely figures in his poetry.

A more openly humorous take on Protesilaus' erudition occurs a few lines earlier, at 11.5. The vine dresser explains that he, still unfamiliar with rustic ways, was trying to plant trees on Homer's instructions: "I was planting trees 'tall' (τά τε δένδρα ἐγὼ μὲν παρακηκοὼς τοῦ Ὁμήρου μακρὰ ἐφύτευον), as I had heard from Homer" (*Od.* 18.359). He had taken the verse to mean that he should place most of the sapling above ground rather than under it, hence planting it "tall". Protesilaus, however, corrects⁵⁰ the vine dresser's literal interpretation, asserting that "tall" actually means "deep", as he illustrates by reference to *Il.* 21.197: τὰ φρέατα μακρά, "tall [i.e., deep] wells." This episode recalls the traditional didactic notion of Homer as encyclopedia (agriculture is often one of the subjects invoked) that we saw Strabo grappling with (cf. 1.2.4 on Odysseus as dispensing sage advice on farming), and that formed a central part of the defense of Homer's poetry from the fifth century onwards.⁵¹ Protesilaus is elsewhere imagined as familiar with such claims; he can rattle off a paean to Homer's poetic genius that sounds like something out of Maximus of Tyre's *Discourses* or Ps.-Plutarch's *On Homer*. Homer "played every poetic mode" and outperformed every other poet; he chose the greatest subject, the Trojan War, and depicted the full variety of human life – military activity of every type, as well as dancing, songs, love, feasting, farming, seafaring, and the making of arms, not to mention the diversity of human character and appearance (25.2–3). Here the convention is played up for laughs: the vine dresser's ridiculous attempt to plant trees according to Homer – just what one would expect from a *pepaideumenos* thrust into the fields – is then 'corrected' in an equally sophistic manner by the rustic hero-ghost's philological intervention.

The anecdote also calls attention to a further curiosity of Protesilaus' scholarly portrait – he is intimately familiar not only with Homer, but also

⁴⁹ The lines were well known (e.g., quoted by Plut. *Mor.* 498c; Grossardt [2006], 419, s.v. 12.3 for more examples). In his *Dialogues of the Dead*, Lucian imagines Protesilaus, like Thersites and Nireus (see above, 159–60), as self-consciously describing himself in Homeric terms (although here Homer is not explicitly mentioned): the hero complains to Aeacus about leaving behind a "half-complete home" (ἡμιτελῆ ... τὸν δόμον; cf. *Il.* 2.701: δόμος ἡμιτελής) and a widowed wife (*DMort.* 27[19], 1).
⁵⁰ The word used is διορθοῦται, evoking the terms of Alexandrian textual criticism (*diorthôsis*: edition).
⁵¹ See Ch. 1: 10–12; Ch. 3: 64–66.

with the Homeric critical tradition, or, to put it more accurately, with the episodes and passages that were the focus of critical debate. I discussed earlier Protesilaus' parroting of well known anti-Homeric condemnations;[52] he also alludes to problems such as the construction and destruction of the Achaean Wall (27.7–8); the divinity of Achilles' horses (50.1–3); the relative ages of Patroclus and Achilles (49.1); the description of Sarpedon's death (39.4); Hector's four-horse chariot (19.2); Odysseus' defeat of Ajax in wrestling (35.8), etc. Some especially interesting examples occur in the course of his novel version of the Mysian expedition (23.1–30), the legendary 'pre-quel' to the Trojan War in which the Greek forces land in Asia Minor but end up attacking Mysia and their king Telephus in the mistaken assumption that it was Troy. In Protesilaus' version, however, the war was not a mistake, and his new account, "ignored by Homer" (Ὁμήρῳ . . . ἠγνοῆσθαι: 23.1; cf. 14.1), serves as a 'correction' of the paltry treatment given to the hero by Homer; now Protesilaus, along with other neglected heroes such as Nireus, Sthenelus, and Palamedes, joins Achilles as one of the foremost protagonists of the most glorious war that no one has ever heard about.

A notable feature of Protesilaus' account is his frequent reference to Homeric passages as support for a tale that, as I have mentioned, he claims Homer ignored. For instance, when he refers to allies of Telephus from upper Mysia, he explains that these were the people "whom the poets call *Abioi*, shepherds of horses, and drinkers of their [i.e., the horses'] milk" (οὓς Ἀβίους τε οἱ ποιηταὶ καλοῦσι καὶ ἵππων ποιμένας καὶ τὸ γάλα αὐτῶν πίνοντας: 23.10). On the one hand this is a clear, and rather gratuitous reference to Hom. *Il.* 13.5–6: "the close-fighting Mysians, the noble Mare-milkers, consumers of milk, and the *Abioi*, most virtuous of men" (Μυσῶν τ' ἀγχεμάχων καὶ ἀγαυῶν ἱππημολγῶν, || γλακτοφάγων ἀβίων τε, δικαιοτάτων ἀνθρώπων).[53] But Protesilaus is not just alluding to Homer, but also offering a solution to a celebrated 'problem' of Homeric criticism. After all, these lines had inspired intense debate among ancient scholars of Homer and geography: Ephorus, Aristarchus, and the historian Nicolaus of Damascus (late first century BCE) had all weighed in on various problems presented by the verses.[54] The word *abioi* was particularly mysterious: Strabo, in a characteristically long discussion (7.3.2–7), argues that

---

[52] See above, pp. 177–8.

[53] As Grossardt (2006), 469–70, s.v. 23.10, points out, "poets" is no doubt a rhetorical plural for "Homer," as also at 39.4, etc.

[54] Ephorus *FGrH* 70 F 42; Aristarchus: Sch. A ad *Il.* 13.6a; Nic. Dam. *FGrH* 90 F 104. For an overview of Hellenistic debates on *Il.* 13.3–6, see Ivančik (1996).

hippêmolgoi, g(a)lactophagoi, and *abioi* are merely epithets Homer uses for the Scythians rather than, as Apollodorus had asserted, the names of fictitious tribes invented by Homer (*FGrH* 244 F 157). The question of whether *abioi* was a proper name or a descriptive adjective also arises in the scholia (Sch. A ad *Il.* 13.6d), where further questions are posed: did the word derive from *bios* ("life") or *bia* ("violence")? If the former, what did *a-bios* ("without life") signify? A nomadic lifestyle ("without [a settled] life")? Posidonius took "without life" to mean 'live apart from women,' and adduced as evidence a novel (and intriguing, for us at least) interpretation of Homer's description of Protesilaus' house in *Il.* 2.701 (δόμος ἡμιτελής): "[Posidonius] believes that a life without a woman is "half-complete" (ἡμιτελῆ), just as he believes that Protesilaus' house was "half-complete" (ἡμιτελῆ) because it had no spouse" (Posid. F 277a2 = Str. 7.3.3).

Is it going too far to see an echo of Posidonius' discussion in Protesilaus' otherwise unmotivated mention of the "Abioi" in *Heroicus* 23.10? Perhaps, but at the very least Protesilaus, by treating *abioi* as a proper noun denoting a particular people while glossing *hippêmolgoi* and *g(a)lactophagoi* as adjectives describing them, is not only vouching for the truth of his new story through its correlation with the world described by Homer, but also chiming in on a controversial issue of Homeric scholarship.

An even better example is the extensive commentary appended to the description of the Greek landing at Mysia, which was made difficult due to the inexperience of the Arcadians who ran aground with some of their ships.[55] "For Homer says, as you surely know, that the Arcadians were neither sailors before Troy nor skilled in seafaring deeds, but that Agamemnon gave them sixty ships and led them to sea even though they had never sailed before" (23.15). The Arcadians' lack of naval prowess (*Il.* 2.603–14) was a surprisingly well-known Homeric detail, but this was probably due to the fact that Thucydides had used the information in his *Archaeology* to support his claims about Agamemnon's naval power: (καὶ Ἀρκάσι [sc. Ag.] προσπαρασχών, ὡς Ὅμηρος τοῦτο δεδήλωκεν: 1.9.4). Protesilaus shows that he has Thucydides' passage in mind when he makes another allusion to it a few lines later. One of Thucydides' arguments in his calculation of

---

[55] A passing reference is also made to the lack of writing among the heroes, perhaps alluding to another debate in Homeric scholarship. For instance, Aristarchus had argued, as part of his general primitivist view of heroic society, that writing did not exist in the heroic age (e.g., Sch. A ad *Il.* 7.187; Schmidt [1976], 213–14). As noted above (p. 180 and n. 16), some scholars see here a subtle refutation of Dictys' work, which presupposes the existence of heroic writing.

Greek troop-numbers was the hyper-rationalized and somewhat pedantic point that "it is not likely that many extra *passengers* (περίνεως) sailed apart from the kings and high officers" (1.10.4). In the *Heroicus*, Protesilaus provides the needless detail that upon landing, the Greeks "all immediately leapt from their ships (except for the helmsman and a *passenger*" (πλὴν κυβερνήτου καὶ περίνεω: 23.17)). Once again, the plausibility of his narrative is backed up by its 'fit' with Homeric detail, and is allied with a subtle allusion to the critical tradition; to Thucydides' point is added the necessity of a helmsman, and in a nod to his concerns, only one passenger per ship is permitted.[56] The way that Protesilaus weaves in traces of Homer and Homeric criticism into his narrative certainly shows off his erudition but it also plays off of the technique of discovering 'hints' of the truth embedded in Homeric poetry as validation of one's 'new' account.

PROTESILAUS, HOMER, AND THE PAST

The characterization of Protesilaus as Homeric reader and critic appears more anomalous when considered against the rest of his representation in the *Heroicus*. The revelation of his Homeric interests and the anecdotes I described above are told in the midst of an extensive description of Protesilaus' current existence and activities as a ghost. His tomb, sanctuary, and appearance are vividly portrayed, as are his exercise regimen, prophetic and healing powers, and earthly manifestations (9–16). The following section (17–22) adds more stories concerning the appearances of other heroes who died in the Troad – Hector, Ajax, Antilochus, Patroclus, and Palamedes. This whole part of the *Heroicus* is imbued with a numinous sense of the divine; the vine dresser's territory and the Troad are marked as the location where the supernatural is commonplace, where the heroes have a very direct impact on the lives of its inhabitants.[57] Unlike his references to Homer, little about the vine dresser's description of heroic activity in the Troad advertises itself as insincere.[58] Maximus of Tyre (*Or.* 9.7) tells stories of Achilles on Leuke, the 'White' Island, in the Black Sea similar to those told at the end of the *Heroicus* and reports that the Trojans of his day say they have seen Hector "sweeping over the plain"; Arrian also reports sightings of Achilles on Leuke (*Peripl. M. Eux.* 23.4). As C. P. Jones has recently

---

[56] For a different interpretation of the Thucydidean allusion, see Grossardt (2006), 474, s.v. 23.17.

[57] Mantero (1966), 48–99.

[58] Although see Whitmarsh (2004), 249: "the text teasingly strains its readers' credulity with the marvelous proposition of a metaphysical dynamism still permeating the landscape of Greece."

argued, "even a sophisticated reader of Philostratus might have been ready to believe, not merely that Protesilaus issued oracles, but that he appeared to especially faithful devotees, and gave them privileged information from beyond the grave."[59]

The apparent seriousness with which Philostratus describes Protesilaus' and the other heroes' activities has persuaded scholars interested in the religious atmosphere of the Empire that the *Heroicus* reflects Philostratus' commitment to the belief in the heroes and the reinvigoration of cult practice.[60] The problem then has been to correlate this objective both with the revisionist tales of the Trojan War that fill the rest of the dialogue and with the incongruous characterization of Protesilaus as Homeric critic. One solution is to argue that the critiques of Homer support the larger ideological project: Teresa Mantero, for example, posits that the Homeric sections of the *Heroicus* rehabilitate the specific heroes Philostratus is interested in reviving – Protesilaus, Palamedes, and Achilles. Another is to presume that the 'serious' portrayal of Protesilaus' epiphanies bestows upon his pronouncements on Homer the status of "revealed knowledge": "The word of the hero who has returned to life and speaks to his worshippers thus has ultimate truth value in the dialogue."[61] What generally goes ignored in these readings, of course, is the playful way in which Philostratus portrays Protesilaus' interest in Homer, and indeed Homeric revision in general,[62]

---

[59] Jones (2001), 148. On such 'close encounters,' see Lane Fox (1986), 137–50 (144–8 on the *Heroicus*); Jones (2001), 146–8; and Zeitlin (2001). For Achilles' cult on Leuke, see Hedreen (1991).

[60] Eitrem (1929); Betz (1996); Maclean and Aitken (2001), lxxxii. Mantero (1966) is the most comprehensive and influential statement of this position; see 13–18 for her survey of earlier scholarship on the issue. Philostratus' connections to the Imperial court of the Severans are well known: among other things, he had studied rhetoric with Antipater of Hierapolis, who would later become Caracalla's teacher, and mentions that he was a member of the "circle" (τοῦ . . . κύκλου) of the empress Julia Domna, who had prompted him to write his *Life of Apollonius of Tyana* (*VA* 1.3. For detailed discussion of Philostratus' biography and court connections, see Flinterman [1995], 15–28; Whitmarsh [2007], 32–5, expresses some reservations about the alleged closeness of Philostratus' relationship with the Severans). It has often been suggested that the *Heroicus* might have been inspired by Caracalla's visit to Achilles' tomb in 214 (Huhn and Bethe [1917]; Eitrem [1929], 1; Anderson [1986], 241). Is its reassertion of archaic Hellenic religion a reaction against the perceived syncretistic tendencies of the later Severans (Aitken [2004], 275–80)? Or is its emphasis on the Greek-barbarian polarity an effort to support Alexander Severus' campaign against the Sassanid Empire in the early 230s (Shayegan [2004])? Or is it alluding to attempts by the 'Syrian' women of the Severan imperial household to highlight their Hellenic piety (Aitken [2004])? For an incisive critique of this sort of historicizing, see Whitmarsh (2007), 35–8; Grossardt (2006), 34–46, is a more comprehensive, yet similarly critical, overview.

[61] Mantero (1966); Maclean and Aitken (2001), lxii.

[62] The tendency to downplay, or disregard, Philostratus' gently mocking and comical tone also leads to serious distortions in Mestre (2004), who reads the *Heroicus* (wrongly in my view) as a serious attempt to renew faith in Homer and the Homeric tradition, in which Philostratus modifies Homer for the transformed culture of Imperial Greece, by making the heroes more morally acceptable and instilling a renewed sense of Greek identity.

not to mention the fact that Philostratus could hardly have 'believed' in the new version of the Trojan War that Protesilaus, via the vine dresser, lays out.[63] A better solution is that proposed by Graham Anderson and Ewen Bowie, who also see the extensive description of Protesilaus' current activities and epiphanies as establishing his authority as a critic, but take its primary function as a *Beglaubigungsapparat* that teasingly 'vouches' for the sophistic, knowing Trojan fictions and Homeric 'corrections' that follow.[64] Such a "framing of the far-fetched by the credible" is familiar to readers of the ancient novel and travel-tales, which frequently justify their narratives by similar appeals to 'truth' (cf. Dio's use of the Egyptian priest in his *Trojan Oration* [Ch. 4: 108–12]).[65] In the case of the *Heroicus*, however, it seems odd that the 'frame' would be so extensive if its main purpose was simply to authenticate the source of the *Heroicus'* Homeric criticism; there is no real parallel for this elsewhere. I would argue rather that the remarkable feature of the *Heroicus* is the (at times unwieldy) combination of contemporary heroic narrative *and* Homeric criticism, and to subsume one to the other, as the real theme of the text, eviscerates the tension that makes the *Heroicus* so interesting.

One thing the juxtaposition of heroic ghosts and Homeric criticism allows Philostratus to explore is the relationship between the present and the heroic, Homeric past. As Tim Whitmarsh has remarked, the emphasis on the heroic epiphanies and interventions can be seen as a re-assertion of the importance and power of archaic energies, which still maintain their strength millenia later.[66] In this sense, Protesilaus plays a key role as a link between the present and the past. A number of scholars have noted the similarities between the atmosphere of the *Heroicus* and that of Dio's *Borysthenitic Oration* (*Or.* 36) and *Euboean Oration* (*Or.* 7) or Philostratus' own anecdote about the so-called 'Heracles' of Herodes Atticus in his *Lives of the Sophists* (533–4).[67] These works center on figures who function as living embodiments of the past and speak to the Second Sophistic desire to travel back in time: Dio's rustic Euboean hunters and primitive, archaic

---

[63] Grossardt (2006), 74–83, demonstrates this conclusively, even if not all of his arguments are equally persuasive.

[64] Anderson (1986), 241–57; Bowie (1994).

[65] Quote from Bowie (1994), 186. Cf. 184–5: "The possibility that there had been such an encounter . . . all this permits the reader a self-indulgent *frisson* of satisfaction. With one part of her mind she knows that it is a Philostratean illusion, with another she can toy with the notion that this source might really provide extra information that only the privileged readers of this work can share."

[66] Whitmarsh (2004), 245; (2009).   [67] Most notably Anderson (1986), 252–3.

Borysthenites, and Philostratus' 'Cynic Superman' Agathion.[68] The fascination with these individuals stems from their preservation of archaic attitudes, values, and even language, untainted by the corruption of the modern era. In some ways, Protesilaus fits well into this group. He has something of an archaic simplicity about him in his traditional virtues, laconic wisdom, defense of the countryside, and advocacy of the old religion. Likewise, interacting with Protesilaus permits one to bypass the effects of time: the vine dresser observes that the hero's sanctuary is in disrepair and "time has worn his statue down" (περιτρίψας δὲ αὐτὸ ὁ χρόνος: 9.6), but nevertheless asserts, "this is of no concern, for I associate with him, see him, and no statue would be more delightful to me" (ἐμοὶ δὲ οὐδὲν τοῦτο· αὐτῷ γὰρ ξύνειμι καὶ αὐτὸν βλέπω καὶ οὐδὲν ἄν μοι γένοιτο ἄγαλμα ἐκείνου ἥδιον: 9.7). Protesilaus provides immediate access to a long lost past, an intimate and powerful connection that goes far beyond that enabled through material remains and artifacts. In him, the vast temporal distance separating the heroic past from the contemporary world is collapsed.[69]

What doesn't quite fit, however, is his interest in Homer and his knowledge of Homeric criticism. In fact, it seems that Philostratus is keen to emphasize this peculiarity, when he informs us that Protesilaus has *read* Homer despite the fact that epic poetry (ῥαψῳδία) did not exist until after the Trojan War (7.5) and that the alphabet was only invented at Troy by Palamedes (33.11)! The primitive survival figure is usually imagined as pre-poetic and hence more sincere and honest; Agathion criticizes tragedy (which he has heard while seated at the top of Mt. Parnassus) for its pleasurable depiction of immoral activity, and poetic "myths" as "advisers of wicked deeds" (Philostr. *VS* 553–4), while the Euboean hunters' general ignorance of the (corrupting) trappings of civilization is reflected in the fact that they do not even know what a theater is (Dio Chrys. *Or.* 7.24). The one exception, Dio's Borysthenites, provides a telling contrast to Protesilaus. The Borysthenites are obsessed with Homer – in fact they refuse to read any other poet, and almost all of them, according to Dio, are able to recite his poetry from memory (36.9). As befits their Black Sea location, they are particularly fond of Achilles, whose tomb and cult on Leuke is close by. In a sense they love Homer because they are Homeric: emulating Achilles, wearing their hair long in Homeric fashion, and constantly engaged in warfare against barbarians. The Borysthenites' archaism and

---

[68] On Dio's *Or.* 7 and 36, see Moles (1995). On Agathion, see Kindstrand (1979–80); Swain (1996), 79–83; Whitmarsh (2001), 105–8.
[69] Billault (2000), 136–7.

past-ness are implicated in their identification with Homer and their complete inability to maintain a critical distance from his poetry. For Dio, their enthusiasm, along with their other 'archaic' qualities, is admirable because it is uninfected by the doubts and pedantries of the Homeric interpretative tradition. But it also becomes the object of Dio's gentle condescension and ironic teasing because of the naïveté inherent in that prelapsarian innocence. If one sets Protesilaus beside the Borysthenites, one can see that it is not just the interest in Homer, but the familiarity with Homeric criticism and awareness of the revisionist tradition in particular that marks Protesilaus as 'modern' despite his otherwise archaic credentials. In this respect Protesilaus embodies the conflicted fantasy of the *pepaideumenos* himself, maintaining an 'ancient' ethical and religious worldview while continuing to adopt a sophisticated 'modern' attitude toward the representation of the past by Homer.[70] In his very being he is a figure, a hero, from the distant past who has nonetheless gained, through his study of Homer, a certain self-consciousness about his pastness.

BELIEF, SKEPTICISM, AND HOMER

A cornerstone of this 'modern' attitude is the skepticism with which Homer's reliability is treated by Protesilaus, who is figured not just as any kind of Homeric critic, but one who 'cross-examines' Homer and assesses the historical truth of his poems in the tradition of Herodotus, Strabo, and Dio. One of the issues Philostratus explores in the *Heroicus* is how the modalities of belief proper to Homer and Homeric criticism overlap and come into conflict with those required by the discourse of heroic *daimones*. As I discussed above, the interchange between the Phoenician and the vine dresser over Protesilaus' eyewitness status stages an amusing confrontation between the Phoenician's 'rational' expectations characteristic of Homeric revisionism and the vine dresser's 'supernatural' explanation based on Protesilaus' powers as a ghost (7.1–6). The message there was that the Phoenician's reliance on historiographical standards of plausibility and verisimilitude had no place in such a context, and this seems further supported by the tenor of the opening chapters. The landscape inhabited

---

[70] The case of Agathion is similar, yet with a subtle difference. Protesilaus' 'archaic' qualities (stemming from his status as a survival from the past) are at odds with his modern erudition, an attribute only appreciated in and characteristic of the Imperial *present*. Agathion, on the other hand, owes both his primitive simplicity *and* the effortless Attic dialect that does not quite 'fit' with it, to his antiquity and pre-modern purity. The contradiction at the heart of Agathion thus results from overbundling him with incompatible 'archaic' traits, while that of Protesilaus arises from introducing a jarring 'modern' attitude to an otherwise suitably 'archaic' character.

by the vine dresser and Protesilaus is a mystical one, redolent of divinity, (τὸ μέρος τοῦ ἀγροῦ . . . θεῖον: 5.2; the Phoenician is described as having arrived "at the behest of a god" [κατὰ θεόν: 6.2; 6.7]). And the heroes are capable of extraordinary, superhuman deeds – Protesilaus can throw a discus "over the clouds" (13.2), floats on the air when he runs (13.3), and can heal diseases (16.1–2). Hector directs a river onto a road to kill an impious Assyrian youth (19.5–7); ghosts appear covered with dust, sweat, or blood on the Trojan plain portending drought, rainstorms, or plague (18.2). The Phoenician's initial skepticism at such tales, which we outlined earlier – his *disbelieving* attitude toward the fantastic (ἀπίστως διακεῖσθαι πρὸς τὰ μυθώδη: 7.9) and his refusal to believe that the heroes appear to people ("I don't *believe*" [ἀπιστῶ]: 3.1, 7.11) – is inappropriate in such a context.

This neat conflict between belief and disbelief, the rational and the supernatural, between proof and faith, is rendered a bit more complicated in chapter 8 of the *Heroicus*. In this strange, yet important excursus the vine dresser catalogues a series of giant bone discoveries in order to convince the Phoenician of the great size of the heroes, which the Phoenician had declared "false and implausible" (ψευδῆ δὲ καὶ ἀπίθανα: 7.9). Here the vine dresser depends upon traditional arguments of proof and demonstration – eyewitness testimony and the material evidence of bones – to make his case for the supernatural. Although the vine dresser begins with hearsay stories, he quickly moves on to remains that he claims to have seen himself: that of a giant killed by Apollo near Sigeum, an unidentified one on Lemnos, another at Naulochus that the vine dresser offers to take the Phoenician to at that very moment (8.6–12).[71] The vine dresser's anecdotes certainly activate "a specifically Herodotean play with the value of travel and autopsy,"[72] but they also recall the 'eyewitness' accounts purporting to tell of 'unbelievable' sights that so vexed Lucian in the preface to his *True Stories*.

In fact, Lucian's *The Lover of Lies*, a dialogue also discussed in this context in the last chapter and expressly focused on the question of belief (its alternate title is the *Unbeliever* [Ἄπιστων] and the words πίστις and πιστεύω appear repeatedly throughout the text), offers a close parallel to the situation depicted in the *Heroicus*.[73] Tychiades, the Lucianic stand-in narrating the story to his interlocutor, is an avowed skeptic much like the Phoenician,

---

[71] On giant skeletons and the *Heroicus*, see Jones (2000) and Rusten (2004).

[72] Whitmarsh (2009), 209.

[73] Similarly, in the *Heroicus*, the vine dresser repeatedly employs the verb "disbelieve" (ἀπιστέω). He begins his argument by declaring to the Phoenician that "you will not disbelieve (ἀπιστήσεις: 7.12) any of these things," and the word appears twice more in 7.12, and subsequently at 8.1, 8.2, 8.12, twice in 8.17, and twice more in the Phoenician's declaration of conversion at 8.18.

while the vine dresser's role is taken up by a series of philosophers who relate tales of magic, ghosts, and paranormal activity, often appealing to autopsy in an attempt to convince Tychiades to 'believe' in the supernatural. Just as in the *True Stories*, the object of Lucian's fascination and scorn is the incongruity between fantastic content and the authoritative claims of autopsy and experience legitimating that content. In *The Lover of Lies*, however, he dramatizes the difficulty facing the skeptic when attempting to rebut someone who claims to have seen something fantastic. Tychiades can only repeatedly and unpersuasively assert the inherent impossibility of the supernatural activity that his interlocutors claim to have witnessed, and he ends up leaving the gathering in disgust.

Philostratus deals with this basic dilemma in a typically more ambiguous manner. On the one hand, he draws attention to the primacy of eyewitness testimony over less direct means by having the vine dresser first tell stories from hearsay (e.g., "my grandfather told me that he saw . . . ": 8.1), which the Phoenician duly criticizes as unreliable. The authority of the vine dresser's subsequent stories, based on autopsy, is thus underlined and meant to be definitive. But several things about this exercise in persuasion are a bit puzzling; not only is its inordinate length (to be attributed perhaps to Philostratus' fascination with the subject)[74] out of proportion with its modest conclusion – that the heroes were indeed much larger than humans in the present – but it fails to address the more substantial claim doubted by the Phoenician: that the heroes live on after death and manifest themselves to the living. The Phoenician's declaration of his conversion (8.18) glosses over this fact: he admits, "I was ignorant of these great things [i.e., bones] and foolishly disbelieved" (ἐγὼ δὲ μεγάλα μὲν ἠγνόουν, ἀνοήτως δὲ ἠπίστουν), but then immediately leaps to the conclusion that "Protesilaus' [current] activities . . . are no longer unbelievable" (μηκέτ' ἀπιστούμενα). The ease and rapidity with which the Phoenician is divested of his vaunted skepticism appears to signal the Phoenician's gullibility rather than the vine dresser's persuasive power.[75] It also further complicates the criteria for belief; what are we to make of the vine dresser's claims to eyewitness testimony here? After all, Philostratus had already problematized the Phoenician's reliance on these kinds of historiographical standards in

---

[74] In his *Life of Apollonius of Tyana*, Philostratus has Apollonius say: "I acknowledge that giants did exist and that gigantic bodies are brought to light all over the world when tombs are broken open" (*VA* 5.16.1).

[75] So Whitmarsh (2004); Grossardt (2006), 47–8, 76–7. The Phoenician is thus unlikely to function as the 'model' for the reader, as supposed by Mantero (1966), 73; Beschorner (1999), 217; Maclean (2004), 133.

the passage discussed previously, poking fun at the Phoenician's assumption of Protesilaus' restricted eyewitness viewpoint. Are appeals to 'rational' arguments even appropriate for authenticating supernatural material?

The slight, yet significant tension arising from these exchanges is reflected in the figure of Protesilaus as well as the dialogue as a whole. The stories that the vine dresser tells of the present-day ghosts emphasize their superhuman powers and the extraordinary nature of their epiphanies, implicitly refuting the Phoenician's critique that they are "false and implausible." But when the vine dresser relates Protesilaus' 'true' descriptions of the heroes during the Trojan War, it turns out that nearly everything fantastic, supernatural, or implausible is eliminated from the traditional legends, in keeping with the rationalizing tendencies of Homeric historical criticism.[76] I mentioned above that Philostratus' account of the heroic past has much in common with that of Dictys and Dares, who downplay the divine and fantastic elements of the tradition in favor of a more mundane, verisimilar narrative. But this naturalizing impulse is evident in many of the authors I have looked at in this book – Homer's story is divested of anything improbable or fabulous that might engender 'disbelief' or else is attacked for those same 'lies.' Despite his own semi-divine status, Protesilaus' critique of Homer is no different; the gods are virtually absent from his account, and his dismissal of the pleasing, yet implausible 'myths' of the *Odyssey* could have been taken from Eratosthenes or Lucian:

Protesilaus does not permit us to listen (ἀκούειν) to the stories about Polyphemus, Antiphates [king of the Laestrygonians], Scylla, the tales of Hades, and what the Sirens sang, but [demands that we] stuff wax in our ears and refuse them, not because they are not full of *pleasure* and capable of *entertaining* (οὐχ ὡς οὐ πλέα ἡδονῆς καὶ ψυχαγωγῆσαι ἱκανά), but because they are *implausible* and *invented* (ἀλλ᾽ ὡς ἀπίθανά τε καὶ παρευρημένα); he orders us to sail past the islands of Ogygia and Aea, and how goddesses loved him, and not to come to anchor near these *myths* (τοῖς μύθοις). (34.4–5)

The rationalizing tendency is especially pronounced in Protesilaus' description of Achilles at the end of the dialogue, where any fantastic element associated with Achilles in Homer is either rejected or explained away. Thus his 'divine' armor was "not as Homer represented it" (οὐ τὸν Ὁμήρου τρόπον); the fact that it was divinely made and indeed everything depicted on it was "invented by Homer" (ἐξευρῆσθαι τῷ Ὁμήρῳ). In reality, Achilles' original armor, which he never lost and which Patroclus never wore, was not decorated at all, but constructed of materials that

---

[76] On rationalizing Homer in the *Heroicus*, see Mantero (1966), 161–7; Grossardt (2006), 80–2.

blended into each other and thus shone in different colors like a rainbow. This was why it was celebrated as having been beyond even Hephaestus' skill. (47.1–5). The alleged immortality of his horses was also "fabricated by Homer" (μεμυθολογῆσθαι τῷ Ὁμήρῳ: 50.2). Nor did Achilles ever fight the river Scamander, which in any case, he could have easily avoided. Rather, Protesilaus "tells a *more plausible* version of these events" (πιθανώτερα δὲ τούτων ἐκεῖνα, οἶμαι, δίεισι: 48.13) in which no mention is made of Achilles' encounter with the Scamander; the Trojans are driven into the river and massacred, not by Achilles alone, but by the Greeks as a whole. The contrast between the tone of the present-day heroic ghost stories and that of the Homeric revisions is brought out by a comparison of this episode, in which the Scamander's rising up against Achilles is rejected (διαγράφει) by Protesilaus, with the miraculous story told by the vine dresser in the first part of the dialogue in which Hector's ghost commands a formerly tiny river to rise up to an immense size, flood a road, and kill a boy who had insulted him (19.5–7). Moreover, when Protesilaus describes sections of the Achilles' legend not covered by Homer, such as his birth and upbringing, he has no such compunctions about indulging in more fantastic, divine, and 'mythical' narratives.

Homer in the Heroicus

The characterization of Protesilaus as a Homeric reader, critic, and revisionist thus embodies many of the tensions simmering underneath the surface of the *Heroicus*: between present and past, the rational and the supernatural, skepticism and belief. Protesilaus' status as a *daimon*, who appears to the vine dresser, dispenses archaic wisdom, cultivates an air of religiosity, and instills awe in those who look upon him contrasts with his pastimes of reading Homeric poetry and scrutinizing its historical content. Yet throughout the text, the authority of Protesilaus, as hero and ghost, is opposed to that of Homer, whom Protesilaus praises as a poet, yet discredits as a historian. Philostratus addresses these underlying tensions in yet another exchange between the vine dresser and the Phoenician: the late but essential discussion of Homer in chapters 43 and 44 of the *Heroicus*. The passage is best known (and deservedly so) for its surprising disclosure that Homer raised Odysseus from the dead, but has not otherwise inspired much commentary.[77] In many ways, however, it is one of the most important sections of the *Heroicus*, the moment when Homer and the heroic

---

[77] Grossardt (2006), 652, sees it as a comment on Platonic literary theory, especially that of the *Ion*.

daimones are revealed to be closely interrelated and when questions about history, truth, and the means by which these are attained and presented are answered.

The conversation about Homer takes place right after the long series of heroic descriptions that constitutes the central part of the *Heroicus* (26–42) and serves as a transition to the climactic account of Achilles' life and afterlife (45–57) that concludes the dialogue. Rather than narrate Protesilaus' version of the Trojan War in sequence, the vine dresser organizes the new information hero by hero, Greek and Trojan, offering a verbal portrait of their appearance as well as scattered comments about their activities, either correcting, supporting, or supplementing what Homer had said about them.[78] This portion of the text is almost entirely a monologue; the Phoenician speaks his first words at 33.38, seventeen pages into the vine dresser's account, and only pipes in two more times, at 36.2 and 40.1, and none of these interruptions are more than two lines in length. It is only when the vine dresser pauses before tackling Achilles that the Phoenician offers up a long impromptu speech of his own, the first expression of his own opinion since the 'Homeric' section began with the account of the Mysian expedition at ch. 23. The topic, an encomium to Homer's historical knowledge, is a bit curious, given that the bulk of the vine dresser's recently concluded account related information *not* mentioned by Homer, such as the detailed descriptions of each hero's appearance and the sordid tale of Palamedes' demise. The Phoenician, however, is impressed with how much Homer actually got right, and offers up a stirring paean to the poet:

You have swayed me so much with respect to Homer's poems that even though I had already considered them as *divine* and beyond human capability (θεῖά τε αὐτὰ πέρα ἀνθρώπου), I am now more *amazed* (ἐκπεπλῆχθαι), not only at the epic composition (οὐκ ἐπὶ τῇ ἐποποιίᾳ μόνον), nor if some *pleasure* (ἡδονή) pervades the poems, but much more by the names of the heroes and their genealogies, and, by Zeus, by the telling of how each of them killed someone or was killed by another. For it is surely no wonder, in my opinion, that Protesilaus, being a ghost, knows these things (δαίμονα ἤδη ὄντα οὐδὲν οἶμαι θαυμαστὸν εἰδέναι ταῦτα), but from where did Homer get Euphorbus, the Helenuses and Deiphobuses, and, by Zeus, the many other men from the enemy forces whom he mentions in the catalogue? For Protesilaus testifies that Homer did not make these things up (τὸ . . . μὴ ὑποτεθεῖσθαι), but composed a narrative of true events which had actually occurred (γεγονότων τε καὶ ἀληθινῶν ἔργων ἀπαγγελίαν ποιεῖσθαι), except for a few that he intentionally seems to have transformed for the sake of *variety* and to render his poetry *more pleasurable* (ἑκὼν μετασκευάσαι ἐπὶ τῷ

---

[78] On this section, which I do not discuss further, see Beschorner (1999), 221–4.

ποικίλην τε καὶ ἡδίω ἀποφῆναι τὴν ποίησιν). This is why it seems to me quite correct what some say: namely that Apollo composed these poems and attributed them to Homer. For it is more likely that a god would know these things than a man. (43.2–5)

This is the first time we hear anything in detail about the Phoenician's opinion of Homer, and on the one hand it confirms his interest in evaluating the historical content related by the poet. He comes across here, however, not as an impartial critic, but as a fanatical "believer" in Homer's reliability; his appreciation for Homer's "divine" poetry, far from being shaken by Protesilaus' repeated additions to and corrections of the poet's account, has only been increased. The Phoenician even undermines the vine dresser's earlier privileging of Protesilean omniscience, marveling at Homer's knowledge of the Trojan forces precisely because that information was difficult to obtain for someone *without* supernatural powers, and dismisses Protesilaus' ghostly knowledge as unworthy of admiration (οὐδὲν οἶμαι θαυμαστόν: 43.3). The forceful and unusual nature of the Phoenician's praise of Homer's historical skills is underlined by his subtle transformation of traditional remarks on the "divine" nature of Homer's poetry. Earlier, in ch. 25, Protesilaus had praised Homer in the standard manner: Homer "fashions [his poetry] with *divine* skill" (δαιμονίως ἐξειργάσθαι: 25.4), and his godliness is the result of his *poetic* qualities – the "grandeur" and "pleasure" of his vocabulary (μεγαλορρημοσύνην; ἡδονῇ: 25.2), his choice of subject (ὑποθέσθαι), and "the *variety* of his characters" (εἴδη τε ἀνδρῶν καὶ ἤθη ποικίλα: 25.3).[79] According to Protesilaus even the theomachy in *Il.* 21, although intended allegorically by Homer, is poetically brilliant: *divine* and *amazing* (πρὸς ἔκπληξιν καὶ θεῖα: 25.9).

Here in ch. 43, however, the Phoenician is just as "amazed" (ἐκπεπλῆχθαι: 43.2) at Homer's capacious knowledge of the historical truth (which Protesilaus had severely criticized as inaccurate) as Protesilaus was at his poetic abilities in ch. 25. Homer's divinity is attributed by the Phoenician *not* to his poetry's "variety" or "pleasure" (ποικίλην τε καὶ ἡδίω: 43.4), which are brushed aside, but to the historical skills that allow him to produce a narrative of "true events which had actually occurred" (43.4). In fact, the Phoenician's radical reassignation of Homer's divinity to his capacity as historian runs against, not only Protesilaus' views, but those of the literary critical mainstream as a whole, which almost unanimously reserved the highest praise for Homer as a poet and rarely singled out

[79] Protesilaus also "marvels" (θαυμάζει: 25.6) at Homer for his ability to correct other poets' faults in a discreet manner.

his historical accuracy as warranting similar distinction. The Phoenician's use of ἐκπεπλῆχθαι ("to be amazed") here is a deliberate and pointed choice; Imperial critics often comment on poetry's ability to instill a sense of ἔκπληξις ("amazement") in the listener, but they generally characterize such "amazement" as stemming from the poet's use of myths, falsehoods, or fictions.[80] Protesilaus' point about the theomachy in 25.9 was on these lines; the episode is obviously a fiction, but excusable because of its impressive and awe-inspiring effects on the reader.[81] The Phoenician's historical interests have resulted in quite a different response: he acknowledges the pleasure and beautiful composition of Homeric poetry, but is "amazed" by the accuracy of the historical content, and this is what he identifies as the source of the poet's divinity.

HOMER'S SOURCE

The Phoenician's investment in Homer's historical authority stems from his astonishment at Homer's profound knowledge of the details of the Trojan War. His question – where did Homer get his information? – thus seems natural for such a critic. But in fact the issue is not explicitly raised in any of the texts examined in this book so far. Advocates of Homeric correctness like Strabo maintain that Homer was representing heroic reality, but never provide a clear explanation of how he knew about it in the first place; they even seem reluctant to consider Homer's date in this context, even though they express opinions on this topic elsewhere in their work. The lack of such discussions in Herodotus, Thucydides, and Dio is perhaps less unusual given their criticisms of Homer's inaccuracy. Nevertheless, all three presume that the poet knew the truth, even if he did not follow it, and suggest that he left hints or signs of that truth hidden in his poetry; despite this, they never specify how he knew that truth. This absence is rendered all the more conspicuous given the fact that every one of these authors explicitly acknowledges that Homer lived well after the events he sings about and therefore could not have witnessed or experienced them.

The question is explicitly posed and/or answered only in the more recondite corners of Homeric revisionism. Lucian, who intentionally sidesteps the entire issue of Homer's historical reliability in the *True Stories*, uses it to set up a joke in *The Rooster*. When Micyllus asks the rooster-Euphorbus

[80] Str. 1.2.17; Plut. *Quomodo adul.* 16C, 17A, 20F, 25D; [Longin.] *Subl.* 15.2; Max. Tyr. *Or.* 17.4b; [Plut.] *Vit. Hom.* 5–6.
[81] Cf. 14.2, where Protesilaus criticizes those who focus solely on Achilles and Odysseus "due to their *amazement* at Homer's poems" (κατὰ ἔκπληξιν τῶν Ὁμήρου ποιημάτων).

whether events at Troy happened as Homer told them, the response –
"Where did [Homer] get his knowledge?" (Πόθεν ἐκεῖνος ἠπίστατο: 17) –
parallels the Phoenician's query to the vine dresser (Ὁμήρῳ δὲ πόθεν μὲν
Εὔφορβος). In *The Rooster*, however, the question is rhetorical; Homer, the
rooster implies, did *not* know the truth, and in fact: "When those events
were happening, he was a camel in Bactria." Ptolemy the Quail provides
more concrete (if contradictory) answers to the mystery of Homer's sources
when he cites Trojan War narratives composed *before* Homer;[82] unlike the
Troy Romances of Dictys and Dares, these works are not meant as older and
more accurate *replacements* of Homer, but as the original documents from
which Homer derived his own poetry.[83] But to claim, as Ptolemy does, that
Homer plagiarized the work of Musaeus' daughter Helen or an Egyptian
woman named Phantasia only begs the question of where *they* got their
information; Ptolemy's revelations tease us not only by their implausibility,
but because they deepen the mystery instead of resolving it.

The Phoenician's posing of the question then, signals that we are yet
again moving into territory occupied by the fictive and fraudulent representatives of Homeric revisionism. How could Homer possibly have
known all of this material? The irony here, of course, is that the historically
obsessed Phoenician, who prides himself on his rationalism and skepticism, is so astounded by Homer's historical prowess that he is forced to
propose an equally outrageous divine solution – that Homer was really
Apollo in disguise (43.5). Now it is the vine dresser who takes on role of
rational critic as he reassures the Phoenician that "the poet Homer did
exist and the poems were composed by a human being" (43.10),[84] that he
lived 160 years after the Trojan War (43.8),[85] and that the famous story of
his contest with Hesiod, won, unjustly, by the latter, was indeed true. His

---

[82] See Ch. 1: 19–20, and above, 179.

[83] The confusion between these two functions might help to elucidate the odd remarks made by the
Suda about Corinnus of Ilium and by John Malalas about Sisyphus of Cos (cf. 179 and n. 12 above).
The *Suda* claims that Homer based his poetry on the earlier poems of Corinnus, despite the fact
that it seems *prima facie* unlikely that a follower of Palamedes, a hero notoriously absent from
Homer's account, would have produced an epic sharing much in common with Homer's. Malalas
(*Chronographia* 132, 19–133, 2 Dindorf) contends that Homer composed the *Iliad* after finding
Sisyphus' work, a similarly strange conclusion given that the three references to Sisyphus by Malalas
are a long speech by Teucer to Neoptolemus on the death of his father Achilles (a non-Iliadic event),
and two radical rationalizing revisions of the Polyphemus and Circe episodes from the *Odyssey*. One
explanation might be that the idea that a work purporting to be pre-Homeric must also have been
one of Homer's sources was powerful enough to override clear indications that such works were
written in competition with Homer, as alternate versions of the Troy legend.

[84] Cf. 43.7: "He existed, friend, the poet Homer existed and sang" (γέγονε γάρ, ξένε, γέγονε ποιητὴς
Ὅμηρος καὶ ᾖδεν).

[85] The vine dresser lists two other possible dates (24 years after the Trojan War, 127 years after [at the
time of the Ionian migration]), before settling on 160 years after the Trojan War, when the Contest

explanation of how the poet gained so much accurate information about the war is correspondingly prosaic: "He knew the names and collected the deeds (τὰ δὲ ὀνόματα ᾔδει καὶ τὰ ἔργα ξυνελέξατο) from the cities which each [hero] led; for he went around Greece at a time after the Trojan War (μετὰ χρόνον τῶν Τρωικῶν) which was not yet sufficient for the events around Troy to have been obscured (ἐξαμαυρῶσαι)" (43.11).[86] The idea that Homer traveled around gathering information recalls similar suggestions by Strabo (e.g., 1.1.2; 1.2.29) and Dio (*Or.* 11.15); like those writers, the vine dresser maintains a studied vagueness concerning the details.

At this point, however, the vine dresser suddenly abandons the sobriety of his previous remarks and offers a completely different answer to the Phoenician's question:

But he *learned* (ἔμαθε) these things in another way, *supernatural* and advanced in wisdom (δαιμόνιόν τε καὶ σοφίας πρόσω). For they say that once, Homer sailed to Ithaca because he had heard that the soul of Odysseus still breathed, and that he raised him from the dead. When Odysseus arose, he asked him about the events at Troy (τὰ ἐν Ἰλίῳ), and he said that he knew and remembered everything (ὁ δὲ εἰδέναι μὲν πάντα ἔλεγε καὶ μεμνῆσθαι αὐτῶν) but that he would not tell anything he knew unless he should obtain as payment from Homer praise in his poetry and a hymn to his wisdom and courage. When Homer had agreed to these things and said that he would *gratify* him in his poetry to the best of his ability (ὅ τι δύναιτο χαριεῖσθαι αὐτῷ ἐν τῇ ποιήσει), Odysseus went through everything *truthfully and just as it happened* (διήει Ὀδυσσεὺς πάντα ξὺν ἀληθείᾳ τε καὶ ὡς ἐγένετο). For souls never lie before the pit and blood. As Homer departed, Odysseus shouted, "Palamedes is prosecuting me for his murder; I know that I am guilty and I will definitely pay the penalty in some way, for the judges here are harsh, Homer, and my punishment is close, but if the people of the upper world do not realize that I have done these things to Palamedes, then the circumstances here will destroy me less. Do not bring Palamedes to Troy, do not employ him in the army, do not say that he was wise. Other poets will say these things, but they will not seem *plausible* because you have not mentioned them (πιθανὰ δὲ οὐ δόξει μὴ σοὶ εἰρημένα)." This was the encounter (ξυνουσία) between Odysseus and Homer, and Homer thus *learned the truth* (οὕτως Ὅμηρος

---

of Homer and Hesiod took place. The same date is mentioned (although with no reference to the Contest) in *Vit. Hom.* 6 West (*Vita Hesychii* [*Suda*], o 251]) 4. On the dating of Homer in antiquity, see above (Ch. 2: 25–6; Ch. 3: 55).

86 To some degree this biographical interlude resembles some of the *Lives of Homer* known to us from antiquity; like Protesilaus, the authors often list a range of possible dates for Homer and also sometimes refer to his travels. As I mentioned above (Ch. 3: 54) these travels are rarely undertaken expressly for historical inquiry; rather they are either inferred from Homer's knowledge of dialects ([Plut.] *Vit. Hom.* 2.8), and geography (*Vit. Hom.* 5 West [Procl. *Chr.*] 8), or are related to his occupation as a poetic performer (*Vit. Hom.* 6 West [*Vita Hesychii* (*Suda* o 251)] 6; *Vit. Hom.* 9 West [*Vita Scoraliensis* 11] 5). The one exception is *Vit. Hom.* 2 West (Ps.-Hdt.) 7, where Homer is said to have learned about Odysseus from the inhabitants of Ithaca.

τὰ ἀληθῆ μὲν ἔμαθε), but he altered many things for the benefit of the story that he planned (μετεκόσμησε δὲ πολλὰ ἐς τὸ συμφέρον τοῦ λόγου ὃν ὑπέθετο). (43.12–16)

The key to this brilliant and outlandish anecdote lies in its concluding sentence, which is basically a paraphrase of Herodotus' famous judgment on Homer's awareness of Helen's stay in Egypt: "It seems to me that Homer also knew this story; but seeing that it was not as well suited to epic poetry as the one which he used, he omitted it (μετῆκε)" (2.116.1). As we have seen, this idea underlies the Homeric criticism of Thucydides, Strabo, and Dio, who all presume that Homer knew the truth, but chose not to tell it for some reason (i.e., exaggeration, entertainment, deception). What never gets explained, however, is how Homer learned the truth in the first place. In fact, Protesilaus himself is guilty of this; in ch. 24 he asserts (as reported by the vine dresser) that Homer had "intentionally omitted" (ἑκόντα . . . παραλιπεῖν: 24.1) the 'true' account of the Mysian expedition from his poetry, implying that Homer knew the story. Protesilaus accuses Homer of doing so in order to "gratify" (χαριζόμενος: 23.29) Helen and adds the more general charges that Homer exaggerated Achilles' exploits and left Palamedes out to appease Odysseus.[87] But he never addresses why Homer should have been aware of the truth at all. It is only now, much later in the dialogue, that the vine dresser reveals in one fell swoop both Homer's reason for his favoritism of Odysseus (χαριεῖσθαι: 43.13) *and* his source of information.[88]

Seen from this perspective, Philostratus' anecdote becomes a comic 'solution' to a question that so many of his predecessors avoided asking. Like them, he accounts for why Homer "altered many things" (43.16) (because he was forced by Odysseus *not* to tell the truth, omitting all mention of Palamedes and glorifying Odysseus beyond measure). He thus follows Dio (*Or.* 11.35) in attributing Homer's deviation from the truth not to any poetic motive, *à la* Herodotus, Thucydides, and Strabo, but to a more

---

[87] Cf. my discussion above (131–4) of Homer 'gratifying' the Greeks in Dio, *Or.* 11.11; 35.

[88] Grossardt (2009), 76–80, sees a parallel to this interview in the story told about Homer's encounter with Achilles' ghost in *Vit. Hom.* 7 West (*Vita Romana*) 5. There Homer prays at Achilles' tomb to see the hero in all his battle glory, but is blinded by the hero's divinely made armor. In exchange he receives the gift of poetry from Thetis and the Muses. The story explains Homer's blindness and poetic genius by linking them with a ghostly encounter, but there is no indication that Achilles is the *source* of any information. Grossardt claims that the "art of poetry" (ἡ ποιητική) granted to Homer by the Muses "almost certainly also implies . . . the factual knowledge about the Trojan War and about Odysseus' travels" (77). Perhaps, but that is not made explicit in the *Vita* nor in the version told in the scholia to Plato's *Phaedrus* (ad 243a).

typically historiographical concern: bias, in this case a concern to flatter and "gratify" Odysseus. But Philostratus also explains the previously
neglected question of how Homer "learned the truth" – with the disclosure that the poet had raised Odysseus from the dead and interviewed
him. And in a clever twist, the two explanations are inextricably linked;
Homer could obtain his knowledge of the true story from his supernatural
eyewitness source only if he agreed not to follow it in his own account.
The situation Homer finds himself in, knowing the truth, but forced to
lie as the condition for that knowledge, is a wry comment on the central
problem faced by historical critics of Homer: how to reconcile Homer's
knowledge of the truth with the fact that his narrative was not completely
true.

Philostratus' 'solution' also further problematizes the relationship
between rational and supernatural that runs through the dialogue. The historical core of Homeric poetry – "everything just as it happened" (43.14) –
was usually defined in opposition to its fantastic, mythic, and incredible
elements, and virtually all attempts to locate history in Homer begin by
eliminating anything that seemed supernatural, divine, or impossible. The
Heroicus is no different; as I noted above, Protesilaus' 'true' version of
events basically adheres to this rationalizing principle. But now Homer's
knowledge of the 'truth' and his historical reliability are revealed to be
dependent upon a supernatural, ghostly source, and one moreover, that
Homer raised from the grave by the techniques laid out in the *Nekuia*, one
of the episodes in his poems Protesilaus had earlier considered mythic and
"implausible" (ἀπίθανα: 34.4).[89] Moreover, by linking Homer with heroic
ghosts, Philostratus pays homage to the Stesichorean tradition of Homeric revision, with a characteristic twist: while Helen's ghost had restored
the poet's sight when he retracted his 'false' version and told the 'truth,'
Odysseus' ghost tells Homer the truth, but then commands him to relate
an account that is *not* true. But Philostratus' attempt to re-integrate the
supernatural roots of Homeric historical criticism back into the tradition
seems like a calculated effort to destabilize the entire process of establishing
the truth, by questioning its ultimate source.

The obvious parallelism between Homer's "encounter" (ξυνουσία) with
Odysseus and the "association" (τὴν ξυνουσίαν: 7.1) of the vine dresser
and Protesilaus serves to further complicate the relation between truth,
authority, and the supernatural. As I discussed earlier, the vine dresser's
claim of a close rapport with a heroic *daimon* was certainly provocative, but

---

[89] 34.4: "the tales of Hades"; cf. Luc. *Philops.* 2.

not necessarily outside the limits of contemporary standards of plausibility. But surely the reader's willingness to believe would have been tested when that same vine dresser, on the information of his ghostly friend, suddenly reveals, nearly two-thirds into the dialogue, that centuries ago Homer learned the truth *in the same way* that the vine dresser has learned it – by interviewing the ghost of a hero. In terms of the ongoing contest between the Phoenician and the vine dresser, the revelation is a riposte to the Phoenician, who had disparaged the vine dresser's source, Protesilaus, because his ghostly knowledge gave him an unfair advantage over Homer. The joke is on the Phoenician when he is told that his beloved Homer gained his knowledge from the very same kind of supernatural source that he had just belittled. On the other hand, as Peter Grossardt has emphasized, the agreement between Homer and Odysseus to suppress certain truths could very well cast suspicion, retroactively, on the veracity of the vine dresser's account, dependent as it is on a heroic ghost who might have laid similar restrictions upon the telling of the 'truth.'[90] Given what we now know about the reliability of heroic ghosts, why should the vine dresser's account be trusted any more than Homer's?

The Homer interlude is thus a pivotal moment in the *Heroicus*; Homer is belatedly described and the sources of his knowledge finally revealed, but the answers have destabilized the entire bases on which the dialogue had been constructed. In one fell swoop Philostratus 'explains' both how Homer knew the truth and why he refused to tell it, a culminating blow in his continued play with the conventions and methods of Homeric historical criticism. The 'truth' of Philostratus' Homer is revealed as contingent, motivated by the same kind of 'favor' or 'gratification' as was Dio's patriotically and politically motivated Homer; and like Lucian, Philostratus posits close collusion between Homer and Odysseus, although now the relation between poet and character has been transformed into one between poet and 'real' hero. But perhaps most significantly, Homer has been revealed as the vine dresser's predecessor, his spiritual ancestor, learning the truth from the 'best' possible source, the ghost of a hero. A link, comical as it may be, has been established between the present and the past, and most importantly perhaps, it turns out that believing in Homer and believing in ghosts, which were the opposing ideas on which the dialogue had been structured up to this point, amount in the end to the same thing.

---

[90] Grossardt (2006), 662, s.v. 43.16, although he perhaps places too much emphasis on this reading.

CONCLUSION: FICTIONAL HEROES

The connection between Homeric past and heroic present is further spot-lighted in the section on Achilles that immediately follows the discussion of Homer. The excursus, which is in many ways the high point of the dialogue, is far longer and much more detailed than that dedicated to any other hero (twenty-three pages in Kayser) and the only one that moves chronologically through the hero's life, from birth to death (44.5–52.2; 196–206 K), and that treats, at considerable length, his life *after* death (52.3–57.17; 207–18 K). In addition, the literary experimentation that characterizes much of the *Heroicus* becomes bolder and more self-indulgent here. Philostratus virtually abandons his attempts to authenticate the 'truth' of his stories, and in fact one almost feels as if he has lost control of the dialogue, as one sees him veer from intricate descriptions of Thessalian cult practice[91] to a macabre tale of Achilles' ghost tearing a young girl limb from limb, from recitations of a hymn to Thetis and a poem ascribed to Heracles, to the bizarre account that concludes the work: an Amazon attack on the island of Leuke that ends with their own horses devouring them, and their scattered limbs and half-eaten corpses washing up on shore.

Within the seeming chaos of this section, one scene shows Philostratus knowingly connecting his Achilles narrative with the inquiry into Homer and history that occupied most of the earlier part of the dialogue. He carefully paints a haunting picture of Achilles and Helen in love on Leuke, the island that, in his version, has been created specifically for them as their resting place after death (54–5). The legend of the heroes on Leuke was traditional, as I mentioned in the last chapter, and may have influenced Lucian's depiction of the Island of the Blessed. Philostratus similarly plays on the ghosts' self-consciousness of their status as subjects of poetry by reversing the conventional (and temporal) hierarchy and having the heroes sing in honor of the *poet* and his deeds; at sunset Achilles and Helen "are said to drink together ... and sing of their love for each other, the songs of Homer on Troy, and of Homer himself" (54.12).[92] The vine dresser reveals that Protesilaus knows the song Achilles composed in honor of Homer,[93] and when the Phoenician asks to hear it, the vine dresser,

---

[91] Rutherford (2009).   [92] Cf. Luc. *VH* 2.15: the heroes sing Homer's poetry.

[93] On Achilles as poet in the *Heroicus*, see Miles (2005). Achilles of course is depicted as playing the lyre and singing at *Il.* 9.185–91. Philostratus relates an anecdote about the young Achilles' desire for musical skill at 45.7; the hero had asked Calliope to grant this wish, but was told that he should concentrate on his military skills, and that "there will be a poet in the future whom I will send forth to sing your deeds."

somewhat surprisingly, complies, reciting a short lyric poem that invokes Echo to "sing to me of divine Homer // glory of men (κλέος ἀνέρων) // glory of our labors // because of him I did not die // because of him Patroclus // is mine, because of him my Ajax // is equal to the immortals, // because of him Troy, sung by the wise as captured by might // gained glory and did not fall" (54.3).[94]

This remarkable, clever scene represents Philostratus' attempt to construct a continuation of Achilles' story that references, but is no longer bound to Homer and the past, in which the hero's ghost, unlike Lucian's heroes in the *True Stories*, lives a life of his own in Philostratus' own Imperial present. The fact that Achilles and Helen are living and singing *right now* is implied by the visits made by Protesilaus' to their island, but is also made explicit when the vine dresser mentions that, while Achilles sings a number of songs, the one he will recite to the Phoenician is a *recent* work; in fact, Achilles just composed it "last year" (πέρυσιν: 55.2)! This jarring temporal reference suddenly underlines the way that Philostratus has collapsed the distant past and the immediate present; the vine dresser's narrative of Achilles, which had begun with his birth from a goddess in the heroic age extends right up until the time of the dialogue itself.

The story of Achilles and Helen on Leuke is also a good example of how Philostratus' 'fictions' become bolder and more imaginative near the end of the dialogue, despite the fact that they are still meant to be 'true', vouched for and witnessed by Protesilaus (who is said to visit Leuke often). Not only does he actually depict the kind of non-canonical romantic union Lucian teased us with but refrained from representing (Cinyras and Helen, Odysseus back with Calypso), but the details of Protesilaus' story test the limits of the reader's belief in his authority. Lucian coyly alludes to new poems by Homer, whetting our curiosity with a couple of verses; Philostratus presents us with a complete poem *on* Homer composed by *Achilles*, and passes it off as the genuine article, garnered from an eye-, or better ear-witness. If Lucian had depicted the heroes in a strictly bounded world in order to emphasize the self-contained fictional nature of Homeric poetry, Philostratus crosses those Homeric borders into the uncharted territories of heroic fiction.

---

[94] Grossardt (2006), 46, sees the recital of the poem as the *Heroicus'* climax, "a grand homage to the power of poetry," where Philostratus admits that, for all of the talk of *daimones* and heroic epiphanies, in the final analysis it is Homer and the literary tradition that have bestowed immortality on the heroes. On the poem's metapoetic associations, see also Grossardt (2004). On the poems in the *Heroicus*, see Bowie (1989), 221–4.

The *Heroicus* concludes with a final exchange between the Phoenician and the vine dresser that almost ostentatiously calls attention to the games Philostratus has been playing with truth and fictionality throughout the dialogue.[95] After the Phoenician expresses his satisfaction with the vine dresser's heroic tales, he requests an ethnographic account of the under-world: "the Cocytus and Pyriphlegethon rivers, the Acherusian Lake . . . the Aeacids [Minos, Rhadamanthus, and Aeacus], their courts and prisons" (58.1). This is a clear allusion to two of the most famous 'myths' or 'fictions' of antiquity, the visits to the underworld by Odysseus in the *Odyssey* (*Od.* 11) and by Er at the end of Plato's *Republic* (10.614b–21d), and perhaps also a nod to Lucian's stay on the Island of the Blessed in his *True Stories*. In fact it was due to the influence of such stories that descriptions of the underworld came to be considered the quintessential examples of fantastic, false 'myths' in antiquity. Thus when the vine dresser *agrees* to consult Protesilaus and then report the 'truth' about the underworld to the Phoenician on the next day, it is hard not to escape the feeling that Philostratus is giving his readers one last signal that the 'truth' of his entire dialogue was nothing other than an effect of an ambitious fictional experiment.[96]

Like Dio and Lucian before him, Philostratus employs the critique of Homer's role as historical witness as a means of exploring and interrogating the Imperial faith in the authority and 'truth' of Greek tradition. But he accomplishes this in a far more indirect fashion, in an unwieldy, loosely structured, non-linear text that jumbles together the fantastic and the ratio-nal, the ancient and the modern – framing his 'true' story of the Trojan War with a vivid portrait of archaic heroes revitalized in the Imperial land-scape, and imbuing one of these ghosts, Protesilaus, with the erudition and critical devotion necessary for a proper assessment of Homeric reliability.[97] The parodic treatment of authoritative claims to truth that runs through the *Heroicus* is one way that Philostratus mocks the presumptions that underlie the Imperial reverence for the Greek past. He reveals that Homer learned the 'truth' from Odysseus' ghost in exchange for lying about him in his poetry, thereby laying bare the contingency of the poet's account of

---

[95] The last tale told by the vine dresser is the long and grisly account of the defeat of the Amazons at the hands of Achilles (56.11–57.17), which, like his version of the heroes on Leuke, is unparalleled (although a number of recognizable elements from the legendary and historical tradition can be detected: Grossardt [2006], 755–69), and dated with curious precision: to "the Olympiad in which Leonidas of Rhodes was first victorious in the *stadion*" (ca. 164 BCE: 56.11).

[96] Cf. Grossardt (2006), 94–6, on the *Heroicus* as Philostratus' practical demonstration of his implicit but never fully articulated concept of fiction.

[97] Grossardt (2006), 96–120, goes so far as to describe the *Heroicus* as an "adding up" (*Bilanz*) of the *entire* ancient poetic, historical, and critical traditions concerning the Trojan War.

events. Moreover this information is disclosed by the curious source upon whom Philostratus bases his own new 'history' – Protesilaus' ghost, who did not witness any of the Trojan War yet knows all about it, who is not only more reliable than Homer, but also one of his most learned critics, and who brings a 'rationalizing' skepticism to Homer's account despite his own supernatural nature. In place of the 'authentic' eyewitness accounts that lay at the base of so many previous Homeric revisions (diaries preserved in tombs, stories preserved in Egyptian temples), Philostratus depicts ghosts (Odysseus and Protesilaus) as the only sources who can reveal the truth (and even they are not to be trusted). Like Dio's *Trojan Oration*, the *Heroicus* calls its own authority into question even as it undermines that of Homer. And while Lucian's *True Stories* emphasized the need to look beyond Homer's connections with 'reality' and appreciate the power of Homeric fiction, Philostratus provides perhaps the most appropriate homage to the inventive qualities of the poet, by not just revising his tales of the Trojan War, but continuing the story of his heroes down into the present day, where they still haunt the imagination of Imperial Greece.

CHAPTER 7

Epilogue

Given the authoritative position of Homer in Imperial society, his symbolic value as the foundation of Greek *paideia*, and his association with the origins of Greek history, the mere invocation of the poet's name (not to mention the quotation of his verses) by an orator, philosopher, or essayist, could be seen as an attempt to inscribe oneself within the Greek literary and cultural tradition. In this sense, the intimate knowledge of Homer and Homeric criticism that Strabo, Dio, Lucian, and Philostratus display in their texts mark them as quintessentially Greek: the frequent quotations and allusions to the poems, the obscure references to scholarly controversies, and the novel 'solutions' they propose to classic Homeric problems speak to a mastery of Greek *paideia* that reflect their place among the Imperial elite. Moreover, by employing their expertise to discuss Homer's relation to heroic history – and in particular whether he accurately depicted that era, its people, and its events – they enmesh themselves in a discourse about the place of the historical (and not just the literary) origins of Greece within Imperial Greek culture. In this book I have traced the ways in which these four Imperial authors formulate their own individual responses to the issue by deploying, in various and inventive combinations, their knowledge of Homer, Homeric scholarship, historiography, and literary criticism. Here, however, I would like to draw out some of the common themes and similarities that tie the authors together, and outline the basic movement of my argument concerning their connection to questions of the past in Imperial culture.

The Imperial writers build upon a way of thinking about Homer and history formulated earlier by Herodotus and Thucydides, the first extant Greek authors who devoted significant space to the question of Homer's reliability. In their critiques of Homer's account of the Trojan War, Herodotus and Thucydides insist that Homer knew the truth, but also maintain that he misrepresented parts of that truth, without ever explaining how these two claims fit together. As historians, their discussion of Homeric poetry centers primarily on its content: they ask whether that content is 'true' (i.e., historical) or 'false' (i.e., invented by the poet, or what we might call 'fictionalized'), and furthermore how one might distinguish the one from the other. Within these conceptual parameters, the central difficulty lay in reconciling the view of Homer as a historian who reflects the realities of the Trojan War, with the view of him as a poet who necessarily writes things that aren't true (i.e., fictions) to fulfill some 'poetic' aim (usually ill-defined: e.g., exaggeration, bias, generic 'appropriateness').

This is the precise dilemma that Strabo sets out to resolve, responding both to the newfound centrality and universality of Homer in the Hellenistic world and his own urge to assert the continuing relevance and value of Homer and the heroic age in the Roman Empire. To do so, he lays out a portrait of Homer as an intrepid historian, dedicated to the truth, thus explaining what the Classical historians left unexamined – why Homer *wanted* to tell the truth at all. But like them, he runs up against the difficulty that Homer was also a poet, and undeniably included a lot of 'myths' or fictional material in his poetry. To explain why someone as historically minded as Homer would do such a thing, Strabo points to his poetic objective of entertaining his audience. But in his desire to find as much 'reality' in Homeric poetry as he can (even in the most unlikely places, like the Phaeacian tales), Strabo is forced into envisioning a 'hinting', enigmatic poet considerably at odds with the conscientious historian he had taken such pains to depict. The failure of Strabo's vigorous efforts brings to light the fundamental tensions that underlie any model positing Homer as historian *and* poet. But they also reveal how any attempt to establish Homer's accuracy as a historian has to follow in Strabo's footsteps – viewing the poet as a real person, setting him at a particular place and time, and articulating the intentions that motivated the composition of his poetry.

Strabo's work also clarifies the extent to which the study of Homeric history and geography was caught up in questions of Greek identity, linked to the desire of cities and individuals to locate some authoritative link to the Greek heroic past. For Strabo, too, Homer and the heroic past embody the defining characteristics of 'Greece' in opposition to Rome. Strabo's defense and scholarly engagement with Homer is not only an assertion of his own place in 'Greek' culture, but also a defense of the continuing value of the ancient literary and historical traditions of Greece. Strabo's vision of Homer and the heroic age and their importance to Greek self-definition is essential to keep in mind as the focus shifts to the three Second Sophistic writers, for whom doubting and undermining Homer's relation to history becomes a way of critiquing such high estimations of the past and the motivations behind them.

One way in which the Second Sophistic authors accomplish this is by sketching their own counter-portraits of Homer. These are undertaken for the same methodological reasons as Strabo's – to ground explanations of Homeric poetry's mixture of heroic history and poetic fiction in a biographical conception of the poet. But unlike Strabo, they exploit the fact that thinking about Homer as a real historicized person, and not an ethereal, divinely inspired, canonical authority figure, was an easy way to expose him to ridicule. Dio thus turns Strabo's portrait of the poet as historian upside-down: he envisions a Homer that has *no* devotion to history or the truth, *no* desire to 'instruct' his audience, and in fact is dedicated to lying, and motivated to do so by his eagerness to flatter his listeners. Dio takes the historicization of Homer even further than Strabo does, placing him in a specific political situation that explains his lies about the Trojan War as a tradition 'invented' by Homer in order to assuage fears of an imminent Asian invasion of Greece. By asserting that Homer was untrustworthy precisely because he was 'Greek' and trying to bolster his compatriots' confidence in their achievements, Dio targets the unthinking reverence with which the Greeks under the Empire (represented, paradoxically, in the speech by the Greek inhabitants of Roman 'Troy,' or Ilium) took solace in their glorious past.

A similar logic informs the depiction of Homer in Philostratus' *Heroicus*, in which the vine dresser reveals that Homer learned about the Trojan War not only by inquiry and travel (the Strabonian model) but from a conversation with the ghost of Odysseus, whom Homer had raised from the dead; the outlandish tale parodies (in a more indirect fashion than Dio) assertions of Homer's reliability as well as his access to the heroic age. The information Odysseus provides is true (the method Homer uses prevents ghosts from lying), but comes with a catch; Homer buys his access to the truth by agreeing to lie about Odysseus in his poetry. Like Strabo and Dio, Philostratus comes up with a reason for why Homer sometimes told the truth and sometimes lied, but he also wittily 'solves' a dilemma that none of his predecessors had even addressed – how Homer gained knowledge of the truth in the first place. Finally, in the *True Stories*, Lucian reports his conversation with Homer himself (or at least his ghost), in which he displays his contempt for historicizing criticism of Homer either by pointedly ignoring issues of Homeric 'reality' or by implying that such information contributes nothing to the proper appreciation of his poetry. Biographical readings are similarly mocked: Lucian's Homer was originally Babylonian, but that revelation does not produce any significant reinterpretation of his poetry either. Rather it seems to emphasize that neither Homer's ethnicity or his origins are as important as the poetic world and characters he has created, a suggestion that is supported by Lucian's representation of the Homeric heroes on the Islands of the Blessed as literary figures, unable to break out of their classic poetic roles.

Envisioning Homer and his activities, then, becomes a way of expressing doubts not just about Homer as a historian, but about *any* claims of access to heroic history. To this end, the three authors also work hard to undermine the authoritative 'sources' of their own narratives. Lucian is the most explicit, declaring in his preface that nothing he will go on to narrate has ever occurred, and hence should not be believed at all, and continually parodying historiographical clichés of eyewitness narratives throughout the *True Stories*. Dio and Philostratus go about this more subtly by appealing to purportedly more reliable 'sources' than Homer – Dio's Egyptian priest, Philostratus' ghost of Protesilaus – who are gradually revealed, through the self-consciously literary way in which they are portrayed, as convenient fictions authorizing the creation of their author's alternative accounts.

This destabilizing of authority and claims to truth is related to a more general thematization of the interplay between truth and fiction in these texts. What unites the three is not simply that they all offer clearly 'fictional' stories in place of or in competition with Homer's – either calling his 'truth' into question (Dio, Philostratus), or simply ignoring historical reality altogether (Lucian). Rather it is that their works themselves tease the reader by constantly hovering at the borders of credibility – and leave the audience questioning not only the 'truth' of Homer, or even the validity of the corrections of Homer, but the sincerity of the author in proposing them in the first place. The texts prompt their readers to ask, in reference to the authors, precisely those questions that the authors are asking about Homer – Do we believe him? Why should we believe him? Is what he says true? If not, why is he lying?

By couching their discussions and thematizations of Homer, history, and fiction in such complicated and ambivalent texts, Dio, Lucian, and Philostratus manage to problematize the ideological motivations that have placed Homer at the heart of Imperial Greek culture. All three authors are mocking the urge to historicize Homer and use him as the basis of the historical past. But while they seem to put themselves forward as the reporters of the 'truth,' they refuse to completely abandon Homer. There is a realization in all three texts that any 'history' in Homer is inextricable from his fictions, whether one dismisses any vestiges of historical reality as irrelevant to his poetry as Lucian does, or emphasizes how historical 'truth' is always already constructed and 'fictionalized,' even by Homer himself, as Dio and Philostratus do (albeit in quite different ways). The three authors thus fashion a new role for the poet, not as purveyor of wisdom and knowledge, nor as reliable witness of the heroic age, but as a fellow storyteller. In the end, Dio, Lucian, and Philostratus all assert the power of fiction over history, but fiction that *knows* it is fiction, that far from passing itself off as the truth, lays bare its invented and constructed nature.

Works cited

Affholder, C. (1966–7) "L'exégèse morale d'Homère,"*BFS* 45: 287–93.

Aitken, E. B. (2004) "Why a Phoenician? A proposal for the historical occasion for the *Heroikos*," in Maclean and Aitken (2004): 267–84.

Alcock, S. E. (1997) "The heroic past in a Hellenistic present," in *Hellenistic Constructs. Essays in Culture, History, and Historiography*, ed. P. Cartledge, P. Garnsey, and E. Gruen. Berkeley: 20–34.

Allen, T. W., ed. (1912) *Homeri Opera*, vol. v. Oxford.

Aly, W. (1957) "Aut prodesse volunt aut delectare poetae," in *Strabon von Amaseia. Untersuchungen über Text, Aufbau und Quellen der Geographika*. Bonn: 376–85.

Anderson, G. (1976) *Studies in Lucian's Comic Fiction*. Leiden.

(1986) *Philostratus. Biography and Belles Lettres in the Third Century* AD. London.

(1993) *The Second Sophistic. A Cultural Phenomenon in the Roman Empire*. New York and London.

(1996) "Lucian's *Verae Historiae*," in *The Novel in the Ancient World*, ed. G. Schmeling. Leiden: 555–61.

Andreani, M. (1998) "Il naufragio nella *Storia vera* di Luciano," *Patavium* 6 (11): 133–47.

Apfel, H. V. (1938) "Homeric criticism in the fourth century BC," *TAPhA* 69: 245–58.

Arnim, H. von, ed. (1893) *Dionis Prusaensis quem vocant Chrysostomus quae exstant omnia*, vol. I, 2nd edn. Reprinted (1962). Berlin.

(1898) *Leben und Werke des Dio von Prusa*. Berlin.

Asmis, E. (1991) "Philodemus' poetic theory and *On the Good King According to Homer*," *ClAnt* 10: 1–45.

Aujac, G. (1966) *Strabon et la science de son temps*. Paris.

(1969) "Notice," in *Strabon Géographie*, t. I, 1 (*Introduction générale* – Livre I), ed. G. Aujac and F. Lasserre. Paris: 3–57.

Austin, N. (1994) *Helen of Troy and Her Shameless Phantom*. Ithaca, NY and London.

Avenarius, G. (1956) *Lukians Schrift zur Geschichtsschreibung*. Meisenheim am Glan.

Baladié, R., ed. (1978) *Strabon. Géographie*. Tome v, Livre 8. Paris.

Bartley, A., ed. (2009) *A Lucian for our Times*. Newcastle upon Tyne.

Baumbach, M. and Bär, S., eds. (2007) *Quintus Smyrnaeus. Transforming Homer in Second Sophistic Epic*. Berlin and New York.

Berger, H., ed. (1880) *Die geographischen Fragmente des Eratosthenes*. Leipzig.

Bernard, W. (1990) *Spätantike Dichtungstheorien. Untersuchungen zu Proklos, Herakleitos und Plutarch*. Stuttgart.

Beschorner, A. (1992) *Untersuchungen zu Dares Phrygius*. Tübingen.

    (1999) *Helden und Heroen, Homer und Caracalla. Übersetzung, Kommentar und Interpretationen zum Heroikos des Flavios Philostratos*. Bari.

Betz, H. D. (1996) "Heroenverehrung und Christusglaube. Religionsgeschichtliche Beobachtungen zu Philostrats Heroicus," in *Geschichte – Tradition – Reflexion. Festschrift für Martin Hengel zum 70. Geburtstag. Bd. II. Griechische und römische Religion*, ed. H. Cancik, H. Lichtenberger, and P. Schäfer. Tübingen: 119–39. Translated in Maclean and Aitken (2004): 25–48.

Bickerman, E. J. (1952) "Origenes gentium," *CPh* 47: 65–81.

Bigwood, J. M. (1989) "Ctesias' *Indica* and Photius," *Phoenix* 43, 302–16.

Billault, A., ed. (1994) *Lucien de Samosate*. Paris.

    (2000) *L'Univers de Philostrate*. Brussels.

    (2006) "Rhétorique et herméneutique dans le *Discours troyen* (xi) de Dion Chrysostome," *Papers on Rhetoric* 7: 1–16.

Biraschi, A. M. (1984) "Strabone e la difesa di Omero nei Prolegomena," in *Strabone. Contributi allo studio della personalità e dell'opera I*, ed. F. Prontera. Perugia: 127–53.

    (1988) "Dai 'Prolegomena' all'Italia: premesse teoriche e tradizione," in *Strabone e l'Italia antica*, ed. G. Maddoli. Perugia: 127–43.

    (1989) *Tradizioni epiche e storiografia. Studi su Erodoto e Tucidide*. Naples.

    (1992) "'Salvare' Omero. A proposito di Strabone viii 3,16," *PP* 47: 241–55.

    (1994) "Strabone e Omero. Aspetti della tradizione omerica nella descrizione del Peloponneso," in *Strabone e la Grecia*, ed. A. M. Biraschi. Naples: 23–57.

    (1996) "Teopompo e l'uso del mito. A proposito di FgrHist 115 F381," *Hermes* 124: 160–9.

    (2000) "Omero e aspetti della tradizione omerica nei libri straboniani sull'Asia Minore," in *Strabone e l'Asia Minore*, ed. A. M. Biraschi and G. Salmeri. Perugia: 45–72.

    (2005) "Strabo and Homer: a chapter in cultural history," in *Strabo's Cultural Geography. The Making of a Kolossourgia*, ed. D. Dueck, H. Lindsay, and S. Pothecary. Cambridge: 73–85.

Blomqvist, K. (1989) *Myth and Moral Message in Dio Chrysostom. A Study in Dio's Moral Thought, with a Particular Focus on his Attitudes towards Women*. Diss., Lund.

Bolonyai, G. (2001) "The uses of progymnasmata: the case of 'refutations' and Dio's *Trojan Oration*," *AAntHung* 41: 25–34.

Bompaire, J. (1958) *Lucien écrivain. Imitation et création*. Paris.

(1988) "Comment lire les *Histoires vraies* de Lucien?" in *Hommages à Henri Le Bonniec. Res sacrae*, ed. D. Porte and J.-P. Néraudau. Brussels: 31–9.

Bonner, S. F. (1977) *Education in Ancient Rome*. Berkeley.

Bornmann, F. (1994) "Giuoco allusivo e parodia letteraria nelle *Vere storie* di Luciano," in *Storia, poesia e pensiero nel mondo antico. Studi in onore di Marcello Gigante*, ed. F. del Franco. Naples: 63–7.

Bouquiaux-Simon, O. (1968) *Les lectures homériques de Lucien*. Mémoires de la Classe des Lettres ser. 2, t. LIX, fasc. 2. Brussels.

Bowersock, G. W. (1994) *Fiction as History. Nero to Julian*. Berkeley.

Bowie, E. L. (1970) "Greeks and their past in the Second Sophistic," *P&P* 46: 3–41.

(1989) "Greek sophists and Greek poetry in the second sophistic," *ANRW* II.33.1, 209–58.

(1994) "Philostratus: writer of fiction," in *Greek Fiction. The Greek Novel in Context*, ed. J. R. Morgan and R. Stoneman. New York and London: 181–202.

(2009) "Philostratus: the life of a sophist," in Bowie and Elsner (2009): 19–32.

Bowie, E. L. and Elsner, J., eds. (2009) *Philostratus*. Cambridge.

Brancacci, A. (1985) *Rhetorike philosophousa. Dione Crisostomo nella cultura antica e bizantina*. Naples.

Branham, R. B. (1989) *Unruly Eloquence. Lucian and the Comedy of Traditions*. Cambridge, MA.

Bréchet, C. (1999) "Le *De audiendis poetis* de Plutarque et le procès platonicien de la poésie," *RPh* 73: 209–44.

Briand, M. (2005) "Lucien et Homère dans les *Histoires vraies*: pratique et théorie de la fiction au temps de la Seconde Sophistique," *Lalies* 25: 127–49.

Brillante, C. (1990) "History and the historical interpretation of myth," in *Approaches to Greek Myth*, ed. L. Edmunds. Baltimore: 93–138.

Brink, C. O. (1972) "Ennius and the Hellenistic worship of Homer," *CPh* 93: 547–67.

Broggiato, M., ed. (2001) *Cratete di Mallo. I frammenti*. La Spezia.

Bruno Sunseri, G. (1997) "Poesia e storiografia in Eforo di Cuma," *QS* 46: 143–67.

Buffière, F. (1956) *Les mythes d'Homère et la pensée grecque*. Paris.

Bunbury, E. H. (1883) *A History of Ancient Geography among the Greeks and Romans from the Earliest Ages till the Fall of the Roman Empire*. 2nd edn. London.

Burstein, S. (2008) "Greek identity in the Hellenistic period," in *Hellenisms. Culture, Identity, and Ethnicity from Antiquity to Modernity*, ed. K. Zacharia. Aldershot, Hampshire: 59–77.

Butti de Lima, P. (1996) *L'inchiesta e la prova. Immagine storiografica, pratica giuridica e retorica nella Grecia classica*. Turin.

Buxton, R. (1994) *Imaginary Greece. The Contexts of Mythology*. Cambridge.

Caiazza, G. (2001) "Un esempio di interpretazione omerica: Dione di Prusa sulla questione del muro acheo a Troia (*Or.* XI § 76)," in *Ricerche su Dione di Prusa*. Naples: 41–63.

(2002) "Alcune note critico-testuali al *Troiano* (*Or.* xi) di Dione di Prusa," in *Scritti in onore di Italo Gallo*, ed. L. Torraca. Salerno: 123–38.

Caizzi, F. D., ed. (1966) *Antisthenis Fragmenta*. Milan.

Cameron, A. (2006) *Greek Mythography*. Oxford.

Camerotto, A. (1998) *Le metamorfosi della parola. Studi nella parodia in Luciano di Samosata*. Pisa and Rome.

Casanova, A. (2005) "Il *Grillo* di Plutarco e Omero," in *Les grecs de l'antiquité et les animaux. Le cas remarquable de Plutarque*, ed. J. Boulogne. Villeneuve d'Ascq Cedex: 97–110.

Casson, L. (1974) *Travel in the Ancient World*. Baltimore.

Chatzis, A. (1914) *Der Philosoph und Grammatiker Ptolemaios Chennos. Leben, Schriftstellerei und Fragmente (mit Ausschluss der Aristotelesbiographie). Erster Teil. Einleitung und Text*. Paderborn.

Chiron, P. (2005) "Aspects rhétoriques et grammaticaux de l'interprétation allégorique d'Homère," in *Allégorie des poètes, allégorie des philosophes*, ed. G. Dahan and R. Goulet. Paris: 35–58.

Clarke, K. (1997) "In search of the author of Strabo's *Geography*," *JRS* 87: 92–110.
  (1999) *Between Geography and History. Hellenistic Constructions of the Roman World*. Oxford.

Cohoon, J. W. (1932) *Dio Chrysostom*, vol. 1. Loeb Classical Library. New York and London.

Cole, T. (1991) *The Origins of Rhetoric in Ancient Greece*. Baltimore.

Connolly, J. (2001) "Problems of the past in Imperial Greek education," in *Education in Greek and Roman Antiquity*, ed. Y. L. Too. Leiden: 339–72.

Connor, W. R. (1984) *Thucydides*. Princeton.

Cook, R. M. (1955) "Thucydides as archaeologist," *ABSA* 50: 266–70.

Corcella, A. (1984) *Erodoto e l'analogia*. Palermo.

Cribiore, R. (2001) *Gymnastics of the Mind. Greek Education in Hellenistic and Roman Egypt*. Princeton.

D'Ippolito, G. (2004) "L'Omero di Plutarco," in *La biblioteca di Plutarco*, ed. I. Gallo. Naples: 11–36.
  (2007) "Omero al tempo di Plutarco," in *Plutarco e la cultura della sua età*, ed. P. V. Cacciatore and F. Ferrari. Naples: 57–84.

Dachs, H. (1913) *Die λύσις ἐκ τοῦ προσώπου. Ein exegetischer und kritischer Grundsatz Aristarchs und seine Neuanwendung auf Ilias und Odyssee*. Erlangen.

Danek, G. (2000) "Lukian und die Homer-Erklärung (*Verae Historiae* 1, 37 und *Odyssee* 10, 203–9)," *AAntHung* 40: 87–91.

Darbo-Peschanski, C. (1987) *Le discours du particulier. Essai sur l'enquête hérodotéene*. Paris.

de Jong, I. J. F. (2005) "Convention versus realism in the Homeric epics," *Mnemosyne* 58: 1–22.

de Lacy, P. (1948) "Stoic views of poetry," *AJPh* 69: 241–71.

de Lannoy, L. (ed.)(1977) *Flavii Philostrati Heroicus*. Leipzig.
  (1997) "Le problème des Philostrate (état de la question)," *ANRW* II.34.3: 2362–449.

de Romilly, J. (1967) *Histoire et raison chez Thucydide*. 2nd edn. Paris.

del Cerro Calderón, G. (1997) "Las claves del Discurso Troyano de Dión de Prusa," *Habis* 28: 95–106.

Demoen, K. and Praet, D., eds. (2009) *Theios Sophistes. Essays on Flavius Philostratus'* Vita Apolloni. Leiden and Boston.

Desideri, P. (1978) *Dione di Prusa. Un intellettuale greco nell'impero romano*. Messina-Florence.

    (1991) "Dione di Prusa fra ellenismo e romanità," *ANRW* II. 33.5: 3882–902.

Dickie, M. (1995) "The geography of Homer's world," in *Homer's World*, ed. Ø. Andersen and M. Dickie. Bergen: 29–56.

Dihle, A. (1986) "Philosophie-Wissenschaft-Allgemeinbildung," in *Aspects de la philosophie hellénistique*, ed. H. Flashar and O. Gigon. Entretiens sur l'Antiquité classique 32. Vandoeuvres-Geneva: 185–231.

Doležel, L. (1998) *Heterocosmica. Fiction and Possible Worlds*. Baltimore and London.

Dowden, K. (1992) *The Uses of Greek Mythology*. New York and London.

    (2009) "Reading Diktys: the discrete charm of bogosity," in *Readers and Writers in the Ancient Novel*, ed. M. Paschalis, S. Panayotakis, and G. Schmeling. Barkhuis, NL: 155–68.

Drules, P.-A. (1998) "Dion de Pruse lecteur d'Homère," *Gaia* 3, 59–79.

Dubuisson, M. (1987) "Homèrologie et politique: le cas d'Aristodémos de Nysa," in *Stemmata. Mélanges de philologie, d'histoire et d'archéologie grecques offerts à Jules Labarbe*, ed. J. Servais *et al.* Liège and Louvain-la-Neuve: 15–24.

Dueck, D. (1999) "The date and method of composition of Strabo's 'Geography,'" *Hermes* 127: 467–78.

    (2000) *Strabo of Amasia. A Greek Man of Letters in Augustan Rome*. New York and London.

    (2005) "Strabo's use of poetry," in *Strabo's Cultural Geography. The Making of a Kolossourgia*, ed. D. Dueck, H. Lindsay and S. Pothecary. Cambridge: 86–107.

Eitrem, S. (1929) "Zu Philostrats Heroikos," *SO* 8: 1–56.

Engels, J. (1999) *Augusteische Oikumenegeographie und Universalhistorie im Werk Strabons von Amaseia*. Stuttgart.

Erskine, A. (1995) "Culture and power in Ptolemaic Egypt: the Museum and Library of Alexandria," *G&R* 42: 38–48.

    (2001) *Troy Between Greece and Rome. Local Tradition and Imperial Power*. Oxford.

Falappone, M. (2006) "Citazioni della tragedia attica nelle 'archaiologiai,'" in *Memoria di testi teatrali antichi*, ed. O. Vox. Lecce: 67–104.

Farinelli, C. (1995) "Le citazioni omeriche in Erodoto II, 116–17," *AION (filol)* 17: 5–29.

Farrell, J. (2004) "Roman Homer," in Fowler (2004): 254–71.

Fauth, W. (1979) "Utopische Inseln in den *Wahren Geschichten* des Lukian," *Gymnasium* 86: 39–58.

Feeney, D. C. (1991) *The Gods in Epic. Poets and Critics of the Classical Tradition.* Oxford.

Ferguson, J. (1975) *Utopias of the Classical World.* London.

Fernández Delgado, J. A. (2000) "Le *Gryllus*, une éthopée parodique," in *Rhetorical Theory and Praxis in Plutarch*, ed. L. van der Stockt. Leuven: 171–82.

Flinterman, J.-J. (1995) *Power, Paideia, and Pythagoreanism. Greek Identity, Conceptions of the Relationship between Philosophers and Monarchs, and Political Ideas in Philostratus'* Life of Apollonius. Amsterdam.

Floratos, C. S. (1972) *Strabon über Literatur und Poseidonios.* Athens.

Ford, A. (1999a) "Performing interpretation: early allegorical exegesis of Homer," in *Epic Traditions in the Contemporary World. The Poetics of Community*, ed. M. Beissinger, J. Tylus, and S. Wofford. Berkeley: 33–53.

(1999b) "Reading Homer from the rostrum: poems and laws in Aeschines' *Against Timarchus*," in *Performance Culture and Athenian Democracy*, ed. S. Goldhill and R. Osborne. Cambridge: 231–56.

(2002) *The Origins of Criticism. Literary Culture and Poetic Theory in Classical Greece.* Princeton.

Fornaro, S. (2000) "Accuse e difese d'Omero: Platone nell'orazione undicesima di Dione Crisostomo," *Eikasmos* 11: 249–65.

(2002) "Omero cattivo storico: l'Orazione XI di Dione Crisostomo," in Montanari (2002): 547–60.

Fowler, R. L. (1996) "Herodotus and his contemporaries," *JHS* 116: 62–87.

(2000) *Early Greek Mythography.* Oxford.

ed. (2004) *The Cambridge Companion to Homer.* Cambridge.

Frazer, R. M., tr. (1966) *The Trojan War. The Chronicles of Dictys of Crete and Dares the Phrygian.* Bloomington, IN.

French, R. (1994) *Ancient Natural History. Histories of Nature.* New York and London.

Friedländer, L. (1907–13) *Roman Life and Manners under the Early Empire*, tr. L. A. Magnus. London. Reprinted (1979). New York.

Fromentin, V. (1988) "L'attitude critique de Denys d'Halicarnasse face aux mythes," *BAGB*: 318–26.

Fuchs, E. (1993) *Pseudologia. Formen und Funktionen fiktionaler Trugrede in der griechischen Literatur der Antike.* Heidelberg.

(1996) "Die 11. Rede des Dion Chrysostomos als Lügenerzählung," *Lexis* 14: 125–36.

Funke, H. (1986) "Poesia e storiografia," *QS* 12: 71–91.

Fusillo, M. (1988) "Le miroir de la Lune: L'*Histoire vraie* de Lucien de la satire à l'utopie," *Poétique* 73: 109–35. Reprinted and translated as "'The mirror of the moon: Lucian's *A True Story* – from satire to utopia," in (1999) *Oxford Readings in the Greek Novel*, ed. S. Swain. Oxford: 351–81.

Gabba, E. (1981) "True history and false history in classical antiquity," *JRS* 71: 50–62.

(1982) "Political and cultural aspects of the classicistic revival in the Augustan Age," *ClAnt* 1: 43–65.

Gaede, R., ed. (1880) *Demetrii Scepsii quae supersunt.* Greifswald.

Gagarin, M. (1990) "The nature of proofs in Antiphon," *CPh* 85: 22–32.

Gangloff, A. (2006a) *Dion Chrysostome et les mythes. Hellénisme, communication et philosophie politique.* Grenoble.

(2006b) "Mentions et citations de poètes chez Dion Chrysostome: manipulation et statut de la parole mythico-poétique dans le discours sophistique," in *Hôs ephat', dixerit quispiam, comme disait l'autre... : Mécanismes de la citation et de la mention dans les langues de l'Antiquité*, ed. C. Nicolas. Grenoble: 101–22.

(2007) "Peuples et préjuges chez Dion de Pruse et Lucien de Samosate," *REG* 120: 64–86.

Garbrah, K. A. (1977) "The scholia on the ending of the Odyssey," *WJA* n.F. 3, 7–17.

Gärtner, H. (1978) "Zoilos," *RE* Suppl. 15: 1531–54.

Genette, G. (1997) *Palimpsests. Literature in the Second Degree*, tr. C. Newman and C. Doubinsky. Lincoln, NE. Originally (1982) Paris.

Georgiadou, A. and Larmour, D. H. J. (1994) "Lucian and historiography: 'De Historia Conscribenda' and 'Verae Historiae,'" *ANRW* 34.2: 1448–509.

(1998) *Lucian's Science Fiction Novel* True Histories. Leiden.

Geus, K. (2002) *Eratosthenes of Kyrene. Studien zur hellenistischen Kultur- und Wissenschaftsgeschichte.* Munich.

Giangrande, G. (2000) "Sobre el texto de Dión Crisóstomo, *Oratio* XI," *Myrtia* 15: 247–52.

Giannantoni, G., ed. (1990) *Socratis et Socraticorum Reliquiae.* 2nd edn. Naples.

Gibson, C., tr. (2009) *Libanius's* Progymnasmata. *Model Exercises in Greek Prose Composition and Rhetoric.* Atlanta.

Gigon, O., ed. (1987) *Aristotelis Opera. Volumen Tertium. Librorum Deperditorum Fragmenta.* Berlin.

Ginzburg, C. (1999) *History, Rhetoric, and Proof.* Hanover and London.

Goldhill, S. (2002) *Who Needs Greek? Contests in the Cultural History of Hellenism.* Cambridge.

Gomme, A. W. (1945) *A Historical Commentary on Thucydides.* Vol. I: *Introduction and Commentary on Book I.* Oxford.

Graf, F. (1993) *Greek Mythology. An Introduction*, tr. T. Marier. Baltimore. Originally (1987) *Griechische Mythologie.* Munich and Zürich.

Graziosi, B. (2002) *Inventing Homer.* Cambridge.

Grentrup, H. (1914) *De Heroici Philostratei fabularum fontibus.* Münster.

Grethlein, J. (2006) "The manifold uses of the epic past: the embassy scene in Herodotus 7. 153–63," *AJPh* 127: 485–509.

Griffin, N. E. (1908) "The Greek Dictys," *AJPh* 29: 329–35.

Grossardt, P. (1998) *Die Trugreden in der Odyssee und ihre Rezeption in der antiken Literatur.* Bern.

(2004) "Ein Echo in allen Tonarten – der 'Heroikos' von Flavius Philostrat als Bilanz der antiken Troia-Dichtung," *ST* 14: 231–8.

(2006) *Einführung, Übersetzung und Kommentar zum* Heroikos *von Flavius Philostrat.* 2 vols. Basel.

(2009) "How to become a poet? Homer and Apollonius visit the mound of Achilles," in Demoen and Praet (2009): 75–94.

Grube, G. M. A. (1965) *The Greek and Roman Critics.* Toronto.

Gyselinck, W. and Demoen, K. (2009) "Author and narrator: fiction and metafiction in Philostratus' *Vita Apollonii*," in Demoen and Praet (2009): 95–128.

Hall, J. (1981) *Lucian's Satire.* New York.

Halliwell, S. (2000) "The subjection of muthos to logos: Plato's citations of the poets," *CQ* 50: 94–112.

Hankinson, R. J. (1997) "*Semeion e tekmerion.* L'evoluzione del vocabolario di segni e indicazioni nella Grecia classica," in *I Greci. Storia, cultura, arte, società*, vol. II, ed. S. Settis. Turin: 1169–87.

Hansen, D. U. (2006) "Orte ohne Wiederkehr. Überlegungen zu utopischen Städten und Stätten," in *Fremde Wirklichkeiten. Literarische Phantastik und antike Literatur*, ed. N. Hömke and M. Baumbach. Heidelberg: 261–76.

Hansen, W. (2003) "Strategies of authentication in ancient popular fiction," in *The Ancient Novel and Beyond*, ed. S. Panayotakis, M. Zimmerman, and W. Keulen. Leiden: 301–14.

Heath, M. (1989) *Unity in Greek Poetics.* Oxford.

(1998) "Was Homer a Roman?" *Papers of the Leeds International Latin Seminar* 10: 23–56.

(2000) "Do heroes eat fish? Athenaeus on the Homeric lifestyle," in *Athenaeus and his World. Reading Greek Culture in the Roman Empire*, ed. D. Braund and J. Wilkins. Exeter: 342–52.

(2003) "Pseudo-Dionysius *Art of Rhetoric* 8–11: figured speech, declamation, and criticism," *AJPh* 124: 81–106.

Hedreen, G. (1991) "The cult of Achilles in the Euxine," *Hesperia* 60: 313–30.

Henrichs, A. (1987) "Three approaches to Greek mythography," in *Interpretations of Greek Mythology*, ed. J. N. Bremmer. London: 242–77.

Hercher, R. (1855–6) "Über die Glaubwürdigkeit der Neuen Geschichte des Ptolemaeus Chennus," *Jahrbücher für classische Philologie*, suppl. 1: 269–93.

Hesk, J. (2000) *Deception and Democracy in Classical Athens.* Cambridge.

Higbie, C. (1997) "The bones of a hero, the ashes of a politician: Athens, Salamis, and the usable past," *ClAnt* 16: 278–307.

Hillgruber, M. (1994) *Die pseudoplutarchische Schrift* De Homero. 2 vols. Leipzig.

Hintenlang, H. (1961) *Untersuchungen zu den Homer-Aporien des Aristoteles.* Heidelberg.

Hodkinson, O. (2007) "Sophists in disguise: rival traditions and conflicts of intellectual authority in Philostratus' *Heroicus*," *Lampeter Working Papers in Classics* (www.lamp.ac.uk/ric/workin_papers/list_of_papers.html#Hodkinson).

Hofmann, P. (1905) *Aristarchs Studien "de cultu et victu heroum" im Anschluss an Karl Lehrs.* Munich.

Höistad, R. (1948) *Cynic Hero and Cynic King. Studies in the Cynic Conception of Man.* Uppsala.

(1951) "Was Antisthenes an allegorist?" *Eranos* 49: 16–30.

Holzberg, N. (1996) "Novel-like works of extended prose fiction II," in *The Novel in the Ancient World*, ed. G. Schmeling. Leiden: 621–53.

Hornblower, S. (1987) *Thucydides*. Baltimore.

(1991) *A Commentary on Thucydides*. Vol. I: *Books I–III*. Oxford.

Householder, F. W. (1941) *Literary Quotation and Allusion in Lucian*. New York.

Howie, J. G. (1998) "Thucydides and Pindar: the *Archaeology* and *Nemean 7*," *Papers of the Leeds International Latin Seminar* 10: 75–130.

Hude, C., ed. (1927) *Herodoti Historiae*, vol. I. 3rd edn. Oxford.

Huhn, F. and Bethe, E. (1917) "Philostrats *Heroikos* und Diktys," *Hermes* 52: 613–24.

Hunter, R. (2004) "Homer and Greek literature," in Fowler (2004): 235–53.

(2009) "The *Trojan Oration* of Dio Chrysostom and ancient Homeric criticism," in *Narratology and Interpretation. The Content of Narrative Form in Ancient Literature*, ed. J. Grethlein and A. Rengakos. Berlin and New York: 43–62.

Hunter, V. (1982) *Past and Process in Herodotus and Thucydides*. Princeton.

Hussey, E. (1995) "Ionian inquiries: on understanding the Presocratic beginnings of science," in *The Greek World*, ed. A. Powell. New York and London: 530–49.

Huxley, G. L. (1973) "Aristotle as antiquary," *GRBS* 14: 271–86.

(1979) "Historical criticism in Aristotle's *Homeric Questions*," *Proceedings of the Royal Irish Academy* 79: 73–81.

Innes, D. C. (1989) "Augustan critics," in Kennedy (1989): 245–73.

Ivančik, A. (1996) "Die hellenistischen Kommentare zu Homer Il. 13, 3–6. Zur Idealisierung des Barbarenbildes," in *Hellenismus*, ed. B. Funck. Tübingen: 671–92.

Jacob, C. (1994) "L'ordre généalogique. Entre le mythe et l'histoire," in *Transcrire les mythologies. Tradition, écriture, historicité*, ed. M. Detienne. Paris: 169–202.

James, A. and Lee, K. (2000) *A Commentary on Quintus of Smyrna*, Posthomerica V. Leiden.

Johnson, W. A. (2009) "Constructing elite reading communities in the High Empire," in *Ancient Literacies. The Culture of Reading in Greece and Rome*, ed. W. A. Johnson and H. N. Parker. Oxford: 320–30.

Jones, C. P. (1978) *The Roman World of Dio Chrysostom*. Cambridge, MA.

(1986) *Culture and Society in Lucian*. Cambridge, MA.

(1999) *Kinship Diplomacy in the Ancient World*. Cambridge, MA.

(2000) "The emperor and the giant," *CPh* 95: 476–81.

(2001) "Philostratus' *Heroikos* and its setting in reality," *JHS* 121: 141–9.

Jones, H. L., ed. (1917) *The Geography of Strabo*, vol. I. Cambridge, MA and London.

Jouan, F. (1966) *Dion Chrysostome. Discours Troyen (XI) qu'Ilion n'a pas été prise*. 2 vols. Diss., Paris.

(2002) "Mensonges d'Ulysse, mensonges d'Homère: une source tragique du *Discours troyen* de Dion Chrysostome," *REG* 115: 409–16.

Kahles, W. R. (1976) *Strabo and Homer. The Homeric Citations in the Geography of Strabo*. Diss., Loyola University of Chicago.

Kakridis, J. (1971) Ἀεὶ φιλέλλην ὁ ποιητής? in *Homer Revisited*. Lund: 54–67.
    Revised version of (1956) *WS* 69: 26–42.
    (1974) "A Cynic Homeromastix?" in *Serta Turyniana. Studies in Greek Literature
    and Palaeography in honor of Alexander Turyn*, ed. J. L. Heller and J. K.
    Newman. Urbana, IL: 361–73.
Kayser, C. L., ed. (1870–1) *Flavii Philostrati opera auctoria C. L. Kayser*. 2 vols.
    Leipzig.
Kennedy, G. A. (1958) "Isocrates' *Encomium of Helen*: a Panhellenic document?"
    TAPhA 89: 77–83.
    (1963) *The Art of Persuasion in Greece*. Princeton.
    ed. (1989) *The Cambridge History of Literary Criticism*. Vol. 1: *Classical Criticism*.
    Cambridge.
    tr. (2004) Progymnasmata. *Greek Textbooks of Prose Composition and Rhetoric*.
    Leiden.
Kidd, I. G. (1990) *Posidonius. II. Commentary. (ii) Fragments 150–293*. Cambridge.
Kim, L. (2007) "The portrait of Homer in Strabo's *Geography*," *CPh* 102:
    363–89.
    (2008) "Dio of Prusa, *Or. 61, Chryseis*, or reading Homeric silence," *CQ* 58:
    601–21.
Kindstrand, J. F. (1973) *Homer in der zweiten Sophistik*. Uppsala.
    (1979–80) "Sostratus – Hercules – Agathion. The rise of a legend," *Annales
    Societatis Litterarum Humaniorum Regiae Upsaliensis*: 50–79.
König, J. (2005) *Athletics and Literature in the Roman Empire*. Cambridge.
Konstan, D. (2004) "'The birth of the reader': Plutarch as a literary critic," *Scholia*,
    n.s. 13: 3–27.
Koster, S. (1970) *Antike Epostheorien*. Wiesbaden.
Kroll, W. (1915) "Randbemerkungen XXXI," *RhM* 70: 607–10.
Laird, A. J. W. (2003) "Fiction as a discourse of philosophy in Lucian's *Verae Histo-
    riae*," in *The Ancient Novel and Beyond*, ed. S. Panayotakis, M. Zimmerman,
    and W. Keulen. Leiden: 115–27.
Lamberton, R. (1986) *Homer the Theologian. Neoplatonist Allegorical Reading and
    the Growth of the Epic Tradition*. Berkeley.
    (1997) "Homer in antiquity," in *A New Companion to Homer*, ed. I. Morris and
    B. Powell. Leiden: 33–54.
    (2002) "Homeric allegory and Homeric rhetoric in ancient pedagogy," in
    Montanari (2002): 185–205.
Lamberton, R. and Keaney, J. J., eds. (1992) *Homer's Ancient Readers. The
    Hermeneutics of Greek Epic's Earliest Exegetes*. Princeton.
Lanata, G. (1963) *Poetica pre-platonica. Testimonianze e frammenti*. Florence.
Lane Fox, R. (1986) *Pagans and Christians*. Harmondsworth.
Lasserre, F. (1982) "Strabon devant l'empire romain," *ANRW* II.30.1: 867–96.
Legrand, Ph.-E., ed. (1936) *Hérodote. Histoires* Livre II. Paris.
Lemarchand, L. (1926) *Dion de Pruse. Les oeuvres d'avant l'exile*. Paris.
Leyden, W. von (1949–50) "Spatium historicum," *DUJ* 42, n.s. 11: 89–104.
Lightfoot, J. L. (2003) *Lucian. On the Syrian Goddess*. Oxford.

Ligota, C. R. (1982) "'This story is not true.' Fact and fiction in antiquity," *JWI* 45: 1–13.

Lloyd, A. B. (1975) *Herodotus, Book II. Introduction.* Leiden.
(1988) *Herodotus, Book II. Commentary 99–182.* Leiden.

Lloyd, G. E. R. (1966) *Polarity and Analogy. Two Types of Argumentation in Early Greek Thought.* Cambridge.

Long, A. A. (1992) "Stoic readings of Homer," in Lamberton and Keaney (1992): 41–66.

Luce, T. J. (1989) "Ancient views on the causes of bias in ancient historical writing," *CPh* 84: 16–31.

Luraghi, N., ed. (2001) *The Historian's Craft in the Age of Herodotus.* Oxford.

Maclean, J. K. B. (2004) "The αἶνοι of the *Heroikos* and the unfolding transformation of the Phoenician merchant," in Maclean and Aitken (2004): 251–65.

Maclean, J. K. B. and Aitken, E. B., trs. (2001) *Flavius Philostratus.* Heroikos. Atlanta.

Maclean, J. K. B. and Aitken, E. B., eds. (2004) *Philostratus's* Heroikos. *Religion and Cultural Identity in the Third Century* CE. Leiden.

Maeder, D. (1991) "Au seuil des romans grecs: effets de réel et effets de création," *Groningen Colloquia on the Novel* 4: 1–33.

Mal-Maeder, D. van (1992) "Les détournements homériques dans l'‘Histoire vraie' de Lucien: le repatriement d'une tradition littéraire," *EL* 2: 123–46.

Manetti, G. (1993) *Theories of the Sign in Classical Antiquity*, tr. C. Richardson. Bloomington, IN. Originally (1987) *Teorie del segno nell'antichità classica.* Milan.

Mangoni, C., ed. (1993) *Filodemo. Il quinto libro della* Poetica (PHerc. *1425 e 1538*). Naples.

Mantero, T. (1966) *Ricerche sull'* Heroikos *di Filostrato.* Genoa.

Marcozzi, D., Sinatra, M., and Vannicelli, P. (1994) "Tra epica e storiografia: il «catalogo delle navi»," *SMEA* 33: 163–74.

Marincola, J. (1997) *Authority and Tradition in Ancient Historiography.* Cambridge.

Marrou, H. I. (1956) *A History of Education in Antiquity*, tr. G. Lamb. Madison, WI.

Martin, R. P. (2002) "A good place to talk: discourse and topos in Achilles Tatius and Philostratus," in *Space in the Ancient Novel*, ed. M. Paschalis and S. Frangoulidis. Groningen: 143–60.

Matteuzzi, M. (2000–2) "A proposito di Omero 'babilonese' (Lucian *VH* II 20)," *Sandalion* 23–5: 49–51.

Meijering, R. (1987) *Literary and Rhetorical Theories in Greek Scholia.* Groningen.

Meineke, A., ed. (1866) *Strabonis Geographica.* Leipzig.

Merkle, S. (1989) *Die Ephemeris belli Troiani des Diktys von Kreta.* Frankfurt and New York.
(1994) "Telling the true story of the Trojan War: the eyewitness account of Dictys of Crete," in *The Search for the Ancient Novel*, ed. J. Tatum. Baltimore and London: 183–98.

(1996) "The truth and nothing but the truth: Dictys and Dares," in *The Novel in the Ancient World*, ed. G. Schmeling. Leiden: 563–80.

Mesk, J. (1920–1) "Zur elften Rede des Dio von Prusa," *WS* 42: 115–24.

Mestre, F. (1990) "Homère, entre Dion Chrysostome et Philostrate," *AFB* 13: 89–101.

(2004) "Refuting Homer in the *Heroikos* of Philostratus," in Maclean and Aitken (2004): 127–41.

Miles, G. (2005) "Music and immortality: the afterlife of Achilles in Philostratus' *Heroicus*," *AncNarr* 4: 66–78.

Moles, J. L. (1978) "The career and conversion of Dio Chrysostom," *JHS* 98: 79–100.

(1995) "Dio Chrysostom, Greece, and Rome," in *Ethics and Rhetoric. Classical Essays for Donald Russell on His Seventy-Fifth Birthday*, ed. D. Innes, H. Hine, and C. Pelling. Oxford: 177–92.

Möllendorff, P. von (2000) *Auf der Suche nach der verlogenen Wahrheit. Lukians Wahre Geschichten*. Tübingen.

(2006a) "Sophistische Phantastik: Lukians Lügenfreunde," in *Fremde Wirklichkeiten. Literarische Phantastik und antike Literatur*, ed. N. Hömke and M. Baumbach. Heidelberg: 187–201.

(2006b) "Camels, Celts, and Centaurs. Lucian's Aesthetic Concept of the Hybrid," in *Desultoria scientia. Genre in Apuleius'* Metamorphoses *and Related Texts*, ed. R. R. Nauta. Groningen: 63–86.

Momigliano, A. (1990) *The Classical Foundations of Modern Historiography*. Berkeley.

Montanari, F. (1987) "Hyponoia e allegoria: piccole considerazioni preliminari," in *Studi offerti ad Anna Maria Quartiroli e Domenico Magnino*. Pavia: 11–19.

ed. (2002) *Omero tremila anni dopo*. Rome.

Montgomery, W. A. (1901) *Dio Chrysostom as Homeric Critic*. Baltimore.

(1902) "*Oration* XI of Dio Chrysostomus," in *Studies in Honor of Basil Gildersleeve*. Baltimore: 405–12.

Moraux, P. (1987) "Homère chez Galien," in *Stemmata. Mélanges de philologie, d'histoire et d'archéologie grecques offerts à Jules Labarbe*, ed. J. Servais. Liège and Louvain-la-Neuve: 25–37.

Morgan, J. R. (1985) "Lucian's *True Histories* and the *Wonders Beyond Thule* of Antonius Diogenes," *CQ* 35: 475–90.

Morgan, T. (1998) *Literate Education in the Hellenistic and Roman Worlds*. Cambridge.

Mosshammer, A. A. (1979) *The Chronicles of Eusebius and Greek Chronographic Tradition*. Lewisburg, PA.

Most, G. W. (1989) "The structure and function of Odysseus' *Apologoi*," *TAPhA* 119: 15–30.

Nadeau, J. Y. (1970) "Ethiopians," *CQ* 20: 339–49.

Nesselrath, H.-G. (1993) "Utopie-Parodie in Lukians *Wahren Geschichten*," in *Literaturparodie in Antike und Mittelalter*, ed. W. Ax and R. F. Glei. Trier: 41–56.

(2002) "Homerphilologie auf der Insel der Seligen: Lukian, *VH* II 20," in *Epea Pteroenta. Beiträge zur Homerforschung. Festscrift für Wolfgang Kullmann zum 75. Geburtstag*, ed. M. Reichel and A. Rengakos. Stuttgart: 151–62.

Neumann, K. J. (1886) "Strabons Gesammturtheil über die homerische Geographie," *Hermes* 21: 134–41.

Neville, J. W. (1977) "Herodotus on the Trojan War," *G&R* 24: 3–12.

Newby, Z. (2007) "Reading the allegory of the Archelaos Relief," in *Art and Inscriptions in the Ancient World*, ed. Z. Newby and R. Leader-Newby. Cambridge: 156–78.

Ní Mheallaigh, K. (2005) *Lucian's Self-conscious Fiction. Theory in Practice*. Diss., Dublin.

(2008) "Pseudo-documentarism and the limits of ancient fiction," *AJPh* 129: 403–31.

(2009) "Monumental fallacy: the teleology of origins in Lucian's *Verae Historiae*," in *A Lucian for our Times*, ed. Adam Bartley. Newcastle upon Tyne: 11–28.

Nickau, K. (1990) "Mythos und Logos bei Herodot," in *Memoria rerum veterum. Neue Beiträge zur antiken Historiographie und alten Geschichte. Festschrift für Carl Joachim Classen zum 60. Geburtstag*, ed. W. Ax. Stuttgart: 83–100.

Nicolai, R. (2001) "Thucydides' Archaeology: between epic and oral traditions," in Luraghi (2001): 263–85.

(2003) "La poesia epica come documento," in *L'uso dei documenti nella storiografia antica*, ed. A. M. Biraschi, P. Desideri, S. Roda, and G. Zecchini. Perugia: 79–109.

Niese, B. (1877) "Apollodors Commentar zum Schiffskataloge als Quelle Strabos," *RhM* 32: 267–307.

Olivieri, A. (1898) "Gli studi omerici di Dione Crisostomo," *RFIC* 26: 568–607.

Ollier, F. (1962) *Lucien. Histoire vraie*. Paris.

Paassen, C. van (1957) *The Classical Tradition of Geography*. Groningen.

Parry, H. (1994) "The *Apologos* of Odysseus: lies, all lies?" *Phoenix* 48: 1–20.

Paschalis, M. (2005) "Pandora and the Wooden Horse: a reading of Triphiodorus' Ἅλωσις Ἰλίου," in *Roman and Greek Imperial Epic*, ed. M. Paschalis. Herakleion: 91–115.

Patillon, M. and Bolognesi, G., eds. (1997) *Aelius Théon. Progymnasmata*. Paris.

Pavano, A. (1998) "Le redazioni latine e il presunto originale greco dell'opera di Darete Frigio," *Sileno* 24: 207–18.

Pavel, T. (1986) *Fictional Worlds*. Cambridge, MA.

Pearson, L. (1942) *The Local Historians of Attica*. Philadelphia.

Pédech, P. (1964) *La méthode historique de Polybe*. Paris.

Pépin, J. (1976) *Mythe et allégorie. Les origines grecques et les contestations judéo-chrétiennes*. 2nd edn. Paris.

(1993) "Aspects de la lecture antisthénienne d'Homère," in *Le Cynisme ancien et ses prolongements*, ed. M.-O. Goulet-Cazé and R. Goulet. Paris: 1–13.

Pernot, L. (1994) "Lucien et Dion de Pruse," in Billault (1994): 109–16.

Pfeiffer, R. (1968) *History of Classical Scholarship from the Beginnings to the End of the Hellenistic Age*. Oxford.

Phillips, E. D. (1953) "Odysseus in Italy," *JHS* 73: 53–67.

Piérart, M. (1983) "L'historien ancien face aux mythes et aux légendes," *LEC* 51: 47–62.

Pontani, F. (2000) "Il proemio al *Commento all'Odissea* di Eustazio di Tessalonica (con appunti sulla tradizione del testo)," *BollClass* ser. 3, 21: 5–58.

  ed. (2005) *Eraclito. Questioni omeriche sulle allegorie di Omero in merito agli dèi*. Pisa.

Porter, J. I. (1992) "Hermeneutic lines and circles: Aristarchus and Crates on the exegesis of Homer," in Lamberton and Keaney (1992): 67–114.

  (1993) "The seductions of Gorgias," *ClAnt* 12: 267–99.

  (2001) "Ideals and ruins. Pausanias, Longinus, and the Second Sophistic," in *Pausanias. Travel and Memory in Ancient Greece*, ed. S. Alcock, J. F. Cherry, and J. Elsner. Oxford: 63–92.

  (2004) "Homer: the history of an idea," in Fowler (2004): 324–43.

Pothecary, S. (2002) "Strabo, the Tiberian author: past, present and silence in Strabo's *Geography*," *Mnemosyne* 55: 387–438.

Pratt, L. (1993) *Lying and Poetry from Homer to Pindar. Falsehood and Deception in Archaic Greek Poetics*. Ann Arbor, MI.

Prontera, F. (1993) "Sull'esegesi ellenistica della geografia omerica," in *Philanthropia kai Eusebeia. Festschrift für Albrecht Dihle zum 70. Geburtstag*, ed. G. W. Most, H. Petersmann, and A. M. Ritter. Göttingen: 387–97.

Radt, S., ed. (2002) *Strabons Geographika. Band 1: Prolegomena, Buch i–iv: Text und Übersetzung*. Göttingen.

  ed. (2006) *Strabons Geographika. Band 5: Abgekürzt zitierte Literatur. Buch i–iv: Kommentar*. Göttingen.

Ramin, J. (1979) *Mythographie et géographie*. Paris.

Reuter, D. (1932) *Untersuchungen zum Euboikos des Dion von Prusa*. Leipzig.

Richardson, N. J. (1975) "Homeric professors in the age of the sophists," *PCPhS*, n.s. 21: 65–81.

  (1980) "Literary criticism in the exegetical scholia to the *Iliad*: a sketch," *CQ* 30: 265–87.

  (1981) "The contest of Homer and Hesiod and Alcidamas' *Mouseion*," *CQ* 31: 1–10.

  (1985) "Pindar and later literary criticism in antiquity," *Papers of the Leeds International Latin Seminar* 5: 384–9.

  (1992) "Aristotle's reading of Homer and its background," in Lamberton and Keaney (1992): 30–40.

  (1993) "Homer and his ancient critics," in *The Iliad: A Commentary*. Vol. vi: *Books 21–24*. Cambridge: 25–49.

Ritoók, Z. (1995) "Some aesthetic views of Dio Chrysostom and their sources," in *Greek Literary Theory after Aristotle. A Collection of Papers in Honour of D. M. Schenkeveld*, ed. J. G. J. Abbenes, S. R. Slings, and I. Sluiter. Amsterdam: 125–34.

Robert, L. (1980) "Lucien en son temps," in *À travers l'Asie Mineure. Poètes et prosateurs, monnaies grecques, voyageurs et géographie.* Paris: 393–436.

Robinson, C. (1979) *Lucian and his Influence in Europe.* London.

Romm, J. (1990) "Wax, stone, and Promethean clay: Lucian as plastic artist," *ClAnt* 9: 74–98.

(1992) *The Edges of the Earth in Ancient Thought. Geography, Exploration and Fiction.* Princeton.

Rose, V., ed. (1886) *Aristotelis Fragmenta.* Leipzig.

Rosén, H. B., ed. (1987) *Herodotus.* Historiae. Vol. I. Leipzig.

Russell, D. A. (1981) *Criticism in Antiquity.* Bristol.

(2003) "The rhetoric of the *Homeric Problems*," in *Metaphor, Allegory, and the Classical Tradition*, ed. G. R. Boys-Stones. Oxford: 217–34.

Russell, D. A., and Konstan, D. (2005) *Heraclitus*: Homeric Problems. Atlanta.

Russell, D. A., and Winterbottom, M., eds. (1970) *Ancient Literary Criticism. The Principal Texts in New Translations.* Oxford.

Rusten, J. (1980) *Dionysius Scytobrachion.* Opladen.

(2004) "Living in the past: allusive narratives and elusive authorities in the world of the *Heroikos*," in Maclean and Aitken (2004): 143–58.

Rutherford, I. (2009) "Black sails to Achilles: the Thessalian pilgrimage in Philostratus' *Heroicus*," in Bowie and Elsner (2009): 230–47.

Sacks, K. (1981) *Polybius on the Writing of History.* Berkeley.

Sage, M. (2000) "Roman visitors to Ilium in the Roman imperial and late antique period: the symbolic functions of a landscape," *ST* 10: 211–31.

Saïd, S. (1993) "Le 'je' de Lucien," in *L'invention de l'autobiographie d'Hésiode à Saint Augustine*, ed. M.-F. Baslez, P. Hoffmann, and L. Pernot. Paris: 253–70.

(1994) "Lucien ethnographe," in Billault (1994): 149–70.

(2000) "Dio's use of mythology," in Swain (2000a): 161–86.

Santoni, A. (2002) "Miti dell'*Odissea* nel Περὶ Ἀπίστων di Palefato," in *La mythologie et l'Odyssée. Hommage à Gabriel Germain*, ed. A. Hurst and F. Letoublon. Geneva: 145–55.

Saraceno, C. (1998) "Omero, Odisseo e Luciano: una lettura di *Storia vera*, I, 3," *Métis* 13: 401–16.

Scarcella, A. M. (1988) "Mythe et ironie: Les *vraies histoires* de Lucien," in *Peuples et pays mythiques*, ed. F. Jouan and B. Deforge. Paris: 169–76. Reprinted in A. M. Scarcella (1993), *Romanzo e romanzieri. Note di narratologia greca*, vol. II. Perugia: 409–17.

Schäublin, C. (1977) "Homerum ex Homero," *MH* 34: 221–7.

Scheer, T. J. (2003) "The past in a Hellenistic present: myth and local tradition," in *A Companion to the Hellenistic World*, ed. A. Erskine. Oxford: 216–31.

Schenkeveld, D. M. (1976) "Strabo on Homer," *Mnemosyne* 29: 52–64.

Schepens, G. (2006) "Travelling Greek historians," in *Le vie della storia: migrazioni di popoli, viaggi di individui, circolazione di idee nel Mediterraneo antico*, ed. M. G. Angeli Bertinelli and A. Donati. Rome: 81–102.

Schirren, T. (2005) *Philosophos Bios. Die antike Philosophenbiographie als symbolische Form. Studien zur* Vita Apollonii *des Philostrat*. Heidelberg.

Schmidt, M. (1976) *Die Erklärungen zum Weltbild Homers und zur Kultur der Heroenzeit in den bT-Scholien zur Ilias*. Munich.

(2002) "The Homer of the scholia: what is explained to the reader?" in Montanari (2002): 159–83.

Schmitz, T. A. (1997) *Bildung und Macht. Zur sozialen und politischen Funktion der zweiten Sophistik in der griechischen Welt der Kaiserzeit*. Munich.

(2000) "Plausibility in the Greek orators," *AJPh* 121: 47–77.

Schröder, S. (1990) *Plutarchs Schrift* De Pythiae Oraculis. *Text, Einleitung und Kommentar*. Stuttgart.

Schouler, B. (1986) "Le déguisement de l'intention dans la rhétorique grecque," *Ktèma* 11: 257–72.

Scodel, R. (1999) *Credible Impossibilities. Conventions and Strategies of Verisimilitude in Homer and Greek Tragedy*. Stuttgart.

Seeck, G. A. (1990) "Dion Chrysostomos als Homerkritiker (*Or.* 11)," *RhM* 133: 97–107.

Shayegan, M. R. (2004) "Philostratus's *Heroikos* and the ideation of late Severan policy toward Arscacid and Sasanian Iran," in Maclean and Aitken (2004): 285–315.

Shimron, B. (1973) "Πρῶτος τῶν ἡμεῖς ἴδμεν," *Eranos* 71: 45–51.

Skiadas, A. D. (1965) *Homer im griechischen Epigramm*. Athens.

Solmsen, F. (1940) "Some works of Philostratus the Elder," *TAPhA* 71: 556–72.

Speyer, W. (1970) *Bücherfunde in der Glaubenswerbung der Antike*. Göttingen.

Stengel, A. (1911) *De Luciani veris historiis*. Berlin.

Stern, J., tr. (1996) *Palaephatus. On Unbelievable Tales*. Wauconda, IL.

(2003) "Heraclitus the paradoxographer: *On Unbelievable Tales*," *TAPhA* 133: 51–97.

Strasburger, H. (1972) *Homer und die Geschichtsschreibung*. Heidelberg.

Struck, P. (2004) The *Birth of the Symbol. Ancient Readers at the Limits of Their Texts*. Princeton.

Swain, S. (1992) "Antonius Diogenes and Lucian," *LCM* 17.5: 74–6.

(1994) "Dio and Lucian," in *Greek Fiction. The Greek Novel in Context*, ed. J. R. Morgan and R. Stoneman. New York and London: 166–80.

(1996) *Hellenism and Empire. Language, Classicism, and Power in the Greek World AD 50–250*. Oxford.

ed. (2000a) *Dio Chrysostom. Politics, Letters, and Philosophy*. Oxford.

(2000b) "Reception and interpretation" in Swain (2000a): 13–50.

Szarmach, M. (1978) "Le 'Discours Troyen' de Dion de Pruse," *Eos* 66: 195–202.

Tate, J. (1953) "Antisthenes was not an allegorist," *Eranos* 51: 14–22.

Täubler, E. (1927) *Die Archaeologie des Thukydides*. Leipzig.

Thomas, R. (1989) *Oral Tradition and Written Record in Classical Athens*. Cambridge.

(2000) *Herodotus in Context. Ethnography, Science and the Art of Persuasion*. Cambridge.

Tomberg, K.-H. (1968) *Die Kaine Historia des Ptolemaios Chennos*. Bonn.

Too, Y. L. (1995) *The Rhetoric of Identity in Isocrates. Text, Power, Pedagogy*. Cambridge.

(1998) *The Idea of Ancient Literary Criticism*. Oxford.

Torraca, L. (2001) "Roma e l'Europa nella prospettiva di un 'provinciale': Dione di Prusa di fronte all'impero," in *L'Idea di Roma nella cultura antica*, ed. F. Giordano. Naples: 243–76.

Tozzi, P. (1967) "Acusilao di Argo," *RIL* 101: 581–624.

Trachsel, A. (2002) "La Troade: entre espace littéraire et paysage historique," *ARF* 4: 41–53.

(2007) *La Troade. Un paysage et son héritage littéraire: les commentaires antiques sur la Troade*. Basel.

Trapp, M. (1990) "Plato's *Phaedrus* in second-century Greek literature," in *Antonine Literature*, ed. D. A. Russell. Oxford: 141–73.

tr. (1997) *Maximus of Tyre. The Philosophical Orations*. Oxford.

Tsakmakis, A. (1995) *Thukydides über die Vergangenheit*. Tübingen.

Usener, K. (1994) "Diktys und Dares über den Troischen Krieg: Homer in der Rezeptionskrise?" *Eranos* 92: 102–20.

Vagnone, G. (2000) "Note al testo della *Or.* XI di Dione di Prusa (*Troiano*): 1. cc. 20–21; 2. cc. 22–24 (pp. 119–121 v. Arnim)," *QUCC* 65: 107–13.

ed. (2003a) *Dione di Prusa. Troiano. Or. XI. Edizione critica, traduzione e commento*. Rome.

(2003b) "Note al testo e all'interpretazione del *Troiano* di Dione di Prusa," *QUCC* 73: 139–45.

(2007) "Storia e ideologia nel *Discorso Troiano* di Dione di Prusa," in *Costruzione e uso del passato storico nella cultura antica*, ed. P. Desideri, S. Roda, and A. M. Biraschi. Alexandria: 379–86.

Valgimigli, M. (1911–12) "La or. LVIII (Ἀχιλλεύς) di Dione Crisostomo," *BFC* 18: 207–10.

(1912) *La critica letteraria di Dione Crisostomo*. Bologna.

Valk, M. van der (1953) "Homer's nationalistic attitude," *AC* 22: 5–26.

ed. (1971–87) *Eustathii archiepiscopi Thessalonicensis. Commentarii ad Homeri Iliadem pertinentes ad fidem codicis Laurentiani*. 4 vols. Leiden.

Venini, P. (1981) "Ditti Cretese e Omero," *MIL* 37: 161–98.

Verdin, H. (1977) "Les remarques critiques d'Hérodote et de Thucydide sur la poésie en tant que source historique," in *Historiographia antiqua. Commentationes Lovanienses in honorem W. Peremans septuagenarii editae*. Leuven: 53–76.

Veyne, P. (1988) *Did the Greeks Believe in Their Myths? An Essay on the Constitutive Imagination*, tr. P. Wissing. Chicago. Originally (1983) *Les Grecs ont-ils cru à leurs mythes?* Paris.

Vischer, R. (1965) *Das einfache Leben. Wort- und motivgeschichtliche Untersuchungen zu einem Wertbegriff der antiken Literatur*. Göttingen.

Walbank, F. W. (1960) "History and tragedy," *Historia* 9: 216–34.

(1974) "Polybius and the Sicilian straits," *Kokalos* 20, 5–17.

(1979) *Polybius. An Historical Commentary*, vol. III. Oxford.

Walcot, P. (1977) "Odysseus and the art of lying," *AncSoc* 8: 1–19.

Wardman, A. E. (1960) "Myth in Greek historiography," *Historia* 9: 401–13.

Webb, R. (2001) "The *Progymnasmata* as practice," in *Education in Greek and Roman Antiquity*, ed. Y. L. Too. Leiden: 289–316.

(2006) "Fiction, mimesis and the performance of the Greek past in the Second Sophistic," in *Greeks on Greekness. Viewing the Greek Past under the Roman Empire*, ed. D. Konstan and S. Saïd. Cambridge: 27–46.

Weil, R. (1977) "Aristotle's view of history," in *Articles on Aristotle 2. Ethics and Politics*, ed. J. Barnes, M. Schofield, and R. Sorabji. London: 202–17.

West, M. L., ed. (2003) *Homeric Hymns. Homeric Apocrypha. Lives of Homer*. Cambridge, MA.

Whitmarsh, T. (1998) "The birth of a prodigy: Heliodorus and the genealogy of Hellenism," in *Studies in Heliodorus*, ed. R. Hunter. Cambridge: 93–124.

(2001) *Greek Literature and the Roman Empire. The Politics of Imitation*. Oxford.

(2004) "The harvest of wisdom: landscape, description, and identity in the *Heroikos*," in Maclean and Aitken (2004): 237–49.

(2006) "True histories: Lucian, Bakhtin, and the pragmatics of reception," in *Classics and the Uses of Reception*, ed. C. Martindale and R. F. Thomas. Oxford: 104–15.

(2007) "Prose literature and the Severan dynasty," in *Severan Culture*, ed. S. Swain, S. Harrison, and J. Elsner. Cambridge: 29–51.

(2009) "Performing heroics: landscape, language, and identity in Philostratus' *Heroicus*," in Bowie and Elsner (2009): 205–29.

Winiarczyk, M. (2002) *Euhemeros von Messene. Leben, Werk und Nachwirkung*. Munich.

Winkler, J. J. (1982) "The mendacity of Kalasiris and the narrative strategy of Heliodoros' *Aithiopika*," *YCS* 27: 93–158.

Winston, D. (1976) "Iambulus' Island of the Sun and Hellenistic literary utopias," *Science Fiction Studies* 3: 219–27.

Wipprecht, F. (1902–8) *Zur Entwicklung der rationalistischen Mythendeutung bei den Griechen*. 2 vols. Tübingen.

Wolff, M. J. (1932) "Der Lügner Homer," *GRMS* 20: 53–65.

Wright, M. (2005) *Euripides' Escape-Tragedies. A Study of* Helen, Andromeda, *and* Iphigenia among the Taurians. Oxford.

Zeitlin, F. (2001) "Visions and revisions of Homer," in *Being Greek Under Rome*, ed. S. Goldhill. Cambridge: 195–266.

Index

Index locorum

Lightning Source UK Ltd.
Milton Keynes UK
UKHW020415041122
411620UK00025B/903

9 781107 485297